Teaching TV Production in a Digital World

Teaching TV Production in a Digital World

Integrating Media Literacy

Teacher Edition
Second Edition

Robert F. Kenny, Ph.D.

LIBRARIES
UNLIMITED

A Member of the Greenwood Publishing Group

Westport, Connecticut • London

Library of Congress Cataloging-in-Publication Data

Kenny, Robert, 1947-
   Teaching TV production in a digital world : integrating media literacy / Robert F.
Kenny.—2nd ed., Teacher ed.
     p. cm.
   Includes bibliographical references and index.
   ISBN 1-59158-199-0 (pbk. : alk. paper)
   1. Television—Production and direction—Study and teaching (Secondary) 2. Digital
electronics. I. Title: Teaching television production in a digital world. II. Title.
PN1992.75.K44 2004
791.4502'32—dc22   2004057626

Library of Congress Catalog Card Number: 2004057626
ISBN: 1-59158-199-0

First published in 2004

Libraries Unlimited, 88 Post Road West, Westport, CT 06881
A Member of the Greenwood Publishing Group, Inc.
www.lu.com

Printed in the United States of America

The paper used in this book complies with the
Permanent Paper Standard issued by the National
Information Standards Organization (Z39.48-1984).

10 9 8 7 6 5 4 3 2 1

CONTENTS

PREFACE

Just my luck! For over 50 years, the television industry had remained essentially the same, with the latest significant development being color pictures. Then I go and write a book about it and changes start happening on almost a daily basis. To be really honest, it was the concept of rapidly changing environment that inspired me to write this book in the first place. I guess one should be careful what he or she asks for. The idea behind the supporting Web site for this book was to help extend the life of the content in the book, knowing the changes we saw beginning at the end of the 1990s were only the beginning of a long series that would change the face of the industry as we know it.

I am very happy to have the opportunity to provide this second edition of *Teaching Television in a Digital World*. The title is becoming more and more appropriate. The truth is that the evolution of television from the analog into the digital world has been coming for over a decade now, much of it invisible to the audiences other than some subtle changes in the screen layouts and new screen shots made possible by sophisticated digital switching and titling devices. However, as is explained in this edition, the digitization of television actually involves five distinct phases, the first three having matured in their use in commercial television broadcasting for almost a decade: the capture or acquisition of the images in new CCD-based cameras; the manipulation and processing of the screens to add digital titles, transitions, and effects; and the ability to record and store the clips digitally. The last two have only come to fore in the last three or four years. Newer presentation methods including digital comb filters, plasma screens, and new advances in rear projection have produced cheaper ways to present affordable high definition sets. Finally, the transmission and distribution of a digital broadcast signal were first introduced by satellites, expanded upon by cable carriers, and only recently available in open-air broadcasts.

Part of the confusion in understanding the digitization process has been brought on by the fact that there are so many aspects that have been introduced slowly over the years. Understanding just what make television digital requires one to be able to parse the process into these five distinct but overlapping categories. This certainly has made the purchase of a television set that much more confusing.

Even if one can make the distinctions among all these phases, most people have difficulty fully understanding just exactly what a digital broadcast entails so that they can explain it to others. I have to thank one of my professors at the University of Florida, Dave Ostroff, who posed what he called the *cookie example* that was so facile that "even your grandmother would understand it." It goes like this: Let's say you wanted to transmit this chocolate chip cookie from one place to another. In an analog transmission, the cookie is transformed into another analog form, transmitted, and then reconstituted at the other end. In a digital transmission, a recipe is sent and the receiver at the other end makes his or her own cookie. The former is most like what we know as "Beam me up, Scottie" from *Star Trek*. I don't think Gene Roddenberry had any idea that Scottie would actually be cloned in the real world!

At any rate, this new look at digitization is not all that is new with this edition. Several changes and corrections have been made to the various chapters, new lessons added, and others deleted to make the book more in line with the changes happening in the industry. Also, with gracious input from Kathleen Kirby, I was able to straighten out some significant confusion surrounding the television code of ethics in **Chapter 2**. I have to thank her for all her wonderful advice and consent. I think I now have presented a fairer picture of the role the Radio-Television News Directors Association has played in attending to this very delicate issue. The great part of all of this is that not only was I able to attend to the details of exactly what happened to the television code, but through her e-mails I am also able to better explain First Amendment issues as they relate to television, which is particularly timely considering the related cases brought against several broadcasting network owners.

Error corrections aside, there are also other important changes in this edition. **Chapter 1** includes references to the new, updated Web-ASSISTant site, and the chronology has been updated for changes made in lesson sequences and content. In **Chapter 2,** the "Who Owns What" section has been completely rewritten. If you think you've had a bad time lately, imagine how tough it was to follow Comcast's bid for Disney. First it was added, then deleted. Also in **Chapter 2**, changes and updates have been made to the answers surrounding copyrights, and changes/additions/corrections have been added to the Code of Ethics discussions. **Chapter 3** includes an update to the interview process discussions. Lesson 3.2B has been changed to "How Videorecording Works" to take into consideration how CDs record as opposed to videotapes. **Chapter 3** has additional discussions about how YPbPR cables and connectors work. Lesson 3.6, "Wiring a Home Entertainment System," has been replaced with "Bringing Television into the Digital Age."

In **Chapter 4,** I rewrote and updated the section on Rod Serling. I also removed Project #3, "Weather Segment, replacing it with "Book Trailers," a new project that teaches text-to-screen principles and acts as a catalyst for bringing video into the classroom. This project can be done in conjunction with the English classes in which students learn to critically read books as if they are going to make a movie of them. The trailer is a much shorter production and helps teach students how to distill the book's contents down into its essential context. The "Learning Styles Web-Quest" has been removed from **Chapter 5. In Chapter 6,** the history lessons are updated with later materials. Finally, in Chapter 7 I added new Lesson 7.8, "UB the Director," a course-ending culminating activity in which students write out camera shot lists and other directorial activities to describe how a short scene might be produced.

I have to say that writing the second edition was a fun exercise. It made me refocus on the thought that no longer is television the purview of the studio environment. Digitization has democratized the production process so well that video is fast becoming the word processing equivalent in this new, media-centric world in which we are living. I believe that this book can be quite useful in any classroom in the school and has the ability to act as a catalyst to helping schools teach literacies other than media literacy, like reading (as can be derived from the "Book Trailers" lesson) and writing (as can come from the "UB the Director" lesson). It is my firm hope that this book may play a small part in fostering these activities in other such venues.

INTRODUCTION

BACKGROUND

The intent of this book is to present a case for, and to show teachers (particularly new ones) how to, implement a television production program in a different light that is in tune with the changing times. No longer can the primary outcome of a television course be to simply prepare future employees for conventional jobs in the traditional broadcasting industry. In the digital world, video is creeping into the mainstream as an integral part of the digital revolution. Marc Davis (1997) while completing his degree at the Massachusetts Institute of Technology coined the term *garage cinema*, which refers to a growing cottage industry in which anyone with an idea has the opportunity to produce and distribute video products through the Internet. *Desktop television* might also be an equitable label. This extension of the use of video into our daily lives has increased the need to broaden the scope of the television curriculum to include a more intense focus on media and visual literacy.

Conversely, no longer is teaching about television and media issues the sole domain of television production classes. Those who teach other courses like English, life management, and critical thinking also are beginning to spend considerable time on media-related issues. They, too, might easily benefit greatly by the contents of a book containing detailed lesson plans that deal with the effects of the media on our daily lives. The heightened need for media literacy is not a coincidence, nor is it an accident. In 1996, Congress passed an Act that removed most of the controls on the media industry originally put in place by the Radio Act of 1927 and Communications Act of 1934 to quell the chaos that was reigning in the industry during the 1920s and early 1930s. Congress, in passing the **Telecommunications Act of 1996** (which was subsequently updated in Federal Communications Commission [FCC] regulations as recently as the summer of 1999), removed almost entirely all controls central to preventing potential conflicts of interests. Among other things, limits were significantly changed on

- the number of media outlets in a single market one company can own,

- the power of individual television or radio stations,

- cross-over ownership by owners of one type of media (such as newspaper publishers) of another (such as a television or radio station), or

- rates cable operators can charge.

Congress, in exchange for pushing the industry to pay for moving into the digital age, essentially deregulated the entire industry by allowing newspaper publishers and telephone and television companies to enter each other's businesses, and large, multilevel organizations born out of megamergers to take control of media markets. The government's thinking was that the advantages of economic progress and increased technological research and design would far outweigh any potential disadvantages of domination of media markets by a few. As a compromise for offering the industry this financial windfall, the Act also proposed an increase in local access channels on cable systems and a re-institution of the Code of Ethics that was virtually abandoned by broadcasters in the early 1980s.

Whatever good effects the new Act may have on technology, consumerism, and the industry as a whole, educators need to understand the immediate impact these changes must have on curriculum design. Now more than ever, students need to become media-literate citizens who understand the impact media have on their daily lives. Television Ontario defines the *media-literate* person as "one who has an informed and critical understanding of the nature, techniques, and the impact of the mass media." They also identify television as the "most persuasive medium" for children (1996, pp. 1–3). It should be obvious that the new law requires that the term *media literacy* be redefined to encompass all the additional technologies that will surely arise. Already we are witnessing dramatic changes in the way information is being communicated and managed. The technologies of the telephone, television, and computer are merging. Kids are spending more time in front of the computer browsing on the Internet, and educators must help them become more informed about the media and advertising techniques imposed upon them in that medium.

Technology is also changing how advertisers portray their message. New, computer-based editing software allows advertisers to increase dramatically the number of frames per second that viewers are exposed to during a 15-, 30-, or 60-second commercial. Teaching about framing is a core technical concept in television production that leads to an increased understanding of the principles of media and visual literacy. Learning about visual clues like the use of colors, shapes, and mass, as well as on-camera techniques like body language, provides students with a broader understanding of the techniques used by advertisers in the various media formats. In other words, inasmuch as the goals and objectives of technology, visual literacy, and media literacy are inevitably intertwined, so must their definitions be expanded to encompass these new intentions.

The purpose of this book, then, is to use media and visual literacy in these newer and broader contexts. It introduces students to the core principles and methodologies behind producing quality video outputs. Students will learn how to organize their thoughts using storyboards and how to write appropriate scripts for a visual medium that employs both sight and sounds to complement each other. Equipment use is taught in the context of accomplishing the visual effects and goals set forth by the storyboards and scripts. Finally, media literacy is set in an historical context through 10 short sessions describing the history of broadcasting through the present and the future of **narrowcasting,** a term that describes what will certainly become the predominant means of one-to-one communication and information management in the new millennium. Students will benefit by being taught about television production in new and practical terms that will also make them better media consumers.

THE UNIQUENESS OF THIS BOOK

First, this book is aimed at teachers rather than students. A traditional textbook is student-oriented and generally organized into set teaching units. It is usually the focal point of the course syllabus that students follow. Usually there is a supplemental teacher's edition that includes enrichment material, answer keys, and/or mastery exercises at the end of each teaching unit. By default, class syllabi often follow the chronology offered by the textbook company. The traditional television production textbooks teach the basics of producing television programs in a studio environment, often focusing on how to put on a daily newscast or news magazine show.

This book actually does all that. But based on a strict interpretation of this description, this book is not a textbook per se. Rather, it is an instructional guide or course guide, aimed at teachers, supplemented by an optional student's edition (referred to as the *Student Workbook*). The target audience is teachers of a first-year high school television program whose students most likely are ninth graders. However, there are no assumptions in the content that would preclude upperclassmen from taking this course. Although the book is aimed directly at television production, all lessons are structured to guide teachers of different academic disciplines who wish to pick and choose appropriate topics for their own subject areas. There is a certain amount of continuity among the lessons, but they are modular so as to stand on their own merit and provide meaningful content to anyone interested in visual and media literacy.

This book also differs from most texts about television because of its subject matter. It is a book about television, and as such contains information on the production sequence, but the course content is not limited solely to the production aspects of television. Rather, the main goal is to promote visual awareness and media literacy by introducing students to the power of the medium, its traditions, and how to ethically manage it. The lessons introduce the foundations, practices, theories, and traditions of broadcasting, using visual awareness and media literacy as their linchpin. As a point of reference, the lessons point out how, over time, the broadcasting industry has learned to use (and some times misuse) television as a visually intensive medium for conveying and managing the flow of information in society. Media literacy and visual awareness are taught from a producer's point of view. Students end up becoming good consumers of media as a natural by-product of learning how to produce their own authentic productions.

All references to the term *television production* are intended to vividly make the point that nothing in television happens by accident. In their lessons about the production sequence, students learn that everything follows a detailed plan, carries out specific objectives, and is done primarily to meet the need and desire to make money. In their history lessons, students learn that television was not always this way. During the 1950s, television was a live medium that both benefited (from the viewer's point of view) and lost something (from the producer's and advertiser's point of view) from mistakes and miscues that often occurred during a show. Shows were original and fresh but ran counter to the goals of perfection and time management.

The needs of current trends unique to the broadcasting industry are simulated within the classroom environment. Students learn about the need to manage simultaneous projects and the need for accurate record keeping. In addition, they learn how to target audiences, how to market products, and why the industry's motivation to make a profit can be both a positive and a negative factor. This book lays down the foundations of real-life workplace situations and serves as a prerequisite text in a series of several television courses that can be offered to high school students. It integrates neatly into a four-year curriculum plan that gradually and incrementally introduces students to the elements of production.

The premise for taking this approach is threefold:

- Although television is an elective course in most schools, not all students are enrolled by choice. Many first-year television students complete only that year and do not enroll in follow-up courses. Those who do go on to become employed in the industry after graduation are certainly in the minority. Often students are placed in the first-year television course to satisfy district- or state-mandated electives requirements.

- The pressures of putting on a daily show often results in a first-year course being bereft of meaningful content. Often the teacher is bogged down with the show and does not have the time to pay proper attention to the needs of the first-year student.

- Most states cannot agree on benchmark standards that include standards for teaching television. For this reason, television curricula vary widely between and among schools. Often this results in redundancy in course content. Whatever television-related standards do exist fall to the media literacy benchmarks written into the English class curricula and visual awareness issues written under the broad heading of visual arts.

In short, this book shows teachers how to implement a program that uses television to teach about television and about the increasing power that the medium has on our daily lives. In other words, one definition of being media literate incorporates an understanding of television as a medium.

Considerable emphasis is now being placed on the importance of teaching media literacy by including it in many state curriculum standards and frameworks for English and global studies. Amazingly, most standards have overlooked a significant opportunity to use the television curriculum to attain these goals. Television is the very medium that has created the need to teach media awareness. While media literacy is struggling to emerge as a critical course offering, television teachers often struggle with course content for their first-year students, who do not have the skills to make significant contributions to the daily news show.

The instructional style presented in this book is a combination of direct, classroom instruction, group discussion, independent study and research, and written enrichment and review exercises. Direct instruction is used, when appropriate. Information is limited to short sessions of about 25–35 minutes each. This is to allow time in each daily schedule for students to work on projects or other self-paced learning activities, regardless of the bell schedule: traditional classes of 50–60 minutes, block schedules in which students meet every other day, or the 4 x 4 block in which students meet for 90 minutes each day. Varying the instructional methodology allows the curriculum to focus on a series of action projects whose topics embrace and coordinate with several other subject areas already being taught in the school: Some elements of the global studies, English, math, and life management courses are integrated into the instructional plan. The final project is a media contest that simulates the quarterly Sweeps ratings that occur in the television industry. Each class section competes with others through a schoolwide broadcast of their programs, which students vote on.

Like most academic subjects, some portion of student assessment comes from written tests and quizzes. However, as the syllabus suggests, the main form of appraisal can come from the evaluation of the media projects from which students compile personal video portfolios. Teachers who follow the course outline closely will implement a culminating project. *Sweeps* is a team production created by the entire class that is entered into competition against the other class sections. Suggestions for grading all projects, including the final one, are based on predetermined rubrics. If the final *Sweeps* project is used, there is also an added competitive incentive: Students operate in a simulated real-world environment in which all the elements of sequencing a developmental production, including targeting an audience and marketing, are synthesized and rewarded.

Finally, this book is supplemented by, and is integrated with, an extensive Web site. The **Web-ASSISTant** Web site (**http://www.web-assist.com**) supplements each chapter with extensive links to sites providing additional research and a vast array of complementary information. The Web site would be useful to any television production course on its own but is much more valuable when used in combination with this text.

EXPECTED OUTCOMES OF THIS COURSE

The target grade level for this course is first-year television production students in grades 9 to 12. However, because the subject matter is presented from media and visual literacy perspectives, it should also prove useful for anyone interested in literacy issues. Often, English and/or other teachers responsible for incorporating critical thinking content into their courses struggle to find relevant course material.

This course is intended to achieve many general learning goals. These goals differ from specific course objectives in that they are more general and relate as much to the overall learning process as to television production. In short, course outcomes should also be looked at as advantages and additional benefits to students who take this course.

Following is a partial list of the learning outcomes for this course:

- **To foster an understanding of cooperative learning** so that students can become a contributing team member for projects and, ultimately, the *Sweeps* production crew.

- To provide opportunities to learn about the **planning process.** The production sequence requires extensive planning before, during, and after production.

- To develop **research** and **critical thinking skills** as students research the content for their projects, visualize camera shots, write their scripts, and search beyond the classroom for resources to complete projects.

- To develop **leadership skills** as students take turns being responsible for overseeing a particular area of production**.**

- To promote a **sense of ownership** of the learning process; students take a storyline and corresponding production techniques into their own hands and use them in their projects.

- To **improve self-esteem;** youths are provided with an outlet to express their views and ideas through an alternate and valid media format.

- To better **prepare students to enter the workplace,** in which planning, technology, teamwork, and time-management skills are in constant demand.

- To **increase communication skills** by extending student's capabilities into a new medium.

- To cause students to become more **literate consumers of media**, a skill that is becoming increasingly important and complex in the digital age.

The objectives listed below represent, on a general level, the skills that students attain by completing this course. They represent the major learning outcome(s) specific to the media and visual literacy perspectives of this book. Chapter references indicate where each skill is further defined: by type, time constraints, and specific guidelines for how they are to be measured.

Overall, after completing this course, students will be able to

- **write** scripts and storyboards in the broadcast style with scripting queues that show basic knowledge of visual storytelling (**Chapter 4**);

- **exhibit** media awareness as it relates to being able to deconstruct various advertising vehicles found in printed form, on the radio, on television, and on the Internet (**Chapter 2**);

- **exhibit** knowledge of the role ratings play in the economies of the broadcasting industry, how ratings samples are gathered, and the role ratings play in determining *newsworthiness* for news broadcasts (**Chapter 2**);

- **exhibit** visual awareness by using generally accepted visual design principles and proper use of audio to supplement portfolio videos (**Chapter 3**);

- **exhibit,** on written tests and quizzes and through participation in class discussions, knowledge of the history of mass communications and the role it has played in an ever-evolving, media rich society (**Chapter 6**);

- **demonstrate** correct equipment use to create visually appealing images in a storyline (**Chapter 5**);

- **exhibit** knowledge of the TV production team and the role each member plays (**Chapter 7**);

- **exhibit** basic knowledge of body language as it relates to presenting visual clues to one's audience, and of on-camera etiquette as it relates to the Television Code of Ethics and copyright laws (**Chapter 5**); and

- **understand** career and college opportunities in television and video (**Chapter 7**).

Nationally, few standards have been developed specific to television production. However, many states are beginning to develop benchmarks that are synergistic to the goals and objectives stated above.

MORE ABOUT THE WEB-ASSISTant WEB SITE

As suggested previously, the Internet appears to be a source of the most current information. This is particularly true in this television course, in which the concept of incorporating media and visual literacy is relatively new. Although there has been a significant amount of material published for television, most of the innovative materials supporting the projects and activities suggested in this course are now being disseminated online. Moreover, comprehensive resources for a television production program as conceived by this book are often difficult to find in text format.

By now, most teachers realize the potential of the Internet and have already discovered many of the Web sites that support television production. They also know how time-consuming it is to browse for appropriate sites and to keep current with the constantly changing environment in which the Internet exists. Teachers often waste a lot of time researching sites only to find they have moved, or have been deleted, by the time the class needs to use them. To ensure that the challenges and opportunities afforded by the Internet do not also become classroom management problems, the **Web-ASSISTant** Web site is provided with ready-made links that will be continually updated with current information. The Web site provides the following support for teachers and students:

- Each student project and learning activity is supported by specific links to a multitude of Web sites that have been reviewed for appropriateness. They provide background and research material to aid students in gathering information about the topics specific to their projects and activities.

- Teachers are supported on the Web site with additional background in a "Digging Deeper" section, a page containing more detailed information about related topics, located at the end of each chapter. Further information on teaching ideas and other role models for issues related to teaching about and using media is found on the "Best Practices" page. These additional topics also include links to technical information on equipment, lessons that others have developed, Web sites that other television teaching organizations have put together, and Web sites that provide details on state and federal teaching standards. As these Web sites change rapidly, they are listed on the course Web site and updated frequently.

- State benchmarks and learning standards are constantly evolving. The Web site is frequently updated on the "Standards" page with the latest URL locator links to other Web sites that provide details.

In addition, all bibliographic and references to other texts found throughout this book are mirrored on the Web site and are constantly updated. This helps to extend the life of this text and prevent it from becoming out of date. With all the changing technology, obsolescence is a fact of life in this industry. Hopefully, the Web site will help to prolong the useful life of this book. More information on how to use the features of this Web site can be found in **Chapter 1.**

HOW THE CHAPTERS ARE ORGANIZED

For convenience and continuity, the chapters in this book are organized into instructional units based on content. This is intended to help television teachers who are unfamiliar with the broadcasting industry understand course content. The subject matter flows together better so that they may make correlations among common concepts or themes.

Although the chapters in this book are specifically organized around subject content, the term *module* has been carefully avoided when referring to the lessons. *Module* often indicates that all related material is covered contiguously during a continuous time frame. Following a modular format can delay actual hands-on experiences because the syllabus requires that all necessary operating procedures be covered prior to starting the first major hands-on project. On the other hand, there is a tendency simply to begin hands-on activities prior to teaching all there is to know about operating the equipment because students are anxious to work with it. Most teachers do not want their equipment mishandled and consider that the best way to teach is to make sure students understand the production process prior to working with the equipment. However, they cannot teach, and certainly students cannot learn, all there is to know about a well-run production on the very first day. The trick is to begin working very early in the term on simple projects that rely on only the most rudimentary aspects of operating the equipment. That is why the chapters are organized by content but do not follow a contiguous schedule. Students receive instruction on rudimentary operating procedures and then begin their first project, even before they cover the units on editing, scriptwriting, or production planning.

To accommodate the need to intersperse class material with activities, and to correlate like material in different chapters, the subject units are guided by two "Teaching Chronologies." The first is based on a traditional calendar in which students meet for the entire school year. The second is modified for the 4 x 4 block. It might seem that courses like television production are aided by alternative schedules that provide additional work time each day. However, the course is easily suited to both the normal yearlong schedule and the 4x4 block, with its modified class periods taken into consideration. The major difference is that the class lectures and discussions often are the subject of a single class period in the traditional schedule but a subset of a longer class in the block.

The subject matter is taught in short sessions interspersed throughout the entire year or semester. The chronology distributes the learning of academic material with technical training according to appropriateness and timing. Students do not have to wait until they learn all there is to know about production techniques or operation of all the equipment before they get started on simple projects. Learning is reinforced because it is anchored in students reviewing their own mistakes. For example, in the first news reading activity, students are asked to read a news script on camera with no prior class time spent on technique. In a follow-up session students critique their own performance and camera technique, after having been instructed on the proper methods. This also provides the opportunity for students to learn *why* a certain technique or procedure is being suggested.

The chronologies have a few things in common. First, the schedule calls for some projects to run concurrently. This is to accommodate the shortage of equipment that often occurs. By staggering the need for particular editing equipment, for example, teachers are able to avoid the logjam that occurs when all students need to use the same equipment at the same time. This also heightens the need to teach students how to schedule and manage their time. Students learn how to handle multiple simultaneous projects and deadlines, when they can have access to equipment, and how to divvy up the workload. The "Teaching Chronology" can be found in **Chapter 1**, "Class Administration." As its title indicates, the chapter covers the administrative aspects of this course. It sets the tone for instruction, provides suggestions about what to do during the first few weeks of the course, provides a course syllabus and evaluation criteria, and discusses closure: competency evaluation, cognitive testing, and test blueprints.

The format for **Chapters 2** through **7** is identical. The introduction includes background information, general goals, and outcomes for the lessons. Prior to each lesson, a pre-plan agenda prepares the teacher with background information about the subject matter and specifies objectives, possible assessment alternatives, and suggestions regarding class presentation and operation. Each lesson includes an estimated duration. The goal is to limit all class presentations and discussions to no more than 40 minutes so that they may be accomplished within a single class period. If a lesson is expected to take more than one class period, it is broken down into multiple sessions of 25–35 minutes each. The class discussions are provided in enough detail so that they may be used as a script by teachers who are unfamiliar with the subject matter. All lessons are supplemented by the *Student Workbook* to help keep students on task.

Because this book is targeted at the first-year media student, time constraints may limit the amount of material that is covered. Lessons are organized to permit flexibility for teachers to make decisions about course content. Some areas might be covered in more detail, others less. Additional readings and reference material are included in the "Digging Deeper" section at the beginning of each chapter for teachers who wish to focus on a particular subject area.

MORE ABOUT INSTRUCTIONAL METHODS

Class Lectures and Discussions

The acquisition of basic technical and historical knowledge is supported through several short lecture or discussion sessions. These detailed plans are offered simply as a model for dialogue or approach to each session, especially for teachers who might be unfamiliar with certain topics. Students have the same material in their *Student Workbook,* except that their version includes blank spaces to be filled in. In addition, all lessons are preceded by a glossary that includes the terms, concepts, and people being introduced. Those teachers who are familiar with the material may wish to introduce the topics in their own way. The material in the *Student Workbook* would then be used as worksheets for students to fill out on their own as a review or reinforcement exercise.

Note taking, when assisted by an outline structure such as the one provided in the *Student Workbook,* keeps students on task and allows the teacher to review the students' notes regularly to discover whether they have grasped the subject matter. The teacher may also reward students for their organizational skills by grading their notebooks. Because the written tests and quizzes are designed to also accommodate an open-note/open-book format, students are rewarded for their ability to apply information to situations rather than their ability to regurgitate memorized facts. Knowing how to keep accurate written records and notes is a very important and necessary skill in the broadcasting industry. This approach is designed to model that requirement.

All the lecture and discussion sessions are designed so they may be completed within the traditional 45- to 50-minute class period. Some are as short as 20–25 minutes. If a school is on a traditional calendar, the classes can be varied so that a discussion/note-taking session can be followed up with individual and group work. A class on the 4 x 4 block lasts roughly 90 minutes. This means that the same routine of a short discussion interspersed with project work can be followed. The only difference is that the follow-up activities can be done in the same class period rather than the next day. The order in which the sessions are taught does not have to vary regardless of the class schedule, and is handled through the "Teaching Chronology."

Student Projects or Activities

The lecture format is not the only way knowledge is attained and measured. Students actually spend more class time working on projects and learning how to operate the equipment than they do taking notes. In fact, the "Teaching Chronology" calls for a ratio of approximately two to one in favor of time spent on independent and group work. Most projects encourage students to acquire information through their own independent research. This may be accomplished in the school's media center, online in the classroom (if the classroom is wired for the Internet), or at home. Students are encouraged to come up with their own background information and design their own projects and learning experiences. In the Web-Quest exercises, for example, students are invited to search for information about ratings and report back to the class any new information they acquire.. In other cases, they are to transpose blocks of information into answers to "who/what/where/when" questions.

MORE ABOUT THE *STUDENT WORKBOOK*

Lesson notes make up the majority of the content of the *Student Workbook*. Blank spaces are strategically left for students to enter key names, words, or phrases from the glossary presented at the beginning of each session. (See the sample page from the *Student Workbook* on page xxv.) In essence, these are handouts or worksheets to guide note taking during class presentations and discussion sessions. They outline a suggested order in which the topics are to be presented. Space is provided on the worksheets for teachers to interject an independent reading and discussion of the specific procedures and techniques found in the texts being used.

Sample page from *Student Workbook*

Lesson 3.2A

How Television Works

Terminology, concepts, and/or people discussed in this lesson:

color bars	phosphorus coating	frame rate for movies
aspect ratio	electromagnets	frame rate for TV without sound
scanning	RGB chroma	frame rate for TV with sound
rasters	microwave	PHI phenomena
radio waves	frequency	
HDTV	gausing	
resolution	dots	

What Is Television?

Television is best defined as a process of transmitting images through a signal from one place to another. No matter how you transmit that signal, the system must convert images to electronic signals and back again. This process is the heart of television. Although they appear to be identical in outputs, television and motion pictures (movies) are quite different in how they gather and project images.

How Motion Pictures Work

Motion pictures (or movies), are defined as **the process of projecting moving images on to a wall or screen.** Motion pictures and television are both based on the principles of **persistence of vision** and the **phi phenomenon**.

In other words, although there is an illusion of motion, the actual output of both is not really a moving image but rather a series of frames (pictures) presented in sequential fashion. We will demonstrate a rudimentary version of this concept in our *Stop Action* project.

After much experimentation, early developers found that a rate of approximately **16 frames** per second would provide the needed illusion. In our later discussions regarding nonlinear editing and its ramifications for deconstructing subliminal and subconscious commercial messages, we will discover what happens when that rate is increased and/or the frames themselves are shortened. **When sound was introduced to the early motion pictures, the rate per second (frame rate) was increased to about 24 fps.** The international film community, largely due to the leadership of the United States, was successful in maintaining the 24 frame per second rate over time.

How Television Differs from Motion Pictures

Television, on the other hand, went down a different path. It appears as though each country had its own interests in television and was led by its own visionary, who took credit for inventing (developing) it. The United States, Japan, Germany, and the United Kingdom, for example, all have produced their own "father of television." Although this helped speed up the invention and development process, it also resulted in the lack of any single broadcast standard.

Frame rates in television range from **25 to 30** per second. In the United States, the National Television System Committee (NTSC) developed a standard in 1947 for televisions used in the United States that reproduces pictures (frames) at a rate of approximately 30 per second. That is why a television produced for use in the United Kingdom will not work in the United States and vice versa. The frame rates in Europe and Japan evolved to a different standard.

The difference in _____ between television and motion pictures is just one of the reasons a motion picture has to be converted before it can be played on television. It also accounts for some of the loss in quality. A motion picture camera records its images in a very similar fashion to a **roll of still photos**: pictures are in their completed form (and at a rate of 24 frames per second).

Television works differently. The frames are not complete when they are captured and displayed. Rather, the picture frame is composed of thousands of *dots* that are **displayed (scanned) horizontally** from left to right, top to bottom. The television camera records in this sequence, and your television tube displays it in the same manner. In short, the pictures displayed on television are actually scanned in a dual interleaved process. The interleaves are called fields, and together they make up a frame. A frame, then, is displayed only after the television system has done its work by covering the viewing area at a rate of 60 times per second to compose each field. Television works simply because the scanning beam is faster than the human eye, thus making images appear fluid. They produce a *nonflickering* display that handles movement.

MORE ABOUT THE MEDIATED ASPECTS OF THIS COURSE

The Role of Mediation

The definition of *mediation* has narrowed in recent years to suggest that technology (computers in particular) has been incorporated into a course of study for students to take control over their own independent learning (Gifford, 1998). For purposes of this course, that definition is not sufficient. Because this book is aimed at teachers, any form of media used needs to support the instruction and facilitation on the part of the teacher. In addition, the definition of what comprises *media* has been extended to include traditional formats (i.e., printed text) as well as digital (computer, CD, and video). The materials suggested in this book have been selected because it is believed that they can be used by teachers unfamiliar with course, as well as more experienced teachers who seek additional support materials not supplied by their own textbooks. Because the concept of incorporating media and visual literacy into a television course is relatively new, a few books have been suggested as outside reading that provide further research and backup support. The media suggested in this book support the teacher's class preparation and delivery as well as many of the follow-up activities.

Technology Media

Herb Zettl may be one of the most well-known television production educators in this country. He has written several books on teaching television, many of which he has condensed and converted into an interactive CD, *Videolab 2.1*, published by Wadsworth Publishing, which can help both the student and teacher. Although it was originally designed as an instructional aid for one-on-one training, the CD can easily be incorporated into direct instructional sessions and displayed for the entire class, using an inexpensive scan converter. The *Videolab 2.1* lessons are suggested at the appropriate places in this book.

Another interactive CD used by this course is *Understanding the Media*, published by the New Mexico Media Literacy Project. **Chapter 2** contains several lessons dedicated to media literacy. Two sessions deal specifically with the deconstructing process for breaking commercials down into their component parts. The New Mexico Media Literacy Project CD provides a basis for those class discussions and follow-up activities.

Video Media

The large number of instructional videos on the market dealing with television, its history and traditions, and the inner workings of the industry may or may not have something to do with the fact that television reached its 50-year milestone in 1999. There are several videos suggested throughout this book, but specifically, there are four excellent videos that can be purchased with performance rights and cleared for in-class use:

- *Understanding Television* is published by the Discovery Channel School and includes instructional hints and student discussion topics.

- *Headlines and Sound Bites,* also from the Discovery Channel School, features Walter Cronkite discussing how television has evolved into a mass marketing information machine.

- *Big Dream, Small Screen,* from PBS Home Video, tells the story of Philo Farnsworth and how until recently he had not received proper credit for the invention of modern television.

- *Signal to Noise: Life with Television* is a series of three videos produced by GPN of the University of Nebraska at Lincoln. It provides opportunities to teach students how television organizations construct their medium and opportunities for students to make their own decisions about what their personal relationship with television should be.

The videos come with their own lesson plans and suggestions on how to incorporate them into the classroom. Each of the videos is also supported by Internet sites that contain supplementary lesson plans and discussion topics. Some of this material may be suitable for the television classroom. These videos have been incorporated into the appropriate lessons in this book.

Textual Media

Although studio production is not the main focal point of this course, the standard, accepted practices for producing a video show still play an important role in the program. Rather than replicate other readily available television production resources, they are referenced and integrated into this course at the appropriate places. Two books in particular are referenced:

- *Television Production: A Classroom Approach,* by Keith Kyker and Christopher Curchy, is published by Libraries Unlimited. The book is written specifically for high school students and comes with a supplemental teacher's edition, a student workbook, and a video that models some of the projects a television production teacher might want to assign in a studio production course. It introduces production terminology and techniques. Portions of the book are integrated, as needed, into this curriculum as individual reading assignments introducing various lessons in **Chapters 3** and **7** that deal specifically with production and equipment operation. The readings are later reviewed and discussed in class.

- *Television Production,* by Ron Whittaker, Ph.D., is published by Mayfield Press. The substance of this text has also been published as an independent study course on the Internet at **www.cybercollege.com**. Certain lessons in **Chapters 3** and **8** reference some of the production, media literacy, and scriptwriting concepts found on that Web site. Although the text was originally written for college-level students, the writing style is simple and can be used for high school students.

- *Perspectives on Radio and Television: Telecommunication in the United States* (4th ed), by F. Leslie Smith, John W. Wright II, and David H. Ostroff, is published by Lea Publishers. This text describes the field of radio and television in the United States in a manner intended to make the book suitable for the classroom teacher. It is divided by subject to be assigned as and when appropriate, and includes information on ethics, careers, and rivals to the commercial industry.

The background information for **Chapter 6** comes from a number of sources. One important resource is *The Tube of Plenty* by Erik Barnouw, published by Oxford University Press. This is an excellent resource for further information to prepare for the history lessons. Two other books are also used as references for the history lessons. *Three Blind Mice*, written by Ken Auletta and published by Random House, is a behind-the-scenes story about how the three television networks lost their way. *The Last Great Ride,* by Brandon Tartikoff, is a story of NBC's resurgence and how network television has lost its sole proprietorship on the viewing public. The history lessons in **Chapter 6** are based on the information provided by these three books and condensed down into 10 poignant 20- to 25-minute sessions introducing the events that helped shape current thinking and trends in the broadcast industry.

Two books were used as references for course content in lessons dealing with camera operation. *Video Goals: Getting Results with Pictures and Sound*, and *The Bare Bones Camera Course for Film and Video*, both written and privately published by Tom Schroeppel, are excellent books on camera techniques and getting started in video on a shoestring.

Len Masterman has written two excellent books on how to teach media and television that serve as an inspiration for some of the basic tenets of visual and media literacy in this course. *Teaching the Media* and *Teaching About Television* are referenced heavily in **Chapters 2 and 5**. Although these two books were published in the late 1980s and early 1990s, they are both timely and concise in their outlook. Both are well worth the effort to add them to your library.

Several other books are used in the development of this course material and are specifically referenced at the appropriate place. Information on how to obtain copies of all these materials can be found on the **Web-ASSISTant** Web site on the pages dedicated to the subject matter in question. The Internet site is used to keep the material updated and timely as prices, editions, and publishers' special offerings change. It is best to visit the Web site often to stay current.

THE INTERDISCIPLINARY ASPECTS OF THIS COURSE

Although teaching students about visual and media literacy and how to produce television shows is the key premise for this course, other, interdisciplinary aspects are also important. Topics for classroom discussions, activities, and projects all incorporate several of the learning outcomes from other academic areas. There are several examples:

- Many of the goals and outcomes in the scriptwriting and storytelling lessons are quite similar to those one might find in an **English** class. Students learn to express themselves using a visual medium that is supported by storyboards and scripts.

- Many **history** and **global studies** issues are incorporated in the media and broadcast history lessons and demonstrated by students in the *Decades* project.

- The *Sweeps* project covers issues encompassing deconstructing commercials and many of the consumerism issues taught in **life management** classes.

- **Math** plays a small but significant part in discussions about ratings. The ratings system incorporates issues like validity, reliability, blocking, and sampling, which show real examples of some of these fundamental math concepts.

- Special effects and equipment use incorporates many of the same processes incorporated into any **technology** course. In addition, the lessons on deconstructing commercials incorporate a session on how technology enhances the delivery of the advertiser's message.

It is possible to work closely with other subject teachers to formulate a curriculum that is mapped around any one or more of these issues. In fact, in some cases whole communication academies have been set up in schools in which the entire curriculum revolves around using television as one of the central facilitation factors. More information on this concept can be found in books such as *Media Action Projects*, by Dirk Shouten and Brian Watling, and by visiting the "Best Practices" page on the **Web-ASSISTant** Web site.

INCORPORATING THE REAL WORLD INTO THE CURRICULUM

In the real world of television, Sweeps plays a very large role in the everyday life of a broadcaster. The most significant basis for how much the national networks or local stations may charge for a 10-, 15-, or 30-second or a one-minute commercial is viewership. To determine how many viewers are watching a particular program, the networks and local stations participate in a month-long Sweeps ratings contest to attract viewers four times each year. Sweeps takes place during November, February, May, and July. Viewership is determined via a ratings system developed and maintained by an outside company hired for this purpose. Today, the AC Nielsen Ratings Service, Inc., is the most relied upon resource. The term *Nielsens* has become synonymous with ratings within the broadcast industry. Ratings determine the content of television schedules, how much everyone earns, and what viewers discuss around the water cooler at work.

Incorporating the Sweeps concept into this curriculum also provides a significant learning opportunity for students. Each television class section produces a competing seven- to ten-minute show that is broadcast to the entire campus. Each class competes with the others by having peers vote for their favorite. Winners are announced on subsequent daily news programs. Students learn poignant lessons about the real world, in which the winning television shows are determined by how well they are received by their audience, not necessarily by the technical qualities of the program. Students become more media literate by learning the importance of marketing techniques such as establishing a *hook* and the importance of a logical and understandable premise, as well as how to deconstruct commonly used marketing tactics. While the competition provides internal incentives, grades for this contest are awarded based on independent criteria that are checked against a scorecard. These include a combination of how well the class operates together as a team, how smoothly the production process evolves, how closely the storyboard and script-building checklist is observed, and how well the camera and post-production techniques are followed.

The *Sweeps* projects are a course-culminating activity. They represent a full year of activities and learning experiences and how well team members have synthesized the material. The *Sweeps* show must conform to specific criteria designed to internalize the lessons taught throughout the year. All activities and learning objectives in earlier chapters result in teaching students how to put on a show.

Leading up to the final project are several interim activities in which students demonstrate, among other things, that they know or have an appreciation for

- the various jobs in a production team,

- visual awareness,

- team-building and cooperative learning,

- storytelling,

- pre- and post-production techniques, and

- how to market their products.

The projects are found at the appropriate points in both the *Teacher Edition* and the *Student Workbook*. Instructions, goals, and outcomes are listed, as well as suggestions for completing the projects. The **Web-ASSISTant** Web site contains links to sites that supply informational resources and background materials for students to complete their assignments. Students visit the referenced sites, research appropriate background information, and obtain visuals for their productions. There are linked sites for each class activity and project, as well as additional supplementary locations for teachers to use, should they decide to dig a little deeper into a specific subject area.

SUMMARY

This book is dedicated to those who want to implement a meaningful media program in their television production curriculum. It is a complete guide that includes detailed lesson plans, suggested chronologies, supplementary resources, and further readings for teachers to dig deeper into any subject material they wish. The course is supported by an

Internet Web site for both the teacher and students to complete course activities. In short, this book is a compendium of the ideas, concepts, and best practices taken from the best available teaching resources about television. Although suggestions for using various references are integrated directly into the course, final decisions about which materials are used, and to what degree, are left with the teacher. The same may be said for the lesson plans. They are detailed to the point of offering a possible script, but the format also provides an alternative approach for teachers who are more experienced in the subject matter.

The intent is to maintain the currency of the materials used in this book with the timeliness of a coordinating Web site on the Internet. There will also be links to other teaching materials and information on media, visual literacy, video production, media resources, and new technologies, as they become available.

Although this book was written as a complete plan, it is modular enough so that specific lessons can be implemented and integrated into existing courses.

RESOURCES

Davis, M. February 1997. Garage cinema and the future of media technology. *Communications of the ACM* 40 (2):42–48.

Gifford, B. R. Mediated learning: A new model of technology-mediated instruction and learning. *Mediated Learning Review*. Available: www.academic.com/mlreview/. (Accessed May 1, 1998).

Ontario Ministry of Education. 1996. *The common curriculum, Grades 1–9*. Toronto: Government of Ontario Bookstore Publications.

CHAPTER 1

Class Administration

For continuity purposes, the chapters in this book are organized topically. However, there is no requirement that they be covered in the exact order in which they are presented. In fact, it is strongly recommended that the lessons be taught in an alternative order. This textual organization might be frustrating to those who prefer their textbooks to be sequenced chronologically, with subject matter grouped in thematic units and taught in the same sequence the book is written. But to accommodate the major goals and objectives of this course, a decision was made to modify the traditional textbook approach.

The first goal of this course is to use media and visual literacy as its approach to television production. However, it also attempts to move away from the traditional deficit view of media education toward the "acquisition model" referred to by Kathleen Tyner in *Literacy in a Digital World: Teaching and Learning in the Age of Information* (1998, p. 131). In short, this book tries to balance the educational needs that require an academic review of our media culture with the practical and technical aspects of teaching television and multimedia production. Students generally enjoy discussing literacy topics in class, but they are also quite anxious to learn how to operate the equipment. Often they view formal class time as limiting the amount of time they have to work with the equipment. It might seem easier just to give in to these pressures and dispense with the classroom discussions. However, that would obviate a very significant teaching opportunity. As the broadcast industry is often blamed for creating the need for media education, it should be obvious that a good place to teach media literacy is in a television class. A good trade-off in course design appears to be the interspersing of short, formal classroom sessions with practical, portfolio-building activities. To do this, the recommended course sequence had to be modified.

The second major goal of this book is to present the subject matter in an iterative fashion to minimize the amount of rote memorization required of the students. Where possible, the rule of threes is used: Students are provided the opportunity to work with the material on as many as three different occasions. They are first presented with the materials during note-taking sessions. They are then either given the same materials several times during subsequent exams and quizzes, or they get to review the same materials as advanced organizers at the beginning of subsequent class discussions. Finally, they are actively engaged in using the information during small group and individual activities, and this serves as the basis for portfolio projects. Integrating the subject matter in this way requires that the materials be presented in a concept-mapped manner. An example might be the various class sessions covering a sequence that teaches verbal and nonverbal storytelling. A teacher might cover lesson content from the various chapters on media literacy, equipment operation, scriptwriting, and visual literacy that all tie together in building-block fashion. The lessons from different chapters are interspersed throughout a set time span and are all covered together. For example, the teacher might begin with basic camera operations, apertures, and framing from **Chapter 3**, then move on to the basics of scriptwriting and storyboards in **Chapter 4**. Next, the teacher might incorporate some sessions that cover visual literacy from **Chapter 5** (e.g., the principles of visual design) and then review Lesson 4.6. This lesson set then would wrap up with a review session called "Video Devises to Supplement a Teleplay or Newscast" from **Chapter 4,** in which students are taught that a scriptwriter is responsible for determining not only how thoughts are verbally expressed during a teleplay but also how some might be visualized using nonverbal communication. To aid in the learning process, test questions about the content of these lessons are repeated in different forms on sequential quizzes, depending on how the subject matter is covered in the individual lessons. The portfolio projects then gradually incorporate these same alternative perspectives in building-block fashion.

Although a concept-mapped textbook offers obvious advantages, the potential for inadvertently overlooking some important details of a particular subject is heightened because the content does not flow in chronological order. To maintain subject-matter integrity and continuity, a compromise was struck to organize the book by subject matter and then cross-reference it with a teaching chronology. The teacher may choose to follow one of two different, but similar, teaching chronologies:

- one that accommodates the traditional calendar and is organized for a semester system, in which students take courses for standard periods of time (one hour or less) throughout an entire school year, or

- one that serves a nonstandard format such as block schedules, in which students meet for extended time periods either daily or every other day during the course of the year.

The block schedule chronology could also be modified to fit the needs of those who wish to select only portions of the course because of the limited student interaction.

It is important to note that the teaching chronologies are only models. A teacher may strictly adhere to them or use them as a catalyst for an individual plan. However, to take full advantage of this alternate approach, it is highly recommended that the teacher become acquainted with the "Teaching Chronology" and then adopt a useable teaching sequence. This book has been written to accommodate just about any lesson sequence.

THE PURPOSE OF THIS CHAPTER

This chapter serves as a catchall that ties together all the administrative details. Because the book is a course guide and not a traditional textbook, some fundamental information on how to run the course needs to be covered first. In short, this chapter is a toolbox for the teacher that contains, in addition to the "Teaching Chronology," the following information:

• the philosophy behind using the **Web-ASSISTant** Web site,

• suggestions for the first few weeks of class,

• information on using the lessons in conjunction with the *Student Workbook,* and

• suggestions on how to build an assessment blueprint.

In addition, this chapter provides a class syllabus and grading policy and introduces the appendixes. **Appendix A** contains an alphabetized listing of terms, people, and phrases, with cross-references to the chapter and lessons in which they appear. This should act as a guide for students to prepare for final exams and to look up information, should the teacher decide to follow an open-book policy for the quizzes. The appendixes contain hard copies of the following forms used in this course:

Appendix A: List of Terms and Corresponding Lessons

Appendix B: Daily Activity Sheet

Appendix C: Equipment Competency Checklist

Appendix D: ENG/Segment Footage Log

Appendix E: Interview Worksheet

Appendix F: Project and Activity Planning Sheet

Appendix G   Segment Checklist/Scorecard

Appendix H: Portfolio Assessment Scorecards

Appendix I: Storyboard Worksheet

Appendix J: Alphabetic Listing of Mediated Resources

INTEGRATING THE WEB-ASSISTant INTO THE LESSONS AND ACTIVITIES

Because this course is mediated through videos, CDs, and the Internet, there are many additional support materials referred to throughout this book. A supplementary Web site (**www.web-assist.com**) created specifically for this course provides direct links to most of the materials for those who wish to purchase them. In addition, the site also contains information on obtaining template data files formatted to accommodate class administration, the PowerPoint slides, and the text itself. The information can also stand alone as a valuable resource tool for anyone interested in media education and is divided into separate frames. One frame links to pages supporting the chapters in this book. These pages provide links to additional research materials and information on prices and how to obtain the reference materials described in each chapter. This text cross-references to the Web site throughout where is appropriate. Each chapter also contains a "Digging Deeper" section that provides supplementary material for teachers or students who wish to review more, in-depth information from the class discussions. Usually, the material is provided in the form of a link to other Internet Web sites containing this information. When no online sites are available, information, direct links, or both are provided to obtain text materials.

Another frame on the **Web-ASSISTant** Web site provides links to information of a general nature for use in class or to add to teachers' general knowledge. The sidebar frame is broken down into two broad sections, one for teachers and the other for students. The teacher section has two subheadings: "Teaching and Learning" and "Research and Support." The student section is broken down into a section for project support and one for activities. There are seven page headings in the teacher section:

Page	Description
"Moments"	These are "additional teaching moments" that have been inspired by students, teachers, and readers of this book. They include short lesson plans of these corollary plans along with links to Internet sites and other materials in support of the lessons.
"Best Practices"	Dedicated to those sites and mediated activities that support media and teacher education.
"Standards"	List of Web sites at which educational teaching standards for media education may be found. Sorted by state and educational organization.
"HD/Digital TV"	List of links and information concerning the change to high definition and digital broadcasting that is supposed to take place by 2006.
"Hall of Fame"	A list of online sites about those individuals who have made significant contributions to either media education or the television broadcasting industry. Many of the locations are Web sites developed by students, who constructed them as class projects, and they are offered as models.
"Media Literacy"	An extensive list of text and Internet-based resources for teachers of media education, provided by Kathleen Tyner.
"Technology (Support Links)"	Links to Web sites that provide specific information on use of equipment, in-depth information on the latest trends in the industry, and sites posted to the Internet by other teachers of television and multimedia.

Because the **Web-ASSISTant** Web site is a living document, it will be in a continual state of change and will be constantly refined and modified. The pages are intended to demonstrate latest technologies and techniques, models, and thoughts on the various underlying topics and objectives of this course: media and visual literacy, mediated instruction and learning, and the broadcasting industry. Among the links provided on the Web site are shortcuts to sites where suggested reading texts, CDs, and videos may be purchased. All research links are reviewed regularly to ensure that they are still active and valid. Additional ones are added as seen fit.

THE LESSON SEQUENCE

As discussed previously, there are two teaching chronology models with identical sequences. The difference between them lies in the time needed in between each class session and the total elapsed time allowed for completing the projects. The first model supports those schools on a traditional calendar. The second chronology model reflects a 4 x 4 block schedule, in which students meet every day for approximately an hour and a half. These students complete the course in a single term. There are several other variations of these two schedules. Some schools operate on an A/B block, in which students meet every other day. The 4 x 4 block accommodates these schools with minimal modification.

All sessions are designed so they may be completed within a single class session, regardless of school calendar. Schools on a traditional calendar may have to intersperse class sessions and project work sessions on separate days. Those on a block schedule should be able to conduct the class sessions with the time left over for project work within the same class period.

Teaching students how to manage multiple simultaneous projects is a practical goal of this course. On many days, more than one project or activity will appear in the same timeslot. Due dates are scattered. Some projects may even end on the same day, or within a few days of each other. Students will have to learn how to plan their own time, taking into consideration conflicts in the availability of editing equipment, priority and critical path items, availability of talent, and so forth. Inserting these complications is intentional; it helps to schedule limited equipment and is a normal part of the learning process that television students must go through to improve their time-management skills.

The "Teaching Chronology" chronologies on the following pages summarize suggested activities by week. **Understand that they are models only.** They may be modified to suit the individual needs of each teacher. School holidays and vacations are not taken into account and will have to be accounted for, based on individual school calendars. All activities are cross-referenced to the specific chapters in the book in which they are described more fully.

TEACHING CHRONOLOGY

Model 1—Traditional Schedule

Note: Although the chronology generally follows the lesson format from the book, there are some differences in the titles found here in order to draw attention to those specific points that need to be focused on. Hopefully these differences are not significant enough to prevent you from following along with the program. The lesson and chapter numbers are an exact match.

Week 1

Class work → Chapt 1-Class Administration → Acceptable Use Policy:
Class work → Chapt 1-Class Administration → Class Role and Seat Assignment
Class work → Chapt 1-Class Administration → Class Syllabus and Grading
Class work → Chapt 1-Class Administration → Outcomes and Course Objectives
Class work → Chapt 1-Class Administration → Personal Objectives
Class work → Chapt 2-Media Literacy → Introduce News Analysis
Class work → Chapt 1-Class Administration →Introduce Web-ASSISTant Web Page
Class work → Chapt 1-Class Administration → Television and Media Production Needs Assessment
Class work → Chapt 1-Class Administration → Introduce Equipment Competencies

Week 2

Class work → Chapt 1-Class Administration → Hand out *Student Workbooks*:
Class work → Chapt 2-Media Literacy → Lesson 2.1A-Media Paradigm
Class work → Chapt 2-Media Literacy → Lesson 2.2-Copyrights
Class work → Chapt 2-Media Literacy → Lesson 2.2-Internet-Copyrights
Class work → Chapt 1-Class Administration → Personal Collage (Visual Story)
Class work → Chapt 2-Media Literacy → Assign Timeline Survey
Class work → Chapt 2-Media Literacy → Lesson 1-Review News Analysis
Class work → Chapt 2-Media Literacy → Video-Headlines & Sound Bites or Signal to Noise

Week 3

Class work → Chapt 2-Media Literacy → Review Timeline Survey
Class work → Chapt 2-Media Literacy → Optional Activity -*Decisions/Decisions*-50 min.
Class work → Chapt 3-Equipment Basics → Lesson 3.1B-Assign Kyker/Curchy Text Lesson 1
Class work → Chapt 3-Equipment Basics → Lesson 3.1B-Introduce Camera Parts
Projects/Activities → Proj 1-*Still Shots* → Introduce *Still Shots*
Projects/Activities → Proj 1-*Still Shots* → Bring in Pictures for *Still Shots*

Week 4

Class work → Chapt 2-Media Literacy → Lesson 2.4A-Video *Against All Odds* - Blocking & Sampling
Class work → Chapt 2-Media Literacy → Lesson 2.3-Censorship Versus First Amendment
Class work → Chapt 2-Media Literacy → Lesson 2.3-Code of Ethics
Class work → Chapt 2-Media Literacy → Lesson 2.4B- Ratings and Rankings Web-Quest
Class work → Chapt 2-Media Literacy → Review Nielsen Research Findings
Projects/Activities → Proj 1-*Still Shots* → Work on *Still Shots*

Week 5

Class work → Chapt 3-Equipment Basics → Lesson 3.1B-Apertures (Lens Versus F-Stop)
Class work → Chapt 3-Equipment Basics → Review Kyker/Curchy Text Lesson 1
Class work → Chapt 3-Equipment Basics → Lesson 3.2-Video *Understanding Television*
Class work → Chapt 3-Equipment Basics → Introduce Zettl's *Videolab 2.1*
Class work → Chapt 3-Equipment Basics → Lesson 3.1-Review Questions

Class work → Chapt 3-Equipment Basics → Lesson 3.2A-How Television Works
Class work → Chapt 3-Equipment Basics → Lesson 3.2B-How Videorecording
Class work → Chapt 1-Class Administration → Quiz 1
Projects/Activities → Proj 1-*Still Shots* → *Work on Still Shots*

Week 6
Class work → Chapt 1-Class Administration → Review Quiz 1
Class work → Chapt 3-Equipment Basics → Lesson 3.3-Assign Kyker/Curchy Text Lesson 2
Class work → Chapt 3-Equipment Basics → Lesson 3.5-Editing
Class work → Chapt 7-Production Process → Lesson 7.2-Implementing the Project Plan
Projects/Activities → Proj 2-*Stop Action* → *Introduce Stop Action*
Projects/Activities → Proj 1-*Still Shots* → *Work on Still Shots*

Week 7
Class work → Chapt 6-History of Broadcasting → Lesson 6.1-Pre-Marconi Era 1870–1900
Class work → Chapt 3-Equipment Basics → Review Kyker/Curchy Text Lesson 2
Class work → Chapt 3-Equipment Basics → Work on Assemble Edit (Numbers Project)
Projects/Activities → Proj 1- *Still Shots Due This Week*
Projects/Activities → Proj 2-*Stop Action* → *Work on Stop Action*

Week 8
Class work → Chapt 3-Equipment Basics → Assign Kyker/Curchy Text Lesson
Class work → Chapt 4-Writing for a Visual Medium → Lesson 4.1- Storyboards
Class work → Chapt 6-History of Broadcasting → Lesson 6.2-TV-Everyone Gets into the Act 1900-1919
Projects/Activities → Proj 2-*Stop Action* → *Work on Stop Action*:

Week 9
Class work → Chapt 4-Writing for a Visual Medium → Script Quest
Class work → Chapt 3-Equipment Basics → Review Kyker/Curchy Text Lesson 3
Class work → Chapt 4-Writing for a Visual Medium → Review Research
Projects/Activities → Proj 2-*Stop Action* → Work on *Stop Action*

Week 10
Class work → Chapt 4-Writing for a Visual Medium → Lesson 4.2- Active Versus Passive Voice
Class work → Chapt 3-Equipment Basics → Lesson 3.5-Character Generator
Class work → Chapt 3-Equipment Basics → Lesson 3.4A-Framing and Focusing a Picture
Class work → Chapt 3-Equipment Basics → Zettl's *Videolab 2.1*-Framing Sequence
Class work → Chapt 3-Equipment Basics → Zettl's *Videolab 2.1*-Depth of Field Sequence
Class work → Chapt 4-Writing for a Visual Medium → Lesson 4.6-Video Devices
Class work → Chapt 4-Writing for a Visual Medium → Lesson 4.3-Get the Lead Right
Class work → Chapt 6-History of Broadcasting → Lesson 6.3- Birth of Broadcasting 1920–1940
Projects/Activities → Proj 3-*Book Trailers* → Introduce *Book Trailers*
Projects/Activities → Proj 3-*Book Trailers* → Book Trailers Storyboard Due This Week
Projects/Activities → Proj 2- *Stop Action*-Due This Week

Week 11
Class work → Chapt 3-Equipment Basics → Lesson 3.3A-Audio Considerations
Class work → Chapt 3-Equipment Basics → Lesson 3.3B-Cables and Connectors
Class work → Chapt 3-Equipment Basics → Lesson 3.5-Insert Edit Due This Week
Class work → Chapt 4-Writing for a Visual Medium → Optional Lesson-Visual Storytelling
Class work → Chapt 3-Equipment Basics → Lesson 3.4C-Basic Camera Moves
Class work → Chapt 1-Class Administration → Quiz 2
Class work → Chapt 1-Class Administration → Review Quiz 2

Class work → Chapt 3-Equipment Basics → Lesson 3.4A-Assign Kyker/Curchy Text Lesson 4
Class work → Chapt 4-Writing for a Visual Medium → Lesson 4.4-Newswriter's Dazzling Dozen
Projects/Activities → Proj 3-*Book Trailers* → Work on *Book Trailers*

Week 12

Class work → Chapt 2-Media Literacy → Bring in Commercial to Show in Class
Class work → Chapt 3-Equipment Basics → Zettl's *Videolab 2.l*-Lens/Focus Sequence
Class work → Chapt 6-History of Broadcasting → Lesson 6.4-Babes in Broadcastland 1920–1930
Projects/Activities → Proj 3-*Book Trailers* → Work on *Book Trailers*

Week 13

Class work → Chapt 3-Equipment Basics → Review Kyker/Curchy Text Lesson 4
Class work → Chapt 3-Equipment Basics → Zettl's *Videolab 2.1*-Visual Forces Sequence
Class work → Chapt 1-Class Administration → Quiz 3
Projects/Activities → Proj 3-Book Trailers → Work on *Book Trailers*

Week 14

Class work → Chapt 3-Equipment Basics → Assign Kyker/Curchy Text Lesson 5
Class work → Chapt 3-Equipment Basics → Lesson 3.4-Visualizing:
Class work → Chapt 5-Developing Visual Acuity → Introduce News Reading 1
Class work → Chapt 5-Developing Visual Acuity → Work on News Reading 1

Week 15

Classwork → Chapt 6- History of Broadcasting → Lesson 6.5-Making Order out of Chaos 1927–1934
Class work → Chapt 6- History of Broadcasting → Lesson 6.6-Notes and Video-*Big Dream, Small Screen* -Part 1
Class work → Chapt 6- History of Broadcasting → Lesson 6.6-*Big Dream, Small Screen*-Part 2
Class work → Chapt 7-Production Process → Lesson 7.5-ENG Assignments
Class work → Chapt 7-Production Process → Review Kyker/Curchy Text Lesson 3
Class work → Chapt 5-Developing Visual Acuity → News Reading I Due This Week
Projects/Activities → Proj 3-*Book Trailers* → Work on *Book Trailers*

Week 16

Class work → Chapt 6- History of Broadcasting → Lesson 6.6-Video-*Big Dream, Small Screen* -Part 3
Class work → Chapt 6- History of Broadcasting → Lesson 6.6-Going for Broke 1935–1945
Class work → Chapt 1-Class Administration → Quiz 4
Projects/Activities → Proj 3-Book Trailers → Work on Book Trailers
Projects/Activities → Proj 4-*Instructional Video* → Introduce *Instructional Video*

Week 17

Projects/Activities → Proj 3-Book Trailers → Book Trailers-Due this week
Projects/Activities → Proj 4-*Instructional Video* → Work on *Instructional Video*
Projects/Activities → Proj 5-Interview/Newscast → Introduce *Interview for a News Magazine*

Week 18

Class work → Review for Midterm Exam
Class work → Midterm Exam
Projects/Activities → Proj 4-*Instructional Video* → Work on *Instructional Video*

Week 19

Class work → Chapt 5-Developing Visual Acuity → Lesson 5.1-The Making of *Citizen Kane*
Class work → Chapt 5-Developing Visual Acuity → Lesson 5.2-Body Language
Projects/Activities → Proj 4-*Instructional Video* → Work on *Instructional Video*

Week 20
    Class work → Chapt 5-Developing Visual Acuity → Lesson 5.3-Principles of Visual Design
    Class work → Chapt 5-Developing Visual Acuity → Lesson 5.3-On-Camera Etiquette
    Class work → Chapt 5-Developing Visual Acuity → Introduce News Reading 2
    Projects/Activities → Proj 4-*Instructional Video* → Work on *Instructional Video*

Week 21
    Class work → Chapt 5-Developing Visual Acuity → Lesson 5.3-Principles of Visual Design-Manipulating Moods:
    Projects/Activities → Proj 4-*Instructional Video* → Work on *Instructional Video*
    Projects/Activities → Chapt 5- → Work on News Reading 2
    Class work → Chapt 5- Developing Visual Acuity → Introduce Interview Segment:
    Projects/Activities → Proj 5-Interview/Newscast → Work on *Interview for a News Magazine*

Week 22
    Class work → Chapt 1-Class Administration → Quiz 5
    Class work → Chapt 2-Media Literacy → Lesson 2.6-War of the Worlds
    Class work → Chapt 6-History of Broadcasting → optional Video *45/85 American History Since WWII*
    Projects/Activities → Proj 4-*Instructional Video* → *Instructional Video*-Due this week
    Class Work → Chapt 5-Developing Visual Acuity → Work on News Reading 2
    Class work → Chapt 4-Writing for a Visual Medium → Opt. Review Act.: UB the Director

Week 23
    Class work → Chapt 5-Developing Visual Acuity → Lesson 5.2C-How to Conduct an Interview
    Class work → Chapt 6-History of Broadcasting → Lesson 6.7A-The Birth of Television 1945–1975
    Class work → Chapt 5-Developing Visual Acuity → Newsreading 2 Due This Week:
    Projects/Activities → Proj 5-Interview/Newscast → Work on *Interview for a News Magazine*

Week 24
    Class work → Chapt 6-History of Broadcasting → Lesson 6.8-Last Great Ride 1975–1985
    Class work → Chapt 2-Media Literacy → Lesson 2.5-Deconstructing Commercials
    Class work → Chapt 5-Developing Visual Acuity → Video-*Speak Up on Television*
    Projects/Activities → Proj 5-Interview/Newscast → Work on *Interview for a News Magazine*

Week 25
    Class work → Chapt 2-Media Literacy → Lesson 2.5B-Advertising Tools and Techniques
    Projects/Activities → Proj 7-*PSA/Commercial* → Introduce *PSA/Commercial*
    Projects/Activities → Proj 7-*PSA/Commercial* → Work on *PSA/Commercial*
    Projects/Activities → Proj 6-*Decades* → Introduce *Decades*

Week 26
    Class work → Chapt 6-History of Broadcasting → Video *Quiz Show*
    Projects/Activities → Proj 6-*Decades* → Work on *Decades*
    Projects/Activities → Proj 5-Interview/Newscast → Work on *Interview for a News Magazine*
    Projects/Activities → Proj 5- *Interview for a News Magazine* Due This Week

Week 27
    Class work → Chapt 7-Production Process → Lesson 7.1-ASSURE Planning Model
    Class work → Chapt 7-Production Process → Lesson 7.3-Production Scheduling
    Class work → Chapt 7-Production Process → Lesson 7.6-In-Studio Etiquette
    Projects/Activities → Proj 7-*PSA/Commercial* → Work on *PSA/Commercial*

Week 28
    Class work → Chapt 7-Production Process → Lesson 7.4 Production Crew Responsibilities
    Class work → Chapt 7-Production Process → Lesson 7.7-Post production

Class work → Chapt 1-Class Administration → Quiz 6
Projects/Activities → Proj 7- *PSA/Commercial* Due This Week
Projects/Activities → Proj 6-Decades → Work on *Decades*

Week 29

Projects/Activities → Proj 8-*Sweeps* → Introduce *Sweeps*
Projects/Activities → Proj 8-*Sweeps* → Last Year's *Sweep*s
Class work → Chapt 3-Equipment Basics → Lesson 3.6-Bringing TV into the Digital Age

Week 30

Class work → Chapt 3-Equipment Basics → Work on Numbers Project:
Class work → Chapt 6-History of Broadcasting → Lesson 6.9-The Birth of Tabloid Television 1986–1999
Projects/Activities → Proj 8-*Sweeps* → Work on *Sweeps*

Week 31

Projects/Activities → Proj 6-*Decades* → Work on Decades
Projects/Activities → Proj 8-*Sweeps* → Work on *Sweeps*
Class Work → Chapt 7-Production Process → Lesson 7.8-UB Director

Week 32

Projects/Activities → Proj 6-*Decades* → Work on *Decades*
Projects/Activities → Proj 8-*Sweeps* → Work on *Sweeps*
Class Work → Chapt 7-Production Process → Lesson 7.9-Segment Checklist

Week 33

Projects/Activities → Proj 6-*Decades* → Work on *Decades*
Projects/Activities → Proj 8-*Sweeps* → Work on *Sweeps*

Week 34

Projects/Activities → Proj 6-*Decades* → Work on *Decades*
Projects/Activities → Proj 8-*Sweeps* → Work on *Sweeps*

Week 35

Projects/Activities → Proj 6-*Decades* → Work on *Decades*
Projects/Activities → Proj 8-*Sweeps* → Work on *Sweeps* **Exam Week**
Class work → Chapt 1-Class Administration → Final Exam Review
Class work → Chapt 1-Class Administration → Final Exam

Model 2—4 x 4 Block

Week 1

Class work → Chapt 1-Class Admin/Assessment → Acceptable Use Policy

Class work → Chapt 1-Class Admin/Assessment → Class Role and Seat Assignment

Class work → Chapt 1-Class Administration → Class Syllabus and Grading

Class work → Chapt 1-Class Administration → Outcomes and Course Objectives

Class work → Chapt 1-Class Admin Administration → Personal Objectives

Class work → Chapt 1-Class Admin Administration → Introduce Web-ASSISTant Web Page

Class work → Chapt 1-Class Admin Administration → Television and Media Production Needs Assessment

Class work → Chapt 2-Media Literacy → Introduce News Analysis

Class work → Chapt 2-Media Literacy → Video *Headlines & Sound Bites* or *Signal to Noise*

Class work → Chapt 1-Class Administration → Hand out *Student Workbook*

Class work → Chapt 2-Media Literacy → Lesson 2.1A-Media Paradigm

Class work → Chapt 2-Media Literacy → Lesson 2.2-Copyrights:

Class work → Chapt 2-Media Literacy → Lesson 2.2-Internet-Copyrights

Class work → Chapt 1-Class Administration → Personal Collage (Visual Story)

Class work → Chapt 3-Equipment Basics → Lesson 3.1A-Basic Care of Equipment

Class work → Chapt 2-Media Literacy → Assign Timeline Survey

Class work → Chapt 2-Media Literacy → Lesson 2.1B-Review News Analysis

Class work → Chapt 3-Equipment Basics → Lesson 3.1B-Introduce Camera Parts

Week 2

Class work → Chapt 1-Class Administration → Introduce Equipment Competencies

Class work → Chapt 2-Media Literacy → Review Nielsen Research Findings

Class work → Chapt 2-Media Literacy → Review Timeline Survey

Class work → Chapt 2-Media Literacy → Optional Activity-Video- *Decisions/Decisions*-50 min.

Class work → Chapt 3-Equipment Basics → Assign Kyker/Curchy Text Lesson 1

Class work → Chapt 2-Media Literacy → Lesson 2.4A-Video *Against All Odds*-Blocking and Sampling

Class work → Chapt 2-Media Literacy → Lesson 2.4B- Ratings and Rankings Web-Quest

Class work → Chapt 3-Equipment Basics → Lesson 3.1B-Aperture (Lens Versus F-stop)

Class work → Chapt 2-Media Literacy → Lesson 2.1B-The Makings of a Newscast

Class work → Chapt 2-Media Literacy → Lesson 2.3-Censorship Versus First Amendment:

Class work → Chapt 2-Media Literacy → Lesson 2.3-Code of Ethics:

Class work → Chapt 2-Media Literacy → Lesson 2.4-Surveys

Projects/Activities → Proj 1-*Still Shots* → Introduce *Still Shots*

Projects/Activities → Proj 1-*Still Shots* → Bring in Pictures for *Still Shots*-

Projects/Activities → Proj 1-*Still Shots* → Work on *Still Shots*

Week 3

Class work → Chapt 3-Equipment Basics → Lesson 3.2-Video-*Understanding Television*

Class work → Chapt 3-Equipment Basics → Lesson 3.2A -How Television Works

Class work → Chapt 3-Equipment Basics → Review Kyker/Curchy Text Lesson 1

Class work → Chapt 3-Equipment Basics → Lesson 3.2B-How Videorecording Works:

Class work → Chapt 1-Class Admin/Assessment → Quiz 1

Projects/Activities → Proj 1-*Still Shots* → Work on *Still Shots*

Projects/Activities → Proj 2-*Stop Action* → Introduce *Stop Action*

Projects/Activities → Proj 2-*Stop Action* → Work on *Stop Action*

Week 4

Class work → Chapt 1-Class Admin/Assessment → Review-Quiz 1

Class work → Chapt 3-Equipment Basics → Lesson 3.3-Assign Kyker-Curchy Text Lesson 2

Class work → Chapt 3-Equipment Basics → Lesson 3.1-Review Questions

Class work → Chapt 4-Writing for a Visual Medium → Lesson 4.1-Story Boards
Class work → Chapt 3-Equipment Basics → Lesson 3.5-Character Generator
Class work → Chapt 3-Equipment Basics → Lesson 3.5-Editing
Class work → Chapt 3-Equipment Basics → Introduce Zettl's *Videolab 2.1*
Class work → Chapt 6- History of Broadcasting → Lesson 6.1-Pre-Marconi Era 1870–1900
Class work → Chapt 3-Equipment Basics → Lesson 3.1B-Apertures
Projects/Activities → Proj 1-*Still Shots* → Work on *Still Shots*
Projects/Activities → Proj 2-*Stop Action* → Work on *Stop Action*
Projects/Activities → Proj 1- *Still Shots* Due This Week

Week 5

Class work → Chapt 3-Equipment Basics → Review Kyker/Curchy Text Lesson 2
Class work → Chapt 6-How History of Broadcasting → Lesson 6.2-Everyone Gets into the Act 1900–1919
Class work → Chapt 1-Class Admin/Assessment → Quiz 2
Class work → Chapt 1-Class Admin/Assessment → Review Quiz 2
Projects/Activities → Chapt 3-Equipment Basics → Lesson 3.5-Assign Assemble Edit (numbers Project)
Projects/Activities → Chapt 3-Equipment Basics → Lesson 3.5-Work on Assemble Edit (numbers Project)
Projects/Activities → Chapt 3-Equipment Basics → Assemble Edit Due This Week
Projects/Activities → Proj 2-*Stop Action* → Work on *Stop Action*

Week 6

Class work → Chapt 3-Equipment Basics → Lesson 3.3-Assign Kyker/Curchy Text Lesson 5
Class work → Chapt 4-Writing for a Visual Medium → Lesson 4.1- Storyboards
Class work → Chapt 3-Equipment Basics → Lesson 3.3A-Audio considerations
Class work → Chapt 3-Equipment Basics → Review Kyker/Curchy Text Lesson 5
Class work → Chapt 4-Writing for a Visual Medium → Optional Pre-Lesson Web-Quest
Class work → Chapt 6-History of Broadcasting → Lesson 6.3-Birth of Broadcasting 1920–1940
Class work → Chapt 4-Writing for a Visual Medium → Review Optional Pre-Lesson Web-Quest
Class work → Chapt 3-Equipment Basics → Lesson 3.3B-Cables and Connectors
Class work → Chapt 3-Equipment Basics → Assign System Setup Review Activity
Class work → Chapt 5-Develop. Visual Awareness → Introduce News Reading 1
Projects/Activities → Chapt 5-Developing Visual Acuity → Work on News Reading 1
Projects/Activities → Proj 2-*Stop Action* → Work on *Stop Action*

Week 7

Class work → Chapt 7-Production Process → Lesson 7.2-Implementing the Project Plan
Class work → Chapt 3-Equipment Basics → Lesson 3.4A-Assign Kyker-Curchy Text Lesson
Class work → Chapt 3-Equipment Basics → Go Over System Setup Review Activity
Class work → Chapt 6- History of Broadcasting → Lesson 6.4- Babes in Broadcastland 1920–1930
Class work → Chapt 6-History of Broadcasting → Lesson 6.5-Making Order out of Chaos
Class work → Chapt 4-Writing for a Visual Medium → Optional Lesson Visual Storytelling
Class work → Chapt 5-Developing Visual Acuity → Work on News Reading 1
Projects/Activities → Proj 2-*Stop Action* → Work on *Stop Action*
Projects/Activities → Proj 3-*Book Trailers* → Introduce *Book Trailers*
Projects/Activities → Proj 3-*Book Trailers* → Work on *Book Trailers*

Week 8

Class work → Chapt 4-Writing for a Visual Medium → Active Versus Passive Voice
Class work → Chapt 5-Developing Visual Acuity → Work on News Reading 1
Class work → Chapt 3-Equipment Basics → Review Kyker-Curchy Text Lesson
Class work → Chapt 1-Class Administration → Quiz 3
Class work → Chapt 4-Writing for a Visual Medium->Lesson 4.2-Visual Storytelling
Class work → Chapt 5-Developing Visual Acuity → News Reading 1 Due This Week
Projects/Activities → Proj 2-*Stop Action* → Work on *Stop Action*

Projects/Activities → Proj 3-*Book Trailers* → Introduce *Book Trailers*
Projects/Activities → Proj 3- *Book Trailers* → Work on *Book Trailers*
Projects/Activities → Proj 2- *Stop Action* Due This Week

Week 9

Class work → Chapt 6- History of Broadcasting → Lesson 6.6- Going for Broke 1935–1945
Class work → Chapt 6- History of Broadcasting → Lesson 6.6-Notes and Video-*Big Dreams, Small Screen*-Part 1
Class work → Chapt 6- History of Broadcasting → Lesson 6.6-Notes and Video-*Big Dreams, Small Screen*-Part 2
Class work → Chapt 6- History of Broadcasting → Lesson 6.6-Notes and Video-*Big Dreams, Small Screen*-Part 3
Class work → Chapt 1-Class Admin/Assessment → Quiz 4
Projects/Activities → Chapt 3-Equipment Basics → Lesson 3.5-Assign Insert Edit (Numbers Project)
Projects/Activities → Chapt 3-Equipment Basics → Lesson 3.5-Work on Insert Edit (Numbers Project)
Projects/Activities → Proj 3-*Book Trailers* → Work on *Book Trailers*
Projects/Activities → Proj 4-*Instructional Video* → Work on *Instructional Video*
Projects/Activities → Proj 3- *Book Trailers* Due This Week

Week 10

Class work → Class work → Chapt 3-Equipment Basics → Lesson 3.6- Bringing Television into the Digital Age
Class work → Review for Midterm Exam
Class work → Midterm Exam
Projects/Activities → Proj 4-*Instructional Video* → Work on *Instructional Video*

Week 11

Class work → Chapt 5-Developing Visual Acuity → Lesson 5.1-The Making of *Citizen Kane*
Class work → Chapt 5-Developing Visual Acuity → Lesson 5.2-Body Language
Class work → Chapt 6-History of Broadcasting → Lesson 6.7A-The Birth of Television 1945–1975
Class work → Chapt 3-Equipment Basics → Lesson 3.5-Work on Insert Edit
Class work → Chapt 3-Equipment Basics → Lesson 3.5-Insert Edit Due This Week
Class work → Chapt 5-Developing Visual Acuity → Introduce News Reading 2
Class work → Chapt 5-Developing Visual Acuity → Work on News Reading 2
Projects/Activities → Proj 5-Interview/Newscast → Introduce *Interview for a News Magazine*

Week 12

Class work → Chapt 3-Equipment Basics → Lesson 3.4A-Framing and Focusing
Class work → Chapt 3-Equipment Basics → Zettl's *Videolab 2.1*-Framing Sequence
Class work → Chapt 3-Equipment Basics → Zettl's *Videolab 2.1*-Depth of Field Sequence
Class work → Chapt 3-Equipment Basics → Lesson 4.2 Visual Forces:
Class work → Chapt 3-Equipment Basics → Zettl's *Videolab 2.1*-Visual Forces Sequence
Class work → Chapt 4-Writing for a Visual Medium → Lesson 4.6-Video Devices
Class work → Chapt 6-History of Broadcasting → Lesson 6.8-The Last Great Ride 1975–1985
Projects/Activities → Chapt 5-Developing Visual Acuity → Work on News Reading 2
Projects/Activities → Proj 5-Interview/Newscast → Work on *Interview for a News Magazine*
Projects/Activities → Proj 6-*Decades* → Introduce *Decades*
Projects/Activities → Proj 6-*Decades* → Work on *Decades*

Week 13

Class work → Chapt 3-Equipment Basics → Lesson 3.4C-Basic Camera Moves
Class work → Chapt 5-Developing Visual Acuity → Lesson 5.3-Principles of Visual Design
Class work → Chapt 5-Developing Visual Acuity → Lesson 5.3-On-Camera Etiquette
Class work → Chapt 3-Equipment Basics → Zettl's *Videolab 2.1*-Lens/Focus Sequence
Class work → Chapt 6-History of Broadcasting → Lesson 6.9-The Birth of Tabloid Television 1986–1999
Class work → Chapt 6-History of Broadcasting → Video-*Quiz Show*
Class work → Chapt 5-Developing Visual Acuity → Lesson 5.3-Principles of Visual Design-Manipulating Moods

Projects/Activities → Chapt 5-Developing Visual Acuity → News Reading 2-Due this Week
Projects/Activities → Proj 5-Interview/Newscast → Work on *Interview for a News Magazine*
Projects/Activities → Proj 6-*Decades* → Work on *Decades* Project

Week 14

Class work → Chapt 1-Class Admin/Assessment → Quiz 5
Class work → Chapt 5-Developing Visual Acuity → Scene-Building Worksheet
Class work → Chapt 7-Production Process → Lesson 7.6-In-Studio Etiquette
Class work → Chapt 2-Media Literacy → Lesson 2.5B-Review Advertising Tools and Techniques
Class work → Chapt 2-Media Literacy → Lesson 2.5-Deconstructing Commercials
Projects/Activities → Proj 5-Interview/Newscast → Work on *Interview for a News Magazine*
Projects/Activities → Proj 6-*Decades* → Work on *Decades*
Projects/Activities → Proj 8-*Sweeps* → Introduce *Sweeps*
Projects/Activities → Proj 8-*Sweeps* → Last year's *Sweeps*
Projects/Activities → Proj 8-*Sweeps* → Planning Time
Projects/Activities → Proj 8-Sweeps → Work on *Sweeps*

Week 15

Class work → Chapt 2-Media Literacy → Bring in Commercial to Show in Class
Class work → Chapt 7-Production Process → Assign Kyker-Curchy Text Lesson 3
Class work → Chapt 7-Production Process → Lesson 7.1-ASSURE Planning Model
Class work → Chapt 7-Production Process → Lesson 7.3-Production Scheduling
Class work → Chapt 7-Production Process → Lesson 7.4 Production Crew Responsibilities
Class work → Chapt 7-Production Process → Lesson 7.5-ENG Assignments
Class work → Chapt 7-Production Process → Lesson 7.7-Post-production
Projects/Activities → Proj 5-Interview/Newscast → Work on *Interview for a News Magazine*
Projects/Activities → Proj 6-*Decades* → Work on *Decades*
Projects/Activities → Proj 8-*Sweeps* → Work on *Sweeps*

Week 16

Class work → Chapt 7-Production Process → Review Kyker-Curchy Text Lesson
Class work → Chapt 5-Developing Visual Acuity → Lesson 5.2-Video-*Speak up on Television*
Class work → Chapt 2-Media Literacy → Lesson 2.6-War of the Worlds
Class work → Chapt 1-Class Administration → Quiz 6
Class work → Chapt 7-Production Process → Lesson 7.8-UB Director
Projects/Activities → Proj 5-Interview/Newscast → Work on *Interview for a News Magazine*
Projects/Activities → Proj 6-*Decades* → Work on *Decades*
Projects/Activities → Proj 7-Commercial → Introduce PSA/Commercial
Projects/Activities → Proj 8-*Sweeps* → Work on *Sweeps*

Week 17

Class work → Chapt 7-Production Process → Lesson 7.9-Segment Checklist:
Class work → Chapt 5-Developing Visual Acuity → Lesson 5.4-Learning How to Learn
Projects/Activities → Proj 5-*Interview for a News Magazine* Due This Week
Projects/Activities → Proj 6-*Decades* Due This Week
Projects/Activities → Proj 7-*PSA/Commercial* → Work on *PSA/Commercial*
Projects/Activities → Proj 8-*Sweeps* → Work on *Sweeps*

Week 18

Class work → Chapt 1-Class Administration → Final Exam Review
Class work → Chapt 1-Class Administration → Final Exam
Projects/Activities → Proj 7- *PSA/Commercial* Due This Week
Projects/Activities → Proj 8-*Sweeps* → Broadcast and Vote

THE FIRST FEW DAYS

The first few days of class are special. They are also critical for assuring the overall success of the class. First, your students will be quite anxious to get going on the equipment. However, it is necessary to cover some specific items that, if they are not covered very early, will lose their impact. The first few days provide the opportunity for the students to get to know each other. In addition, the media issues are quite important to the overall tone of the class, and it is very important to set the context in which the class discussions will operate. Teenagers do not innately understand that the specific media and visual awareness issues even exist, let alone that they need careful consideration. Setting up the contextual background to describe the issues is important in creating relevance, a necessary learning prerequisite.

During the first few days of class things can be quite chaotic: Students being added to and withdrawn from the class roll, and so forth. It may be quite difficult to get very far into course content until the classes are finalized. Yet the schedule is so full of content that you cannot afford to lose too much time. The first few days are a perfect time to go over your syllabus and class rules and introduce some of the history, traditions, and fundamentals of media and communications. The early days of the term provide an opportunity to lay the groundwork for some of the media education and visual awareness sessions. The news-media filtering paradigm, how broadcasters make money, and how newsworthiness is determined, as well as how newscasts are assembled, are good media topics that are useful for any student. Anyone who happens to drop out of the course will still be able to come away with some usable information. Much of the media literacy course material is also appropriate for life management and English classes. The first few days are also a good time to consider how to manage the cooperative learning environment in which the group-based projects must operate. Initiating some basic team-building activities is necessary and is also a great ice-breaker to provide useful information about individuals in class with regard to their work-ethic, existing knowledge about course content, and interpersonal and communication skills.

SHORT-TERM GOALS FOR THE
FIRST TWO WEEKS OF CLASS

Following are activities that are best covered early in the course. Because they are general in nature, they are not covered specifically in any other chapters in this book.

1.   Assess Existing Knowledge

Some students may come to class with television production experience from another course. Most programs are independently constructed, based on the individual school's needs and perceptions of the value of a television class. Because there are no standardized benchmarks, students will arrive with a mix of experiences. Some will overestimate how much they know and will try to convince the teacher that they do not need to sit through classes that cover the basics. A needs assessment is a good way to determine existing knowledge and to balance some inflated egos of those who believe they are already experts in the field. The following is a sample of an assessment questionnaire that represents some of the key issues presented in this course. Because it is a sample, it may be used as is or be modified to suit individual needs. Multiple-choice questions may be better suited to pre-needs assessments. The intent of a fill-in-the-blanks style instrument is to have students note one of two things: whether they know what the terms mean, or simply whether they have ever seen them before. Both forms of identification yield information the teacher can use. Regardless of format, some type of pre-needs assessment should be done.

The following represents only a partial listing of the terms introduced during this course. It is not intended to show complete knowledge of the entire course. It serves only to identify a cross-reference of those materials taught in the course to provide to the teacher with an idea of the level of magnitude of the students' preexisting knowledge.

Sample Television and Media Production Needs Assessment

Following is a partial list of terms and concepts that we will be covering in this course. This is not a test. Rather, it is an attempt to find out how much you already know. It is not intended to be a complete list, but represents some of the core concepts. Be as honest as you can about answering the questions.

1. True or False: Marconi invented the Radio.   **T   F**

2. True or False: Television was first thought of during the late 1800s.   **T   F**

3. What does the *chroma key* on the A-V board do?

    _____

4. What does the viewfinder on a camera do? _____

5. What is meant by the expression, "The viewfinder often does not always tell the truth"?

    _____

6. Name four pieces of information the viewfinder provides:

    1. _____ 2. _____ 3. _____ 4. _____

7. What does the term *white space* mean?

    _____

8. What is a storyboard? _____

9.–11. What is a copyright? _____

        a patent? _____

        a trademark? _____

12.   For each of the following terms:
        1) circle the words you recognize or have seen before
        2) define the ones that you feel you know

audio dub _____

2nd generation _____

sticks _____

ENG _____

RCA _____

VU meter _____

footage _____

13.   What does the term *Sweeps* mean, with regard to television broadcasting?

_____

14–15. How do television stations/networks make their money?

_____

Name three things upon which they base how much they charge for their services:

1. _____   2. _____   3. _____

16.   What does the f-stop in a camera do?

_____

17.   In a 10:1 zoom what does the 1 stand for?

_____

18.   What is a CCD?

_____

19.   What is audio dubbing?

_____

20.   Define the term *media literacy*.

_____

2. Build a Consensus Toward a Class Code of Ethics

Attempts have been made by broadcasters to regulate their own activities regarding on-air conduct, copyrights, and show content. Introducing the broadcaster's code of ethics provides an easy segue into the same issues as they relate to class activities. Decisions will have to be made rather early about how copyrighted material will be used and permitted in class. Discussions regarding industry rules and regulations should take place very early in the term. This will place the issue in a real-world context and will make it easier to deal with when situations arise. In most cases, media students become very sensitive and sympathetic to the copyright issues. They also take ownership of the problem after they take part in establishing a code of ethics.

Because the Internet is integrated with class activities, adopting an acceptable use policy (AUP) is a good strategy and should be done early in the course. This is a self-monitoring and self-regulating agreement among students, their parents, and the school that governs what is acceptable behavior when using the Internet. There are two schools of thought about using the Internet. There are those who wish to protect students from ever encountering unacceptable sites, through censorship and filters. Others feel that teaching appropriate use is best. Often, schools refer to this as a technology code of ethics and handle this on a schoolwide basis. If you follow the latter path, you certainly should insist that an AUP be used. Other examples are provided via links to the Internet on the **Web-ASSISTant** Web site. The sites provided directly by the **Web-ASSISTant** Web site have been reviewed to ensure as much as possible that they contain only appropriate material. However, because the Internet changes so rapidly and the links provided are external to and not owned by the **Web-ASSISTant** Web site, there can be no guarantees. Spending a few moments reviewing your school's AUP is time well spent during the first few days of class.

3. Introduce the Technology of Television

The Discovery Channel School has produced a great video, *Understanding Television*, that is copyright cleared for presentation in class. It is a solid introduction to the course during the first few days. The video provides a balanced background for the topics that will be covered over the course of the term. It may be necessary to replay portions of this tape throughout the course as the specific topics are introduced in detail. The video runs for approximately 50 minutes and comes with a teacher discussion guide. The tape is organized into two sections. The first introduces many of the technical terms and concepts found in **Chapter 3**. The second explores digital and high definition concepts that are covered in **Chapter 7**. This is one portion of the tape, in particular, that will probably serve the class well if it is replayed just prior to conducting those discussions.

The video is supplemented by its own Web site. Links to that Web site, as well as information on how to obtain the video, can be found in the "Digging Deeper" section of the **Web-ASSISTant** Web site.

4. Students Should Establish Their Own Personal Relationship with the Media

Educators tend to frame media studies in the negative because it is much easier to do and is often considered politically correct. However, the goal of this course is to balance any critique with positive experiences. It is critical, therefore, to spend time introducing both sides of the issue. There are several mediated resources that have already been mentioned; the New Mexico Media Literacy Project CD, the *Headlines & Sound Bites* video, and the *Signal to Noise* series all help to make these points. However, a serious discussion should take place about the positive aspects of the media, covering such things as

- new interactive technologies;

- the integration of the Internet, computer, and telephone with television;

- the increased access everyone has to information; and, especially,

- the increased ability students have to learn from other's use of media and transfer this newly found knowledge to other learning experiences.

It is also very important that no targeted value judgments about the media be made. The teacher's role is to present the facts and allow students to make informed decisions about what they see and hear so they may establish their own relationship with the media. This may be difficult, but it is the only way students will become lifelong learners who can think for themselves. It is important to take the lead from the news anchor's code of ethics: that editorializing be clearly identified ahead of time and not commingled with the presentation of the facts.

5. Assign the First Visual Story

Because you will be faced with students from various backgrounds, you will need to determine how well individual students will work together, who has had prior television experience, and, generally, which students you will be able to count on during the sessions. You will need to know who prefers to work in the background, who wants to be on-screen talent, and so forth. An activity that seems to work well in helping introduce students to one another is to have students create a cover page for their *Workbook* that contains a pictorial story and/or symbolic representation about themselves: what they like to do, their favorite colors, music, and the like. The objective is to introduce the emphasis being placed on developing visual and nonverbal communication capabilities. This will also provide an idea of a student's visual orientation. Lack of artistic skill should not be a drawback. In fact, it may even be an opportunity to test resourcefulness. Students may supplement their covers with pictures cut out of a magazine, photos, and so forth. In short, this is their first attempt at trying to tell a story using only visual clues.

Because it is also a way to benchmark your students' visual acuity, it is best that this assignment be given with minimal instructions. These collages should not be critiqued for their technique (use of colors, location of pictures, and etc.). Students will be able to use this first assignment as a pretest to measure their ability to create a visual story at the time they enter the course. After participating in lessons about the use of visual cues, using video equipment and multimedia to create visual imagery, how to supplement videos with audio, and so forth, they should be able to look back on these first assignments and critique them, describing what they would do differently. This provides them with another feedback mechanism at the end of the course to see how much progress they have made.

6. Introduce How the Internet Is Integrated into the Course

In the future, as students become more Internet-active on their own outside of school, teaching them how to access the Internet may not be an important initial learning activity. Even so, it is a good idea during the first few days to spend some time on the Internet in teams to help determine which students work well together. A useful and fun activity is a Web scavenger hunt, which consists of a question sheet that students fill out in teams using information they gather from the Web. There are two activities using content from media education that can be used. A Web-Quest is a useful project to help students get started. This activity covers information that will help students become more knowledgeable about television ratings. Information they find will help them take a more active part in discussions about Sweeps and the issues surrounding how broadcasters earn money. The second activity is an activity sheet on copyrights in which students are led to several sites that discuss copyrights and responsibilities, and it ties in very well with the literacy theme. All references, activities, and follow-up work for both activities may be found on the **Web-ASSISTant** Web site. Using the provided sites should cut down on the time it takes to have students research this information. Even the most Internet-active students could use more experience developing critical thinking skills necessary to perform research efficiently. Younger students tend to have knowledge of only one or two of the more popular search engines or directories, and these might not be the best ones to use in an educational environment, severely limiting their ability to access the material they need.

7. Set the Ground Rules for Equipment Usage

The most important psychological factor for students during the first two weeks is to overcome their anxiety about working with equipment. There is one school of thought holding that students should simply begin because everyone learns best by doing and by learning from mistakes. Other teachers will want students to learn everything there is to know about the equipment prior to allowing them to touch it. The best approach lies somewhere in between. There is an old joke that goes:

> *If you give an infinite amount of monkeys an infinite number of typewriters and provide them with an infinite amount of time, eventually, they might re-create Shakespeare.*

The brunt of jokes like this usually is those people who never seem to be able to complete their work on time. As a teacher, you have to draw the line somewhere. You will never have enough time to teach enough skills so that students do not make any mistakes while creating their projects. A teacher's job is to facilitate growth by providing students with enough knowledge to get started and then provide them with small tasks to accomplish their goals.

This strategy accomplishes two things. First, it gives students the opportunity to use the equipment earlier. Second, it teaches them how to transfer knowledge. Newly acquired skills from earlier projects will help them take on the more the complex issues in later projects. In addition, there is some truth to the theory that students learn best in problem-solving environments. They tend to remember how to operate the equipment when they learn how to solve specific problems they encounter. This is the philosophy behind the sequencing of the projects. It is also the rationale behind the sequencing of class sessions in the "Teaching Chronology."

During the first week, students are presented with a small activity to introduce them to basic ground rules for using equipment, along with a few basic operating instructions. Their first task is to work in teams and assess their partners' initial operational skills. Afterward, the class gets back together to discuss their first activities and what they have learned. The second hands-on session (which takes place a few days later) covers using cameras to accomplish specific tasks and introduces the first project. This way, students are given the opportunity to learn basic handling procedures and class rules prior to getting too involved with project details.

8.   Introduce Ground Rules for Cooperative Learning Activities

Developing teamwork is the critical path toward making cooperative learning a success, especially with socially conscious teenagers. Younger students sometimes have a hard time coping with being placed on teams where other members are not personal friends. A good way to emphasize teamwork and to ensure that team projects are a success is to spend some time during the first few days playing team-building games. *Decisions-Decisions: Violence in the Media,* published by Tom Snyder Productions, is a media-assisted simulation game in which students form teams to role play. This activity actually accomplishes two distinct goals. Besides team building, *Decisions-Decisions* is also an educational aid that introduces some very important media issues. How this activity fits into the educational framework is covered in detail in **Chapter 2**. The emphasis here is to stress the role the game can play in helping to teach students how to set goals and to deal with assorted complications and influences from biases, preconceived opinions, assorted unrelated facts, and potentially false assumptions that might cause them to stray from their target. All of these are very common to one who is faced with tough decisions and deviations when trying to implement a plan to attain set goals and objectives. This game also introduces a few new vocabulary concepts: the difference between opinion and fact and how biases, preconceived ideas, and assumptions can taint results.

This activity can be completed within two or three standard 50-minute classes or one or two 90-minute block periods.

For those who do not wish to invest the time in taking on a full program like *Decisions/Decisions*, there are several other shorter simulation and team-building games. The **Web-ASSISTant** Web site directs students to a couple of locations that offer online books and reference materials.

HOW TO USE THE *STUDENT WORKBOOK* IN CLASS

The boldfaced and underlined words in the lessons in the teacher's guide refer to the items that are left blank in the *Student Workbook*. The teacher's edition lesson plans contain the identical text as the *Student Workbook,* with the missing words underlined. Students are to fill in the missing word to complete the sentences as you discuss them. This will enable you to determine that each student is staying on task. Generally, students are quite concerned about missing any words, so you will be able to gauge if they are at least writing the words down in their *Workbooks*.

The advantage of using lesson plans is obvious, but using them properly in class is crucial. It is not suggested that the teacher simply read from the scripts. This approach will severely limit the interaction between teacher and student that occurs during open discussions. However, on occasion (especially in the beginning of the term), following the script very closely makes a lot of sense. Students will get accustomed to filling in the blanks in their *Student Workbooks*. This concept is not always evident to students and will have to be reinforced. Sometimes, several verbatim repetitions of the facts may be required for some students to get all the information. Others will not bother to write anything down at all. The script-with-blanks format aids the process of identifying those students who are off-task or are not writing down the correct information. It follows that those who do not get the information written down are probably not on task and have developed poor learning habits. Some students are poorly motivated and register for an elective course simply because they perceive it to be an easy grade. A structured note-taking session is an easy way to identify these students.

Each session contains a set of review questions for students to synthesize and summarize what they have learned. These may be assigned as homework assignments or in-class reviews.

THE PROJECT SEQUENCE

The projects follow a specific sequence intended to build a knowledge base requiring increasing technical knowledge, familiarity with scriptwriting, using storyboard techniques, and knowledge of the production process. The first two projects (*Still Shots* and *Stop Action*) require only a rudimentary knowledge of how to use the camera and how to put a story together. Neither requires a script or on-camera talent. The story must be told visually and accompanied with appropriate music. These projects are designed so that they may be introduced during the first week or two of class. They teach how to

- turn the camera on and use the still button,

- audio dub,

- add titles using a character generator or PowerPoint, and

- edit.

The *Stop Action* project also introduces the concept of persistence of vision, which is essential to an overall understanding of how television works.

More than likely, students will encounter some small technical problems completing these two projects. This is a planned part of the learning process. The need to solve these problems is a good motivator.

Project #3 (*Book Trailers*) is very similar to music videos, but with the added idea of learning how to translate textual information into visual. Students decide on the essence of the selected book (that is, if they were able to boil the book down into three or four sentences that describe the essence of the book, what would they say?). The resulting product could include stills, movie clips, animation, and on-screen acting. It is a wonderful activity that also introduces students to the art of storytelling. For that reason, it is best to select from fictional books rather than nonfiction. The *Instructional Video* project (#4) requires that students further refine their scriptwriting capabilities and may be their first on-screen experience. They further their work with the three-part storyline (beginning/middle/ending) and the use of visuals to supplement their message content. The fifth project is an *Interview*. In this video, students learn about b-roll footage and secondary camera shots. The *Decades* (#6) and *PSA/Commercial* (#7) projects refine students' visual communication abilities by teaching them how to combine visual imagery with scripts, to sell a product or idea, and to create moods using video. *Sweeps* (#8) is a class project in which students use production planning and storyboards to pull several unrelated sequences together.

The projects are sequenced chronologically and introduced at the appropriate place. That does not imply, however, that they are to be introduced in linear fashion. The "Teaching Chronology" shows that they are, in fact, introduced on an overlapping schedule. This has been done for two reasons. First, economic constraints most likely mean that there probably will not be enough equipment to go around. There may be enough cameras to allow several small teams to share. Editing equipment is getting cheaper, but it still costs so much that it is very likely groups will have to share. The editing station will most likely become a bottleneck to production. Phasing the projects in so that each will be at a different stage of completion at any one time will place less stress on the schedules and relieve the bottlenecks. The ostensible reason for phasing in projects, however, is to teach students the concept of managing multiple projects at once. The production scheduling sessions take into account this approach to planning. The problem encountered with equipment shortages is, in fact, teaching students about reality. Equipment availability is a serious issue to contend with, even in professional studios.

TELEVISION COMMERCIALS AND MUSIC VIDEOS AS MODELS

Television commercials are suggested in several different contexts throughout this course. The most obvious use is in **Chapter 2.** Class sessions show students how to deconstruct commercials into smaller parts. Deconstructing commercials is key to understanding how television producers impose their views on the viewers, affect them psychologically, and create the need to purchase products, take action, or believe the philosophy being sold. The fact that commercials are a construct means that they have something positive to offer that is much more significant than simply introducing a self-defense tactic to protect students from the evils of advertisements. Advertisers spend so much time and money producing short segments (15–30 seconds) that each commercial contains considerable technique, technology, and transferable knowledge. That makes commercials probably the perfect model to demonstrate how videos are to be made. They contain all the learning components that we attempt to demonstrate in this course, and, certainly, they contain all the elements producers wish to produce in their programs. Commercials have a definite script, storyboard, and set of objectives. Their producers have analyzed their audience, targeted their market, and figured out how to influence the viewer in the way they intend. Commercials are also motivational. Teenagers love to watch them, love to discuss them, and probably are more familiar with them than with anything else on television. Asking them to bring in examples and explain the video techniques that they discovered while watching specific commercials does not even sound like homework to them.

Similar ideas can be expressed about music videos. They are not as perfect a product, but they do tell stories visually. Teens are familiar with the lyrics of the music and can easily explain the visual semiotics incorporated into the video. Most contemporary music videos are high tech and include several examples of messaging constructs. Students love to watch them and may be more articulate about them than about any other example.

Students also love to make commercials and music videos of their own. To increase the learning experience, though, it is important to insist that they identify beforehand the technique(s) and psychological tools they are using in their construct. Students love to wing it, so asking them to spec out their design elements is an important component to ensure that some preplanning has taken place.

COURSE CONTENT AND GRADING

Following is a sample course syllabus that may be modified to suit individual needs and may be distributed during the first days of class and at parents' night activities. It is recommended that percentages be attached to individual goals to represent the emphasis placed on each one and the relative importance each represents to the overall course content. Tests and quizzes should then be coordinated that incorporate proportional representation.

Sample: Class Syllabus and Grading Policy

The purpose of this course is to provide opportunities for students to learn elements of media and visual literacy and to develop introductory skills in television and multimedia production.

Course Content

Includes an overview of television and the television team; careers in television and video; the history of mass communications, with special emphasis on radio and television history; an orientation to writing for television as compared to other media; and the use of basic television equipment, with special emphasis on developing a visual awareness for the video medium.

Basic Educational Mission Statement

To stimulate students' awareness of their own relationships with media and to learn how media organizations construct their information flow, in order to transfer this new-found knowledge via action projects that will make them better analyzers of information and better communicators, both as receivers of information and as distributors.

Intended Outcomes

After completing this course, students will be able to demonstrate competency in certain learning areas. Following is a partial listing of those competencies, along with a list of how closure will be obtained:

Desired Outcome	Chapter	How Demonstrated
Exhibit knowledge of the history of mass communications and the role television has played.	6	Tests & Quizzes
Exhibit *media awareness* as it relates to various communications vehicles such as newspaper, radio, and television.	2	Review Activities Tests & Quizzes Project #7: Commercial
Identify different types of script copy.	3	Class Activities Tests & Quizzes
Write script in the broadcast style with scripting queues.	3	Project #3: Book Trailers Project #8: Sweeps
Produce a television segment, including a storyboard, script, audio mixer, and special effects instructions.	7	Project #5: Interview Project #8: Sweeps
Exhibit knowledge of the television production team and the role each member plays.	7	Class Activities Tests & Quizzes Project #8: Sweeps
Exhibit knowledge of ethical awareness as it relates to proper on-camera etiquette and fundamental U.S. copyright laws related to mass communications.	2	Class Activities School Broadcasts Projects
Demonstrate correct equipment usage.	3	Competency Checklist
Exhibit an understanding of basic statistical concepts of sampling, reliability, and validity and the role these play in proper survey gathering.	2	Tests & Quizzes Class Activities

List the principles of visual design as they relate to communicating content.	5	Tests & Quizzes Projects (all)
Recite how body language plays a role in communicating (or, in fact, hiding) feelings and emotions.	5	Tests & Quizzes On-air Activities

GRADES

Grades will be obtained through four distinct forms of assessment. Each will play a role in final calculations according to the chart below:

Tests/quizzes………..…......................................20%

Includes tests, quizzes, and final exam. These will measure attainment of cognitive objectives, based on the study blueprint handed out at the beginning of the school session. All tests and quizzes are open-book.

Portfolio Assessment…..................................30%

Both the *Student Workbooks* and video portfolios will be graded. Students will be rewarded for keeping accurate notes and records of accomplishments in their *Student Workbooks* once each grading period. Portfolio projects will be graded according to performance-based assessment scorecards. Record keeping is an important part of job performance evaluation in the broadcasting industry. To emphasize this important activity, students will be awarded points for keeping current with class notes and production planning. Portfolio assessments for each project will be completed in a similar manner and will carry equal weight. In addition, students may pick one project they determine their best work from their portfolios to submit for grading against their own assessment criteria.

Equipment Competencies………...................20%

Students will receive credit for demonstrating their ability to operate the equipment per operator's handbooks and written instructions handed out in class. Assessment will be in the form of points awarded and recorded on a competency checklist containing a list of the appropriate equipment..

Participation/Work Ethic...............................30%

Includes all group projects, in-class, and Sweeps activities. Assessment will be accomplished through awarding points each week, based on the teacher's perceptions of the contribution to class discussions, independent work on class assignments, general work ethic, and team-building activities with fellow classmates.

Because most work is done in class, attendance is extremely important, just as it is in a real-world work environment. All work must be made up in order to receive any credit. Deductions will be made for late work.

Throughout the session, students will receive progress reports that incorporate the above. They will be in the format of a performance review similar to that which adults receive at their jobs.

TESTS AND QUIZZES

All written exams should be designed to accommodate the use of open books. Test questions should be designed so that allowing students access to their *Student Workbooks,* class materials, and texts will not detract from the educational experience. Unfortunately, the open book testing concept in this course is not based on a strong research premise, as there appears to be a "dearth of literature in this area" (Feller, 1994, pp. 235–238). Rather, it is based on a practical evaluation of the state of affairs in the broadcasting industry, where record keeping is crucial to survival. Networks and stations must prove they have complied with FCC regulations by submitting detailed logbooks. Sponsors require very specific billings and proof statements as to when their commercials ran. A television classroom better simulates real-world situations if it introduces and encourages detailed record keeping on the part of its students.

Open-book testing also entails changing the method of teaching to make it compatible. Such a technique requires special teacher and student preparation to implement it. For example, students are not asked to memorize a list of dates and names. However, they are asked to explain why specific events happened at certain times rather than others. They might be asked to explain why the television golden age took almost 20 years to develop, as opposed to the radio age, which blossomed within two years of its emergence on the broadcasting scene. In other words, the tests and quizzes concentrate on giving students every opportunity to show what they can accomplish when given the tools of the subject. Technical questions center on why something did not work as expected. Cognitive literacy, then, implies that students understand the meaning of events and situations, rather than simply feed back facts.

The tests and quizzes should be considered learning opportunities. The midterm and final should be cumulative. The quizzes can actually be used to teach course content. A good analogy is a sports team that uses the regular season to prepare for the play-offs. Because champions are determined during play-offs, the regular season can be used to get the team in shape. The quizzes in this course equate to the regular season, in which season standings (grading periods) are to be considered as benchmarks. As questions often build on each other, they may be asked in several ways on different tests throughout the course. The redundancy also helps reinforce knowledge acquisition. It is common to use fill-in-the-blank questions the first time questions are asked, only later to include them as multiple choice or true/false questions. If a question is phrased properly, it may be asked in several different ways to indicate that the student is moving up Bloom's Taxonomy ladder.

Using questions that may be answered by information provided later within the same test or quiz also helps to teach the art of visual thinking and observation. Several hints are provided throughout each quiz, including clues that there might be more than one correct answer to a question by indicating more than one test question number for a particular question (e.g., a question that contains three correct answers is listed as question number 1–3). The same technique of answering an earlier fill-in-the-blank question by making it a choice in a later multiple-choice question can be used in this circumstance. The earlier quizzes should start out as mostly fill-in-the-blank questions. Later, as they begin to refer to the materials more often, the same subjects may be covered as a multiple-choice question that requires more critical thinking, as compare and contrast questioning.

The quizzes and exams provided are models. They may be modified, based on how closely the "Teaching Chronology" is followed. It is not uncommon to move some questions from one test to another or to add questions because it was discovered that students require additional learning opportunities. In some cases, test questions are redundant because they cover the same content areas in several different ways. This is intentional. Questions may be asked several times to reinforce learning, or to accommodate including the number of questions that is equal to the percentage dictated by the test blueprint.

BUILDING A TEST BLUEPRINT

Lesson outcomes and objectives are mainstays of any syllabus. However, not all objectives are created equal. Some learning activities may be deemed more important to overall course goals than others. To balance the evaluative emphasis placed on objectives in correct correlation to their associated valuation, it may be best to weigh each objective in terms of its representation on tests and quizzes. This is done in an assessment blueprint. A blueprint, also often referred to by instructional designers as a table of specifications, is nothing more than entering each objective, as expressed on the syllabus, in a spreadsheet, and then counting the number of questions from all tests and quizzes. The objectives might even be classified according to learning domains or to Bloom's Taxonomy. The teacher may then use the blueprint to determine how much emphasis to place on the learning outcomes associated with each objective. Portfolios can also be assessed in similar fashion by weighting points assigned to each objective.

The most common use for test blueprints is to cross-reference course objectives, but it may also be used to measure the relative emphasis on any factor the teacher wishes to survey. For example, the sample blueprint below measures the relative importance placed on each of the chapters in this book, as measured by the percentage of test questions that directly relate to each chapter. The resultant percentage of questions pertains to each chapter:

Chapter 1:	Class Administration	10%
Chapter 2:	Media Literacy	20%
Chapter 3:	Equipment Basics	20%
Chapter 4:	Writing for a Visual Medium	10%
Chapter 5:	Developing an Acuity for a Visual Medium	15%
Chapter 6:	The Birth of Radio and Television	15%
Chapter 7:	The Production Process	10%
		100%

The results may or may not be surprising. Notice that only 45 percent of course content (and corresponding emphasis on tests in our example) pertains directly to those topics found in a traditional television production course. However, the figures properly reflect the relative emphasis the book places on media literacy, history, and visual awareness. The relatively low scores for production and scriptwriting reflect the fact that this course is aimed more at using video as a vehicle to communicate a visual message than at studio production. Although it has its own chapter, production is relegated to a secondary level, that being one of several different turnouts in the video and television domain. The same might be said of scriptwriting. Scripts are, of course, extremely important to television, but they play a secondary role in this course because more importance is placed on introducing students to the world of nonverbal communication. In fact, students do not write their scripts until project #4 (however, storytelling *is* introduced in project #1 and followed-up on in project #3). Production involves more of a planning process that is generic to any industry. When students are finally immersed in production techniques unique to television in the second year, they have a frame of reference to go by.

Some may view test blueprints as being too restrictive. Indeed, they are not meant to become a rule, but rather a model, which may be modified to suit needs. Certainly if students are having a difficult time handling certain cognitive aspects, then subsequent exams should be reconstructed to retest those points. In addition, instructional time does have a tendency to be interrupted by assemblies, fire drills, and so forth. There is therefore a need for some type of tracking mechanism. The blueprint provides a way for teachers to track back to the syllabus to be sure that they are spending the correct proportion of time and including the correct emphasis when things get off track.

One comment: Perhaps zeroing in on tests and quizzes as the sole source of blueprinting does not properly reflect the true emphasis being placed on each outcome. This is because other forms of evaluation take place. Both portfolio assessment and competency benchmarks are used extensively. The blueprint concept has been introduced solely to provide an evenhandedness to testing and to counter a tendency to overlook written evaluations in a subject area that incorporates a high number of objectives written for the kinesthetic domain.

The first step toward correctly following the intent of any lesson plan is to ensure that students are taking down the information being discussed during class presentations. It is often difficult for students to simultaneously write quality lesson notes in their *Student Workbooks* and follow class lectures. The fill-in-the-blank note-taking format provides a means to adjust the pace of the class. The teacher can determine whether certain information or a section is to be left out because it is too difficult or because time is short. The script provides a means for the teacher to note any content that was not covered in an individual class and to decide whether the test or quiz should be altered. These changes can then be easily tracked back to the course blueprint to ensure the proper representation is still being achieved based on the weight assigned to each objective.

PORTFOLIO ASSESSMENT

One reason cognitive requirements can be modified to include open-book testing is that student performance is evaluated on several different levels. Projects are evaluated using an assessment scorecard. A scorecard is not exactly the same thing as a rubric. Rubrics suggest that a specific set of guidelines be followed, with very limited flexibility. A model approach is preferred when there are many similarities. Using a model implies that changes may be made, based on the variations in goals and objectives of each project. Those modifications are spelled out in the "Project Planning Considerations" section for each project. It is also not an intention of the scorecard to provide the ability to assign an exact number grade to each project. The scorecard does allow you to come up with a very specific grade; however, there is also a lot of room for interpretation. This is intentional. Grading creativity can be a frustrating task. There must be enough opportunity in the assessment phase of each project for the student and teacher to have a meaningful dialogue about the strengths and weaknesses of each completed project. Often this conversation leads to the students being harder on themselves. Usually, a compromise grade is agreed to. The idea is for students to learn from each project as they progress through the year. Stressing that the students will have the final say in which project is presented as the term project implies that they also will have developed the ability to critique their own work fairly and honestly. This is a large part of the self-awareness process that is so important to the objectives and outcomes of this course.

EQUIPMENT COMPETENCIES

A second alternative evaluation process occurs in the area of equipment competencies. Evaluating student competencies on equipment is a significant part of the syllabus. It is important that students be able to demonstrate that they know how to operate the equipment. It should be stressed, however, that it is more important that they know how the equipment works conceptually. Each studio will have different brands of equipment. Each brand has its own quirks and specific procedures. Students should be taught how a function is performed so that all they have to do when going into a new studio is to reorient themselves to how that specific equipment accomplishes the required task.

Grading competencies is a pass/fail effort. The "Equipment Competency Checklist" in **Appendix C** shows a sample list of equipment that students are qualified to operate. The procedure is simple. Students are handed the checklist early in the term. They are tasked with taking the responsibility to show their teacher that they know how to operate the equipment by making an appointment. Once the teacher is convinced that the student knows how to operate that equipment, the checklist is initialed and dated. Once all the required equipment is dated and checked off, the checklist is turned in and points are awarded for completing that step.

PARTICIPATION AND WORK ETHIC

There are eight projects and several other activities assigned during the course. Some of these other activities are graded; others are not. To continue to encourage students to maintain a consistent workflow, they also receive an evaluation for participation. There has been considerable research on separating assessment and dealing with disruptive classroom behavior. Focusing on evaluating classroom activities in terms of work ethic mirrors employee performance evaluations that occur annually (or more often) in a real-world work environment.

The idea is simple. Busy students are happy students who are also engaged in learning. As long as the lessons are structured and well-planned, and students remain focused on accomplishing tasks, they tend not to make bad behavioral judgments., If they know that they will be able to work on their projects afterward, they tend to stay on task during class discussions. This means that the teacher must maintain a tight schedule during direct instruction sessions. They must be able to commit to spending only the time allotted for each session, unless it appears that students are actively engaged in a discussion. If the time frame is not met, the teacher must be willing to make up for it at another time. Shorten another session to make students feel that you value your time commitments as much as you expect them to. This builds up mutual respect between students and their teacher, making classroom management a much easier task.

RESOURCES

Feller, M. 1994. *Studies in educational evaluation: Open-book testing and education for the future.* Vol. 20, pp. 235–238. London: Elsevier Science Ltd. Available: www. ehhs.cmich.edu/ins/open.perf (Accessed April 2, 2004).

Tyner, K. 1998. *Literacy in a digital world: Teaching and learning in the age of information.* Mahwah, NJ. Laurence Erlbaum Associates.

CHAPTER 2

Developing a Literacy for Television and the Media

INTRODUCTION AND LESSON GOALS

In a television course, the context of *media literacy* may be looked upon and approached in many different ways. Television Ontario describes a media literate person as one "who has an informed understanding of the nature, techniques, and the impact of the mass media" (1995, p. 2). For purposes of education, they also define television as "the most pervasive medium" (1995, p. 2), with the understanding that teaching media literacy in school is an important task.

However, recent technological developments may make the defining of **media** solely in terms of **television** too narrow. Current definitions of *media literacy* also have to take into consideration the vision held by companies like Microsoft, AT&T, AOL, and BellSouth. In today's world, the futures of television, the telephone, and computers are moving along increasingly parallel pathways. Although students may never do their homework on the family television set, television will become more interactive and will, in the not-too-distance future, encompass many of the characteristics of the family computer. At the same time, your computer will take on many of the characteristics of your television. It will be able to easily handle real-time moving images just like your television does. In addition, long distance telephone charges as we know them may soon disappear. With current technology, it is now possible to also connect your PC directly to the Internet using the electrical outlets in your house.

With these changes in mind, perhaps there is a broader definition that can be applied. In 1996, the National Communications Association adopted the following two criteria at a workshop sponsored by the Aspen Institute. As shown in the brochure announcing their workshop, an effective media participant can demonstrate:

- the effects of the various types of electronic audio and visual media, including television, radio, the telephone, the Internet, computers, electronic conferencing, and film, on media consumers; and

- the ability to identify and use skills necessary for competent participation in communication across various types of electronic audio and visual media.

This broader definition takes into account the new digital technologies on the horizon.

THE IMPACT OF TECHNOLOGY ON TELEVISION

The future impact of all this new technology on the school curriculum will be astounding. For example, in just a few years, using products like the new Microsoft Longhorn operating system, people will be accessing information from the Internet right from their desktop or software application without really having to do anything, not even open up a menu. The definition of a Web page will change from something that resides on an Internet service provider, as it does now, to any source document residing anywhere in your computer. In other words, a word processing document that contains hyperlinks automatically becomes a Web page. This is certain to have an affect on how we look at textbooks in the future. Most will be closely tied to the Internet to remain current. Because a computer will be provided with continual access to the Internet, a text with links will be able to receive updates automatically. Currently, most current Internet sites are text-based. In the near future, sites will become increasingly interactive, using computers, video, and text.

Technological advances will have a tremendous effect on television viewing for entertainment purposes. Although no one knows for certain that the days of one-to-many prime time viewing are numbered, there is considerable evidence that the television ratings system (and corresponding system for providing commercials) will evolve into a more interactive process. Information on viewing habits will be gathered online on a one-to-one basis. Viewers will be able to watch any show, when they want it, on demand, without having to videotape it during its normally scheduled time period. Already, companies like TiVo have put on the market the personal video recorder (PVR), which contains a hard drive that allows viewers to stop a show to answer the telephone and then continue where they left off. This same machine can be programmed to reflect one's viewing preferences, find shows that meet those criteria, and capture them for later viewing on a predetermined basis. In other words, the current definition of *prime time* will certainly be challenged. Current definitions of media literacy have to include the possibility of these new communications methodologies.

Technological developments are also causing significant changes in how programs are being constructed. Advertisers certainly have access to the same academic research that points to the facts that

- media carry with them the same interpretations of reality as do real events,

- viewing traumatic events has a significant positive effect on a viewer's ability to remember an event that takes place right afterward, even if that event is a very negative one, and

- arousal (regardless of whether the arousing event is positive or negative) also has a considerable effect on a viewer's attention span and motivation (Lang, 1995).

It shouldn't be surprising that the favorite forms of arousal come from sexual imagery, images associated with speed (like rocketry), and images that have a high degree of movement (Thorson and Friestad, 1985). Technology certainly carries with it the ability to accelerate images. More and more producers are using quick cuts and cut-frame editing techniques made available to them through nonlinear, digital editing packages that are now becoming affordable to even the smaller production houses. It should not be surprising then, that advertisers continue to put pressure on the networks to produce more of this kind of content. Not only do they want to advertise on shows with overt sexual and action-adventure content, but they also are becoming more savvy about when to run their ads within a show. Viewers are more likely to remember things right after a negative or generally arousing scene (Thorson and Reeves, 1985).

Although the need to teach media literacy is not a direct result of these new strides in technology, these increasingly sophisticated information management-type viewing systems are giving rise to significant justification for teaching television as an information-processing medium. The following quotes from the Media Literacy On-line Project's Web site are the founding principles behind many of the lessons found in this chapter. The boldface has been added for emphasis and was not a part of the original document.

- "Television is **manufactured.**" In other words, television is not a window on the world, or a mirror of society. It is not accidental, capturing reality when, as luck would have it, a camera happened to be turned on. Rather, television is carefully constructed by teams of communication workers. Nothing you see or hear on television is left to chance.

- "Television has **commercial implications.**" This means television is a viable business. Its primary goal is not to entertain or to inform, but to make money. The product being bought and sold is the audience: you are the product. Commercial considerations shape what we watch on television.

- "Television has **social and political implications.**" Although television is not real, it influences our behavior in the real world. Television shapes constituencies and influences the political process. Political decisions in the United States are increasingly played out during prime time.

- "Television carries **value messages**." Although balance and objectivity are journalistic ideals, television is not value-free. It imparts the values and ideologies of its producers."

- "Television has its **own unique language**." We learn to make sense of television by observing codes and conventions until we understand its grammar, its transitions, and its unique form of narrative structure.

- "Audiences are **active**." Audiences do many things while watching television, but on some level, they must participate in the communication process by making sense of the images and sounds they see on television. The audience does not always get the same meaning that producers intend.

- "Television has **unique aesthetic form**." It is an immediate, close-up medium where pictures override sound. Commercial television's time limitations are its major constraint; its immediacy its greatest asset. Audiences derive great pleasure from television. It has the potential for beauty and artistry that transcends its limitations. (Media Literacy On-line Project, 1996)

In practical terms, teaching media literacy should include schooling on consumerism in some form. There was a time when the need for teaching this so-called protectionist or deficit aspect of media literacy was not as timely as it is today. The idea was to teach students to be **eventual** consumers who would make purchases when they started to earn expendable incomes. However, the need to teach consumerism may be more pressing. Many news sources report that today's youth between the ages of 14 and 25 have, on average, between $50 and $100 per week in disposable cash for discretionary spending. Advertisers now realize that this target market is a multi-billion dollar industry. And their efforts are paying off. Bob McCannon from the New Mexico Media Literacy Project jokingly quips that if you want to retain teenagers' attention, "all you have to do is show them a commercial every seven minutes" (McCannon, 1998). He may have been using a bit of hyperbole to indicate his assumptions about teenage consumerism, but he was probably closer to the truth in a way even he did not realize. In short, students generally enjoy watching commercials. Many may not know who their congressperson is or know anything about current events, but most can probably list all the details about every commercial they have seen in the past 10 days. Using commercials as a teaching vehicle is a great hook. Teenagers love watching and talking about commercials. Critiquing them creates an immediate impact and leads to interesting group interactions and critical thinking sessions.

The danger of what is happening in commercials is not simply that businesses are trying to sell something. Commercialism has gone on since the beginning of time and is at the core of a capitalist economy. However, information and message management have now infiltrated all aspects of our daily lives. In other words, being media literate implies that we are able to recognize that we are continually being sold something. Students have the same need to identify and learn the goals, purposes, tools, and intended outcomes of all communications, regardless of media type or purpose.

What makes this even more of an issue for a class about television is that this type of salesmanship has also crept into the process of providing news coverage. The concept of **newsworthiness** has taken on new meaning: **infotainment.** New words have crept into our newscast vocabulary like **sound bites, spin doctors,** and **paparazzi**. To quote the back cover of *The Cronkite Report* video used in these sessions:

The media lack objectivity. News is often inaccurate. Producers seek to entertain rather than inform. Coverage is too negative. These are just some of the things the working press have to say about the state of their own profession. (Discovery Learning Channel, 1996)

The point this video makes is that news is often selected, packaged, and presented, not based on its news value, but on how many commercials the newscast can sell. This viewpoint appears to be backed up by other sources (Freed, 1999). It is important to note that younger high school students generally have no concept of how the media make money. Certainly, they may have some idea that money is involved, but only in general terms, such as that celebrities are rich and that movies cost a lot to make and that special effects add to the cost of movies. What they may not realize is how intrinsic money is to the daily operation of television. A good way to prove this point is to ask the basic question on the pre-test/pre-needs questionnaire:

How do television networks/affiliate stations make money?

The corollary question is to ask during Lesson 2.1 is:

How are stories selected for newscasts?

Most will answer the first question incorrectly and will probably continue to answer it incorrectly on quizzes up until the final exam. Answers to the second question are taught very early on in Lesson 2.1B, "The Makings of a Newscast," as posted by Dr. Ron Whittaker on his Web site (www.cybercollege.com).

A new wave of information management has crept into our political system. We sometimes hear how politicians make choices about governing based solely on the results of popularity polls. In 1998, a movie was released called *Wag the Dog*. This movie probably cannot be played in the classroom due to its "R" rating, but many students probably have seen it. Its premise, the making of a fictional war to save the popularity of a presidency, gives one pause. Although there is no hard evidence, many felt that this fictional account may not have been far from the truth in the middle of the debates about impeaching the president that year. Another movie of this same genre is *Primary Colors,* in which John Travolta manages his presidential campaign through the media. Although it is a fictional account, it serves as a great learning set/advanced organizer:

Do you think presidents have ever used the media to their advantage?

Do you think a Wag the Dog *scenario could ever actually happen in this country?*

Technological advances, the growth in the management and manufacture of information, and the increased potential for the integration of hidden messages and agendas without our knowledge through television advertising have made the need to educate more compelling. The selling of products and ideas does not solely reside in the standard, clearly identifiable media marketing campaigns, as we have known them, or within the confines of the medium itself. They are becoming increasingly ingrained in those areas previously commercial free. For example, many people are walking billboards for private causes, clothing manufacturers, or their favorite rock groups. By wearing brand logos on their clothing or T-shirts they display various messages. The same is true for bumper stickers on automobiles.

TOWARD AN ACQUISITION MODEL

The advancement of media education in this country has been slowed by an apparent rift between those who teach literacy from the negative (deficit) point of view and those who believe that there should be a more positive spin to it. The main difference between these two approaches to media literacy is the intent or desired outcomes for their programs. Although a critique of the media occupies a considerable portion of the agenda of this course (at least in the initial sessions), the end or desired outcome of media education in this course is to cause students to establish their own, personal relationship with the media. Students are asked to critically review what is happening in the industry to decide for themselves how they should react to the bombardment of media. They can, then, decide the role television and other media will play in their lives.

From there, they will be able to take the first steps toward becoming **creators of media.** This course takes its lead from media educators like Dirk Shouten and Kathleen Tyner, who refer to an "acquisition model," a term first coined by R. Desmond in his 1997 book *Media Literacy in the Home: Acquisition vs. Deficit Models.* By first understanding the power of the media, students will become better communicators through their use. Many educational institutions such as The Ontario Ministry of Education also favor this proactive approach:

> Media literacy is concerned with helping students develop an **informed and critical understanding** of the nature of the mass media, the techniques used by them, and the impact of these techniques. More specifically, it is education that aims to **increase students' understanding and enjoyment** of how the media work, how they produce meaning, how they are organized, and **how they construct reality**. Media literacy also aims to provide students with **the ability to create media** products. (1996, pp. 6–7)

The need to become more sophisticated creators of media will become much more important in the future. New technologies are already beginning to cause a complete paradigm shift in the connotation of the term **television broadcasting**. Soon an entire new industry will emerge in which individuals will broadcast commercially from their homes. **Garage cinema** is already a reality in an amateurish sort of way (Davis, 1997). Movies like the *Blair Witch Project* should serve as an example, at least as representative of the genre. Recall the woman who recently gave birth over the Internet. Others (like the experiment in which students set up a camera in their dorms) are recording their entire daily lives for all to watch. The movies have made two forays into the subject with films like *EdTV* and *The Truman Show*. The idea that someone can create his or her own commercial media business took shape recently when a young man opened up his own radio station over the Internet after being turned down for a job as a disc jockey at a local radio station.

TOWARD A HORIZONTALLY INTEGRATED MEDIA CURRICULUM

Possibly because the term **literacy** has traditionally been associated with the reading curriculum, the goal of teaching media literacy have often been relegated to the school's English department. However, a more meaningful way to attack the issue might be to offer it horizontally across the curriculum using thematic mapping. A horizontally integrated curriculum provides an opportunity for social studies, English, and life management teachers to work together. A properly devised television curriculum can supplement this horizontal curricular view (see Figure 2.1).

Figure 2.1. Media Literacy Thematic Diagram.

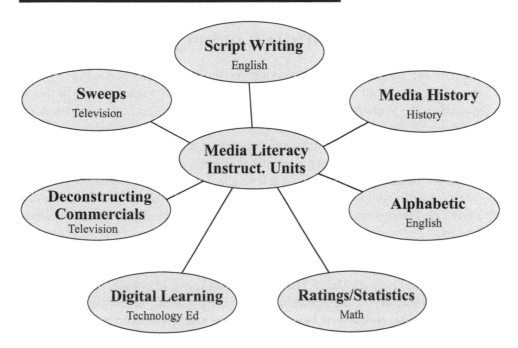

Combining criteria to teach the linguistic and communication aspects of being media literate (English class), its social aspects (social studies and debate), and its consumerism (life management), will reinforce learning. By incorporating subject matter from other content areas into show topics, students will learn how ingrained media are in their lives, and how dependent they are on a media-rich environment. The television production class, especially a first-year course, may be a good way to bridge the gap between subjects. Instead of focusing entirely on studio broadcast production, first-year students could work with their peers in other curricular areas to build authentic productions around media themes. This approach would provide the opportunity to expand to impact of the television class to a far wider range of students.

SUMMARY

In learning how to deconstruct media, students also learn their own constructions. They learn about communications in the context of message design, persuasive writing, and creating a personal communications style. They then use these newly discovered cognitive skills to create media of their own. The opportunity to use that very medium that has contributed so greatly to creating the need for media education is just too wonderful to pass up. It has been a startling revelation to review so many school-based television production programs throughout the country (through an evaluation of textbooks, videos, and on the Internet) only to find that many may have missed a wonderful teaching moment. The need for incorporating media and visual education into the television curriculum is born out of the necessity of media teachers to become promoters and advocates for media education in elementary and secondary education. By learning its traditions, history, and etiquette, student will better be able to maintain the self-policing traditions instituted by the National Association of Broadcasters in 1952 and reintroduced by the Telecommunications Act of 1996 (Federal Communications Commission, 1999). This, in turn, will help to advance the cause for continuing the television curriculum in schools.

DIGGING DEEPER

Sources for additional information on media literacy are becoming more readily available every day, both in print and online. All references to the sources in this section are repeated on the **Web-ASSISTant** Web site, where direct links and additional information on these and other reference materials can be found. The Web site is used to update information found in this text and other mediated resources.

There are three books in particular that should be read by teachers trying to prepare themselves for teaching students about television. The first two, *Teaching About Television* (Macmillan Press Ltd) and *Teaching the Media* (Comedia/MK Media Press), were written by Len Masterman. These two books are compendia of thought on the issues surrounding media education and the problems students and teachers face when trying to participate in media education programs.

The third book, *Educating Students in a Media-Saturated Environment* (Technomic Press), was written by John Davis. Davis promotes the use of popular music, movies, videos, and both commercial and educational television to help students and teachers study how all media affect children on both the cognitive and emotional levels.

There are several sites on the Internet that provide insights into media education. The **Web-ASSISTant** Web site provides several links, both to places to obtain copies of these three books and to information on how to obtain all the mediated and textual resources at the end of the "Chapter Two" page. Most are links to **super sites** that provide numerous links to other sites of similar interest. One particular educational site noted on the "Best Practices" page was created by Public Broadcasting in support of the 1998 elections. The *30-Second Candidate* provides lesson plans and discussions about the development of the 30-second commercial and how it has affected political races. It provides a good second look at commercials, how they are constructed, and how they attempt to influence our thinking. This could be a useful ancillary lesson to integrate into the curriculum.

Dr. Ron Whittaker, at **www.cybercollege.com/televisionnews.html,** discusses the *Decline of Television News Credibility*. This is an excellent article about what has happened to television news coverage. It can be used as supplementary reading or to stimulate class discussion.

One additional link may be of interest. The *San Jose Metro*, a newspaper in Silicon Valley, California, published a story in its January 23, 1997, edition about a program being aired on a local PBS station, *Fear and Favor in the Newsroom*, a documentary about how big money influences the media. This compelling article discusses the difficulties the independent moviemakers had getting anyone to air their program. This show is finally working its way around the country and may be generally available in the near future. In the meantime, the news article is an opportunity to make a point, especially in Lesson 2.1A, The Media Paradigm.

SEQUENCING THE LESSONS IN THIS CHAPTER

The lessons in this chapter were written in contextual sequence: They have continuity with regard to subject matter and can be taught in the exact order in which they are presented. However, to take advantage of the opportunity to reach the specific goals attempted by this book, it might be better to consider following the suggested sequence as outlined in the "Teaching Chronology" found in **Chapter 1.** At a minimum, it makes sense to at least consult the prescribed format to make an informed decision.

Lesson 2.1

Lesson Planning Considerations

(**Approx. Time**: 35–45 minutes)

Agenda

The media sessions begin with the news. The news filtering session (Lesson 2.1A) can be taught quite early in the school year because

- it lays the foundation for the whole television ratings/Sweeps system, as described later in this lesson set;

- it is a quick introduction to the news gathering process;

- it provides quick insight into how much students know about the industry;

- it is supported by an easy activity (News Analysis) that can get a student's whole family involved in discussions about our literacy theme;

- it doesn't require much previous knowledge of the technical aspects of commercials and commercialism;

- it identifies for students early on how intertwined the objectives of other businesses have become with the products produced by the broadcasting industry; and

- it forces students to quickly form their own personal relationship with the media.

In Lesson 2.1A, you are introducing the media paradigm. Many students do not know what a paradigm is. You will know you have succeeded if, at the end of the lesson, students can describe to you what elements might cause a paradigm shift, and the effect the profit motive has on the content they see on television.

Objectives and Outcomes

These lessons on media literacy have several objectives, as outlined by the concerns expressed above. All class sessions, activities, and projects have been designed to accommodate three domains in Bloom's Taxonomy: the cognitive, the affective, and the kinesthetic.

After participating in this lesson, students are expected to

- describe, and later assess, the media-filtering paradigm;

- describe how owners, advertisers, the government, and media markets may influence what gets aired on television; and

- listen to a newscast and identify the appropriate newsworthiness criteria for each story.

Mediated and Textual Support

The Discovery Channel School offers a video that serves as a good introduction to the principles that are covered in these media literacy sessions: *The Cronkite Report: Headlines & Sound Bites*. It comes with a four-page teacher's guide and is supported by in-depth materials provided on its own Web site. The video provides a good backdrop for the topics covered in the first lesson and should be shown as a separate session, just prior to beginning the first lesson.

Another video that will help orient students to the concepts found in these lessons is *Signal to Noise,* distributed by GPM, at the University of Nebraska at Lincoln. *Signal to Noise* is a three-part series that premiered on public television during the summer of 1996. It takes a critical look at the power, business, and allure of television. The videos are broken down into manageable segments that hold the students' attention. The segment approach empowers the teacher to control the time commitment for the specific literacy aspect and still leaves class time to work on projects and activities.

Ron Whittaker, whose online course may be found at **www.cybercollege.com**, under "TV Production Support," provides the list of newsworthiness criteria used in Lesson 2.1B, which is used with his permission. This site also offers several essays on the issue of media literacy that might prove worthwhile as background information. Dr. Whittaker provides limited copyrights to teachers who want to use this material in class, as long as proper reference is made.

Information on how to get to this site and how to obtain all the mediated and textual resources mentioned in this chapter and in the GPM video may be found on the **Web-ASSISTant** Web site.

Lesson Readiness

The lesson begins with an advanced organizer in the form of a game. It is one that most children have played before, "Whisper Down the Alley." They should find it easy to use as a bridge to the new information being delivered in this lesson. You start by thinking up a sentence that includes a person, whom you call by name, an action that this person did, and a time and place that the action happened. You then whisper all this information into the ear of the first person. Then that person whispers it to the next, and so on until the message gets all the way across the room to everyone in the class. Then you ask the last person to repeat out loud what he or she heard and compare it to what you said to the first person. Everyone will be amazed at how different the final version is from the original, regardless of how many times they have played this game. As much as any other activity, this acts as a wonderful introduction to the topic of news filtering and how it is a miracle that a news story actually ends up being accurate on the network or local news. Along the way, someone handling the story might have a private agenda and modify the story a bit.

Now, you have your students perfectly prepared for the story you are about to weave about the news gathering process.

Closure

Students will demonstrate attaining the cognitive objectives by their active participation in class discussions and by correctly answering questions found on quizzes.

Lesson 2.1A

The Media Paradigm

Pre-Lesson Activity

Whisper Down the Alley (Telephone)

Student Instructions:: This is a game you probably have played before. Some call it **Telephone**. Your teacher is going to whisper something into the ear of the first person. In return, that person repeats it to a second person, and so on, until everyone has had a turn. The last person in line will repeat out loud what he or she heard. There is a good chance that it will not be the same as what the first person heard. Why did this happen? This demonstrates how eyewitness accounts can vary and how the news can get changed from the time it happens to when it is reported on television, even if no one had a reason to change it. What do you think might happen if you add to that mix a news reporting agency that wants to change the news for some reason? Has this ever happened before? We will discuss these issues in this class

Terms

local media market	sponsors	public broadcasting
media market	EFP	associated press
media paradigm	GE	devising commercial rates
disinformation	ENG	how stations and affiliates make money
commercial	CBS	government

Lesson Notes

Often you hear that an issue is *more complicated than it looks*, or that a solution to a problem is more difficult than it appears on the surface. The reason behind these comments is generally that there are several, interrelated circumstances, people, or events that affect an issue or problem unexpectedly. Any change also might have an effect on the problem or issue at hand. This often changes the perceived solution to a problem or understanding of the issue. In some cases, the proposed alteration may even make the problem worse. Because the issue is so complicated, quite often these interdependencies are investigated and then described in terms of some type of visual pattern or example. We refer to these visualizations as a **paradigm**. A paradigm is a way of thinking or a school of thought about a complicated issue that is visually represented in graphic form.

Trying to redefine a complicated issue in simple terms so that everyone can understand it may be likened to trying to hit a moving target. Have you ever been involved in a situation in which you thought you knew the answer to a complicated problem, but just when you were about ready to define a solution, something changed and your solution was not correct, or your solution only made matters worse? Surprises happen when you do not understand the ramifications of all the issues surrounding the situation and the interrelationships among the surrounding factors. Such changes are often referred to as **paradigm shifts**. Trying to predict the weather might be a good analogy. Meteorologists are often wrong in their forecasts because there are some unaccounted for factors that can influence weather that even the most sophisticated software packages cannot consider. A weather report on television tries to explain the forecast by showing it in terms of simplified boxes, charts, and diagrams. A television weather report qualifies as a good example of a paradigm shift.

What we see on television is the result of many complicated situations and influences. We need to describe what these are, so we have developed a paradigm of our own (see Figure 2.2).

Figure 2.2. Media Paradigm.

To get the full impact of this diagram, you have to understand how broadcast (both over the air and cable) stations and networks make money. We will have a separate session on the mechanics, but for now, you need to know that the expression *time is money* applies directly to broadcasting. Stations and networks in the United States make money through sponsors. Our system is unique in the world. How it came about will be the subject of our history sessions. In exchange for money, a network or station usually provides a product or service. In broadcasting, the service is called a <u>**commercial.**</u> The basis for how much a station or network charges for the commercial is as follows:

How much a network or station/affiliate may charge for a commercial:

	Variables
Commercial $ =	**time** (how long the commercial runs and what time of day),
Times	**when** the commercial runs
Times	the **rate** determined by ratings (how many watch)
Times	the **number of** times the commercial **runs**

We will be learning about the variables in future classes. We will learn why the time of day is important and how the rate is determined. For now, you need to understand that a station's or network's survival depends on its sponsors.

You also need to know that there is a difference between commercial sand and noncommercial stations and networks. The latter are known as **public broadcasting** stations and networks. Again, we will learn how these originated, but for now you need to know that they depend on donors and public funds from the government to stay in business.

It is important to understand the interrelationship between a media outlet and its sponsor to make sense out of the information-filtering paradigm.

The Media Paradigm

Figure 2.2 represents a news media filtering diagram. To understand the concept, you also need to understand that every single story you see on the news travels through these filters somehow. The box at the left represents the news event as seen and reported by those whose responsibility it is to report the event. Those who report an event are called **ENG** or electronic **n**ews **g**atherers. An ENG team is a small group, normally made up of an on-screen talent and a cameraperson. Sometimes an audio technician is included.

What Is an ENG?

You may or may not be aware that there are companies in existence whose sole job is to report news events all over the world. A local station might use these companies or simply have its own people on staff. Often stations in a larger city will also rely on independent contractors to report events. The most vivid example is those traffic reports you hear on the radio every seven minutes. These companies are hired by several stations to track and report the news. On a national and international scale there are companies like the **Associated Press** that report on significant events. If the event is of sufficient importance or duration (like the Super Bowl), the network will hire an **EFP** (electronic **f**ield **p**roduction) unit. An EFP is the same as an ENG but is equipped with a significant amount of equipment to actually edit, fade between cameras, add sound, reply, and so forth. In other words, an EFP is a ministation on wheels.

There are at least two potential influences on the ENG and EFP. First, they **make a determination that an event is newsworthy** in the first place. If they do not report on it, it did not happen, so to speak. Can you think of a possible circumstance that might cause an ENG not to report an event?

Teacher's Note: At this point, ask the students to come up with examples. Their examples will probably not be of a political nature. But you might feel the need to interject that some people feel that some reporters will not report on an issue because it does not fit a political profile of some type. Assuredly, you have your own examples. (Recall the Dan Rather incident during the 2004 presidential campaign.)

In summary, there are potential influences that determine if and how an event is reported.

The center box in the paradigm pattern is the **local media outlet** for reporting the news, which is either a major network or an independent station. We will see in our scriptwriting activities that what someone writes and how one reports it (inflection of voice or facial expression) both have an influence.

Outside influences are represented by the boxes above and below the center box. Three different possibilities come to mind. One is the local **station/affiliate ownership**. This could be as simple as a **company decision to report or not report** an event on basis of what they determine to be newsworthy. This decision could be based on ownership issues. Not every ENG story makes it to the show. We will see in the surveys we do this week that each station reports things a different way, at a different time, or not at all.

Who Owns What?

The idea of consolidation in broadcasting that was initiated by the Telecommunications Act of 1996 and aided by several additional provisions in later laws has escalated to the point where the majority of holdings in most broadcasting outlets (as well as more and more local affiliates and other news sources) is now held by a very few large, powerful media giants. These holdings have become prominent in the news lately through stories such as Comcast's now withdrawn tender offer to purchase all of Disney's holdings. If such a merger had taken place, it would have made Comcast the largest of the media giants in the United States. With almost $46.5 billion in revenue (2003), Comcast tops the list, followed by Time Warner ($39.6 billion in 2003), Viacom ($26.6 billion), News Corp ($19.6 billion), and NBC/Universal ($14.5 billion) (*Columbia Journalism Review*, 2004).

Teacher's Note: This is the time to review company ownership relationships. When discussing these relationships, be sure to point out why they are covered in this course. Discuss the potential for ownership to color news or program content. Give some concrete examples. You also could discuss significant ownership changes that have recently occurred.

The fact that several media companies have merged has made a lot of news lately, sometimes not too complimentary to the government, the president, or the FCC. The large volume of media mergers is the result of promises made almost 10 years ago as a part of the move to digital and high definition television. Networks and affiliates were being required to spend millions of dollars on new equipment to support this migration. As a part of these negotiations, the rules for cross-ownership were relaxed, and continue to be so. For further information on this interesting topic, see Joel Brinkley's *Defining Vision: How Broadcasters Tricked the Government into Inciting a Revolution in Television.*

The following list was considered accurate at the time of publication. As it changes often, you may wish to update it. The *Columbia Journalism Review* carries a list online (www.cjr.org/tools/owners/index.asp).

- Disney owns ABC, ESPN (Hearst owns 25 percent), ABCFamily, Disney Channel, and 10 ABC affiliate stations; 37.5 percent of A& E Network; 39.6 percent of E! Entertainment Television, and 50 percent (along with Hearst) of Lifetime Cable Network; and Touchstone TV, along with several movie studios and radio networks.

- GE owns NBC/Universal, which owns CNBC, MSNBC (a joint venture with Microsoft), Bravo, Sci-Fi, Trio, Telemundo, and USA. Its holdings also include Universal Studios and several themes parks, including Universal Studios Orlando.

- Fox (a public company that is 82 percent owned by Rupert Murdock's News Corporation) owns Fox Broadcasting, all Fox News & Sports outlets, 35 Fox-owned affiliate stations, 21 regional cable television networks, Speed Channel, Fox Movie Channel, and the National Geographic Channel, and is a partner with Hughes Electronics, which operates DirecTV, and several other interests, including Madison Square Garden, Radio City Music Hall, and several sports teams.

- Time Warner owns TNT, HBO, TBS Superstation, Cinemax, The WB (along with a 22 percent interest by the Tribune Corp), and CNN and all its affiliates; Compuserve, AOL, and Netscape; and the Atlanta Braves.

- VIACOM owns CBS, CMT, SpikeTV, UPN, TVLand, Nickelodeon, MTV, VH1, Comedy Central, Showtime, Affinity, BET, and Showtime, along with Blockbuster, several movie studios, and Viacom Outdoor (advertising).

- Comcast owns The Golf Channel, Outdoor Life Network, a major holding in E! Entertainment Television (along with Disney), AT&T Broadband, Comcast High Speed Internet, 21 percent of Time Warner subsidiary TWC Cable Systems, and several sports teams in the Philadelphia area.

- Univision owns TeleFutura Network. (*Columbia Journalism Review,* 2004)

Teacher's Note: It might be fun to speculate on how a news story might be positioned or influenced if it happened to be good or bad news about the parent company. Remember that we are talking possibility here. However, Congress was so concerned about the content of news for over 50 years that it passed laws to control who owned what stations and the public's right to knowledge through the Radio Act of 1927 and the Communications Act of 1934.

The next potential influencer, noted by the box at the top of the diagram, is the **government**. Several times throughout history governments, in the name of national interest, have withheld information from the public. For example, in the United States the Warren Commission, which undertook the task of investigating the assassination of President John F. Kennedy, locked its records up for several years. During the Vietnam War, the U.S. military was accused of misrepresenting the number of U.S. casualties in an elaborate **disinformation** campaign of deliberately provide misleading information (not to be confused with *misinformation*, that is, information disseminated during a time of crisis that might be accidentally wrong due to the confusion surrounding the events).

Sponsors certainly have the potential to influence the news. As you know by now, all programming is paid for by sponsorships and advertising. In the next session we will do a case study to show how that works. But for now, just understand that a sponsor, through this business relationship, has the potential to influence a story, the same as an owner does.

The box to the right in Figure 2.2 represents the **local media market:** that's you and me. The local market is a significant influencer. Not every type of news story is shown in the same manner in each city and town. What plays well in New York City might not play in Orlando, Florida, or Lincoln, Nebraska. The simplest example is the weather—mostly local. As another example, a report on the wheat crop might get more coverage in Lincoln than in New York.

Teacher's Note: Even if there are no political issues, students should understand how the potential influences affect what news is reported, and how. Imagine the potential danger should these influencers be overlooked. We started the discussions with the general feeling that the media are extremely powerful. Steps had been taken to regulate the industry in terms of how many stations one company could own, whether it could own all the media outlets in a single city, and so forth. This course will cover these issues as we follow the history of broadcasting.

Follow-up Activity

News Analysis

Student Instructions: You are to watch the news for the next three evenings. You are to watch three news programs, at a different time each night.

For this assignment, you are to watch the news on _____.

Then compare your answers and prepare a chart for the rest of the class. Your chart should answer the following questions:

1.   How many news stories are there on average in a half-hour news show?
       Night 1: _____ Night 2: _____ Night 3: _____

2.   How much time (on average) is spent on each story? _____ _____ _____
                                                          min.   min.   min.

3.   What is the news flow? If you were a stranger from out of town, what impression about this city would you get?
       Night 1: _____.
       Night 2: _____.
       Night 3: _____.

4.   Which is the most important news item from the entire broadcast? How do you know?
       _____
       _____
       _____

5.   Is there a slant or opinion that is obvious? Why do you think the selected stories were used?
       Night 1:_____ Night 2: _____ Night 3: _____

6.   If you were the news director, what flow would you use? Which stories would you delete and which would you put in their place?
       _____
       _____
       _____

Lesson 2.1B

The Makings of a Newscast

Terms

timeliness	proximity	exceptional quality
possible future impact	prominence	shock value
consequence	human interest	number of people involved
pathos	conflict	
titillation component		

Lesson Notes

Newscasts do not happen by accident. In fact, you will see by the end of this course that the goal of broadcasting is to ensure that **nothing** happens by accident. We have already seen today how the different influencers play a role in swaying what is shown during a newscast, or at least how much play a story might get or when it is shown. Much has been written about the effect the content of the story has on its newsworthiness.

Let's take a look at some of the things we found out in the Follow-up Activity and try to relate them to our discussions regarding how a story is selected and what effect the influencers might have on those decisions.

Selection criteria for the stories that end up being shown:

Timeliness	How recent is it?
Proximity	How close is it?
Exceptional quality	How important is it?
Possible future impact	How does it affect the future?
Prominence	How important is the person involved?
The # of people involved or affected	How many are involved?
Consequence	What is the impact?
Human interest	Is there a human interest story there? (Question: Are animal stories human interest stories?)
Pathos	Is there human suffering?
Conflict	Are there people fighting?
Shock value	Is it shocking? (example: Jerry Springer show)
Titillation component	Are there sexual overtones?

We could say that each item on this list could be affected one way or another by the influencers we have discussed. Can you think of how any of the items on the list might be affected by the government, a sponsor, an owner, the local market, or an ENG group?

Teacher's Note: At this point, spend some time reviewing the meaning of the terms involved with this paradigm and how they affect whether a story is chosen and how an influencer might sway a media outlet to
1. change the story content,
2. change the amount of time a story might get on the newscast,
3. change when the story is played, and
4. eliminate the story altogether.

One of the things that should become obvious from our review of this list is that only a few can be reasonably managed to affect any ratings increase. If you understand the reasoning that stations and networks exist primarily to make money, then it should be easy to understand why conflict, shock value, and titillation are used so often and as lead stories during newscasts.

Teacher's Note: Class discussions will center on findings from the news analysis. You will definitely see a trend in how news directors use shock value, conflict, and titillation to gain ratings. You should also get some idea about how the local stations play the news for ratings. Chances are that sometime during the course of your class discussions, some important news story will break. Try to spot examples you can use in class to make your point about the news being used as a marketing tool for local stations to increase ratings. Local news programs are also considered cash cows to local stations. Commercial time does not have to be shared with their affiliate networks. Newscasts are therefore a large source of revenue for local stations.

Lesson 2.2

Copyrights and Responsibilities Web-Quest

Lesson Planning Considerations

(**Approx. Time:** 25–35 minutes)

Agenda

For a television/media teacher, the ethical treatment of copyrights may be difficult. This is not a difficult concept to teach. However, there is a temptation to indoctrinate students about copyrights and then ignore them in school productions. Many people are simply under the false impression that schools have some type of special exemption (called **fair use**) and do not have to follow the general rules everyone else does. This is simply not true. There are exceptions for classroom situations, but generally everyone is obligated to honor the same copyright laws, especially for productions that are broadcast campuswide. Simply put, if the production is to be made for use by an audience and/or broadcast anywhere (even within the confines of the school campus), copyright laws must be observed. This applies to sight (pictures, still shots, movie clips, and so forth) and sound (music, recorded speech, and so forth).

This puts an extra burden on the television classroom. Copyright enforcement has generally been weak, but that slackness may be changing soon. It is important to cover these issues, especially because this class comes in contact with copyrighted material so often. Teachers should adhere strictly to their school copyright policies to protect themselves. If there is no policy, they should work on a committee to create one. In many cases, the school's media coordinator might be a great resource for this purpose.

There are several sources for copyright-free music. The best way to approach this is to adopt a policy that states **when in doubt, it's safest to assume that the material is copyrighted.** This might be a hard pill to swallow. Students will want to use the latest music videos taken right off their televisions, the latest CDs for background music, and so forth. Teaching students to understand and respect copyright laws requires that they be followed, even when it hurts. Using a music or video cut for an individual project that is to be placed on one's portfolio is one thing. But these clips should not be used in conjunction with schoolwide productions, especially video yearbooks, without permission. Teaching the rules of copyright is a very important function of a television class. The First Amendment right of free speech protects the intellectual property of speakers, writers, artists, and composers.

Objectives and Outcomes

As a result of this lesson, students will be able to

• compare, and later defend, arguments about First Amendment rights and censorship;

• define and understand the NAB television Code of Ethics;

• compose and employ a class code of ethics for on-air presentations; and

• respect and follow copyright laws in their own projects.

<u>Mediated and Textual Support</u>

If you want to get into a lot of detail about this subject, there are several sources. In addition to those sources listed for the web-quest, the "Digging Deeper" section at the end of "Chapter Two" on the **Web-ASSISTant** Web site provides several Internet references on copyright law.

<u>Lesson Readiness</u>

Students participate in a web-quest as a means to becoming oriented to the problems and misconceptions concerning copyrights. More than likely, they will come to class with several extraneous questions and what ifs about copyrights. Limit the time spent on these issues rather than stimulating their interest in the topic. There is an orientation questionnaire that covers many of censorship issues. Students are to come to class with a written opinion about the issues.

<u>Closure</u>

Closure will come when students can participate in class discussions. They are also asked to construct a class code of ethics for on-screen behavior that is based on traditions, understanding of copyrights, and ethical behavior.

Pre-Lesson Activity

Copyright Versus Public Domain

Student Instructions: Today we are going to search on the Internet about copyright. Go to the **Web-ASSISTant** Web site (www.web-assist.com). From there, go to **Student Activities: Copyrights** and follow the instructions. You are to bring back to class the information you find and participate in discussions. You are to develop an opinion about copyright laws and be prepared to discuss any knowledge that you did not have beforehand.

In the time allotted, see how many answers to the following questions you can find:

What things does a copyright cover? **Rights to creative works**

When is a copyright registered? **Immediately upon completion of the material**

How long does it last? **Depends on when the work was created. The Sonny Bono Copyright Term Extension Act of 1998 extended many copyrights by 20 years. For works created after January 1, 1978, a copyright lasts for the life of the author plus 70 years. In the case of a joint work, copyright lasts for 70 years after the last surviving author's death. For anonymous works and works made for hire, copyright lasts 95 years (for example, the copyright on cartoon characters like Mickey Mouse) from the year of first publication or 120 years from the year of creation, whichever ends first.**

What happens to the copyright when someone dies? **See above answer**

What about the Internet: are creative works also protected? **The same rules apply**

How are copyrights enforced overseas? **International treaties**

What are patents and trademarks? Patents protect **inventions**. Trademarks cover **logos and symbols**.

What is fair use? **The following comes directly from Section 107 of the Copyright Act of 1976. Limitations on exclusive rights: Fair use:**

"Notwithstanding the provisions of sections 106 and 106A, the fair use of a copyrighted work, including such use by reproduction in copies or phonorecords or by any other means specified in that section, for purposes such as criticism, comment, news reporting, teaching (COMMENT: including multiple copies for classroom use), scholarship, or research, is not an infringement of copyright.

In determining whether the use made of a work in any particular case is a fair use the factors to be considered shall include—

1. the purpose and character of the use, including whether such use is of a commercial nature or is for nonprofit educational purposes;

2. the nature of the copyrighted work;

3. the amount and substantiality of the portion used in relation to the copyrighted work as a whole; and

4. the effect of the use upon the potential market for or value of the copyrighted work.

The fact that a work is unpublished shall not itself bar a finding of fair use if such finding is made upon consideration of all the above factors."

What is the affect on fair use made by the DMCA?

(This could be a lengthy discussion, but it is essential for students to understand that copyright is a two-edged sword). By prohibiting the ability to copy electronic media, the ability of those wishing to take advantage of fair use may be severely limited. For example, a teacher or library is no longer able to reproduce portions of works for classroom use, and a critic is no longer allowed to use a video clip to demonstrate a point. This is an ongoing issue and is being met with considerable opposition. There are several Web sites devoted to this cause. Go to www.askjeeves.com and ask "what is fair use?" and several links will pop up.

Teacher's Note: At this point, the teacher should introduce the concept of copyrights and fair use and how they affect using materials in the classroom. Procedures should be tied to individual school policies.

Opinion questions: Based on our discoveries today, please answer the following in your own words:

What are the implications of copyrights for our projects? _____.

Considering the copyright and trademark issues above, why do you think a Talent Release Form is necessary in television production? _____

Terms

copyright laws	public domain	trademarks
patents	talent release form	international treaties

Teacher's Note: Students have a natural curiosity about copyright and tend to ask trivial what-if questions. You can allow these discussions to go in any direction you want, but you may find it best to limit the time you spend on copyrights to about 30–45 minutes. Be sure to cover the basics within that timeframe and be sure to introduce your own class rules about how you will enforce and respect the copyright laws within your project outlines. An optimal situation is to take the class to a computer lab or the media center where all students can have access to computers at the same time, and have them complete the questions for class discussion.

Lesson Notes

In the activity that began this lesson we learned how the rights of individuals to free speech are preserved and protected. That same right also protects ownership of what is said or otherwise communicated (**performed, written, painted, mimed, or recorded**). The right of an individual to retain ownership of his or her original thoughts or works of art is protected by the First Amendment under **copyright laws**. Stated another way, this is a *right to copy*. The opposite of copyright is **public domain**. Contrary to the belief of many, there is no in between. Either a work is copyrighted or it is public domain (copyright free). Once given up to the public, a work cannot be copyrighted again. Even the owner of a copyright cannot state that his or her work is given to the public domain but with conditions. There is no *almost* when it comes to the public domain.

The law indicates that when the copyright holder dies, the copyright continues for up to 75 years (recently extended for up to 95 years). Some estates will assume responsibility for a work to protect it.

A copyright is immediate and does not have to be registered. Some time ago, this was not the case. You actually had to register your work to protect it. A poem is copyrighted as soon as it is written. Every original work is protected, even your homework answers. The reason you might register your work or otherwise show evidence of publication is to protect its origination date and time. For example, if there is a dispute, and you have proof that your work predated another's, the one who has proof stands the better chance to get credit for the work. That is why some people have actually sent the written document to themselves in a self-addressed, stamped envelope, to show the postmark as proof of its creation date. Registration is no longer required, but it does help make the case for ownership. Many corporations go through the registration process because they have so much money at stake.

Copyright protects works of art. **Patents** protect inventions. **Trademarks** protect products and corporate logos. Although the underlying concepts are similar, rules for registration vary greatly.

In the media industry, we deal with copyright a lot. We have to be cognizant that copyright accompanies published music and visual images that we will want to use in our productions. As a general rule, we will assume that everything is copyrighted, even the things we find on the Internet, unless we are shown otherwise. Therefore, any project we intend to broadcast or show to an audience will be protected under the copyright laws.

There is a thing called *fair use*, which allows use of copyrighted work without permission if the portion is under 500 words. However, because this can be confusing, it is best to be a conservative in this area.

You may wonder how copyrights are protected overseas. This has been and is a cause for serious concern. You may have read or heard that countries like China have been ostracized for lack of adherence to copyrights. They have been accused of allowing companies to illegally copy music onto CDs and then sell them on the black market. This is something that nations are coming to grips with through **international treaties**.

Closer to home, we respect copyright laws as best we can. No permission to use material is to be assumed. Unless you have it in writing, then you must assume that it has not been granted. For that reason, we will ask everyone who appears as talent on any of our productions to sign a **talent release form**. This is to protect us both. The talent are giving us permission to use their images in our shows. By signing the form, they acknowledge that they might appear in one of our. They have the right to (or waive the right to) review any production in which they appear prior to its being shown.

Lesson 2.3

Broadcast Code of Ethics

Lesson Planning Considerations

(**Approx. Time:** 25–35 minutes)

Agenda

So far, we have posed to the students some of the problems and issues facing the broadcasting industry. By presenting problems first, we have provided an opportunity to show the derivation of the self-regulatory steps the industry has taken. This session is intended to reinforce the need for regulation and to point out how the industry has responded. Many of the ethical issues are probably also being reviewed in social studies and/or civics classes.

Redundancy is a good thing. In a television and multimedia production class, we view ethics issues as behavioral. In a civics class, ethics are examined from a sociological viewpoint. Often social studies discussions are accompanied by debates on such nebulous topics as whether violence in the media begets violence in society, or whether censorship overrides one's First Amendment rights. In a television class, our discussions take a more pragmatic approach. We discuss the need for and the traditions of self-regulation, as well as appropriate on-air demeanor in the classroom and for programs broadcast on campus. These issues used to be fairly straightforward; all the television teacher had to say was "if it is okay for prime-time television, then it is okay for our shows." However, things have become more complicated. No longer does this statement cover the gamut of what is considered acceptable behavior and wording on shows appearing on commercial television. One has to wonder what went wrong.

The Code of Ethics is covered in this lesson, although it was essentially killed by the broadcasting industry in 1983, after a protracted legal battle with the U.S. Justice Department. In 1979, the Justice Department, under the Sherman Act, filed an antitrust suit against the National Association of Broadcasters (NAB), who were thought to have been using certain provisions of the Code to monopolize advertising rates. In *United States v. National Association of Broadcasters*, the court held that the multiple product rule of the Code, which prevented advertisers from advertising more than one product in a 30-second commercial, was per se illegal since it had the effect of increasing the demand for and price of commercial time. Although the Code was ultimately abandoned, many of its provisions were not challenged. There are provisions in the 1996 Telecommunications Act for a voluntary Code to be reinstituted. However, as of the publishing of this text, no overt action has been taken by the NAB to do so. In fact, the frameworks followed in today's programs are based on a "Statement of Principles" adopted by the NAB in 1990 and reaffirmed in 1992. Additional information on the provisions of the 1996 Act, along with the history of the Code, can be found on the **Web-ASSISTant** Web site under "Digging Deeper."

Although there have always been implied obligations under the public trust provisions in the 1934 Communications Act, adherence to the statutory code has mostly been voluntary. No federal agency requires owners and/or station managers to operate their affairs in an ethical manner. One also has to consider that there are also implied "degrees of ethicality" (Smith et al., 1998, p. 458). How well managers and owners fulfill these requirements has traditionally been left up to self-regulation.

However (thankfully) there is one broadcasting organization that has always had the highest regard for ethical standards. The Radio–Television News Director Association (RTNDA), which is not affiliated with the NAB, has consistently reaffirmed its stand on ethical on-air behavior. The following summary was taken from the RTNDA Web site:

> **PUBLIC TRUST:** Professional electronic journalists should recognize that their first obligation is to the public.
>
> Professional electronic journalists should:
>
> - Understand that any commitment other than service to the public undermines trust and credibility.
>
> - Recognize that service in the public interest creates an obligation to reflect the diversity of the community and guard against oversimplification of issues or events.
>
> - Provide a full range of information to enable the public to make enlightened decisions.
>
> - Fight to ensure that the public's business is conducted in public.

Professional electronic journalists should (this has been paraphrased from the Web site):

- Gather and report news without fear or favor, and vigorously resist undue influence from any outside forces, including advertisers, sources, story subjects, powerful individuals, and special interest groups.

- Resist those who would seek to buy or politically influence news content or who would seek to intimidate those who gather and disseminate the news.

- Determine news content solely through editorial judgment and not as the result of outside influence.

- Resist any self-interest or peer pressure that might erode journalistic duty and service to the public.

- Recognize that sponsorship of the news will not be used in any way to determine, restrict, or manipulate content.

- Refuse to allow the interests of ownership or management to influence news judgment and content inappropriately.

- Defend the rights of the free press for all journalists, recognizing that any professional or government licensing of journalists is a violation of that freedom.

The full text of the RTNDA doctrine can be found on their Web site, **www.rtnda.org/ethicscoe.shtml**.

From a teacher's point of view, this is a relief. Although following these provisions is still voluntary, a television teacher desperately needs something to point to with regard to ethical behavior, even if it is only in the newsroom.

One also needs to make the distinction between broadcast television and cable and satellite. The foundation of any argument about on-air conduct must be traced back to the Communications Act of 1934, which contains specific language about acceptable use of specific words. This Act only applies to over-the-air broadcast. Cable and satellite broadcasts are excluded from this regulation. All recent FCC actions in raising fines imposed against broadcasters to as much as $500,000 per infraction for offensive materials apply only to the open airwaves, which are to be safe-guarded by the "in the public trust" wording found in the 1934 Act.

Author's Note: At the time of publication, on-air (in)ethical behavior had been in the news a lot. Certain networks and on-air talent like Howard Stern were being cited (and their distributors assessed large fines) for "unbecoming behaviors." These fines, according to some, were based on the provisions of the 1934 Communications Act, as explained above, that specifically forbid explicit descriptions of reproductive organs and/or sexual acts. On the other hand, there are many who dispute the FCC's ability to control what is being said or displayed in radio or on television, based on First Amendment principles. Over the years the courts have upheld a different standard for over-the-air broadcasters than for cable and satellite based on the fact that access to the electromagnetic spectrum is tightly controlled due to its limited capacity. This seems to be the best argument for why some limited content regulation (such as indecency regulation) has been upheld for broadcasters but not for other media (such as cable and/or satellite transmissions).

Objectives and Outcomes

As a result of this lesson, students will be able to

• discuss the differences between freedoms provided in the First Amendment and censorship,

• form an opinion about how this relationship should work in the context of a broadcast, and

• describe the need for a Talent Release Form.

Mediated and Textual Support

If you have time, you may wish to use the optional Web-Quest on censorship. The *Web-ASSISTant* Web site provides links to the various locations where the answers to the questions can be found.

Lesson Readiness

The censorship questionnaire should help to orient students to the context in which censorship will be discussed in class.

Closure

Students should be able to express their opinions regarding censorship and to formulate a class code of ethics.

Pre-Lesson Activity

Censorship Questionnaire

Student Instructions: You are to fill out before class the following questionnaire about your personal views on censorship, First Amendment rights and responsibilities, and ethical on-the-air behavior. You may ask your friends, other teachers, and parents for help. This will be mostly a group discussion centering on the need for differing regulations, with the class hopefully coming to the conclusion that self-regulation is best. You may use these discussions to preface an introduction into your own rules for in-class productions.

1. In your opinion, what makes the broadcast industry different from other entertainment media with regard to rules for appropriate behavior?

   In the entertainment media, one usually makes an overt act to participate. That person has to purchase the newspaper or magazine, purchase a movie ticket, and so forth. With television and radio, the medium does the acting; once it is turned on, it invades your household. In the early years, citizens did not even have much of a choice with regard to which channels they watched or stations they listened to. [As an aside: We will learn in our history lessons that early regulations controlled how many licenses were awarded in each locale and who owned which media outlets (unlike newspapers or cable, —both of which have a history of being unregulated monopolies). Also mention public trusts provisions in 1934 Communications Act.]

2. How have the choices made available by cable television and satellites changed the television industry?

   First, there are more choices. No longer do the big three networks (ABC, NBC, CBS) own the airwaves, so to speak. Next, there are premium channels like HBO, which viewers have to purchase. Then there is pay-per-view.

3. What does the term *prime time* viewing mean, and what role does it play in determining on-air behavior?

   Prime time traditionally has been the time between 8PM and 11PM ET. These have been considered prime slots for selling commercial advertisements, because the largest audiences will be watching during these hours. Prime time also implies that younger viewers (viewers 18–34) are watching and that these time slots would be prime for complaints if programming did not reflect middle of the road attitudes and behavior. Even though prime time is becoming less prime with all the available choices, it still affects programming choices made by the major networks.

4. Why did the broadcasting industry choose to self-regulate its behaviors?

Like radio, television was initially viewed as a news and communications medium rather than an entertainment vehicle. Journalists live by a certain code of their own (such as checking out each potential story with a minimum of two independent sources). [As an aside: In our history lessons we will learn about the long-time close ties between broadcasting and the military.] In the early days, each network hired a staff of censors who had the job of reviewing all scripts for each show. Traditionally, the National Association of Broadcasters (NAB) has taken on the task of self-regulation and enforcement.

Terms

allegedly	tabloid television	smut
paparazzi	redeeming social value	sound bites
media circus	the television code of ethics	spin doctors
obscenity		

Lesson Notes

Over time, market forces and changing standards for behavior have chipped away at our traditional views of what is deemed **appropriate behavior**. In the early years of television, the NAB (National Association of Broadcasters) had worked hard to maintain a self-regulating committee to monitor and enforce on-camera behaviors. By 1953, they had instituted a voluntary code, which included a network or station's right to display the seal of approval. However, as a result of a succession of legal battles regarding free speech and antitrust, this code has fallen away with no replacement. Stations and networks have been forced to deal with the elements of the code on their own. We will review the provisions of the original code in order to to find out how television has evolved in the past 15 years without a code to follow.

NAB Code of Ethics

Look at the following list of inappropriate subject matter. The items all came from the National Association of Broadcasters Code of Ethics. Which ones do you think are still in effect? Based on what you see on television today, how are some of the more popular television shows stretching the limits of decency?

Teacher's Note: The Radio and Television News Director's Association (RTNDA) has posited its own code of ethics. The full text of the RTNDA doctrine can be found on the Web site, www.rtnda.org/ethics/coe.shtml. It may be useful to explore this list also and use it in class to elicit student opinions about which of these are being violated or followed during newscasts.

The following should be avoided:

* **Profanity**, **obscenity**, **smut**, and **vulgarity** even when likely to be understood by only a part of the audience.

* **Words describing sex acts** or specific parts of the human anatomy.

* Words (especially slang) derisive of any **race**, **color**, **creed, or nationality**, except where use would be for the specific purpose of effective dramatization, such as combating prejudice.

* The presentation of techniques of crime in such detail as to **invite imitation**.

* Creation of the state **of hypnosis** by act or demonstration on the air and hypnosis as an aspect of parlor game antics to create humorous situations within comedy situation.

Other Guidelines

* **Avoid attacks** on religion and religious faiths.

* Law enforcement and legal advice **for a fee** must not be offered.

* **Avoid** such exclamations as **flash or bulletin.**

* **Avoid showing** on-the-scene **betting** on sporting events.

* Providing **answers to contestants on quiz shows** is prohibited.

* Avoid depicting **inhumane** treatment of animals.

* Segregate **news from opinion**.

The Code of Ethics was originally drafted in 1952, and by the early 1980s it was out of favor because of political pressures and infighting in the association NAB. Over time, there has been a gradual erosion of the will to enforce these premises in the United States. Other countries, like Canada, still seem to be observing their codes of ethics. As recently as 1996, the U.S. government, as a part of the compromise to remove almost all existing regulations on the industry, has attempted to get the industry to reinstitute a national code of behavior. Whatever ethical behavior exists in television today is mostly based on fears of public or sponsor reprisal (market forces) and lawsuits.

Teacher's Note: In early 2004, as a result of the infamous "Janet Jackson incident" at that year's Super Bowl, public outcry over this "envelope pushing" came to a head. The FCC issued fines to major media companies for misconduct. Although certain vulgarities were tolerated, explicit depictions would be punished. The pressure increased to the point that some media companies began firing disc jockeys and show hosts to avoid financial penalties. It appears that the pendulum had begin swinging back. These news items make good classroom discussion topics.

Some of these rules may seem ludicrous by current standards. The framers of the code were apparently worried about the negative effect television might have on its viewers. Although for the most part broadcasters still exhibit some restraint, an increasing number of **shock jocks,** tabloid news shows (**tabloid television**), exotic talk shows, and "reality" shows have stretched the limits of regulation. The quest to retain audience market share has increased the pressure to push the envelope.

Only the last standard in the second list above (**segregate news from opinion**) appears to have remained intact. The continued tradition of segregating fact from opinion may be driven more by a fear of lawsuits than a general consensus about right and wrong. There is still legal protection against deliberately spread false accusations, in the form of **libel or slander lawsuits**. From time to time a tabloid or magazine is sued by a celebrity because that celebrity thought an article deliberately harmed his or her reputation. Although libel may be difficult to prove, the law appears to have tempered the temptation to spread rumors. On the other hand, the threat of a libel suit could discourage the publication of an investigative story for fear of reprisal and lengthy, expensive lawsuits.

Often you will hear a news reporter use the term **allegedly**, although the evidence appears to be overwhelming (i.e., the accused is shown to have done the deed on camera). *Allegedly* is used when an accused person has not yet been convicted (innocent until proven guilty). The reference is generally removed from the broadcast as soon as the trial is over.

Another term that seems to allow individual interpretation with regard to whether a code has been violated is **redeeming social value.** This t equates to permitting a local rendering of what is obscene or vulgar and leaves the door open to interpretation. Many take this to mean that, as long as there is a storyline, anything goes. The intent of this expression is to narrowly define vulgarity to mean that something is only obscene if it is shown only for its titillation or shock value without some higher purpose, such as making a statement or to spark some type of public discussion.

There are several groups that think things have gone too far. Public opinion may be the best regulator. In the school, the concept of playing to a captive audience is more apparent because there is only one "channel." and the shows are broadcast campuswide. The need for self-regulation is even greater than in the general public. For that reason we must compile our own list of rules for on-air dress and appropriate behavior.

Various practices have given rise to four terms that are becoming quite common when referring to a media event:

- **Media circus:** This term refers to a situation or event about which the reporting media go so berserk that the clamor caused by the media contingent completely overshadows the event itself. Recent examples are the O. J. Simpson trial in 1996 and the Monica Lewinski scandal in 1998, in which instances the media actually created the news rather than simply reporting it. Some feel that this type of behavior is an abuse of the concept that the public has the right to know. You may even hear a television or radio newscaster quote someone who may have been interviewed or appeared on an earlier edition of one of their own shows. That quote or series of statements then becomes the story rather than remaining a supporting statement.

- **Paparazzi:** This term comes from a central character in an old Frederico Fellini classic. In this movie, Paparazzo was a photographer who hounded the main character to get a story. The pejorative term refers to those photographers who work for the tabloids and do anything to get the photograph they want.

Teacher's Note: Recall that in 1997 Princess Diana was killed in a car crash while attempting to avoid the paparazzi Some students may remember the incident; it should make for lively class discussion. Can you think of other incidents?

- **Sound bites:** This term refers to short catchphrases or sentences, often used during political campaigns, that draw attention to a main point. Often, a commercial or politician says so much during a campaign, and air-time is so limited (newscasts often limit a segment to 30 seconds or less) that the supporters want only the most concise bits repeated over and over so viewers will remember them.

- **Spin doctors:** This term refers to highly paid professional promoters and public relations teams hired by politicians, whose one-and-only function is to spin (turn) an unfavorable news story into a favorable story for their candidate.

Follow-up Activity

Class Code of Conduct

Student Instructions: To better understand the concept of self-regulation, we are going to design our own code of conduct for class projects and broadcasts. Because we have a **captive audience** at school that is even more defined and more "captive" than the general public, we have to hold ourselves more accountable than commercial television does. We have our own definition of a **prime time** when almost all of the student body watches our productions. The list you develop should contain the class code of conduct to be used when we appear on any program produced in this course.

With regard to showing programs in class, we agree:

_____

_____

With regard to showing programs on campus, we agree to:

_____

_____

Talent Release Form

We have briefly discussed the need for a talent release form that supports copyright obligations. There is also a need for the show producers to secure from the on-air talent an agreement that indicates that they agree to abide by the same designated code of rules and procedures we have set up. The release form, then, has two purposes. It is necessary that anyone who appears on camera as talent (not a part of general field footage) sign this release prior to the show in which he or she appears.

> ***Teacher's Note:*** Hand out talent release forms at this time and review any questions with the students.

Optional Activity

Decisions-Decisions: Violence in the Media

Lesson Planning Considerations

(**Approx. Time**: 55–75 minutes)

Agenda

The following activity is based on an online computer game called *Decisions-Decisions: Violence in the Media*, published by Tom Snyder Productions. The site contains video clips, support materials, and a teacher's guide. The site may be accessed at **ddonline.tomsnyder.com/issues/tvviolence/intro.cfm**. Students are faced with a series of difficult decisions while playing the roles of key members of an in-house advertising team for a major snack food company. To help them decide wisely, they receive advice from four expert advisors who provide information in a series of scenarios printed in handbooks that accompany the software. Through this simulation game, students explore media violence and develop an understanding of the media paradigm presented in Lesson 2.1A.

Students divide up into six groups. Because this is a team project, it is an opportunity for the teacher to form project groups and to use this program as a test to determine how well the newly formed groups interact. The program can be set up so that each group competes individually, or it can be set up for each group to work independently, but in a controlled manner where the teacher calls each team up to the computer to enter its answers in turn.

The teacher

- prepares the class with an overview and set-up,

- organizes the class for either a whole-class discussion or multiteam environment, and

- runs the computer program.

That's about it! As the computer actually runs the simulation, the teacher plays an advisory role and facilitates the activity, in which the students actively participate. Because this session runs about 50 minutes, it will take one class period for schools on a traditional calendar. It can also be broken down into two separate sessions. The computer stores the answers for each team so that the class can go back to them the next time.

Objectives and Outcomes

This exercise provides the following activities and outcomes for students:

- It uncovers a real-world dilemma through a critical reading of the scenario in the student reference books included with the program.

- They learn to prioritize goals.

- They are able to offer multiple perspectives on complex problems.

- They learn to come to a consensus.

- They learn how to deal with the consequences of their choices.

- They analyze business choices often made in the broadcasting industry.

Mediated and Textual Support

Decisions/Decisions: Violence in the Media is a computer simulation game published by Tom Snyder Productions. It explores the complexities of grappling with television violence and provides a first-hand opportunity to make decisions that will affect an outcome, causing students to have to live with the results. Information on how to order this simulation game can be found on the **Web-ASSISTant** Web site.

Lesson Readiness

By the time students get to this activity, they have had the session on the media paradigm (Figure 2.2). They can be oriented to the context by simply reviewing the aspects of that diagram. The diagram introduces how various ownership and commercial interests affect the content of shows. This session only reinforces the impact a sponsor might have on show content.

Closure

Students should be able to discuss the outcomes of the game and describe why their team scored the way it did.

Lesson 2.4

Lesson Planning Considerations

(**Approx. Time:** Discussion Activity 1: 15–25 minutes; *Against all Odds* Video: 25–30 minutes; Internet Activity: 35–40 minutes)

Agenda

This lesson is actually preceded by one outside activity and one in-class activity. The in-class session is a Web-Quest designed as a group critical thinking activity. Students are to find on the Internet the answers to the questions and determine in class discussions the effect problems in determining exact ratings criteria have on the economy of broadcasting. The out-of-class activity is a survey in which students poll individuals to find out what the participants feel is the most significant event that happened during the 1950s or 1960s in the world of mass communications. The intent is to demonstrate apparently contradictory results. The first activity is to show that survey taking and polls are extremely accurate, if done properly. By tracking their responses on a board, students will see first-hand how a sense of trends starts to appear while taking a survey. The Web- Quest introduces, among other things, the Nielsens, one of the most well-known media research companies in the world. Although the Nielsen system can be extremely accurate, it does have its problems. The Web- Quest found under **Student Activities** on the **Web-ASSIS-Tant** Web site, also introduces some of the more inventive ways in which technology will help to solve some of those problems.

The third part of this lesson is to watch a video segment from the *Against All Odds* series produced by CPB/Annenberg that covers how survey results can become biased. Once students are introduced to the concept that ratings are the most significant source of revenue for the media and that several problems are involved in obtaining ratings results, they will better understand how the system has become so convoluted. They should also get a sense of the contradictions that exist. Apparently, there are insurmountable problems in the information-gathering routines, yet the economy of the industry is founded on this less-than-perfect system. Even more amazing is the fact that political popularity polls also run on similar systems, and these appear to have become a significant contributor to decisions our government officials make in running our country.

As a result of taking a survey, students will learn many things. The first lesson falls into the realm of organizing and sequencing a production, so it could have been put in Chapter 7. However, through this lesson students will learn something about the ratings system and poll taking in general, so it could have just as easily ended up in this chapter. Because of its fundamental nature, this lesson is taught very early in the term. The activity will help students understand how the entire ratings system is flawed and why the industry is striving to make one-to-one marketing a reality.

It is very important to introduce the idea that their own beliefs are not necessarily those of others, especially to younger students. One of the founding principles of visual literacy training for students is to learn that everyone has individual tastes and desires unique to themselves. Younger high school students have not grasped the concept that a world exists beyond themselves. What they see as white may indeed be black. Another student's taste in music or fashion, show format, and so forth may not be the same as their own. Another way to point out this important concept to students is to have them conduct a survey about a topic. The topic could be about a personal preference, a moment in history, or a subject of your own.

In keeping with the television theme, the suggested format for the lesson is to have students ask eight individuals about developments that took place within the past century in the media industry. There is nothing scientific about the number eight. A sampling of four was tried, but a sense of the trend was not evident when the number was too small. Also, students need to learn how difficult it is to get the proper number of respondents.

After taking the survey, students should reach an informed opinion, based solely on the eight results. They will think that eight people are enough, until they find that the others in the class have different answers, as evidenced by the chart you will develop. A trend should start to emerge. If one does not, you can use the results as a teaching moment to demonstrate the need for a sufficient number of responses before a trend can develop.

If a trend becomes evident, it will visually demonstrate that poll taking is essentially a numbers game. The more responses, the more likely the poll will be accurate. Your teaching point should come to the same conclusion. You should not be able to accurately determine the "winner"; only a trend should be evident. This lesson on trends should help you introduce the videos in the next session. Blocking and sampling cover the population issues. The video on reliability and validity covers issues like the questioning style, the number of questions asked, and so forth.

Regardless of the responses, the discussions in class will be memorable. Students may simply learn that not everyone has the same opinions about *anything*, and that those surveyed will *always* offer an opinion, whether or not they any knowledge of the subject matter. Students will develop a basic understanding of how responses stratify. Most importantly, they will see for themselves that their own opinions are not necessarily those of others. Only when they begin to see this will they start to understand the concept of catering to an audience. Understanding these concepts makes a good introduction to the lessons on the production sequence. Understanding one's audience is the first item on the list.

The results of a survey will vary considerably. If a student asks eight different people, there will be eight different responses. Ask students to reveal their answers and record them on the board. Students will probably be frustrated over how difficult it is to get accurate information. At first, the results will be quite scattered. Students will then see a tendency toward some answers chosen more frequently than others, as the results are combined with those of the other classes. This is a very dynamic and visible exercise in which students actually get to witness first-hand what the term *central tendency* means. It also provides a good segue to discuss sampling and blocking, validity, and reliability, the cornerstones to an accurate ratings system.

You probably have already taught the lesson on media filters, in which you discussed how television networks and stations make money. This will result in another discussion and lead-in to television **ratings**. You are now in a position to take your students to the media center or computer lab to find out how the ratings system works and what some of the problems are with it. For this activity, students are to follow the **Ratings and Rankings Web-Quest** found at the **Web-ASSISTant** Web site, which will take them through the Nielsen ratings system. Because the videos may not have been shown yet, students may be wondering how a sample can project what the population as a whole thinks or will do.

Objectives and Outcomes

At the end of these sessions, students should be able to

- describe the survey process in terms of sampling, validity, and reliability and how these affect outcomes;

- understand the various ways in which the interviewer has influence on the outcome of a survey;

- describe the greatest advantage and disadvantage of the Nielsen system; and

- describe how technology will effect a change in the way ratings will be surveyed in the future.

Mediated and Textual Support

A good format for the history survey can be found at the *Media History Project* at **www.mediahistory.umn.edu/index2.html.** The *Media History Project* provides a timeline of the history of communications all the way back to 40 B.C. It might be useful to choose a decade during the twentieth century to make sure that your students find interviewees who have an opinion on the issue at hand. Which decade you pick does not matter. The sample instructions in this session happen to choose the 1950s because it is far enough back so that the range of answers will vary widely. This is intentional. Students need to understand how results tend to scatter, the fewer results there are. However, they also tend to consolidate, as more answers from the other classes are included. This understanding is crucial to their understanding of the role statistics play in the ratings system. Sputnik always seems to be a good topic for the 1950s. You will have the most fun if the results are somewhat scattered but end up providing some type of trend.

A classroom presentation and discussion follow based on portions of the video *Against All Odds,* produced by CPB/Annenberg. The lesson on blocking and sampling (tape 13) presents an interesting example of how this statistical concept is used by a potato chip manufacturer to determine quality control. The reliability and validity lessons have short clips on how these are used in day-to-day survey situations. Then they present the session on survey bias. Information on how to obtain this video is found on the **Web-ASSISTant** Web site on the "Chapter Two" page.

The last portion of this lesson is another Web search. This time, students use the questions below to conduct a cyber scavenger hunt. In the process, they learn about some of the problems companies like AC Nielsen have in maintaining an accurate ratings base and what is being done now and planned for the future to correct these problems. This exercise introduces the basic concepts of how to determine ratings, how to maintain accuracy, and how to plan technologies. The **Web-ASSISTant** Web site provides links for students to find the answers.

Class discussions on ratings center around the elements of the current ratings system and perceptions of any pitfalls, as well as what might be done about them.

Once you convince students how the process works in theory, they are ready to validate the notion they already have: that it is not a perfect world, and there is the possibility of a breakdown.

Lesson Readiness

Start this session by posing the following two thoughts:

1. With all the varying opinions around, it is amazing that companies like AC Nielsen can actually determine a trend regarding shows people watch.

2. With all the people living in the United States, how can AC Nielsen gather the information needed to say that a million viewers are watching show "X" or do not like show "Y"? Do they actually survey one million people?

You should allow about 40 minutes for this part of the exercise. When the students finish, they should be able to carry on an intelligent conversation about the ratings system, what its problems are, and what appears to be on the horizon to fix them. The *Against All Odds* video should help students understand the theories behind how to make the numbers come out right.

Closure

Students will participate in class discussions based on their Web-Quest activities and be able to answer the review questions at the end of the sessions.

Lesson 2.4

Video: Blocking, Sampling, and Poll Taking

Pre-Lesson Activity

Timeline Survey

Student Instructions: Using the printout that has been provided in class, you are to take the timeline and ask, in an opinion poll, which event is the most significant of that decade, as it relates to progress in communications. You are to take an opinion poll by asking eight people what they consider the most significant event from the list provided that happened in the world of communications during the 1950s. You are to do this out of class and bring the results back for discussion. Mark each person's response on your handout with a simple check mark. You may wish to ask why each one was picked, in order to add to the classroom discussions.

Teacher's Note: The timeline comes from the *Media History Project* (www.mediahistory.umn.edu/index2.html), which provides an excellent timeline of communications events, 400 B.C. to date.

We are going to watch a portion of a video called *Against All Odds*. Although the main purpose or this video is teach statistics, the segments we are going to watch contain several interesting pieces of information about surveys and poll taking that are relevant to our session on ratings. The first clip deals with sampling and how this technique can improve or detract from the predicted results. Then we are going to look at an interesting segment on how to take polls and how the way they are conducted can influence results. You have already encountered some of these problems in the polls you have taken. After discussing this video, you are later going to find out more about the Nielsen ratings system and some of the problems it has getting accurate results. As you will find out in class, the Nielsen system is largely based on the same concepts that go into surveys and requires the same care and quality control.

When we are finished with all three of these sessions, you should have a good idea how important the ratings are to television and how imperfect the methods of getting these ratings are.

Three Important Concepts in Polls/Surveys

For the purposes of this session, you need to know what the following concepts are and how they affect the outcomes of surveys and polls. In the space provided, write down

1. a definition for each concept and one example,

2. an example of how results may be corrupted if incorrectly done, and

3. how each concept may be a positive influence if it is treated correctly.

Sample

Definition: **Selecting a portion of the population from which you are trying to draw poll.**
Negative Influence: **Hard to get a good random sample; can be manipulated/biased.**
Positive Influence: **Best way to be able to select a portion of the population and extrapolate results.**

Validity

Definition: **Asking the correct questions that pertain to the answers you are seeking.**
Negative Influence: **Results will be biased if asking wrong questions.**
Positive Influence: **If done correctly, can predict results of population.**

Reliability

Definition: **Asking the questions correctly to get results.**

Negative Influence: **Could be a valid question, but if you ask it incorrectly, results could still be biased.**

Positive Influence: **Valid, reliable questions asked of a random sample can predict results with very few people.**

Lesson 2.5

Lesson Planning Considerations

(**Approx. Time:** 25–35 minutes each)

Agenda

This lesson on deconstructing a commercial is what many believe media literacy to be about. Although it fits only the narrower definition of media literacy as discussed earlier, it does have a role in the curriculum. The problem is to take it out of context and make this aspect of media literacy the major part of the curriculum. This negative approach is often the only one followed because it is often the easiest to explain. Concerns about consumerism do appear to have merit. Recent polls have indicated that students between the ages of 14 and 25 have at their disposal between $85 and $100 per week. The importance of learning how to look at commercials and make rational buying decisions is increasing exponentially.

It will take a little while to get accustomed to using the New Mexico Media Literacy Project CD. In preparation for the class, you might want to use movie clips from the CD other than the specific ones that were selected for this lesson. The basis for selection was somewhat arbitrary but had to do with appropriateness and timeliness of material. Commercials tend to become dated quickly and some work better in different parts of the country. Therefore, each example should be reviewed before using it in class. The CD contains so many examples that picking a sample set for class should not be a problem. The problem is to pare them down to present during one or two 25–minute lessons. The specific set of commercials presented in this lesson have been selected only as models, and these choices are based on one person's opinion of their potential learning value. All the examples on the CD are valuable and come with discussion topics and thinking questions. Teachers may want to design their own set.

Objectives and Outcomes

After participating in this lesson, students will be able to

- identify attributes of persuasion;

- define and provide examples of connotation and denotation;

- list the effect of audience on word choice, format of verbal or written message, and method of persuasion;

- identify traditional arguments associated with persuasion;

- identify the different techniques and rhetorical structures advertisers use to persuade an audience; and

- compose a 15- or 30-second commercial that clearly demonstrates an understanding of selected methods and tools of persuasion.

Mediated and Textual Support

This class is based entirely on an interactive CD called *Understanding the Media,* (often referred to as New Mexico Media Literacy Project). The value of the New Mexico Media Literacy Project CD is that it outlines general and specific deconstructing tools and also provides class discussion topics with possible answers. Although there is a recommended sequence for using the New Mexico Media Literacy Project CD, no claim is being made that this is the only way to go through the CD. In fact, the program was designed specifically to provide the teacher with the most flexibility. Although some scenes are shown more than once, their effectiveness is not reduced by the fact that they were used in another context.

Using the CD provides a great deal of flexibility in how much detail to go into (and, therefore, how much time you wish to spend). This class is designed as a 50-minute session or as two 25-minute periods over two days.

The class on technology is optional, especially if you do not have access to editing software. It does make the point of how the changes we describe are actually carried out by producers of advertising.

The effectiveness of this session is extended through the use of some type of mediation, even if it isn't the lessons provided on the New Mexico Media Literacy Project CD. Several Internet sites provide interesting in-class activities and support for class discussions. The **Web-ASSISTant** Web site provides several links in the "Digging Deeper" section under "Chapter Two."

Lesson Readiness

Students love to watch commercials. This is a mediated session that includes watching commercials. Play a couple of commercials just before class begins; students will pay attention to them. By asking students how they accomplish their goals, you will orient them to the context in which the commercials are to be covered in class.

Closure

Students are to bring in examples of commercials as a follow-up activity. They are also asked to respond to written questions on quizzes.

Lesson 2.5A

Deconstructing Commercials

Terms

construct	**techniques**	**analyze the audience**
differing meanings	**techno effects**	**value messages**
pacing	**satire**	**emotional transfer**
deconstruct		

Lesson Notes

In this lesson we are looking at commercials in a way that perhaps you never have done before. We are going to analyze television commercials in two ways. First, we are going to look at how they are put together, what their objective is, and how this is accomplished. Second, we are going to relate the composition of the commercial using the tools we have already started to implement in the making of our own videos: the **use of color, lines, and mass** from our elements of design class; **the use of camera and post-production techniques** from our last session on manipulating moods; and **body language**, where it is appropriate.

The term **media literacy** has been defined in several ways. For the purpose of this class, we borrow from the one provided by Canadian Public Television:

> The media-literate person is one who has an informed and critical understanding of the **nature, techniques**, and the **impact** of the mass media. For children, the most pervasive medium is television. Media Literacy: Teaching about Television focuses on the tools they **need for television literacy**: **the ability to make rational judgments** about what they see on television. (Ontario Ministry of Education, 1995).

This definition will serve as the guideline we use to ensure that you have grasped the subject material. Through the identification of the **tools** you will need to deconstruct commercials, you will also be more able to make judicious determinations for yourself about how to react to them.

Remember, the first and foremost tool the designer of a commercial uses is to attempt to increase the probability that you, the viewer, will make an **emotional** decision, not an intellectual one. To fend this off, you need to be able to think with your head, not your heart.

First, we must define our main tool of self-defense. We often refer to the need to **deconstruct** a commercial. Deconstructing, for our purposes, refers to the process of breaking a commercial down into its basic component parts to analyze it. This term has been carefully chosen. A commercial does not happen by accident. In fact, *nothing* on television is the result of an accident; everything we see and hear is done for a specific reason or **objective**. As a matter of fact, the first thing we teach you about making a video project in this class is the need to **analyze the audience** and determine an **objective** for each scene or camera shot.

Deconstructing something means to parse something into its component parts to analyze it. This is similar to the notion we might have of a competitor trying to take our product apart to discover our secret ingredient or process.

To make this notion of deconstructing happen, we need to invent some tools. Rather than reinventing the wheel, we will use an interactive CD produced by the New Mexico Media Literacy Project. The CD (see Lesson 2.5B) identifies two types of tools, aptly named **General Methods** and **Specific Tools**.

Our **General Methods** are:

- The **construct:** how the commercials are put together.

- The **techniques** used: specific conceptual designs.

- **Value messages:** hidden meanings and interpretations.

- **Differing meanings:** things mean different things, based on the age of the viewer.

- **Emotional transfer:** to get the viewer to make emotional versus rational decisions.

- **Pacing:** frame speed influences emotional transfer.

- **Techno effects:** raising the emotional level has become much easier with increased technology.

We will now look at how each of these concepts works in a commercial environment.

Constructing Reality

Teacher's Note: The specific commercials picked out for this exercise are purely arbitrary. It was felt that they represent a good cross-section. However, the teacher may pick any he or she feels will get the point across.

#1: George Strait Beer Commercial

The first commercial is one in which George Strait is selling something. The method used is **satire** (making fun of a situation). Although there is nothing wrong with this form of humor, it is often not understood by youngsters, those who often watch the shows in which this commercial appears. Is George telling the truth? Does this commercial show that it is acceptable to lie? If so, about which subjects?

Teacher's Note: If you have covered the lessons in **Chapter 3** on the use of camera angles to define the relationships between individuals, you should be able to use discussions about *Citizen Kane* as a follow-up to these points.

#2: Diamonds Are Forever

Are diamonds forever? Are they unique? Remember, advertisers often turn the very weakness of their product into a selling point to dispel rumors about using child labor.

How does the use of a black-and-white image change or color our impression? What is the black-and-white imagery used for in this commercial? **Emphasis**.

#3: Child Labor

How does this image of who those experts are that are cutting your diamonds change your impression of their worth? (Show child labor.)

#4: Bottled Water

Does anyone miss the point of how advertisers have created the ability of bottled water producers to actually charge for something that is already available to all of us for free?

Specific Techniques

#1: Special K Commercial

Advertisers spend, on average, $**20–40** million per campaign on advertising campaigns. For this reason, understand that nothing happens by **accident**. In order for advertisers to get their money's worth, each scene is loaded with stimuli. Every scene has only one objective: to **emotionally stimulate you to purchase a product**.

Teacher's Note: The FTC calls this puffery and allows it under FTC regulations regarding what ads are allowed and not allowed to say. Because factual information opens the ads up to liability and FTC rules, regulation has the effect of pushing advertisers to resort to puffery.

#2: Scene from the Movie *Falling Down*

Which emotions does this trailer evoke? Look at the number of scene changes within this short trailer. Can you say why there are so many?

_____

_____

#3: RCA Commercial

What can you tell me about the use of colors and light? Who is the intended audience? How do you know this?

_____

_____

Value Messages

#1: HBO Movie Director

There are 47 scenes in this 30-second commercial (some using **cut-frame** technology). What is the central message? How do colors, lighting, and shadows evoke an emotion? How about the music?

_____

_____

#2: Differences Between Men and Women

What visuals can you see that might hint at sexual overtones?

_____

_____

Commercialism

#1: *Baywatch* Teaser

This has been rated as the number one television show in the world. What is the obvious central theme or hook? Did you know that the swimsuits were individually tailored for each star?

_____

_____

#2: The Speaker's Beer

What does this photo tell you about *Time Magazine's* possible political slant?

_____

_____

Differing Meanings

#1: Pizza Commercial

What does Jimmy Johnson tell you about lying? This is satire again. It may be okay, depending on when the commercial is run.

_____

_____

Emotional Transfer

#1: Little Debbie

What techniques or music does the advertiser use? Can you see the products in each scene? How about the use of cute, cuddly images to sell a product that is full of sugar and, essentially, bad for you, if eaten in excess?

_____

_____

Pacing

Pacing deals with memory function and emotional arousal. If you recall, in earlier discussions we learned that television, when it first appeared, ran at approximately 24 frames per second. Now most commercials run at about 30. The brain can intellectually absorb things at a rate of 8 frames per second.

Look at #1, the Coors Ad, #3, the violent interjection in the Olympics ad and #4, the laugh track in the football commercial. Play them at regular speed, and then slow each one down to show the interjections and unnoticed stimuli.

Techno Effects

The discussions about the use of this tool, in essence, enhance the discussions about pacing and rapid inputs of external stimuli. The use of computer graphics, camera angles, framing (close-ups), reaction shots, and quick cuts taken together can create quite an arousal.

Look at the *Dragon Heart* trailer at regular speed and then in slow motion.

Lesson 2.5B

Review

Terms

symbolism	stacking the deck	nostalgia/timing
hyperbole	testimonials	bribery
repetition	füherprinzip	nationalism
humor	name calling	group dynamics
the big lie	band wagon	
maybe		

Lesson Notes

In the last session, we concentrated on the general tools advertisers use in producing commercials. As we discussed, general tools are the building blocks on which the scheme for the commercial is erected. They are used in the planning and construction phases of development. Today, we are going to look at some of the more specific methods or formulae they use. These are, by nature, much more subtle and therefore much more insidious

General Methods

Let's begin with a review of the general tools from our last session. We said that there are several methods advertisers use to get the viewer in the mood to buy the product they are advertising. As a review, enter in the box the name of the method that is described with the example.

METHOD	DESCRIPTION	EXAMPLE
Emotional Transfer	is used to get the viewer to make emotional versus rational decisions. This is the most important hidden agenda behind all commercials. All other general tools are used to cause emotional transfer.	Little Debbie Foods
Constructing Reality	is how the commercials are put together.	G. Strait beer commercial
Techniques	are specific conceptual designs.	Special K, *Falling Down*, RCA commercials
Value Messages	are hidden meanings and interpretations.	HBO movie director commercial
Differing Meanings	means that something has a different meaning or connotation, based on the age of the viewer.	Jimmy Johnson pizza commercial
Pacing	is the frame speed that influences emotional transfer.	Little Debbie Ad, Coors Ad, Olympic Ad
Techno Effects	raises the emotional level by making it easier to affect the pacing.	*Dragon Heart* Trailer

Specific Tools

The specific advertising methods are easy to spot, once you become familiar with them. They are taught as a part of the curriculum of every advertising course. Understanding the specific tools is essential to your ability to decode advertising images and enable you to unravel their hidden meanings and subtleties.

There are dozens of specific tools used by advertisers. We are going to review many of them today and demonstrate some of them. Note that the word *emotion* comes into play again in many of these concepts. The following are intended to invoke powers of persuasion or propaganda-style messaging. When you look at these tools, try to identify the coloration, body language, or other psychological factor that helps to influence the mood.

TOOL	MEANING	EXAMPLE
Symbolism	These are the words, designs, places, music, and persuasive techniques to attach emotional content to something else.	Marlboro cigarettes satire
Hyperbole	hype or exaggeration, glittering generalities	Ford commercial
Humor	surprise (sometimes it works, sometimes it does not)	Monday Night Football —Andre Agassi
The big lie	There is no **evidence:** you need to pick words apart.	President Bush speech
Maybe	outrageous claims.. Maybe *you* could win too!	Lottery commercial
Repetition	This is a biggie. How many times have you seen a local car dealership commercial? It is better to purchase 100 15-second spots that 50 30-second ones.	Local car dealership commercials
Nostalgia/timing	the good old days	Relating the cell phone to the two-way radiophone from World War I
Bribery	value-added extras, coupons, and so forth.	Coupons
Nationalism	What do padlocks have to do with solving social problems? No one shoots a lock. What do master locks have to do with a woman alone in a parking garage?	Master Lock commercial
Group dynamics	building alliances. what are spin doctors? What body language techniques are being used?	President Clinton speech
Stacking the cards/deck	telling only part of the story	Crime statistics; political ads
Füherprinzip	body language, visual imagery. Which of the two has better karma?	*Time* magazine covers
Name calling	political dirty tricks	Political ads
Bandwagon	Everyone's doing it!	How many times have you used this one on your parents at home?
Testimonials	use famous people to gain sympathy	LaToya Jackson Psychic Hotline

Lesson 2.5C

Technology's Effect on the Media

Technology plays an extremely important role in helping advertisers obtain the results they seek. There have been significant advances in editing techniques, animations, and special effects. Today, we are going to review a couple of examples from the CD. Then, if there is time, you will look at a typical nonlinear editing system. It is not the intent to make you experts, only to show you how technology changes editing criteria and helps to speed up the framing process to heighten the emotions advertisements try to elicit.

Discussions on Use

> **Teacher's Note:** The following clips come from the New Mexico Media Literacy Project CD, under "Techno Effects."

We are going to watch two video clips. The first is a Pepsi ad featuring polar bears that ran during the 1999 Super Bowl. The second is a Dr Pepper Ad. We also have a newspaper article discussing violence in children's cartoons.

As always, you should keep in mind the following three primary axioms we discussed in earlier classes that guide all advertising campaigns:

- Advertising is not **reality**, but most people do not know this, especially younger audiences. Advertisers construct their own view of life and want you to buy into it

- Advertisers spend **$20–40 million** on each ad campaign. They want return for their money.

- Nothing on television happens by **accident** (that is the primary difference between television of the 1950s and today).

Now, go to the CD and click on **Technology** under the main menu. The discussion boxes will help the class activity. When you move forward using the right arrow button, you will come to some discussion boxes that have a sample. Click on the sample until you find the Pepsi and Dr. Pepper ads. If you go back using the **Return** button, you can follow along with the discussion boxes and use as many as you wish.

Nonlinear Editing

For this activity, Adobe Premier, Apple iMovie, or any other digital editing package may be used. The key points to bring out are that the whole notion of framing rates has changed. In our first few classes, we discussed the fact that television traditionally has used about **24–30** frames per second. As seen on the New Mexico Media Literacy Project CD, the human brain processes things in as few as **8** frames (i.e., one-third of a second). This technique is called "fast cutting."

The second major change is the concept of **cut frames**. With Adobe Premier, you can load on to the screen the sample (they use a trapeze sequence). With nonlinear editing, you can cut the frames as short as you like. You can stitch these cut frames together to make an entirely new sequence of shortened frames. When you play them on a screen, the movements appear so fast that your brain does not have time to let your consciousness know that you have seen them. This is very easily demonstrated on the editing software.

Questions

1. Under normal conditions, what is the number of frames the human mind can absorb and intellectually process? **8 frames or 1/3 second**

2. What is the framing rate for television? **30 fps**

3. How much do advertisers typically spend on ad campaigns? **$20–40 million**

4. In this lesson, we learned two important characteristics of television advertising:

    a) **Nothing** happens by accident.

    b) Advertisers attempt to create or construct their own sense of **reality**.

Follow-up Activity

Examples of Commercials

Activity Planning Considerations

In class show examples of some ads and video clips from the New Mexico Media Literacy Project CD. Ask the students to write down what tools and methods were used as the premise or hook. After the students review all the examples you give, go over them and discuss them. This activity can be done in class and should take about 10–15 minutes.

The New Mexico Media Literacy Project CD has a "Helpful Hints" section on the main menu. Under each heading, there are some good examples that have not been shown before, so you can use them in this activity. You may or may not wish to use this activity as a graded exercise.

Student Instructions: To be sure that you have understood these concepts, complete this out-of-class assignment. Bring in two magazine advertisements or video clip(s) of a television spot (or one of each). For each one, write down at least one general tool and one or two specific methods that were used as the main premise or hook for the ad. Be prepared to present your example to the class.

How You Will Be Evaluated

This is a point-gathering activity. No specific grade will be given, other than points being awarded for your bringing in two examples on time. Your presentations will earn you points for class participation.

Due: _____

Example/Clip #1: _____

General Tool Used: _____

_____

_____

_____

Specific Method: _____

_____

_____

_____

Example/Clip #2: _____

General Tool Used: _____

_____

_____

_____

Specific Method: _____

_____

_____

_____

Lesson 2.6

War of the Worlds

Lesson Planning Considerations

(**Approx. Time:** 45–50 minutes)

Agenda

Students have already heard of Orson Welles because of having seen *Citizen Kane*. The *War of the Worlds* radio performance actually preceded the movie by about three years, making Mr. Welles about 23 years old at that time! Welles was well-known in Hollywood and had a reputation when he produced *Citizen Kane*.

The main goal of this session is to show how Welles introduced a problem into our society. Because of the many hysterical reactions to broadcast, the industry has to provide warnings to an unwary public. Welles actually did issue a warning at the beginning of the broadcast, but it was not heard by anyone tuning in late. Remember that the country was in the throes of a depression and fears and anxieties were running high. Most of the broadcasting regulations we have in this country were adopted because of similar misunderstandings

The program provides considerable opportunities for class discussion on such topics as **mob psychology**, First Amendment rights and responsibilities, and whether a few overreactions require that the rest of society lose a little more of its freedom.

Objectives and Outcomes

At the end of this session, students will

• understand how the *War of the Worlds* broadcast actually caused some people to take their lives,

• form an opinion about whether this type of thing could ever happen again and what precautions the industry should put in place to safeguard against it, and

• learn that this has already been done in the Code of Ethics.

Mediated and Textual Support

The **Web-ASSISTant** Web site provides links to several sites that describe further background material to be used in conjunction with the playing of the *War of the Worlds* tape or disc.

Lesson Readiness

Many students have already heard of this event. Ask students if they have ever heard the expression *there's a sucker born every minute*, a statement attributed to P. T. Barnum but actually made by his competitor, banker David Hannum (Silverman, 1999). Ask them if they know what it means and if they can cite examples of this being true. Then ask if they believe that someone could ever put a hoax over on the American public through broadcasting a fake show about a space invasion.

Closure

Students will cite instances in which they have seen television, CD manufacturers, and motion picture studios warn viewers of potential hazards prior to the beginning of shows (including the new rating system).

Censorship Versus Free Speech Revisited

On the evening of **October 30, 1938, America went to war with Mars!**
Listeners turning on their radios that evening heard an announced program of dance music interrupted by a series of startling news bulletins. A scientist at a Chicago observatory had just seen "several

explosions occurring on the planet Mars." News bulletins followed that a "huge flaming object" had fallen to Earth on a farm in Grover's Hill, New Jersey. A militia was sent and horrified radio listeners heard it wiped out before their very ears by what appeared to be a visitor from another planet. More landings were reported in Buffalo, Chicago, and St Louis. An anxious radio audience came to the awful conclusion that the Earth was the target of a full-scale invasion by visitors from Mars!

Questions

After listening to this program, answer the following questions:

1. Who wrote and produced this show? What other artistic endeavor was this person involved with?
    Orson Welles; Citizen Kane

2. At what time of year did the broadcast air? Do you think this was deliberate?
    Right before Halloween; certainly

3. It was reported that people were so taken by the believability of the broadcast, some even jumped off bridges to their death. Why do you think so many people "fell" for it?
    Not enough warnings; anxieties due to Great Depression

4. Do you think this type of thing could happen ever again? Why or why not?
    P. T. Barnum was said to have said that there's a sucker born every minute; It could but less likely due to regulations.

5. What ramifications do you this broadcast had for its originator of this program? (How was he received by the public after this incident?) (Remember, he was the same person who later caused a furor with *Citizen Kane*. He was not that well-liked before the incident.)
    Developed a reputation as a rule breaker; may have caused him problems getting movie released

6. After this broadcast, the FCC initiated certain controls (warnings at beginning and at each commercial break) to help prevent people from falling for this type of gag again. Do you think these types of controls are necessary? Why or why not? What about free speech?
    Possible answer: Some feel that the government needs to step in when the industry cannot figure out how to control itself. With free speech comes responsibilities. If the public cannot manage responsibilities for themselves, the government needs to ensure the overriding rights of the public.

Portfolio Project #7
PSA or Commercial

Teacher's Note: Remember, this book is not sorted in the same order as the course schedule. This is because we skip around a lot to improve learning. The projects and lessons in this book are grouped by topic. Although the project listed here is the first one presented in the book, it is not the first one taught during the year. Please refer to the Teaching Chronology for more information regarding the sequencing of the classes and activities.

Project Planning Considerations

Agenda

Commercials are a great model for demonstrating video production techniques. Because marketing campaigns are so expensive, more time, money, and energy per second go into making a 15-second commercial than into any other type of production. Commercials are perfect representations of scriptwriting that supplements the video images, editing, special effects, and production planning. In short, making a commercial provides a great opportunity for students to show that they have learned the elements contained in just about all the lessons and earlier video activities found in this book. Yet the commercial is not the final project. The *Decades* project is not as sophisticated, but it is used for students to demonstrate their understanding of the role television plays in our daily lives. This is most effectively done after they have participated in just about all the history lessons. The Sweeps project is last because it involves a complete production schedule that includes the class in various roles. The commercial project has been inserted as close to the end of the course as feasible.

Mediated and Textual Support

How much additional technical support to provide for this project is a personal choice. Certainly commercials do not have to contain digitized special effects to be persuasive. However, if any software is available, it will not hurt to allow students to use it, unless the special effect becomes the main focus rather than finding other ways to develop a persuasive video. Sometimes allowing students to modify existing videos demonstrates their creative talents.

Student Instructions: Your team is to create a 15- or 30-second commercial or public service announcement (PSA). It does not have to contain any special effects, but it should show evidence that you understand the persuasion aspects that go into making commercials. Your title screen should clearly designate which of the general methods or specific tools you employed. Your product may be original, or you may make a new commercial for an existing product. You may employ a methodology or theme used by an existing commercial and apply it to your product. The commercial should be *exactly* 15 or 30 seconds long.

How You Will Be Evaluated

The project will be evaluated using the same scorecard used for the others, with the following modifications:

Criterion #1: Because making commercials is an exacting science, yours must be exactly 15 or 30 seconds. Points will be deducted for any projects that miss the mark by more than 5 seconds either way in consideration of the fact that this is your first timed project.

Criterion #2: The title page should designate the general method or specific tool employed vis-B-vis our class discussions.

RESOURCES

Columbia Journalism Review. 2004. cjr.org/tools/owners/index.asp (Accessed September 14, 2004).

Davis, M. 1997, February. Garage cinema and the future of media technology. *Communications of the ACM* 40 (2).

Desmond, R. 1997. Media literacy in the home: Acquisition vs. deficit models. In R. Kubey (Ed.), *Media literacy in the information age.* New Brunswick, NJ. Transaction Books, pp. 323–343.

Discovery Learning Channel. 1996. *The Cronkite report: Headlines and sound bites* [Video].

Federal Communications Commission. 1996, February 8. *The telecommunications act of 1996.* Available: www.fcc.gov/telecomm.html. (Accessed September 14, 2004).

Freed, K. *Deep media literacy: A proposal to produce understanding of interactive media.* Available: www.media-visions.com/ed-deepliteracy.html. (Accessed September 14, 2004).

Lang, P. J. (1995). The emotion probe: Studies of motivation and attention. *American Psychologist* 50 (5): 372–385.

McCannon, Bob. 1998, October. As quoted from New Mexico Media Literacy Project presentation at the Florida Association of Media in Education (FAME) Conference, Ft Lauderdale, FL.

National Communications Association. 1996, June. Media Literacy Workshop at an Aspen Institute Workshop. Available: www.natcom.org/instruction/K-12/K12stdspr. htm. (Accessed September 14, 2004).

Ontario Ministry of Education. 1989. *Media literacy guide: Intermediate and senior discussions.* Toronto: Ontario Ministry of Education.

Ontario Ministry of Education. 1995. *The common curriculum, Grades 1–9.* Government of Ontario Bookstore Publications, Toronto, Ontario, Canada.

Silverman, S. P. T. Barnum: How he changed the English language forever. *Useless information.* Available: home.nycap.rr.com/useless/barnum/index.html. (Accessed September 14, 2004).

Smith, F. L., J. W. Wright, and D. H. Ostroff. 1998. *Perspectives on radio and television.* (4th ed). Mahwah, NJ: Lawrence Erlbaum Associates.

Thorson, E., and M. Friestad. 1985. The effects of emotion on episodic memory for television commercials. In P. Cafferata and A. Tybout (Eds.), *Advances in consumer psychology.* (Lexington, MA: Lexington Press, pp. 131–136.

Thorson, E., and B. Reeves. 1985. Memory effects of over-time measures of viewer liking and activity during programs and commercials. In R.J. Lutz (Ed.), *Advances in consumer research*, vol. XII. New York: Association for Consumer Research.

Tyner, K. 1998. *Literacy in a digital world: Teaching and learning in the age of information.* Mahwah, NJ. Laurence Erlbaum Associates.

Whittaker, R. n.d. Television Production Cyber Course. Available: www.cybercollege.com. (Accessed September 14, 2004).

CHAPTER 3

Equipment Basics

INTRODUCTION AND LESSON GOALS

It would appear that learning the equipment might be the best place to start in a course about television. However, in the "Teaching Chronology," formal training on the equipment does not start until the second or third week. There are two schools of thought on the best way to get started. The traditional approach has been to require students to first master all the cognitive skills prior to allowing them to handle the equipment. Other educators feel there are many disadvantages to technique-led practices. (Kizlik, 1998). Regardless of the certain dangers in giving in to the temptation to simply begin, many educators also believe that students learn best from solving the problems they create (Shouten and Watling, 1997).

PROBLEM-BASED LEARNING

We compromise. Instruction begins with classes on minimal equipment functions, care, and handling procedures. Subsequently, we begin with a couple of short and carefully guided exercises and activities. This plan relieves some student anxiety. Younger students want to handle the equipment as soon as possible and become bored quickly if the projects are delayed too long. All the projects in this course are spaced and placed in the "Teaching Chronology" in a **building-block** fashion that progressively requires more knowledge and understanding as the projects are introduced. The first few projects center on framing and focus control and are not constrained by scripts. In the beginning, they require only minimal knowledge of storyboards and camera operation. Students need only know how to turn on a camera, use a few of the basic buttons, and read only a few indicators before they attempt to shoot footage.

This quick-start approach encourages students to solve problems. This method will results in situations such as over-exposed or out of focus footage. These problems create the need for students to learn how to make corrections to make their work come out better. The most common errors can then be made into test questions to help them internalize operational procedures on a cognitive level.

There is considerable research in learning theory that supports problem-based instruction. Driscoll made a case for the idea that "students learn most about a particular subject when they learn how to obtain knowledge for themselves" (1994, p. 22). This instructional methodology has merit, especially in hands-on instructional environments. Only after students see their own footage do they fully understand the need for proper lighting, framing and focus, or post-production editing. This problem-resolution approach works well because it presents students with a rationale and a frame of reference when the techniques are later introduced in class sessions.

GOALS OF EQUIPMENT TRAINING

Most of the class sessions entail direct instruction. Students follow along in their *Workbook* by filling in underlined spaces that have been strategically left blank. Retention of the information is encouraged through follow-up exercises, independent reading from the supplementary texts, and additional hands-on work. Experienced television teachers may note that the specific equipment operational information presented in this book is minimal. This recognizes that the procedural instruction content depends largely on the brand of equipment at each school. Reference is made throughout the lessons to consult other texts and online resources to obtain the specific details on operation of equipment. This book should be regarded simply as an organizational companion to these other references.

Thus, the instructional orientation of this book with regard to equipment training is to provide enough generalized content and technical orientation to teach students how video equipment can be used to accomplish the specific outcomes associated with the **acquisition model** for media literacy, as explained in **Chapter 2,** and **visual acuity,** as explained in **Chapter 4**. Developing a visual sense for, and a literacy of, the media is the most important outcome for this course. Instruction on the use of equipment is therefore aimed toward that end. *Visual literacy* and *media literacy* are similar in meaning but are approached differently. Visual literacy is developed through visual awareness, an understanding of how to use the equipment to create an environment, image, or thought. Media literacy is discovered through analysis and synthesis of the underlying thoughts or agendas that bombard viewers in a media-centric world. Students are taught how to use the camera and post-production equipment with an emphasis on showing them how to imbed a story visually and how to evoke an emotional tie with their viewers using a visual medium. In short, they are introduced to the tricks of the trade so that they may know how to deconstruct it for themselves.

Because equipment training occurs so early in the schedule, its goals are quite simple:

> • *Goal 1: to provide just enough knowledge of the equipment to get students started using it very early in the training cycle.*

The timing of this session ensures the safe and careful operation of the equipment and may precede any detailed lessons on how the various parts of the camera function. Students seem to learn better when they have some problem-solving basis for learning.

Choose a small problem for them to solve with the camera (like close-up still shots). Provide one that demonstrates how you would like theirs to look, and ask them to make theirs like the model. This gets them to turn the camera on and off, to learn how to focus, to zoom, and to use the still button. Knowing about the charge-coupled device (CCD), all the things found in a viewfinder, zoom ratios, and so forth is not critical for this session. Students are operating the camera within the first three or four days of the term.

- *Goal 2: to show students how to find the information they need, through the use of user manuals and other resources, to make them self-sufficient.*

This course requires a great deal of individualized and group instruction. Students who are working on their own must be able to work independently on their activities while you are helping another group. However, you will probably find, as a result of one of the activities associated with this lesson, that reading a manual is not as straightforward as it seems. As anyone who has struggled to put together a child's gym set by reading an instruction manual knows, it takes practice (and patience) to go through the books. At a minimum, you should go through the manuals once yourself and check off the things you want the students to find. The exercise at the end of this chapter will familiarize students with manuals.

Learning how to read instructions is a guiding principle of this course. The speed at which technology is changing the industry suggests an open-book approach to testing. Students work with readings, answer review questions, and demonstrate their competency in using the equipment. It is more important that your **lifelong learners** know how to obtain the information they need when they need it, especially if it changes from studio to studio and year to year. Besides, it has not been proven that memorizing all the names of inventors, technical jargon, and so forth associated with this course will help students become better employees, more creative artists, or more highly technical resources for future employers.

USING THIS BOOK IN CONJUNCTION WITH EQUIPMENT MANUALS

Possibly the best source for specific information on equipment operation is the user manuals published by the manufacturers. In additional to the manuals that come with the equipment, there are several online resources about most equipment brands. The **Web-ASSISTant** Web site provides links to several reference sites that contain cross-links to the equipment commonly found in schools today.

Teaching how to independently find information more quickly and efficiently might prove to be the most important lesson teachers involved with technical subjects can provide for students. To promote this concept of self-sufficiency, students are provided with a *Student Workbook* in which they can store information in an organized manner for later retrieval. One session on learning how to read user manuals and how to use the *Student Workbook* to take shorthand notes will do a lot to save students time, as they get going on their projects and come upon an operational procedure that they are not familiar with or have forgotten.

DIGGING DEEPER

Tom Schroeppel has privately published two excellent books on how to use video equipment to attain video production goals. *Video Goals: Getting Results with Pictures and Sound* introduces an approach to using video equipment to make consistently good video programs. The author's suggestions are intended to serve as a basis for developing a successful shooting methodology that is based on individual goals. *The Bare Bones Camera Course for Film and Video* explains, as simply as possible, how to shoot images on film or tape. Both cost around $10 and are goal-oriented in that they are aimed at demonstrating how to use video equipment to attain specific outcomes. Like this book, specific operational instructions for using a particular brand of equipment are left to the equipment manuals. Ordering information may be found in **Appendix J**.

The **Web-ASSISTant** Web site provides additional links to equipment manufacturers and several other resources for further information on equipment operation, fixing malfunctions, and so forth. There are also links to sites that provide supplementary information on some of the additional topics covered in this chapter. For information on digital and high definition television (HDTV), go to the **Web-ASSISTant** Web site. Because Internet links are subject to change, check the "Chapter Three" page on the **Web-ASSISTant** Web site for updates to see if this link is still active. Where possible, an alternative will be provided, should this link be removed in the future.

SEQUENCING THE LESSONS IN THIS CHAPTER

The lessons in this chapter were written in contextual sequence. That is to say, they have continuity with regards to subject matter and can be taught in the exact order they are presented. However, to take advantage of opportunity to reach the specific goals attempted by the course guide, it might be better to consider following the suggested sequence as outlined in the "Teaching Chronology" found in **Chapter 1**. As a minimum, it makes sense to at least consult with that prescribed format in order to make an informed decision.

Lesson 3.1

Lesson Planning Considerations

(**Approx. Time:** 20–25 minutes each)

Agenda

This lesson set is made up of two parts. Lesson 3.1A is a basic introduction to class rules for the operation and care of the equipment. It can be presented anytime during the first week of school. It provides an opportunity to review how to care for the equipment, how to set it up, and then how to use the camera to take good shots. Because the best learning experiences happen when students have to solve problems they have created for themselves, students start using the equipment right after the first session. Students get to shoot single shots of photographs.

Lesson 3.1B is delayed until after students have handled the equipment at least once. The content of this instruction assumes that students have reviewed basic terminology on their own prior to class. Students bring to class the review questions to study as the topics are covered. This set of instructions covers the equipment in a generic way in terms of general equipment care considerations.

Objectives and Outcomes

By the time students complete this lesson, they will be able to

* explain the care, storage, and use of video hardware and software;

* state **house rules** dealing with operating the equipment in a safe and clean manner;

* locate the instructions in the equipment product manuals to successfully determine how to solve selected operational problems without the help of their teacher;

* list the limitations of the viewfinder with regards to framing, lighting, and focusing pictures;

* demonstrate the steps necessary to set up, turn on, and operate a video camera; and

* demonstrate how to load, record, and play a videotape.

Mediated and Textual Support

Lesson 3.1A does not involve the use of any outside materials. Rather, it is an opportunity for students to handle the camera and for the teacher to set some general ground rules for its operation and to introduce the operators' manual(s).

For this portion of the course, there are printed resources. First is a textbook published by Libraries Unlimited: *Television Production: A Classroom Approach,* written by Keith Kyker and Christopher Curchy. (See **Appendix J** for information on how to obtain this text.) The text lessons are introduced as independent study sessions that are assigned to students, graded, and reviewed in summary in class.

The second source is *Videolab 2.1*, an interactive CAI course based on Herb Zettl's *Television Handbook* text and produced by Wadsworth Publishing. Although the depth that this CD goes into is a bit more than what is needed in a first-year course, it is an excellent resource. Only pertinent lessons are referenced in the "Teaching Chronology."

Lesson 3.1B is a good place to introduce Zettl's *Videolab* 2.1 CD because it provides the teacher with an opportunity to demonstrate how the f-stop and settings affect the inner workings of the camera to produce results. Many of the cameras in use by schools do not use f-stop or the zoom ring settings. However, they are important functions to learn because they show how the camera actually works. Much of the information is transferable to the functions of any quality camera and is therefore quite useful.

The last reference is an interactive, self-paced cyber course written by Ron Whittaker, Ph.D., which may be found at **www.cybercollege.com**. This course serves as background information for several of the sessions. It is primarily designed as a self-study course for college students, but much of the material is relevant and easy to understand, even at this level. Dr. Whittaker provides limited performance rights for teachers to download and print portions of his lessons, as long as proper reference is provided. Several drawings of various types of lenses may found under "TV Production Support: Lesson 12- Focal Length & F-stop Myths." He provides in-depth information on lenses in a module called "Lenses—The Focus of Creative Control." There is also a unit called "Video Cameras & Their Operation." Because Internet links are subject to change, check the **Web-ASSISTant** Web site ("Chapter Three" page) for updates to see if this link is still active. Where possible, an alternative will be provided, should this link be removed.

Those who have never seen fixed focal length lenses used on old television cameras might be tempted to take zooming for granted. Because a picture is worth a thousand words, the historic archive site maintained by Chuck Pharis (**www.pharis-video.com**) might prove invaluable. It contains several pictures of older cameras that show the old rotary lens panels on the front of the original studio cameras. Seeing these rotaries seems to help students understand what types of problems the zoom lens helped to solve. Again, because Internet links are subject to change, check the "Chapter Three" page on the **Web-ASSISTant** Web site for updates to see if this link is still active. Where possible, an alternative will be provided, should this link be removed.

Lesson 3.2 uses a video as its source. *Understanding Television*, produced by Discovery Learning Channel. It contains several excellent segments on the various video equipment components that are later reviewed in detail. See **Appendix J** to learn how to obtain this video.

Lesson Readiness

Students are already self-motivated to learn how to operate video equipment. They are particularly interested in seeing themselves and others on camera. However, they generally do not really know what they are looking at when they peer into the viewfinder. The opportunity to focus their attention on framing, zooming, lighting, and focusing comes after they have had to deal with correcting problems they encounter in Project 1. Therefore, the need to ready students is diminished. They do need to become oriented toward proper handling of the equipment. Quite often their own work best prepares students to recognize the need for proper procedures. By allowing them to make a short video that will most likely be full of framing, lighting, and focus mistakes will be the best preparation for future procedural sessions. Lesson 3.1A, therefore, actually acts as the orientation for the real procedural sessions.

The lessons in the Kyker-Curchy textbook (see listing under "Mediated and Textual Support") are assigned to prepare students for the materials covered in Lesson 3.2. The discussion questions that precede this lesson ask students orienting questions. They introduce the need for learning how to adjust focus and light settings, then lead the discussions into the visual literacy issues that will follow in a few weeks.

Closure

By the time students have completed Lesson 3.1, they will have participated in four distinct opportunities to learn about television equipment. First, they will have read the text lesson and answered the review questions. Next, they will have participated in class discussions. They will have watched a video, and, finally, they will have answered the review questions that follow the Kyker-Curchy text. In addition, they will have had the opportunity to handle the equipment and will have begun to work on Project #1. These problem-based activities provide plenty of closure opportunities.

Lesson 3.1A

Basic Care of Equipment

Lesson Notes

Before we begin, there are a few procedural issues we need to discuss. They all involve the basic care and safety of the equipment. When handling a camera, you should:

- *Avoid touching the lens or viewfinder.* As the glass gets oily, it is extremely difficult to keep clean.

- *Be careful where you put the camera down.* Be sure that when you set the camera down, you place it in the middle of a table, or someplace where, if it gets knocked over, it will not fall down.

- *Handle the equipment only when necessary.* You are not to handle the equipment unless it is for training or a shoot.

- *Replace the lens cover* and remove tapes and batteries when finished. At the end of class, you are to put the camera back into its case securely.

- When possible, *use the tripod or sticks.* Unless you are shooting field footage, you need to take every advantage to get the best still shots. This will also help minimize the chance of breaking the equipment.

Teacher's Note: At this point you might go over circled cross-reference numbers from the manuals and point out basic operational procedures for the specific brand of camera you are using. Students may be grouped in teams of two to three if there is not enough equipment to go around. Have them take turns doing basic operations like zooming in and out, changing from picture to picture, and playing back the video in the viewfinder.

Cover such activities as how to put the camera on and off the tripod. Experience has shown that often *set up* and *take down* procedures never get covered and consequently cause considerable difficulty. They should be taught early. Another procedure frequently forgotten is the proper care and cleaning of the equipment. Particular attention should be taken with the lens. It is easily scratched and tends to collect fingerprints. In the viewfinder discussions that follow, students will learn that the viewfinder does not always tell the truth. A dirty viewfinder will distort an image, producing a false image. A dirty lens may not show up until the video is played back on a monitor.

Lesson 3.1B

Basic Video Concepts

Pre-Class Activity

Student Instructions: In preparation for this lesson, turn to the appropriate lesson in *Television Production: A Classroom Approach.* Answer the review questions.

Teacher's Note: You may wish to review the questions in detail at the beginning of this session. An alternative approach is to collect the review questions and grade them as an activity to gain closure.

Pre-Class Discussion

Student Instructions: This session discusses how we adjust focus and light in the camera. Besides correcting problems, your understanding of these processes will actually help you add to your visual abilities.

Teacher's Note: The purpose of asking the following questions is to get students to begin thinking about the shots they take and how to affect a mood or point of view strictly through a visual image. Most students have a good idea of how and when one might want to use dark images to express anger, fear, and so forth. They just never have tied it into a viewfinder before. The answers to the questions will vary. Students need to understand very early that their work does not have to fit a *norm*, as long as there is good reason.

Answer the following two questions in the space provided:

Do you think there might be an occasion in shooting footage when you would actually want to have shots that are too dark or too bright?

_____

_____.

Do you think there might be an occasion in shooting footage when you would actually want to have shots that are out of focus?

_____

_____.

Terms

white balance	lens vs. f-stop	fixed-length lens
variable-length lens	macro lens	zoom lens
charge-coupled device	calibrating	wide-angle lens

Introduction

This course emphasizes the proper use of the camera. When discussing the camera, we are concentrating on just three aspects:

- light settings

- focus

- framing

Although these might seem to be simple concepts, understanding how to use them for your advantage will make you a better videographer.

What the Viewfinder Does

If you learn one thing, it is that a **viewfinder may not always tell the truth**. This is quickly changing as technology gets better in the consumer environment. You may also find that your home-based cameras might actually do a better job than the cameras at school. Simply put, the viewfinder lies. Actually, this may be a lie itself. What I am referring to is the fact that there are many things about the image you find in the viewfinder that require that you look at your shoot on a television monitor to be sure you have good video. This is because many viewfinders

- distort the image because its aspect ratio (width and height) may not be correct,

- produce a distorted or black-and-white image,

- may be out of focus—often the viewfinder has its own settings, and

- may not show proper framing.

The newer home cameras use a monitor-like viewfinder now. But the professional cameras invest more in the technology of producing images than they do in viewfinders. For a purist, the latter adds unnecessarily to the cost of the equipment (they like to make their own light settings with a meter, for example). The main reason for a viewfinder is to show the **relative** position of your subject. *Relative* is a key word here. Again, until you see the image on a monitor, you are only approximating. Although this is not always true, it can account for variances in quality of equipment.

On many cameras, the viewfinder shows many other things. The equipment manual lists all of them. Among the things found in a viewfinder are

- humidity levels,

- amount of tape left,

- battery levels,

- brightness,

- whether zooming is being used, and

- whether the tape is being recorded.

Teacher's Note: Go over other specific instructions for your brand of camera at this time. It is not important to make the students memorize a long list, however. This does vary by manufacturer. A good rule of thumb is to categorize the types of things that a viewfinder can show. Most students get the point quickly, note the major items, and learn where to find the information in the manual. This is a good question to use in an open-book format because it requires the students to look up the information that is found on the numbered reference list (something most younger students do not understand).

Lens Versus F-stop

The relationship between the lens and the f-stop is quite simple. A lens focuses and the f-stop adjusts for lighting conditions. A picture may be out of focus but not blanched, and vice versa.

The f-stop really measures the **Closure** not the **aperture.** The opening has its own designation called an *aperture*. By making the **Closure** larger, the aperture gets smaller, thereby allowing less light in. Pictures are made darker by enlarging the f-stop.

Fixed-Length Versus Variable-Length (Zoom) Lens

There are two kinds of lenses: **fixed-**length and **variable-**length, better known as a **zoom** lens. A fixed lens does not allow you to change the location of the subject to keep it in focus. The lens ratio determines which lens you use.

Teacher's Note: Some students have difficulty with the concept of ratios. Therefore, the idea of a 10:1 or a 25:1 ratio makes little sense to them.

The "1" represents the subject standing at a normal (optimal) distance from the front of the camera (two to three feet, or one meter). Therefore, a subject that is 10 to 30 feet away can be brought in to look as though it is in normal range (two to three feet) with a 10:1 zoom. A subject that is up to 75 feet away can be brought in to normal range with a 25:1 zoom, and so forth.

Maintaining Focus While Zooming

You may encounter problems keeping your lens in focus while zooming. There is a trick to it. The best way to maintain focus is to zoom all the way in to the closest setting and bring the image into focus. Thus, when you zoom in and out, the camera will maintain its focus as you have set it.

Types of Lenses

There are two kinds of specialty fixed-length lenses that you need to know about:

The **macro lens** is a specialty lens used for subjects that need to be viewed at a range closer than the normal one to three feet (like inside a microscope).

A **wide angle lens** is a specialty lens used for wide peripheral vision (like the one used in a peephole in a door. This distorts (flattens) the picture in the middle to gather a wider shot (an example of this is the scene in the movie *Cable Guy* in which Jim Carrey's face is distorted as the camera peeps through the peephole).

> ***Teacher's Note:*** You may wish to show an example of this from the movie or other source. It is quite difficult to show using a still picture.

The CCD

The CCD, or **charge-coupled device**, is a chip inside the camera that converts light energy into electrical energy. It replaced the picture tube in older cameras. The CCD is what makes modern cameras lightweight and inexpensive.

Calibrating and Balancing

Another more generic term you need to understand is **calibrating**, synchronizing, or **balancing** equipment. You will come across this term in reference to audio (zero balancing or phasing) as well as in video (white balancing, color bars).

White balancing is a method to allow those cameras with this feature to automatically adjust for light conditions. A simple procedure is to place a white piece of paper in front of the camera at the "1" position and push the white balance button. The camera will self-adjust to the light automatically after about 3–10 seconds. Although the light may not be totally correct (depending on the lighting system you have), it will be the best your camera has to offer at that point. If you adjust the light, the camera will tend to self-adjust better if it has been white-balanced at least once during the shoot.

Questions

Student Instructions: Answer the following questions in your own words.

1. What does the following statement mean? *A viewfinder may not always tell the truth.* **There are certain distortions, it may not be in color, or the framing might not be correct.**

2. Name four things a viewfinder shows. **<u>Depends on the brand</u>**

3. Lens versus f-stop. The f-stop really measures the **<u> closure </u>** not the **<u>aperture.</u>**

4. Fixed-length versus variable-length (zoom) lenses. In a 10:1 zoom ,what does the "1" stand for? **<u> 2-3 feet (1 meter) </u>.**

5. How do you maintain focus while zooming? **<u>Zoom all the way in. Focus the camera. It will maintain at this point.</u>**

6. Two types of lenses:

    a) What is the macro lens used for? **<u>Extreme close-ups (e.g., in microscopes)</u>**

    b) What happens to the image in a wide-angle lens when it gets too close? **<u>It gets flattened and distorted.</u>**

7. CCD. What did this replace in the older cameras? **<u>Picture tube.</u>**

8. Synchronizing and balancing equipment:

    a) What does the term *synchronize* mean? **<u>To calibrate all parts so they operate in unison</u>**

    b) What does the term *white balancing* mean? **<u>A method to allow cameras with this feature to automatically adjust for light conditions.</u>**

<u>Lesson 3.2</u>

Lesson Planning Considerations

(**Approx. time 3.2A**: 30–40 minutes; **Approx. time 3.2B**: 20–25 minutes)

<u>Agenda</u>

To ensure that students attain the desired outcomes for this lesson, they need to develop an understanding of the differences and similarities between the terms *videography* and *television production*. In context, *television production* refers to the process of putting on a studio-based televised show. It includes pre-planning (storyboards, scriptwriting, and studio set-up), on-air techniques and etiquette, post-production (editing and audio dubbing), and post-show critique (the most often overlooked aspect of putting on a show). Many of these tasks and concepts are borrowed, with permission, from others' work. Often, because we are in a hurry to get a show on, we forget to show the students the value of imagery, proper use of framing, white space, and so forth. These techniques of videography form a proper foundation to, and support the concepts of, visual literacy. If students begin to understand how to manipulate the visual image to get their point across, they will also become more discerning about what the media industry is doing to them as they watch television at home.

There are actually two parts to this story: how television works and how the videotaping process works. What is described in the following session might become outdated in the near future. Everyday uses of digital television and DVD are just around the corner and will be discussed in further detail later in this chapter. Students can benefit a lot from gaining an understanding of video theory. For the purposes of a foundations course, the digitizing of the images and sounds is simply a different method of delivery. Although this may be a gross oversimplification, the basic tenets remain. In addition, it may be quite a while before all schools become fully digitized. Significant space is dedicated on the **Web-ASSISTant** Web site to the digital environment.

Objectives and Outcomes

At the end of this lesson, students will be able to

- describe how the formats for television, motion pictures, and computers vary due to their intended purpose;

- relate the need for and problems with converting television signals into digital format;

- describe flicker rates and how they affect visualization of moving images;

- describe how a picture is translated from light into electrical energy, the role of the vacuum tube, and CCD chip;

- describe the concept of RGB chroma and how blue screening works; and

- describe how videotape recorders record videotapes.

Mediated and Textual Support

The basis to this lesson is a video produced by the Discovery Learning Channel, *Understanding Television,* which outlines the major points regarding how television works. It is a good video that can be played during the first week of school. Many references to it are made throughout the following lesson scripts. To add reinforcement during your sessions, you may wish to play back certain sections individually as a visual aid. Check **Appendix J** to learn how to obtain this video.

This video is appropriate for showing very early in the course schedule. For some, it might be easier to show just before working on this lesson. Because the early part of the school year involves many interruptions, with students making schedule changes and so forth, the video is a good activity to introduce the technical concepts in an entertaining way. The video comes with suggested stimulation questions and review activities in which students use their recall powers to go over this information in earnest.

Lesson Readiness

The video becomes a more effective orientation tool when it is played twice. It is also better received by the students when it is played in separate installments. The tape is organized into two sessions, separated by an intermission. The lesson has been broken down into two sessions that closely follow the tape format. Part Two of the tape also includes discussions about additional aspects of television that are not covered in the lessons (specifically, more in-depth coverage of satellite transmissions and digital television). Depending on the background of your students, you may wish to include these in your viewing or shorten them by playing only small portions.

To begin Lesson 3.2A, play Part One of the tape in its entirety. Later, you can show the tape in short clips as demonstrations during the class discussions. Students are then afforded the opportunity to go over the materials at least three additional times.

Closure

Students will view clips from *Understanding Television* as a review, so they will see the concepts twice. They will read the Kyker-Curchy text and answer the review questions, as well as answer the review questions at the end of this lesson, which will be graded. According to the "Teaching Chronology," students should complete Quiz 3.

Lesson 3.2A

How Television Works

Terms

definition of television	gausing	frame rate for movies
color bars	electromagnets	frame rate for television without sound
aspect ratio	RGB Chroma	frame rate for television with sound
scanning	dots	microwave-based frequencies
rasters	frequency	definition of movies
radio waves	phosphorous coating	high definition television (HDTV)
resolution		

What Is Television?

Television may be defined **as a process of transmitting images through a signal from one place to another**. No matter how you transmit that signal, the system must convert images to electronic signals and back again. This process is the heart of television. While they both appear to be identical in outputs, television and motion pictures (movies) are quite different in how they gather and project images.

How Motion Pictures Work

Motion pictures (movies) may be defined as **the process of projecting moving images on to a wall or screen.** Motion pictures and television are both based on the principles of **persistence of vision** and the **phi phenomenon**. Both refer to a psychological concept in which the mind sees a sequence of still images in a steady motion, at the point in which they are displayed rapidly enough (in this case 15–16 frames per second). In other words, while there is an illusion of motion, the actual output of both is not really a moving image but rather a series of frames (pictures) that are presented in sequential fashion. We will demonstrate a rudimentary version of this concept in our *Stop Action* project (number 2). After much experimentation, early developers found that a rate of approximately **16 frames** per second would provide the needed illusion. In our later discussions regarding nonlinear editing, and its ramifications for deconstructing subliminal and subconscious commercial messages, we will discover what happens when that rate is increased and the frames themselves are shortened. When sound was introduced to the early motion pictures, the rate per second (frame rate) was increased to about **24** fps. The international film community, largely due to the leadership of Hollywood, was successful in maintaining the 24 frame per second rate over time.

How Television Differs from Motion Pictures

Television, on the other hand, went down a different path. Rather than following a single international standard, each country had its own interests in television and was led by its own visionary who took credit for inventing (developing) it. The United States, Japan, Germany, and the United Kingdom, for example, each produced its own father of television who established a personal broadcast standard. Although this helped speed up the invention and development process, in the end it resulted in the lack of any single broadcast standard.

As a result, frame rates in television range from **25 to 30** per second. In the United States and a few other countries like Japan, the National Television Standards Committee (NTSC) developed a standard in 1947 for television to reproduce pictures (frames) at a rate of approximately 30 per second (the actual rate is 29.97). That is why a television produced for use in the United Kingdom will not work in the United States and vice versa. The frame rates in Europe evolved to a different standard. They are referred to as PAL and SECAM. Japan generally follows the NTSC standards because their largest customers are found in the United States.

The difference in **frame rates** between television and motion pictures is just one of the reasons a motion picture has to be converted before it can be played on television. It also accounts for some of the loss in quality. A motion picture camera records its images in a very similar fashion to a **roll of still photos**: Pictures are in their completed form (and at a rate of 24 per second).

Television works differently. The frames are not complete when they are captured and displayed. Rather, the picture frame is composed of thousands of dots that are **displayed (scanned) horizontally** from left to right and top to bottom. The television camera records in this sequence, and your television tube displays the picture in the same manner. In short, the pictures displayed on television are actually scanned in a dual interleaved process, first the odd lines, then the evens. The interleaves are called *fields,* and together they make up a *frame.*

The scanning process is not exactly horizontal, but more diagonal. This diagonal interleaving process was designed to overcome the "flicker" (also called the blanking interval) that resulted from the short time interval that it took the scan to go from the bottom of the frame to the top. To result in a correct 30-second scan, the framing rate had to be doubled. A frame, then, is displayed only after the television system has done its work by covering the viewing area at a rate of 60 times per second. Television works simply because the scanning beam eliminates the flicker faster than the human eye can see, thus making image appear uninterrupted. They produce a nonflickering display that handles movement.

What the Picture Tube Does

How the picture tube actually displays the image is also quite fascinating. A projected (scanned) beam is made up of electrons that produce light when they strike the **phosphorous** coating on the inside of the glass inside the tube. Electrons respond to a magnetic charge. **Electromagnets** are used to control the aim of the beam in a very precise manner. Because this whole process is magnetized, it is possible to damage your television set or at least get a distorted image by placing it too close to a magnetic field, such as those created by large hi-fi speakers. This process is technically called **gausing**. Older television sets had a degausing button on the back to demagnetize this distortion. Newer televisions have a built-in degausing process that resets itself each time the set is turned off and back on again.

Television picture tube images are really made up of **dots**. A scanning beam sweeps across them and makes the lines light up. In a television built for use in the United States there are about 280 dots across one line. There are also 525 lines stacked up. This entire 280 X 525 field is also referred to as a **raster.**

Simple multiplication of the dots per line times the number of lines should tell you how many dots each single image (frame) of a television picture has:

525 lines x 280 dots = 147,000 dots per frame

This bit of information might be seem trivial, but its importance will become obvious when we discuss the differences between analog television video and computer video later in this lesson. The 525 x 280 ratio is **roughly 4 by 3** and is more commonly referred to that way. Screen size is referred to as the **aspect ratio** and makes up the viewing standard for television. Every television set in America, whether it is a 17-inch or a 36-inch screen, maintains this same ratio of lines and dots per line. Movies, on the other hand, operate with many different aspect ratios.

What Is RGB Chroma?

Instead of one scanning beam and one color of phosphorous, color television features three scanning beams activating three basic colors of a prism that can be separated out: **red, green, and blue** (RGB) Chroma. We will go into more detail on this process later in this chapter when we discuss the blue screen process used most commonly by television stations during their weather reports. It is important to note that these three colors of light, when mixed together, create a white beam.

Technically, there are also differences between how a color image and how a black-and-white image are projected. For color images there must be a signal for each of the primary colors used. Because the NTSC wanted ordinary black-and-white televisions to be able to receive the color signals and vice versa, they made a decision to adjust the modulation and the frame rate to 29.97 fps. What were once 60 fields became 59.94 fields alternating back and forth.

Although this may seem trivial, there is some significance here, which will come out in a little more detail when we discuss videotapes and lighting and framing requirements. There are also differences in how we shoot in black and white versus color. We will bring this out in **Chapter 5**, when we provide details on the significance of the use of light and shadow in *Citizen Kane,* a movie that was purposely shot in black and white.

The Role of Color Bars

Teacher's Note: Do not take it for granted that your students know what you are talking about. It might be good to show a set of color bars in class.

Color bars are the basic calibration and reference signal used in color television since the National Television Standards Committee (NTSC) developed the technology that we all now watch daily. Color bars can be used to check transmission paths, signal phase, and recording/playback quality, and to monitor alignment. Without specialized equipment, they permit adjustment of color intensity, tint, and black level (brightness and contrast) on a monitor. Color bars are a great tool for setting up shop quickly. Once you learn what color bars look like, you can eyeball it. With a couple of additional checks, you can really make your setup fairly precise. Generally, if you have access to a color bar, it is a good idea to use one to set up your system, and it should be checked often. Many studios begin each day with a synchronization procedure to ensure the quality of their broadcasts.

Teacher's Note: A complete tutorial on colors, color bars, and eye physics, complete with graphs and picture illustrations, may be viewed at the ntsc.org Web site: **www.ntsc-tv.com/ntsc-index-05.htm.**

How a Television Camera Works

Most parts of a television camera work very similarly to a movie camera; however, because it needs to scan a picture, a television camera requires different technology. Early cameras were quite large (and very expensive) because the imaging device was more like a picture tube found inside a television set (only working in reverse). The tubes had a special layer that was sensitive to light, and as this layer was scanned by an electron beam, the image that was focused on the tube was converted to an electronic voltage that corresponded to the brightness of the image. These tubes were expensive, hot, and heavy, and had a short life span, making them impractical for consumer use. Several years ago, when the computer chip came along, television developers came up with an idea to combine light sensitivity onto a chip receptor called a **CCD** (charge-coupled device). This breakthrough not only allowed cameras to become less expensive but also contributed to cameras becoming quite small and manageable.

The color television camera begins the process of creating a picture on your television screen in the same way: It focuses images on television pickup devices, which convert light energy into electrical energy. But a color television camera has three pickup devices, one for each of the primary colors: red, green, and blue (RGB Chroma).

How a Television Picture Gets to You (Transmission)

In land-based transmission methods, **radio waves** make it possible to get the signal from the studio to your home. These are the same radio waves that carry the news to you on your radio at home or in your car. The only difference is the type of information they are carrying. In conventional broadcast radio, the radio waves carry a sound, or audio, signal, while in television they also carry the video signal.

That is why our history lessons on television begin with Guglielmo Marconi. His discovery of these radio waves became the foundation of the broadcasting industry as we know it today.

Regular television stations use a form of amplified modulation (AM) radio waves to send the video. Since television signals typically take up to 1,000 the spectrum space of audio signals, it is important that channel space be conserved. The rise in the number of local interest television stations, cell phones, and pagers all competing for radio bandwidth explains, in part, the FCC's ruling requiring all television stations and networks to convert to digital signals by the year 2006. This will be discussed in **Chapter 7**.

There are two major types of satellite television systems today. Traditional satellite television uses lower **microwave-based** frequencies. These have been available to consumers since the 1970s and are the systems that require those large ugly dishes. They use frequency modulation (FM) for transmission, the same type and frequency of wave that brings you music on your stereo system at home or in your car.

The new direct satellite systems (DSS) operate at a higher **frequency**, which allows the dishes to be smaller. In addition, the video signals are converted to digital data, which are sent over the satellite link. At the receiver the digital signals are converted back to video (analog) for your television set. DSS signals are generally of higher quality than conventional satellite television.

High definition television (HDTV) is not the same thing as digital television. By the strict definition, high definition television is standard analog television with more **resolution** (that is, lines or "dots" per frame), allowing pictures to be sent with more detail. HDTV may be transmitted using analog or digital signals. In fact, the Japanese have been doing this for over 25 years.

Teacher's Note: For more information on Japan's efforts with HDTV, look up the "MUSE Project" Web site. Or look up the Advanced Television Systems Committee (ATSC) Web site, which has a brief history and timeline of the development of HDTV in the United States.

Based on agreements reached in the Telecommunications Act of 1996 and subsequent annual reports, digital systems will also be high definition when they become generally available. Over-the-air broadcasters will be allocated two transmission paths (one analog and one digital) until at least 85 percent of the local population is able to receive the digital signals. There are more lines in HDTV (either 1080I or 720P, depending on the standard selected by the broadcaster) than in regular television, and the standards for the picture will require it to be wider, making viewing more like going to the movies. The number of lines on programs transmitted in HD format will not fit into the standard 525 x 280 set. Most HDTVs work on a 16:9 ratio.

If you notice the little message on your television just prior to viewing a video you have rented from your video store, the movie has been converted to video for viewing on your television. This message actually refers to screen size. You have also probably noticed some movie trailers that have not been converted yet; with the black lines running along the top and bottom of the screen. When HDTV comes into play, all images will appear like those trailers. Fortunately, the new proposed standards for HDTV in the United States will include digital transmission, which should improve the overall quality of the picture as well as eliminating the need to convert the images (as long as you own a digital television receiver as well).

Computer Video Versus Television Video

Computer screens can have many times more dots on their display screens than do television displays. It is actually a misnomer to call a computer display a video. The computer screen can show a much clearer and sharper image (television has been compared to looking at something through a screen door: it is fuzzy, blocky, and the edges are all funny). We refer to this difference in number of dots as **resolution**.

Computer displays do not interlace two fields because they have not needed to deal with flicker and image movement. Computer screens have a frame rate that varies from **60 fps to 120 fps** depending on the machinery and the software in use. The density of the dots on a computer screen is much higher than a standard television display. That is why a one-to-one alignment of a dot-to-dot playback makes the computer playback less than full-screen.

In short, there are technical compatibility issues between number of display dots and screen rates that cause a conversion to be necessary when you want to display a computer image on your standard television set in your home (or classroom).

The aspect ratio for computers is the same as for television (4:3). This explains the **scanning** that is referred to when one discusses the need for a scan converter to display a computer image (which is digital) on the television screen in your classroom. In short, a digitized picture combines the interleaving process into one step. The screen flicker rate and number of dots per area on the screen are the main physical differences.

Review Activity

Student Instructions: As a result of completing the following chart, you will have a short summary of the differences among television, the movies, and computers. You will also understand why images, within the guidelines of the current state of the art in consumer electronics, have to be converted before they can be shared.

	Television	Motion Pictures	Computers
Purpose (original)	transmit moving images electronically	project images on to a wall or screen	non-moving images
# Frames	25–30	16–24	60–120
Composition	dots/rasters	full frames	dots/rasters
Aspect Ratio	525 x 280 (4 x 3); 16 by 9 for HDTV	various, especially wide-screen.	generally, 4 x 3

Lesson 3.2B

How Videorecording Works

Terms

magnetic tape	VHS	camcorder	CDR-W
tape head	tape generations	footage	CD-ROM
DVD	Pit	land	

Lesson Notes

How Videotape Works

Videotape is a plastic-covered **magnetic tape** that is coated with a layer of microscopic metal particles. These particles are capable of holding a magnetic charge. That charge emanates from the tape head of a videotape recorder. In 1956, two-inch-wide tape was the first broadcast standard. It took four passes to scan a picture. American companies like Ampex ruled the roost for several years. These standards have changed over the years, with several companies vying for their format to become standard. Standards for home use did not come about that easily. The key to being able to make smaller tapes was discovering the idea of making the tape heads inside the VCR rotate so that the images could be captured diagonally, making it possible to record on narrower and shorter tapes.

Sony introduced a beta format in the 1970s, but that gave way to the ¾-inch cassette format championed by JVC. Eventually, the ½-inch **VHS** format came into prominence. These are the tapes that you typically rent from your local video store. All VCRs use video heads that travel across the surface of the tape and leave magnetic traces in the tape's coating corresponding to the video signal. Video players are simply that; they can play back a tape but not record. A VCR (video cassette recorder) both records a tape and plays it back. Originally, broadcasters (and consumers) had to deal with two pieces of equipment: a VCR and a camera.

Teacher's Note: Amazingly enough, students have trouble understanding the term *camcorder.* It takes some beginning students quite a long time to understand the differences between a camera, a VCR, and a camcorder (to be able to compare and contrast them).

In the early 1990s a **camcorder** was invented that combined the aspects and features of a VCR and a camera. The invention of the camcorder made the lives of the ENG team much easier. Today, one will find several television studios utilizing sophisticated camcorders, many of which have all the bells and whistles found on larger equipment .

The recording surface of a VCR is called a **head**. Typically, a VCR will have anywhere between two and six heads. Obviously, the more heads, the better the recording quality. To be able to record, both the tape and the heads are moving. The heads spin at a high rate of speed over the surface of the tape.

During playback, this whole scanning process is reversed. The magnetic traces left on the surface of the tape create magnetic changes in the heads, which are then converted and amplified into voltage, which is routed to the video equipment.

There are two types of recording processes: **composite** and **component**. Composite videotape handles all the signal information as one big wavelength. Component recordings are videotapes that can handle the signal information as separated values involving the luminance (or essential picture brightness and edges) and color values These are technically known as the Y and the C: Y for luminance, C for chroma. The separate components for Y and C make it possible to preserve the quality of the signal as it is recorded and played back. Commercially, the Y/C component recording is referred to as S-video. Computer displays cannot handle component or composite video signals.

In short, it all boils down to a thing called bandwidth, which refers to the megahertz (MHz) ratings. The higher the bandwidth the better the playback quality. The industry standard for naming this bandwidth is commonly called lines of resolution for the horizontal scanning lines (remember the dots?). Professional equipment has more bandwidth (lines) capability than consumer equipment.

Even so, broadcasters loathe tape **generations** (copies of an original). There is an axiom in the industry never to go beyond a second-generation tape at all costs. A first-generation tape is also often called **footage**: raw, unedited tape shot on-site or in the field, by an ENG team. Once the tape has been edited in post-production, it becomes a second-generation tape, and so forth.

How CD-ROMs and DVDs Work

Recording onto digital media like CD-ROMs and DVDs has much in common with, and many difference from, recording on analog media like videotape. In the final analysis, the end result is the same. It all boils down to electrically charging a medium in a way so that it can be sampled, coded, and interpreted by the media reader. In the case of **CD-ROMs,** a laser from the read/write head sends a low-energy light beam toward a compact disk (CD) that is built on using a layer of a clear polycarbonate substance. The layers are made up of several colors (usually green and gold, which reflect the laser beam). The light from the laser cuts a continuous wave pattern in the polycarbonate plastic (often referred to as a **pit** or groove) similar to those on a phonograph record. The laser beam reflects off the groove, making a wave pattern, and reads its frequency patterns. As the head follows the groove, it uses positional information provided by the groove's waves to control the speed of the motor that is turning the disk so that the area under the head is always moving at the same speed. A dye layer is designed to absorb the light at specific frequencies. The resulting distortion (called a stripe) varies according to whether a beam is switched on or off. When the beam hits a stripe the distortion in the groove scatters the beam so that light is not returned to the read head, in contrast to the flat area (**land**) that does. Each time the beam is reflected back to the head, the head generates a patterned pulse of electricity that is compressed, error-checked, and passed along to the computer. The way information is written on CD-ROMs by making these indentations permits them to be only written to only one time. A **CD-RW** is a rewritable disk. Instead of creating grooves and stripes, rewritables actually use dye to store data instead of etching grooves on the disc. CD-RWs use a phase-change metal that permits the disk to be reverted back to its original state so it can be rewritten (recolored, actually) by new data (pulses).

The surface of a **DVD** (digital video disk) is quite similar to that of a CD but is more densely layered so that is can more compactly record more data in a single area. The resulting pits are much smaller, thereby making the DVD capable of holding as much as 8.5 GB (versus 700–850 MB) of data. The write head laser uses a much shorter wavelength, which makes the laser beam narrow enough to read the smaller pits and lands on the DVD surface. The laser head also is constructed differently. It is surrounded by a magnetic coil so that the head can focus on the beam in a more concentrated manner to more accurately read the compacted beam. The DVD also uses a prism-like device that converts the bursts of light reflected back from the flat areas (lands) on the disk to electricity, which the computer interprets as code and data. The construction of the read and write heads allows data (pulses) to be written in multiple layers. The DVDs are capable of writing data (pulses) on both sides of the disk, thereby doubling their potential capacity. However, very few DVD drives are capable of reading both sides; you must remove these double-sided disks and flip them over to read them.

Questions

Student Instructions: This session was based on the video *Understanding Television,* which we viewed earlier. Answer the following questions based on your understanding of our discussions and notes from that video.

1. What is the primary reason that the format differs between television and the movies? **Their purposes are different**.

2. What is persistence of vision? . **Refers to a psychological concept where the mind sees a sequence of still images in a steady motion, at the point in which they are displayed rapidly enough. In other words, while there is an illusion of motion, the actual output of both is not really a moving image but rather a series of frames (pictures) that are presented in sequential fashion.**

3. Why did the frame rate for movies have to be increased from 16 fps to 24fps? **To accommodate sound**

4. What is the frame rate for television? **25 or 30** fps.

5. A movie frame refers to a wholly completed picture. On the other hand, television pictures are captured in a series of **dots**.

6.   What does the term *raster* refer to? **The entire screen area made up of these dots**

7.   True or false, a television signal utilizes radio waves.   T   (F)

8.   The term *resolution* refers to the number of **dots per inch** on a screen.

9.   What does the term *generation* refer to? **Copies of an original, copies of copies**.

10.   What is *footage*? **Original, unedited tape**

11.   What two pieces of electronic equipment make up a camcorder? **Camera and VCR**

12.   Describe the difference between composite and component recording processes by filling in the blanks below:

   Component recordings are videotapes that handle the signal information as separated values involving the luminance (or essential picture brightness and edges) and color values. On the other hand, **composite** videotapes handle all the signal information as one big wavelength.

13.   Based on the preceding descriptions, which one, composite or component, do you think provides a better quality picture? **Component**

14.   Why does a computer image have to be scanned so it can be shown on a television screen? **To be converted to proper raster size and frame rate**

Lesson 3.3

Lesson Planning Considerations

   (**Approx. Time**: 20–25 minutes)

Agenda

   Audio is the type of subject that can be implemented without a lot of discussion. However, to do it right, it needs a series of lessons all its own. This course guide assumes that there is a supplementary technical reference book used. Therefore, a departure from the traditional approach to discussing audio has been taken. Audio is not presented as a standalone subject. The session on microphones is followed by a second session that includes discussions on both audio and video connectors. Mixing is discussed in the lesson about post-production and is presented in terms of an audiovisual (AV) function. The "Teaching Chronology" recommends that the two sessions of this lesson be split into two separate time periods.

   One thing is certain when discussing microphones: There are always going to be more types and styles of microphones on the market than what most school budgets are able to afford. Does it make sense to introduce students to all of them, although they may not see them or use them for the next four years? Maybe so; maybe not. Possibly the best compromise is to put together a session for students that covers the basics with regard to mics and sound-gathering techniques. Then show them the types they actually have in stock to use. An indirect benefit of pointing out all the variables in microphones, cables, and connectors may be to show how places like Radio Shack stay in business. There are so many different types of microphones and connectors; it is amazing that Radio Shack seemed to have all of them covered. After a while, your studio will become a small supply house with small boxes or trays everywhere with little connectors in them that you may no longer remember the use for.

The best way to introduce the topic of audio and to keep it within the time frame and difficulty level for first-year students is to separate it into two discussion topics: a session covering microphones, followed by a session on cables and connectors. Mixing and sound manipulation can be discussed in a later session covering post-production.

Objectives and Outcomes

At the end of these lessons, students will be able to

- recite the differences between transducer and condenser microphones;

- outline the uses for different types of microphones, based on pickup patterns;

- identify, select, and demonstrate use of an appropriate microphone;

- describe the need for different types of cables and connectors; and

- follow a schematic diagram to wire a basic studio and/or home entertainment system.

Mediated and Textual Support

Again, an assumption has been made that some outside source has been used to introduce the various types of mics and connectors. The Kyker-Curchy text *(Television Production: A Classroom Approach)* covers microphones as a separate unit. See **Appendix J** for more information about this text.

The Zettl *Videolab 2.1* CD also has a section on audio. The problem with using any outside resources is that the equipment brands and quality vary greatly from studio to studio and from school to school. It is quite difficult to find any material that covers the information generically so as not to confuse students when the actual equipment differs. For this reason, the Zettl *Videolab 2.1* CD should be reviewed in advance to be prepared to discus them.

The **Web-ASSISTant** Web site also provides information on audio manipulation, using digital technology, in the "Digging Deeper" section on the "Chapter Three" page.

Lesson Readiness

Students are asked to independently read the Kyker-Curchy Text and answer the review questions at the end. The questions are to be completed in advance of the class session for a grade. If you have your students answer the review questions prior to this session, the session will go much smoother. The review questions will help put things into perspective, to extend students' knowledge to the understanding of visual and media literacies, and put into practice a couple of exercises that will help the students remember what they have learned. The class session is used to review the answers to the questions and broaden the scope of the material covered in the text.

Closure

The wiring exercise at the end of this lesson provides an opportunity to evaluate how well students have understood the concepts in this lesson. If you are following the "Teaching Chronology," students should also have completed Quiz 1.

Lesson 3.3A

Audio Considerations

Pre-Class Activities

Student Instructions: Read the appropriate lesson in *Television Production: A Classroom Approach,* and answer the review questions. These are due on the date posted on the assignment board.

Terms

dynamic microphone	omnidirectional mic	lavelier
condenser microphone	phantom power	cartioid
unidirectional mic	AV board	mixing

Two Types of Microphones (Mics)

Audio is a very specialized business. There are about as many different types of microphones as there are differing needs. The more generic a microphone is in covering different uses, the less effective it is in specific cases. Requirements for studio sound are quite different than for outdoor scenes. Sometimes electricity is available and sometimes it is not. Background noise often needs to be filtered out. Windy conditions present their own set of problems. The subject of audio can consume a lot more time than we are going to take in this introductory course. We are introducing microphones based on their

- **transducer,** or method of operation, or their

- **pickup pattern.**

Transducer

Even though you are going to be introduced to three types of microphones, for the purpose of this course, we only need to know about two different types: **dynamic** and **condenser**. We probably will not have the opportunity to work with the ribbon mic because it is not durable enough to use in a classroom situation.

Teacher's Note: Go to the Zettl *Videolab 2.1* CD and click on *audio*. The discussions on connectors in this session actually go into further detail than what is presented on the CD. Therefore, you may wish to skip that section on the CD.

A dynamic mic is very durable and operates off a membrane type of mechanism. It is more mechanical in operation and, therefore, often does not have its own power source. The standard, bulb-type (or ice cream cone-shaped) microphones are generally dynamic mics. Because the dynamic mic requires so little power, the source actually comes from the mixer or camera to which it is connected. In the industry, we call this phenomenon **phantom power**.

While a dynamic mic is good to use on a remote ENG assignment because it is durable, it is not the highest quality you can get. The condenser mic is a high quality mic that operates electronically and requires a small battery. The **lavaliere** or lapel mic is an example of a condenser mic.

Pickup Pattern

Microphones are also defined by their pickup patterns. If a mic has multi pickup patterns, then it is called either **multidirectional** or **omnidirectional**. The microphones that are physically attached to consumer-grade cameras are often omnidirectional. Although there might be an on/off switch on them, they are not as effective as a handheld mic for interviews, for example. On the other hand, background audio is often desired to add "ambience" to a home video shoot, which is one reason (besides making them cheaper) that the consumer-grade equipment uses omnidirectional mics.

If it only picks up a limited area, it the mic is referred to as a **unidirectional** mic. An omnidirectional mic is not as effective in an outdoor scene, for example, when you want to record voices but do not want background noise. The lavaliere or lapel mics are generally unidirectional mics.

Cartioid mics are also generally considered to be unidirectional mics, but they have a "dead zone" where nothing is picked up. In addition, because their pickup pattern is "heart-shaped," they often pick up unwanted audio. The best unidirectional mic is the super-cartioid, or the shotgun mic. The pickup pattern on the shotgun is very narrow and has to be pointed directly at the subject to be effective. However, little or no background noise is usually detected.

The cone-shaped handheld mics used in on-camera interviews also have a heart-shaped (cartioid) pickup pattern but are less directional than lapel mics. This is why during an interview the interviewer has to get into the habit of bringing the mic back and forth between himself or herself and the subject. Otherwise, half the interview will not be audible.

A professional studio will incorporate several different types of microphones all at the same time. You will see a boom mic (which is really a specialized unidirectional mic, also referred to as a *shotgun* mic), a cone mic on a desktop, a lavaliere mic, and so forth. They all have their specific purpose. Blending (also referred to as **mixing**) these all together is the job of the audio engineer. Smaller studios combine mixers for audio and video into an **AV board**. We will go into more depth on how to use mixers during our discussions on post-production.

Lesson 3.3B

Cables and Connectors

Terms

shielding	BNC cable	rf-cable
S-video cable	impedance	RCA cable
jack	connectors	XLR cable
phasing	YPbPr	plug

Lesson Notes

To make more sense out of connectors; we will discuss both video and audio connectors together. RCA made a good case in point when they brought to market a cable that is interchangeable between audio and video connections. We will get to that in a few moments.

The first thing we have to get across is the idea of **shielding**. A shield is a protective covering on top of a cable that prevents interference and loss of signal. Just because a cable has a cover on it does not mean that it is shielded. The shielding usually is in the form of a foil-type substance. Then that foil is covered (normally with black rubberized or plasticized material).

The video cable is the standard cable that you typically see fastened to the back of your television set, which delivers your standard cable stations. This is called a **rf-cable** (for radio frequency) The name relates to the original concept that the term *radio* referred to the radio waves, the technology behind all communications. However, if you notice, this has a screw-on fastener. Although this is good for home use, it is quite a bother for studio operations. If you put on one of these easy-on/easy-off connectors, the line is much more insecure, especially if you are moving equipment around as much as you are in a studio. Therefore, the technical crews needed a solution: a cable with twisty-lock called a **BNC cable** (probably named after the company that invented it and brought it to market). The shielding on a cable is a plastic tube, then a wrapped wire that forms a second connection, followed by a rubber coating. Even minimal signal loss in video transmissions can cause a snowy picture (one with video distortion). Therefore, the connections all have to be made precisely.

There is another specialty cable used in the video industry called an **S-video cable** (for super), also called a Y/C cable. Remember our discussions about Y and C in how television works? The "Y" stands for luminance and the "C" stands for color (chroma). This cable has four little pins inside the cap. Three of the pins are used for the three basic colors (**red, green, blue**). The **fourth pin controls the brightness** or luminance. This cable is very fragile and very expensive. It has limitations on how far the signal will go without some external boost. But it is the best signal transmission source and is used almost exclusively in professional studios.

Audio cables and connectors are a little less sophisticated. Even though there appears to be a multitude of different kinds of audio cables that are used by home stereo sets and computers, inside they are all the same: wrapped or straight copper wire.

Newer, digital televisions that use high definition display techniques have added a newer, higher quality cabling. Known by its acronym (**YPbPr**), this specialty cable works very similarly to the S-video cable. It singles out the blue and red signal, with the green being automatically calculated from the red and blue settings. The "Y" represents the luminance settings. Some believe that this newer cable is of a better grade than the S-video cable, but any differences are negligible and are hardly detectible to the human eye. The whole concept of separating out the different colors from luminance is based on the principle that the human eye is more sensitive to changes in brightness (almost 90 percent more) than to changes in colors. This will be further explained in **Chapter 7**.

A microphone requires a special kind of cable because of its low voltage requirements. Remember, a dynamic mic does not require its own power source. Therefore, any loss of signal from one end to another is crucial. In physics class you will learn about action-reaction. This concept, as it relates to electricity, is called **impedance (or resistance)**. Impedance slows power much like wind drag does a moving car. The more impedance, the more power is required. All cables contain some level of impedance. Zero impedance indicates an incomplete circuit. That is how an ohmmeter works. When an electrician is looking for a broken circuit, he measures impedance in terms of ohms, the unit measurement of impedance. No impedance means an incomplete (i.e., broken) circuit.

However, in a microphone cable, impedance is a problem. In other words, we need to find a cable that is low in resistance. The specialized low impedance mic cable is called **XLR** cable (for extra-**l**ow **r**esistance).

Audio cables are only confusing because of all the adapters required to go from a 1/16-inch mini plug to a 1/8-inch, and so forth. Audio is also confused by the fact that there are usually **two audio** channels for stereo (left and right). After a while, RCA came out with a new convention for cables. Not only does their system now color coat the connectors, but their cable is also interchangeable between audio and video. They named their invention **RCA cables.** Now the **red** connector is for right audio, **white** connectors are for left audio, and **yellow** connectors are for video. Although that is the industry standard, there is nothing to prevent you from using a yellow cable for right audio, for example, just as long as you can remember your own color coding scheme.

The last thing we have to understand is the difference between a **jack** and a **plug**. The easiest way to remember this is to learn that a plug gets inserted into a jack. Jacks are color-coded to correspond with the cable ends. There are two types of jacks: in and out. When you are connecting one piece of equipment to another, you run the cable from the **out jack** to the **in jack**. Because we attach all the pieces in series, we continue this concept from one piece to another, until all the elements of the system are connected. You now have all the information you need to successfully wire a small studio or even your stereo system at home (see **Figure 3.1**).

Figure 3.1. Typical Wiring Diagram for Home Video System.

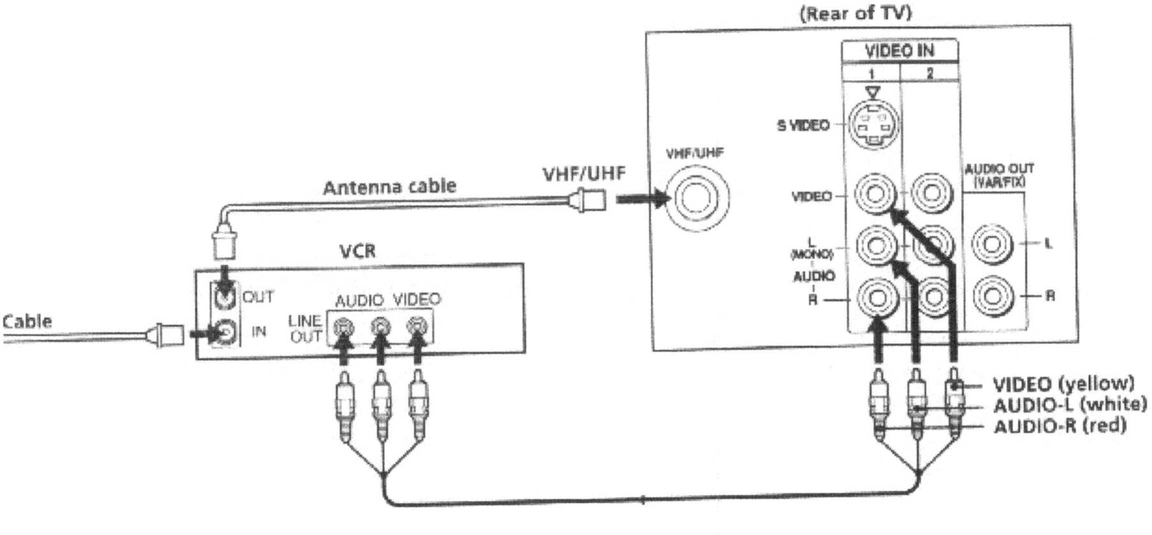

Teacher's Note: You might want to bring in an example of a wiring diagram from a home stereo system to show as an example.

Standardization has finally arrived in the consumer electronics industry. However, it was not always that way. Each manufacturer used unique wiring combinations to hook up its equipment. To accommodate all the different combinations, retail companies like Radio Shack have come to the rescue. If you visit your local Radio Shack store, you will find rows and rows of packages and cables. **Connectors** usually refer to all the types of jacks and plugs that work with the cables they are connected to. Connectors carry the name for their most common use. In other words, a BNC connector is the plug and jack combination that allows the BNC cable to be connected to the equipment.

Another way in which the industry has standardized is by phasing. **Phasing** actually comes from an electrical term and refers to connecting (or setting) the common wires to common wires, the hot wires to hot wires, ground to ground, and so forth. When you plug in a lamp or stereo equipment, you may notice that one prong is wider than the other, requiring you to plug the device in a certain way. This to ensure that the equipment is properly phased with the electrical wiring. The wiring that comes with speaker systems is also phased. Usually there is a copper wire and a silver wire. It does not matter which is used for each connection, as long as the same colored wired is used at the other end (left to right).

It is crucial to the overall effectiveness of your shoot to have all your equipment balanced. Audio is easier to explain than video. For example, look at the dial on a car stereo. When it is **in balance** from left to right, back to front, the indicators are actually set at zero.

Review Activity

System Setup

Student Instructions: For each of the setups listed, select the most appropriate cable/connector (in column B) and provide the reason why it is the most appropriate by circling the correct connector and the reason why that particular connector/cable type should be selected (column C).

A	B	C
When setting up a **microphone** I most want to use a(n)	RCA cable **XLR cable** S-video cable BNC cable rf cable	because it has the lowest resistance because it is the cheapest because it handles colors well because it a universal plug because it has the best quality because it has special security locks
When **wiring** a **home stereo** I most want to use a(n)	RCA cable XLR cable S-video cable BNC cable rf cable	because it has the lowest resistance because it is the cheapest because it handles colors well because it is a universal plug because it has the best quality because it has special security locks
When **wiring** a **studio** I most want to use a(n)	RCA cable XLR cable S-video cable BNC cable rf cable	because it has the lowest resistance because it is the cheapest because it handles colors well because it is a universal plug because it has the best quality has special security locks
When **wiring** an **ENG** I most want to use a(n)	RCA cable XLR cable S-video cable BNC cable rf cable	because it has the lowest resistance because it is the cheapest because it handles colors well because it is a universal plug because it has the best quality because it has special security locks

Lesson 3.4

Lesson Planning Considerations

(**Approx. Time**: 20–25 minutes each)

Agenda

The term *visualizing* covers a lot of ground. Before students can become visually literate in interpreting images, they need to understand how some of these things are accomplished. This lesson is actually broken down into three sessions. The first, "Framing and Focusing," includes concepts of focal length, the various shots (close-up, extreme close-up, headshot, etc.), white space and symmetry, and practical implications for subject placement. The second, "Vectoring and The Z-Axis," covers how these two principles change a viewer's perspective, lead room, and nose room. "Basic Camera Moves" explains how they affect the effectiveness and mood of the shot.

Objectives/Outcomes

As a result of these sessions, students will be able to

• recite and demonstrate the concepts of proper framing,

• recite various types of shots and the general purpose for each, and

• describe the visual concepts of symmetry and balance.

Mediated and Textual Support

The lesson is again supplemented by the Zettl *Videolab 2.1* CD. You will be faced with two major decisions: (1) when to present this material and (2) how much detail from the CD to present.

These sessions are actually spaced out in the "Teaching Chronology" and take place about a quarter of the way into the term. This is because students are anxious to get going. Therefore, you must decide when to allow your students to handle the equipment, before or after they are taught everything there is to know about it. It is like the chicken and egg adage. A good teaching trick is to use problem-based learning and delay the information in these sessions until your students are open to receiving it. If they have some exposure to the camera and have a couple of projects under their belts, their anxiety to get going will be reduced somewhat. In addition, they will be ready to take in the information, especially if you can relate to a need they have created for themselves because they have already made some mistakes. If you take notes throughout the year regarding some problems students had to overcome, or mistakes they made, you can use those notes during these sessions so that the students have something to relate to.

Students are not penalized for making mistakes. Rather, they are rewarded for learning from them. You will read later how the grading system works. Because the projects are apt to get better as time goes along, the system rewards this by allowing students to pick one project from all of them to be submitted for a **portfolio grade**. This concept is discussed further in **Chapter 1** under "Course Content and Grading".

The second problem is how much detail to expose first-year students to. The Zettl *Videolab 2.1* CD covers a lot more information than you will need. The topics selected in these sessions focus on the significant points that will help students get through the projects slated for this first-year course. The Zettl *Videolab 2.1* CD was designed with sufficient detail to make it an effective tool for as many as two or three school years. To alleviate some of the required front-end planning time, an optional class session has been included after *Lesson 3.4* that outlines a suggested navigational path. Although this guide was written as if the CD were to be used at one time after all three sessions have been completed, the suggested video sessions could, in fact, be included as an integrated part of each session in Lesson 3.4, as the topics are being covered. It depends on how the teacher views their effectiveness.

Tom Schroeppel offers two books that contain several hints and techniques about videography. The first is *Video Goals: Getting Results with Pictures and Sound,* which focuses on the idea of making sure that each project has an objective before it is shot. This includes scripts, pre-production, adding sound, and editing. The second is *The Bare Bones Camera Course for Film & Video,* which explains, as simply as possible, how to shoot usable images on film or tape. Information on how to obtain these books can be found in **Appendix J** and on the **Web-ASSISTant** Web site on the "Chapter Three" page.

Lesson Readiness

Students are to read the appropriate lessons in the Kyker-Curchy text (*Television Production: A Classroom Approach*) on their own and answer the review questions and turn them in for a grade. The lesson will be covered within the sessions for Lesson 3.3.

Closure

Students will have begun Project #1 by the time this lesson is covered in the "Teaching Chronology." Showing and critiquing current projects provides an excellent opportunity to bring closure.

Lesson 3.4A

Framing and Focusing a Picture

Pre-Class Activity

Student Instructions: Read the appropriate lessons in *Television Production: A Classroom Approach.* The answers to the review questions are to be handed in on the due date on the assignment board.

Terms

framing	**long shot**	**head room**
nose room	**lead room**	**closure**
symmetry	**focal length**	**cross shot**
white space	**normal setting**	**bust shot**
extreme close-up	**medium shot**	**two shot**
OTS (over the shoulder) shot		

__Framing__ (also referred to as **field of view**) refers to the concept of placing your subject properly in a shot. It involves where to cut off your subject when only part of that subject is to be shown or where to position your subject in profile or moving shots. In short, there are four framing techniques you need to know. We will cover three of them in this session and the last one in Lesson 3.4B when we discuss camera movement.

First, we have several framing concepts to go over. Second, we will learn about *field of view*. *Videolab 2.1* describes field of view as how the subject appears in the camera viewfinder (monitor). Some of the views are new, and some we have gone over already. Can you describe what each one does and when it can be used?

- **Long shot:** used to orient a viewer to the location of the shot

- **Close-up:** used to get the viewer to focus on specific action

- **Extreme close-up:** used to show a reaction, or to elicit an emotion

- **Medium** shot: used as the normal view (the standard two to three feet)

- **Bust shot:** used in studios for newscasts

- **Two shot:** standard interview shot

- **OTS (over the shoulder) shot:** used in interviews as an alternative view, by showing a partial view of the back and shoulder of one of the individuals in the shot

- **Cross shot:** used as an alternative to the OTS shot

Teacher's Note: The industry standard for framing is often referred to as the **rule of thirds.** An alternative approach is to divide the frame into quarters, using dead-center aim to keep the subject in the center of the frame. An analogy is to describe the bull's-eye on a target. *Videolab 2.1* refers to all of the following as subcategories of *lead room* on the CD.

To understand the proper framing techniques to use, we need to know more about some new concepts.

Headroom is the space above the head in a one or two shot. Be sure that there is enough room, but not too much. Using the crosshairs/quadrant rule, the middle of the subject should appear almost **dead center**. This is to eliminate the illusion that makes the subject appear to be pulled toward the edge of the screen.

Nose room is the space between the front of the subject and the left or right edge of the frame. Again, using the dead-center rule, the nose of the subject should remain in the center of the frame as the profile becomes more pronounced.

Lead room is the term used to indicate how a moving picture should be framed. Be careful not to let the subject get too close to the edge of the frame. Again, using the target analogy, if you keep the subject more or less in the **dead center**, you have the best opportunity to keep the subject in the right place.

Teacher's Note: You may wish to skip lead room and nose room until the next session, when the concept of vectors is introduced. If you have not done so yet, this may be a good a time introduce the term *white space*. Although it is not about shooting a person as the subject, it does relate to the concept of symmetry.

Closure relates to an illusion the mind makes automatically to close off or to complete a picture that is partially drawn. This illusion is a factor when shooting a person as a subject. There are certain cut-off points: just below the knee, partially showing the shoulders, and so forth.

Teacher's Note: You may wish to explain how closure also is very useful to a director or cinematographer who wishes to take advantage of the illusion using a series of long/cover shots, followed by a tight shot to give viewers the impression that the scene actually occurs in a place other than on the set. For example, the stadium scenes (i.e., long or cover shots) in movies like *The Waterboy* were shot during an actual football game, but the close-ups were shot using only several dozen extras. The combination of the long/cover shots and close-ups gives the illusion that the scene was actually taking place during the football game. It should not be difficult to come up with several additional examples to make this point.

Any good still shot needs **symmetry** (or balance). If you take a frame and divide it up into four quadrants, the crosshairs represent dead center. Because it is the natural tendency of the viewer to look dead center in a shot, if you do not present a balanced shot, the viewer may become disoriented. Using this crosshairs technique often automatically takes care of the head room problem.

Teacher's Note: Now is also a good time to refer back to an earlier lesson about symmetry and balance, as discussed on the "Portfolio Scorecards." However, it is also important to note that discussions about symmetry and balance assume that the camera person or director actually wants a balanced picture. Sometimes an off-balance picture is what the shot calls for (as in the case in teleplays where the central characters need to be shown having problems, or in a newscast where the subject is moved to the side to make room for b-roll footage, and so forth. At this time, you may wish to explain what b-roll footage is, although it comes up in later lesson notes.).

This discussion also links back to earlier discussions about the storyboard. Recall that each frame needs to have an objective, or purpose. This is how the scriptwriter indicates to the technical crew how the shot should be taken.

While we are on the subject of symmetry, we might discuss what to do with title pages or any cut that includes a page written on a character generator or a PowerPoint® presentation. The proper technique is to provide plenty of **white space**. White space is blank space in the picture that does not cause a mental overload for the viewer. White space **does not refer to the color** of the space, but to the **amount** of space.

Under **focus techniques**, we often classify camera lenses by their **focal length** and **angle of view**. The field of view actually is in the shape of a triangle. The horizon line forms the base of the triangle. The focal length is really the distance between the horizon and the camera. As the focal length changes, so does the angle of view and the magnification of the subject. Essentially, we appear to be bringing the horizon closer. This has the effect of making the object appear farther away. By extending to the horizon, we appear to be bringing the subject closer. Actually, we are changing the angle of view to accomplish this.

Teacher's Note: The Zettl CD provides an excellent moving graphic of this concept.

Like the f-stop, we do the opposite of what we might expect:

A **short** focal length = a **wide** angle of view and the object appears far away.

A long focal length = a **narrow** angle of view and the object seems **closer**.

Use a **normal setting** to get the picture to look like it appears to the naked eye.

Lesson 3.4B

Vectoring and the Z-Axis

Pre-Class Activity

Student Instructions: Read the following passage and answer the question that follows.

During our last session, we discussed framing. We limited our discussions to framing still pictures in which the subject appears facing forward. All pictures have a natural gravitational force drawing the viewer's attention to the center of the shot. We have been referring to the need to maintain symmetry and balance. What we are really saying is that, under normal conditions, the framing of the shot should coincide with that normal gravitational pull. There are times, however, when we will want to cause the viewer to look elsewhere in the picture.

Can you think of a circumstance when you might want to have the viewer look elsewhere, other than the dead center of an image?

For example: When you want to make room to insert footage that shows what the talent is speaking about (often referred to as b-roll footage), such as during a newscast.

Terms

frame	vectoring	z-axis
peripheral vision	tight shot	

Having a viewer look elsewhere is usually done with profile shots or shots in which the subject is moving across the **frame**. Although the concept of maintaining balance is the same, there are differences in how this is done. The natural or gravitational pull that a frame imposes on the viewer is called a vector. The act of making the viewer look elsewhere in the shot is called **vectoring**. In other words, there is an apparent contradiction. Actually the term *vector* refers to two things: the natural pull toward the center that all shots seem to have, and an act whereby the videographer wants to divert viewers' attention away from that natural place they would first look in a shot.

Framing and **vectoring,** taken out of context, are actually opposite in meaning. Taken together, they make up a composite of procedures that allow the videographer to accomplish certain goals.

Vectoring is essentially a framing technique that actually refers to a psychological **movement**, or **direction**. In a moving image, a vector is the direction the subject is actually moving in. We actually see and use vectoring everyday; whether it be a traffic cop pointing to get you to look or move in a specific direction, someone motioning to you to sit down next to them when you enter a room, or a billboard advertisement that states *Made Ya Look*. In still shots, a vector is a directional force causing the viewer to actually look in a certain direction. Understanding the concept of how to manipulate your shots is one of the most important aspects of visual awareness and media literacy, which we will cover in much more detail in **Chapter 4**. For now, we need to learn how to properly frame a shot to either counterbalance the natural effect of vectoring or create a directional force to cause your viewers to look elsewhere.

For a first-year course, learning two basic framing techniques that take vectoring into account should suffice. There are certainly several more techniques and considerations, which you will be learning in future courses.

The **z-axis** is an imaginary line that runs between the lens of the camera and the horizon. Knowing about this line and its effect on camera shots is very important. A focal length change (zoom) in or out makes the horizon appear to be closer or farther away. It also affects the amount of **peripheral vision** (view of what is on either side of you) allowed by the camera. The closer in along this axis you draw the horizon, the more compact the subject(s) appear. This is how you can create an illusion of a crowd scene without actually needing a crowd. Remember what we said about closure? In combination, this effect is used quite often in scenes in which you need a large audience (like a stadium full of people) when you really do not have access to that many people. This is also known as a **tight shot**. Or, you might use it on a street scene that is interlaced with live shots of a similar-looking place. This is how television shows like *NYPD Blue* are able to use a combination of tight shots interspersed with street scenes from New York to create the illusion that the scene is actually taking place on-site in New York. Recall the two camera shots that take **vectoring** into account.

Nose room implies that a profile shot is taken. The subject should be placed right of center for left profiles and left of center for right profiles. This provides for extra room in front of the subject so that there is no distortion (where the nose is pulled toward the edge of the screen).

Lead room is for left-to-right or right-to-left moving pictures, in which a moving subject is framed with plenty of room in front so that it does not appear to be constantly pushing against the edge of the frame.

Recall also that there is a very simple method to accomplish the framing subjects, whether they are frontal, profile, or moving in your pictures. It is referred to as the bull's-eye method. If you take the most important aspect in your picture and ensure that it always remains dead center (in an imaginary bull's-eye you create in the viewfinder), all the framing considerations will take care of themselves. A profile shot will automatically be compensated, and the moving image will never run up against the outside frame. Even extreme close-ups will frame themselves properly. To do this, however, you need to understand that all shots have vectors, and that a good videographer knows what the vector is in every shot.

Basic Camera Moves

Terms

pan	tilt	truck
dolly	pedestal	zoom
rack focus shot		

Lesson Notes

Charlie Chaplin used to make us laugh in his movies by making some foolish move in front of the camera. This kind of shooting (in which the camera remains still while the subject moves about) was fairly standard until *Citizen Kane* came along in 1941. Now it is commonplace for the camera to take part in the activity, and in some cases, actually create an activity. This lesson is intended to show you how basic camera moves can create images and moods and even scene changes.

Pan and **tilt** are camera moves in which the tripod remains stationary. A **pan** is a side-to-side movement. A **tilt** is an up or down movement. Both create an impression on the viewer because the angle of view of the subject changes. A tilt can show superiority (looking down at the subject) or inferiority (the camera is lower than the subject looking up). Orson Welles used these two moves quite effectively in *Citizen Kane*. Sometimes, when you want the camera to act as the eyes of the viewer, the subject will talk directly into the camera. The camera (audience) can simulate a "yes" or "no" response from the viewer by panning back and forth for a "yes" or tilting up or down for a "no." Typically, this is a favorite move on children's shows.

Truck and **pedestal** are two similar moves, but the camera moves along with the subject, either side to side (**truck**) or up and down (**pedestal**). With these two moves, you want to stay even with the movement but not create any particular illusion of height or distance. In the movies or location shots, often the camera is placed on a rail to keep the movements fluid. You may see a similar, but not identical, move in which a crane is used to create the illusion that you are taking off in an airplane.

The zoom has been discussed in earlier sessions. A dolly accomplishes a similar effect. In a **dolly** move, the cameraperson physically moves the entire camera and tripod assembly closer to the subject. A zoom is not really a camera *move* per se, but it does accomplish an effect on the viewer. It is often referred to as a **logical camera move**. If you closely compare a dolly and a zoom, you can easily notice a different effect. A dolly move simply brings the viewer closer to the action for focus. A **zoom**, on the other hand, especially if done quickly, can create an illusion of surprise (quick zoom in) or anxiety (quick zoom out). Perhaps the most effective use of the latter may be seen in the movie *Quiz Show* in the scene in which the protagonist (played by Ralph Fiennes) has an anxiety attack while in the isolation booth trying to make a moral decision regarding telling the truth .

Another logical (as opposed to physical) camera move is the use of focal length change. In a previous lesson we discovered what the effect the x-axis has on the amount of peripheral vision and how to maintain focus during a zoom. However, we can actually use the effect of going in and out of zoom during a **focal length change**. This is called a **rack focus shot**, an effect that has come into vogue during the last 10 years or so. By changing the focus in and out from a subject in the foreground to one in the background and vice versa, we can actually simulate a scene change in which different actions are taking place at the same time. We can also create a situation in which someone appears to be eavesdropping on another's conversation, either on purpose or by accident.

Optional Activity

Lesson Planning Considerations

(**Approx. Time:** 30–35 minutes)

Agenda

An alternative way to use the *Videolab 2.1* CD by Herb Zettl to review the material presented in Lesson 3.4 is to wait until the three sessions are completed. Using the rule of thirds (presenting students with the opportunity to go over material on three separate occasions), it may be better to dedicate one final session to reviewing the techniques using the visual support the CD offers. The movie clips are short and can be covered quickly.

The format and construct of the CD make it an interactive computer-assisted course that is a part of an individualized instructional program. Please keep in mind that its original intent has been modified here. Because its intended audience includes more than first-year students, the CD contains considerably more clips than are needed for this course. The navigational flow suggested below is the result of spending considerable time with the CD to find clips that are the most relevant to the three sessions of this lesson, and it parallels the order in which the techniques are covered. First framing and vectors are reviewed, then the depth of field dimension.

The techniques may be broken down into three major categories: basics of how to frame and focus a shot, how to add depth and energy, and how camera movements provide alternative perspectives. This class session was designed to provide the second of three looks at camera operation (the quizzes and projects being the third).

Understand that this is just one of many ways this CD could be used in class. It is certainly better for the teacher to take the time to sketch out a navigation plan specific to individual class needs.

The suggested path assumes that all three sessions in Lesson 3.4 have already been reviewed in class. An additional opportunity for students to actively engage in learning these concepts is to have them bring in examples from current or past television shows or movies that use these operations. In class, ask students to describe the objective or intent of their use within the context of the movie or television show's premise.

Following is a suggested path for using the *Videolab 2.1* CD to review all three sessions in Lesson 3.4:

At the **MASTER CONTROL**, Click on **CAMERA**:

1. Go to **COMPOSITION** (tape #6)
    _____ Select *Field of View*
    _____ [Go back to **MASTER CONTROL**]

2. Go to **SCREEN FORCES** (tape #5)
    _____ Select *Vectors, Frame edge, Horizon, Balance*
    _____ [Go back to **MASTER CONTROL**]

3. Go to **COMPOSITION** (tape #6)
    Select *Field of view, Head room, Lead room, Background, Closure*
    (Skip *Close-ups* for now, as it will be covered later)
    [Go back to **MASTER CONTROL**]

4. Go to **PICTURE DEPTH** (tape #7)
   Select *Z-Axis & Depth of Field*
   Link to *Rack* (in **FRAMING** (tape #4))
   From *Rack*, Link to *Z-Axis* (in **SCREEN MOTION** (tape #8))
   Select also *Lateral* and *Close-ups*
   Link to *Framing Close-ups* (in **COMPOSITION** (tape #6))
   [Go back to **MASTER CONTROL**]

5. Go to **CAMERA MOVES** (tape #9)
   Select *Zoom, Pan, Tilt, Pedestal, Truck,* then *Dolly.*
   Dolly is selected last because it ends with a comparison of dolly and zoom.

Lesson 3.5

Editing

Lesson Planning Considerations

(**Approx. Time:** 20–25 minutes)

Agenda

Developing a generic training program for equipment is difficult because procedures vary by brand. However, some concepts and definitions are, regardless of the equipment. Terms like assemble versus insert editing, cueing techniques, audio dubbing, adding title screens, wipes and swipes versus fading, and so forth are taught in a similar manner. The only difference is the actual buttons that have to be pushed to accomplish the task. One of the goals of this lesson, then, is to teach post-production on a conceptual level that students can take with them when they move to a new studio environment. These lessons concentrate on the technical aspects of editing. The production aspects of editing (how and when this fits into the overall production plan, creative aspects, and so forth) are covered in **Chapter 7.**

The perspective of this lesson is the actual operation of the equipment. These topics are visited again in subsequent lessons in **Chapter 5,** which covers visual literacy, and in **Chapter 7** in a lesson on post-production functions.

Objectives and Outcomes

As a result of participating in this session, students should be able to describe and perform the following tasks or operations:

- assemble editing;
- insert editing;
- adding wipes, swipes, and fades;
- character generation; and
- audio dubbing.

Mediated and Textual Support

One obvious resource for this lesson is the user manuals. They should be reviewed not for specific content but in light of their organization. Students need to know where they are kept and how to use them as a reference, if they get stuck on a problem. Instruction will most probably take place one-on-one, or in small groups. Therefore, small labels placed on the equipment might prove equally effective as any handouts provided in class.

Tom Schroeppel offers a book that contains several hints and techniques as they relate to videography. *The Bare Bones Camera Course for Film & Video* explains, as simply as possible, how to shoot usable images on film or tape. Information on how to obtain this book can be found in **Appendix J** and on the **Web-ASSISTant** Web site (on the "Chapter Three" page).

The cyber course at **www.cybercollege.com** includes a module on audio that might prove useful. Dr. Ron Whittaker, who developed this Web site, provides limited copyrights to teachers as long as proper reference is made. Because Internet links are subject to change, check the **Web-ASSISTant** Web site (the "Chapter Three" page) for updates to see if this link is still active. Where possible, an alternative will be provided, should this link be removed.

Lesson Readiness

Because students have already completed Project #1, they already have an idea about how editing can correct numerous framing errors. They will have also had an opportunity to use the AV board, so the problem with orienting students in preparation for this lesson is not to get them to understand the need but rather to have them recall the activities they already know and match them with the name of the procedure. The intent of the pre-class activity is to have students recall the kinds of functions they already know how to use, so they can attach the names.

Closure

The list in "Objectives and Outcomes" is only a partial line-up. Obviously, completing this list depends on the exact configuration in your studio. How and when students are asked to display their competencies on the checklist (per the sample provided in **Appendix C**) is also an individual decision.

Regardless of equipment, the *Numbers* project, as outlined below, is a good way to determine if students know how to complete the editing tasks.

Pre-Class Activity

Student Instructions: After each technique below, write post-production activities for each that you have already done on your projects to date and describe how each was accomplished:

Assemble editing _____

Insert editing _____

Adding wipes, swipes, and fades _____

Character generation _____

Audio dubbing _____

Terms

post-production	linear editing	nonlinear editing
assemble editing	insert editing	cut
wipe or swipe	fade	character generator (CG)
audio dubbing		

Lesson Notes

Editing can appear to be more complicated than it looks. It is also made more complicated by the fact that each studio differs in the brands and configuration of equipment (how the equipment is hooked up). The best way to learn this phase of equipment operation is to learn the underlying concepts of editing and become familiar with some standards for design layouts.

Editing as a whole, using the AV board and adding titles and sound, is most commonly referred to as **post-production**. Traditionally, this has been a physical activity. In other words, something is done to the footage tape to physically (electronically) alter it. Digital technologies (i.e., computers) have changed the way in which footage is converted into edited tape; however, the concept remains the same. Some of the differences will be described in this lesson when appropriate. The first difference is how physical and digital editing are referred to. The **standard editing techniques** are most commonly called **linear editing**, because it has traditionally been done in a production line fashion. First, the tape is edited and title pages added, then audio is added or modified, and later some insert editing may take place. The newer **digital editing techniques** are often called **nonlinear editing** because of how it is accomplished. The video is fed into a computer and accessed via a software program, such as Adobe Premier, iMovie, Avid, or Final Cut. All modifications can be completed at once. After editing, the finished product is recorded back onto videotape, or, in some cases, left in digital format to be played directly as a DVD product.

Because the actual procedures of how to accomplish these tasks vary, we are not going to go over them today. Rather, we will be working in small group sessions to teach you how to operate the equipment in this studio. The main goal of this lesson is to discuss the concept behind the tasks involved and review some of the typical configurations in a nonlinear studio. Armed with this knowledge, you should be able to go into most medium-sized studios and become oriented to the new configuration with minimal difficulty.

Analog Editing

Editing refers to the overall process of modifying footage and creating a completed product. Typically, it takes place in the post-production phase. Editing also has a more narrow reference, to the idea of taking the footage and laying it out in the sequence specified by the storyboard. There are two types of analog editing.

Assemble editing refers to the process of arranging the tape in the prescribed order. Footage may be captured in any sequence. Now it must follow the storyboard laid out by the scriptwriter and director. The term refers to the process of adding tape together, back to back, in an assembly line fashion.

Insert editing refers to the process of adding new video footage over the top of existing footage. The audio track may or may not be altered accordingly. This differs from assemble editing because the sequence of the original footage remains intact. This type of editing is useful for instructional videos, in which the talent describes a procedure and wants to visually display how it is to be done. Insert editing is complicated by the fact that it cannot be done to any space on a tape that has any other type of interference on it. (This interference is commonly referred to as **snow**.)

Transitions

Moving from one scene to the next may take place immediately as a **cut**, or by using one or more of several transitioning effects. The following are two of the more commonly used transitioning effects.

Teacher's Note: If the class takes place in the studio and is set up properly, you may wish to show how the following effects look as you are discussing them.

Wipe or swipe is a technique in which the second scene or image gradually replaces the original image vertically, diagonally, or horizontally across the screen. There are several types of boards that provide many different types of transitions. They will be learned as we progress through our projects.

Fade is a transition similar in intent to the wipe or swipe. However, it is accomplished by the original picture growing dimmer and replacing it with a new image that gradually grows brighter. The second image can be a new scene or a blank (e.g., fade to black).

Titles and Credits

All video productions need to have title and credits pages. These can be added in many ways. Most studios have access to a **character generator (CG)** that allows the editing director to add titles that can scroll, fade, or crawl along the bottom of the screen. The colors may be arranged, the fonts changed, and so forth. Some studios are set up to do this digitally through software such as PowerPoint, Hyperstudio, Director, and After Effects. Character generation is the generic term associated with this function, regardless of software configuration.

Adding or Modifying Sound

The process of adding or modifying the sound track is traditionally referred to as **audio dubbing**. This process can only be done to tape that already has a control track that resulted from something being recorded on it. There are generally two sound tracks on standard videotape, allowing several different combinations of sound. In a digital world, this process can be done in several ways. CDs, audiotapes, WAV, and MIDI files, and even sound tracks from other videotapes, may be used. Care must be taken when attempting to audio dub not to overlay the video track. If the wrong buttons are pressed, this could happen. As a part of our individual instruction, we are going to review these procedures.

Preparing New Tapes

In a first year-course, we only concentrate on the basic concepts of post-production. However, there is one procedure or trick we can learn that will add a lot of effect to our videos and is fairly easy to accomplish. If you want to create a video on which the audio track corresponds to the video track (the lyrics are coordinated, or the audio completes at the exact time), audio track must be laid down first. Then, the video is applied using insert editing rather than assemble editing. To do this, you must first understand that a video product's worst enemy is snow, which is really video noise. It is impossible to insert edit or audio dub over snow. Some studios have established a procedure to make all raw videotapes ready for production by first removing all the snow by assemble editing black video on to all new tapes. That way, the editor has the flexibility to insert video on to previously recorded tapes using insert editing and to lay down the audio track first.

Questions

To demonstrate your understanding of the concepts put forth in this lesson, complete the following by writing a short sentence or two describing what caused the problem and how to correct the error.

1. How do you remove snow from in between segments that have been already assemble edited? **You have to re-edit them onto a new tape**.

2. When trying to insert edit, the VCR did not respond. I am certain I followed the instructions correctly (and you have) and that the equipment is not broken. What else might be the problem with the tape? **The tab has been removed, preventing any editing.**

3. When trying to audio dub a tape, you accidentally wrote over a portion of the video. What wrong buttons did you press? **Record button**

4. How to you prepare a new video so that you can immediately insert edit it or lay down the audio track first to coordinate it? **Record a control strip by recording a black or blank section first.**

Review Activity

Numbers Project

Activity Planning Considerations

Agenda

Evaluation of the success of attaining the goals and objectives of this lesson will take place on the "Competency Checklist." However, there is a simple activity to help students demonstrate that they have learned how to assemble edit. In preparation, the teacher records a tape that contains a series of numbers in sequence from 1 to 25. The tape is recorded so that the numbers change every five to ten seconds. Students are then assigned a random series of five to six numbers within the range 1 to 25. Students edit onto their portfolio tapes a segment containing the assigned numbers. The outcome of this activity is for the students to have on their portfolio tapes a segment that is completed in the correct order, for the exact amount of time per the teacher's instructions, and without snow in between segments. The same activity can later be assigned using insert editing as the competency. Once each activity is completed, the student's "Competency Checklist" may be updated. This activity could be completed for any of the techniques discussed in this lesson. Editing is the most important function because it is the foundation of all the others.

(Some teachers may think that this activity is superfluous because of the new nonlinear editing equipment. Although it is true that the exercise was designed around analog editing techniques, a lot can be said about practicing continuity. This activity, if accompanied by asking students to add music, transitions, and so forth, can actually be a good starting project to check out the basics of editing, regardless of the equipment or software being used.)

Student Instructions: For you to show your ability to assemble and insert edit, you will be assigned a specific activity to complete. You will be provided with a master tape with a series of numbers on it. You are also going to be assigned a subset of that series to add to your portfolio tape. You are to add the assigned numbers to your tape in the specific order. Each number must appear on your tape for exactly _____ seconds.

Teacher's Note: The teacher should fill in the blank with an appropriate time.

You are to add those numbers to the tape using assemble editing. Once you complete that task, you will be given another master containing some other scene. You will show you know how to insert edit by overlaying that scene over the top of the assemble-edited portion of your tape.

How You Will Be Evaluated

Once the project is completed, your "Competency Checklist" will be updated. The finished product must have the correct numbers in the correct order and for the correct amount of time, with no snow in between segments. The insert must be placed over the numbers portion of the tape.

Lesson 3.6

Lesson Planning Considerations

(**Approx. Time:** 40–45 minutes)

Agenda

In keeping with the overall intent of this book to introduce literacy about the medium of television and the digital domain, this lesson attempts to transcend any purely technological discussions about how the equipment works to introduce a view of equipment enhancements from a functional and philosophical standpoint. It reviews some of the technical and sociological aspects of the digital process as it relates to television. Rather than concentrating on the technical functions of digital broadcasting, it is an attempt to look at digital convergence from a different point of view. There is a lot of technical information that one could teach a student about how digital electronics works, but there are plenty of books on the market that do just that, and could probably do a lot better job than can be done in one short lesson. Therefore, it is the intention of this lesson to help students understand that the process of converting to the digital domain is complicated because it involves five distinct processes, many of which have been going on for quite some time.

Further, this lesson is intended to demonstrate differences between a "born-digital" medium and one that has been digitized from another form. Simply put, the digitized version of a medium is quite different than something that is created in the digital domain. The implications of converting a medium to a digital environment don't end once the analog waveforms are converted into bits and bytes. A *digital* item implies several additional factors (such as an intent to create a participatory and interactive environment). On the other hand, a *digitized* item often comes up short of the intended outcome. As Janet Murray noted in *Hamlet on the Holodeck* (1998), a medium that is being carefully crafted for the digital domain is has several similar characteristics: They all are (or should be) procedural, participatory, spatial, and encyclopedic. These four terms all have one thing in common: they involve interactivity and immersion, creating a sense that a door is being closed. In other words, creating digital content changes the way content is created. Producers must be able to create these new sensations using intelligence within the technology that provides interactivity for viewers to to synthesize programs to eliminate unwanted content, to provide immediate feedback, and to do so similarly on various platforms like television, a computer, or the newest CG-3 technology telephones. This interplatform shift has a name: *digital convergence*.

Any study of moving television as we know it to a new domain will certainly be inadequate unless we also discuss a new philosophical shift. Looking at digital video requires a whole new perspective on the industry, the way content is created, and the way viewers become participants and producers.

The technology is evolving so quickly that anyone teaching or writing about it in a textbook will be hard pressed to keep up with it for several years to come, which is another reason to take a more philosophical look at the technology of digitization. Hopefully this approach will never become outdated.

Mediated and Textual Support

The basis for discussions in this lesson comes from many sources. If the teacher is seriously interested in pursuing a new look at television and digital video, there are several books on the topic, including the following:

> *Hamlet on the Holodeck: The Future of Narrative in Cyberspace*, by Janet Murray. MIT Press, 1998.

> *Defining Vision: How Broadcasters Lured the Government into Inciting a Revolution in Television,* by Joel Brinkley. Harcourt, Brace, 1997.

Objectives

As stated above, the desired outcome for this lesson is a more extensive and philosophical than what one might expect to find in a series of lessons about equipment. The conversion to the digital domain requires an entirely new line of thinking. The expected outcomes for this lesson typify that process.

At the end of this lesson, students will be expected to

- understand the impact that digital convergence will have on the broadcasting paradigm,

- know the five different processes that are included when considering the digitization of television,

- be able to compare the analog and digital domains from a function and feature perspective.

Lesson Readiness

Teachers can begin discussions about interactivity by asking students if they can name the various ways in which they have seen a program attempting to draw its viewers into a discussion or to create some type of participatory environment. As time goes on, this exercise will become easier and easier. Among the recent choices that students may draw on are voting during an *American Idol* show or a news show asking viewers to phone in or e-mail their responses to a poll. Some might even come up with pay-per-view. The goal behind this exercise is to help students understand that although a digital domain is not required for interactivity, digitization is certainly going to make interactivity more common and easier. The discussions then can go on to cover the need on the part of the show's producers (and sponsors) for this to happen. If these people want and need us to be more participatory to raise ratings, then it is an easy mental leap to see why digital television is something broadcasters want to happen. The trick is to get the American public to want it badly enough to spend the extra money and throw away their old analog sets.

Closure

At the end of this exercise, students will demonstrate their understanding by actively participating in the optional discussion in **Chapter 6.**

Lesson 3.6

Bringing Television into the Digital Age

What Is Digital Convergence?

Terms

capture or acquisition	**broadcast**	**killer app**
transmission or distribution	**narrowcast**	**digital convergence**
manipulation, processing, or operation	**passive viewing**	
recording or storage		
interactive viewing		

Lesson Notes

Before we can begin to understand the implications and impact of the move of broadcasting into the digital world, we have to first investigate and review two very important concepts:

- The timing of the recent publicity and news about **digital convergence** (the merging of computers, television, and cell phones) is no accident. The basis for the move to digital can be traced back to the implementation and reactions to three very important pieces of legislation that continue to help shape the industry.

- The foundations of the technology we currently use in broadcast video were discovered and nurtured more than 150 years ago. Even with digital convergence, the process still boils down to an analog conversion.

The social, legal, and regulatory aspects of how broadcasting (and possibly the Internet) is to be regulated are based on three laws:

- The **Radio Act of 1927,** which added the necessary regulations so that proper controls could be added to an industry that was "behaving badly."

- The **Communications Act of 1934**, which implemented many compromises such as public broadcasting and instituted the traditions of public trust that pervaded most of the discussions of the role broadcasting should play in our daily lives.

- The **Telecommunications Act of 1996,** which removed many of the regulations deemed no longer necessary in a maturing industry and helped broadcasters pay for the expensive digital conversion.

Of the three laws, the last may be credited with creating most of the chatter one hears about moving broadcasting into the digital age. The process began in 1986 when regulators and industry groups made a push to develop a high definition strategy. Converting processes to digital became part of the strategy that attempted "level the playing field" for American electronics firms, which were trying to compete with foreign companies that had been developing high definition systems for years.

The combination of high definition and digital transmissions has become a singular concept (Brinkley, 1997). Many aspects of the so-called **digital convergence** (the combination of television, telephones, and computers) can be attributed to the incentives provided to companies to implement the conversion of the broadcasting industry. All three industries went through a period of very rapid expansion and development at the end of the twentieth century that, in spite of a short period of abeyance during the "dot-com" meltdown in 1999–2002, continues to be very strong.

Understanding the Digitization Process

Digitization in broadcasting involves five separate processes:

- **Capture**

- **Processing**

- **Storage**

- **Transmission**

- **Presentation**

Three of these five processes have been going on for decades in the industry. Technological advances have been taking place in the capturing, storage, and manipulation of images, as will be shown later in this lesson. The recent hubbub over digitization has centered around the transmission and displaying aspects. Although it appears to be a brand new process, digitization still has to deal with the analog world we live in and, in many cases, hybrid conversions.

Capture

The process of capturing an image (still or moving) in cameras is done today with the CCD chip. Although many refer to these CCD cameras as digital, technically they are not. The capture process in a CCD camera does involve sampling (one of the three processes involved with digitization), but it really is doing it in a different format than what television has been doing since Farnsworth's days (converting light into electronics). These so-called digital cameras may use digital processing, but it takes place after the acquisition. A choice can be made by the manufacturer to continue the process in either digital or analog format. The internal conversion process in today's DV cameras makes them more closely related to digital. These cameras actually attempt to categorize and encode the signals after they are captured. But remember that the CCD chips themselves are analog.

Processing

Television systems for years have been dealing with various aspects of processing and operations. For example, all tape recorders have to deal with time-based corrections that are needed due to the technology involved. Producers and directors have been able to take advantage of the conveniences provided by digital effects generators, scopes, and switchers. It wouldn't be surprising if most K–12 studios in the country are now using digital switchers and character generators made relatively cheaply so that most schools can afford them. These devices are more in line with the technical definitions of what is *digital*.

Storage

To appreciate this portion of the process it is important to understand some of the important limitations and benefits surrounding storing data. First, all bits are identical. It doesn't matter what the data consist of; they can be used in general purpose computers. Unlike an analog signal that can be improved after it is captured by things such as time-based coding, improving digital data is limited by the quality of what transpires in the capture process, making the quality of the camera a much more significant piece of the puzzle. You've probably heard of the expression "a picture is worth a thousand words"; in the digital domain, a picture is really worth 4,000 by 3,000 pixels (three colors at 8 to 12 bits each in standard systems). With this calculation, it is easy to understand how file sizes can become fairly large. For example, one 35mm film frame requires 432,000 bits (about 54 MB), or about 4 GB per second (at 72 frames per second), or about 14,400 GB per hour.

Transmission

This is one of the two areas on which most of the recent emphasis has been placed (and the subject of most recent television advertising). As with capturing, the transmission process still is technically mostly analog because it relies on clocks on modems and the analog electromagnetic spectrum. In audio and video, regardless of the transmission process, a transmission and a receiver must be able to synchronize capturing and displaying. Although the data being transmitted may be in digital form, the actual envelope in which a signal is being transmitted still uses spectrum wavelengths. There are subtle differences between an analog transmission and a digital one in what is actually taking place between and inside the television, however.

From a technical standpoint, a digital transmission consumes considerably more channel space. A typical analog channel is allocated about 6Mbs (million bits per second), which easily accommodates the 4.2 Mbs that is required. On the other hand, a digital channel will be allocated approximately 18Mbs. Because there is no more room in their present space in the electromagnetic spectrum, the broadcasting channels are being moved into a higher space.

Teacher's Note: For an explanation of the electromagnetic spectrum and several excellent pictures that can be used in class, go to Electro Optical Industries (EOI), at **electro-optical. com/bb_rad/emspect.htm**, which has graciously permitted us to use this site for this course.

The compromises drawn up during the standards and practices meetings that culminated in the 1996 Telecommunications Act provided multiple transmission standards. For example, networks and/or local affiliates will be able to choose between 1080I (interlaced) and 720P (progressive scanned) broadcast patterns. The choice between the two boils down to how well interlaced patterns work in shows like sporting events, with a lot of switching and frame movement, versus the progressive standard that most closely relates to 35mm film. Although differences in display resolution are virtually indistinguishable, choosing the 720P standard will result in broadcasters being able to transmit multiple programs at once. Over the course of the next several years, broadcasters will continually flip back and forth between broadcast methods. For example, at times during the day they might choose to run standard analog shows (reruns, for example), which allow for up to four shows being transmitted simultaneously. Those broadcasters who utilize the 720P standard will be able to run two shows at once. Those in the 1080I will be limited to one show at a time. Everyone will still have room for two-way data transmission, regardless of the method chosen.

To make this transformation clearer, we can use a simple analogy. Let's say, for example, that we would like to transmit a theoretical cookie from one place to another using the analog process used currently by television broadcasters. First, we need to take the original cookie and transform it into another analogical form (cookie waves?). Then it is transmitted to the second location and transformed back into its original form (kind of like what Gene Roddenberry had in mind with "Beam me up, Scottie") . In a digital world, the original transmission wouldn't be a transformation of the original cookie, but rather a recipe for making cookies. At the other end, the receiver would make its own cookie!

Teacher's Note: The whole idea of the holodeck, as first used in the *Star Trek* series, is the foundation to the storytelling aspects of life in the digital world. For more information on this transformation in thinking about digital storytelling, see Janet Murray's *Hamlet on the Holodeck,* found in the References at the end of this text.

Presentation

This is perhaps one of the most confusing of all the processes, mainly because manufacturers have not been able to standardize terminology or the processes so that the average consumer can easily understand them. We have digital comb filters (which use digital manipulation to clean up interlaced lines for better resolution of images and text), progressive versus interlaced scans (still under debate about which is better, considering that technicians have actually been able to determine a fixed number of lines (720 and 1080 respectively) for each where they are virtually identical), flat screens (which help with distortion but are not digital), and HDTV. The last is the area of most confusion. As discussed in other lessons, the terms *high definition* and *digital* have no relationship to one another. Sure, there's better resolution, but if one also includes a 16:9 aspect ratio, the definition of high definition narrows considerably. The technologies were combined to help stimulate sales of the latter. Many networks and affiliates are broadcasting digitally now, but as of publication of this book, very few shows are both digital and high definition at the 16:9 aspect ratio.

Teacher's Note: A great, easy-to-understand discussion about aspect ratios and how they affect shooting can be found at **www.mediacollege.com/video/aspect-ratio/.**

Comparing Analog Video to Digital

A better way to analyze the analog and digital broadcasting environments might be to compare their features. Following is a simple chart comparing the two feature by feature. Although most of the terms are easily understood or have already been clarified, some may need further elaboration.

Analog	Digital
Broadcast transmissions	**Narrowcast** transmissions
Passive viewing	**Interactive viewing**
Linear editing	Nonlinear editing
Uses lower spectrum	Uses upper spectrum
2 audio channels (stereo)	5.1/7.1 audio channels (surround)
VCR output	DV output
Producer /network control of content	Viewer is producer

The differences between broadcasting and narrowcasting are subtle. Since we already have experiences with broadcasting it may be better to concentrate on narrowcasting. The end result of narrowcasting is the same: communication to a mass audience, done one person at a time. For example, a large group of people may all be viewing the same page on the Internet at the same time, but each at his or her own pace. A television show sent over the Internet would be viewed the same way, with the viewer maintaining control over the time and place.

A digital environment is said to be one in which viewer interactivity is common. One kind of interaction would be to simply determine how and when to watch a show. Of course the broad definition of interactivity means much more than that, including the possibility for two-way transmission of data (e.g., the results of a straw poll, making a purchase, or playing an interactive game).

The differences between linear and nonlinear editing will be discussed on other lessons, as will the use of the electromagnetic spectrum. More audio channels are also made available in the digital domain. Digital is not required for front-to-back surround sound, but true surround sound with separate signals sent to five or seven speakers individually is enhanced greatly with digital signals. The importance of DV output is also discussed in other lessons. In short, the difference is the level of compression offered by DV formats.

Viewer participation in a digital environment is more than selecting viewing times for a show. It also involves the ability for the audience to make scene selections, choose camera views, and even make content modifications. Imagine, for example, a world in which a sports fan could select which team member to watch during a team sporting competition or select a different ending to a favorite show.

An Evolving Participatory Environment

The ability for viewers to become participants in show content has not waited for the digital age to arrive. Producers have a longer history of attempting to bring their audiences into the content cycle. For example, in the 1960s viewers were treated to "sing-a-longs" with *Mitch Miller*, and to paint on the screen during *Winky-Dink*. Pay-per-view is a good example of viewers making content selections. Context-based content changes have been available using Line 21 on the screen, to be used for closed captioning and important weather data. More recently, public-opinion shows have been closely tied to related Web sites at which viewers may send in opinions and vote in straw polls. Personal video recorders like TiVo® permit viewers to create personal prime times (versus actual prime times that have been long established by the networks) that mimic their free times. Microsoft tried Web-TV for a while, with limited success.

But with all the choices for content, picture clarity, and viewer interaction, the key stumbling block to complete integration and conversion to the digital domain still appears to be the lack of a true **killer app,** that one show (like *Bonanza* was for color television) or concept that will convince the majority of Americans that they cannot live without a digital, interactive HD television (or converged machine, whatever we call it). Without the attraction to a mass audience, the pricing for equipment, content production, and delivery will remain high.

Teacher's Note: In the long run, we shouldn't be quite so impatient. Television, and digital video in particular, have evolved and democratized the production process in 50 years, whereas it took 500 years for the printing press to evolve into word processing.

Portfolio Project #1
Still Shots

Project Planning Considerations

Agenda

This project should be assigned very early in the course. It could be delayed until after scriptwriting is introduced, because it covers many of the elements of visualization. This, in effect, is the student's second visual story assignment. In addition, the completed still shots can be used in later classes to point out shortcomings in visual design, equipment technique, and so forth. Students will then learn from their own mistakes. A useful teaching moment presents itself when students are able to describe what they would have done differently on this project, had they had the knowledge imparted during the follow-up lessons.

It may take a while to get the the purpose of this project across because it is the first one. It is not unusual for students to be very literal and to need specific instructions. Most need to be told exactly (almost word-for-word) what they have to do to successfully complete projects. Spelling out the project in great detail is very tempting. However, the benefit of providing explicit instructions has to be balanced against the downside of taking away from the creative aspects of completing the projects. It is good to have examples of previous projects, and it is an even better idea to have examples of projects that have a few flaws in them. Students learn through critiquing even the more obvious shortcomings of others' works.

This project is really about telling a story visually with the help of an audio track. Some teachers use similar assignments that require voiceovers to tell the story. Although that may be a valid alternative approach, the intent is to have the student attempt to focus on the visual aspects. The audio track may be music, sound effects, or voiceovers, but it should be stressed that the audio track supplements and complements the video, not the other way around.

Students will also want to know other requirements, such as how long the recording has to be. It might be good to discuss the length in terms of an average or a target, keeping creativity in mind. There will be plenty of opportunities later in the course to require a specific length. In broadcasting, the timing of the video is an exact science. However, teaching this concept can wait in favor of creativity on this first assignment.

This activity gives students their first opportunity to use the camera for a purpose and to learn some fundamental editing techniques. Because it most likely will be assigned prior to the class session on editing, some students will already know about the content of Lesson 3.5 because it will introduce them to some of the functions through trial and error. In this project, students are graded on their ability to frame pictures, assemble edit them into a sequential storyline, audio dub music, and use the character generator to add the title page. Because this is the first project, you may have to spend a little extra time setting it up. Assessment is aided by scorecard models provided in **Appendix H.** The actual model is formatted specifically for this project.

If the "Teaching Chronology" is being followed, this activity will be assigned prior to Lesson 3.5. Therefore, you may wish to have students take three shots of their pictures to practice framing and focusing. Whether you tell them about any other shortcuts, like the still button on the camera (if it has one), depends on how far you wish to go with the concept of problem-based learning. This project will work either way, because you will have the ability to still the shots on the AV board during editing.

What This Project Is About

A good story does not need any words. Television is a visual medium. A good videographer needs to know how to create visual imagery. The objective of this project is to first show you how, then test your ability, to tell a story visually.

Student Instructions: You are to make a two- to three-minute video using pictures about a common theme. This is a test of your ability to frame and focus still pictures, assemble them into a final version with a continuous storyline, and add a complementary audio track. Unlike the introductory collage, the subject matter can be anything(it does not have to be about you). Examples are such things as

- favorite hobbies, or sports you play;

- favorite rock groups;

- movies you have seen;

- a series of pictures of your new house being built;

- a series of pictures about you growing up; or

- pictures of friends.

You could even do a series of pictures about a wonderful place you know about or would like to visit. The idea is for you to create a mood with the pictures and supplement them with audio. The number of pictures depends on the final length you choose. Too few pictures that are left on the screen too long can detract from a good project.

How You Will Be Evaluated

An assessment scorecard will be used to evaluate this project. As can be seen on the sample scorecard in **Appendix H**, the first section deals with a basic checklist of items such as the following:

- There is a title page.

- The length is within range.

- A story is being told.

In addition, a fundamental conceptual theme is tailored to meet the objectives of each project. For example, Part One is the layout using the following criteria specific to this activity:

Balance—Each frame should hold some type of symmetry. The pictures should take up the entire frame or be bordered and centered.

Unity—Each frame should look the same, unless a difference is planned and provides emphasis or makes a specific point. There should be continuity between pictures.

Emphasis—The storyline should remain constant between pictures. There should be no confusion about why an individual picture has been included. The main idea of the storyline or premise must be clearly understandable.

Teacher's Note: Some students may have a problem identifying a main theme or idea for their project because the concept is almost too basic. When you mention that there must be a storyline, most interpret that to mean that there must be some type of plot involved. All you are trying to get them to do is map an idea conceptually. The best way to explain is through example. It could be about their summer vacation, their house being built, a competition they went to recently, pictures of themselves growing up, a favorite musical group, and so forth. Once completed, you will be using this project to introduce the idea of a storyboard. Because all the pictures are unified, there is no need for a detailed explanation of the shots for each frame. When covering a storyboard for a more complicated project that contains many different shots and angles, the storyboard will be used to indicate each camera shot in terms of angles, lighting, and so forth.

RESOURCES

Brinkley, J. 1997. *Defining vision: How broadcasters lured the government into inciting a revolution in television.* New York: Harcourt Brace.

Driscoll, R. 1994. The act of discovery. *Harvard Educational Review* 31, no. 1: 21–32.

Kizlik, R. 1998. *Strategic teaching, strategic learning, and thinking skills.* Available: www.adprima. com/strategi.htm. (Accessed September 14, 2004).

Murray, J. 1998 *Hamlet on the holodeck: The future of narrative in cyberspace.* Cambridge, MA: MIT Press.

Shouten, D., and R. Watling 1997. *Media action projects: A model for integrating video in project-based education, training, and community development.* University of Nottingham, UK: Urban Programme Research Group, School of Education, p. 16.

CHAPTER 4

Writing for a Visual Medium

INTRODUCTION AND LESSON GOALS

In its finest form, television is about telling a story using visual means. It took a while, but early television pioneers eventually realized that the television medium was not simply "a radio with pictures" (Barnouw, 1990, p. 12). It is a unique medium with its own nuances, strengths, and shortcomings. If anything, a primary premise for this course is to teach that a television segment is only as good as its plan, its vision (no pun intended), and its script. Producers who can bring all the technological enhancements in the world to bear on their productions simply cannot mitigate the basic need for an underpinning of a strong storyline. The temptation is to give in to the desire to fluff up the story with special effects: *all fluff and no stuff . . . all sizzle and no steak.*

For the purposes of this chapter, the term **script** actually refers to three things: the dialogue, the video devices used by the scriptwriter (and interpreted by the director), and any supplemental audio that is used to tell the story. A television script, then, not only tells the talent what to say but also what to do. The script also introduces the director to the overriding mood or feeling of the segment. In other words, the script is the written plan or blueprint for the entire production as visualized by a storyboard. This course makes a distinction between two kinds of script formats. A **teleplay** script is much more detailed and tells a story. A **news script** does not require as much detail because it tells a story of much a shorter length, and it has its own requirements as to writing style. The newscast also has its own form of notation and punctuation to indicate what to say and how to say it. A storyboard is the scaffolding, or schematic, that supports both script formats.

The primary goal of the lessons in this chapter is to introduce students to these two script formats and the importance of storyboards, and to dispel any preconceived notions that scripting, video, and supplemental audio are three separate functions, when, in fact, they all are interdependent. They are all job responsibilities of the scriptwriter.

DIGGING DEEPER

There are several textual and online resources and activities dealing with scripting and storyboards that belong in any teacher's repertoire. Good books that explains how the storyboard fits into the overall production scheme are *Video Goals: Getting Results with Pictures and Sound* and *Bare Bones Camera Course,* by Tom Schroeppel. Information on how to order these books may be found in **Appendix J**.

The **Web-ASSISTant** Web site lists several additional online resources for scriptwriting that can be found on the Internet. These links may be found at the end of the "Chapter Four" page in the "Digging Deeper" section.

SEQUENCING THE LESSONS IN THIS CHAPTER

The lessons in this chapter were written in contextual sequence. That is to say, they have continuity with regard to subject matter and can be taught in the exact order they are presented. However, to reach the specific goals attempted by this course, it might be better to consider following the suggested sequence outlined in the "Teaching Chronology" in **Chapter 1**. At a minimum, it makes sense to at least consult that prescribed format to make an informed decision.

Storyboards

Lesson Planning Considerations

(**Approx. Time:** 25–35 minutes)

Agenda

Students may have trouble visualizing how versatile a storyboard is. This session teaches how a storyboard differs from an outline, and how important a properly thought-out storyboard is to a successful video project. Certainly, younger students will yearn to get started. They will want to wander about shooting footage with no preconceived idea about what or why they are shooting. Aimless shooting is not necessarily damaging, especially in the beginning, when students are getting used to the equipment. However, the teacher should differentiate between using this type of shoot as an orientation to the equipment and permitting an unstructured environment for all production. It is imperative that students learn that even an incomplete storyboard is better than no plan at all.

What students seem to object to most about having to write storyboards is drawing pictures. Creating a storyboard with artistically correct sketches is not the focus of the exercise. Rather, it is intended to get students to begin to think visually through a storyline to be sure all the important shots are included. To get them to think in visual terms, the storyboard should contain some type of visual element to supplement the audio track. That is why the *Stop Action* project (#2) is particularly useful. Placing pictures in a video in a sequential order to tell a story is exactly the same operation as developing a storyboard. In fact, the picture board *is* the storyboard. It is a good idea to have students write down a few simple sentences describing the story they are trying to tell, to number the pictures, and to jot down how each fits into the overall story. In essence, this outlining technique is the first stage of the storyboard development process.

Objectives and Outcomes

At the end of this lesson, students should be able to

- specify the major steps leading to broadcast scripts used in broadcast videos.

- describe four major uses of storyboards in the production sequence. and

- plan and produce a storyboard free of continuity errors for a short teleplay or newscast.

Mediated and Textual Support

As mentioned in the "Digging Deeper" section, there are several sites on the Internet that provide information on how to obtain storyboard software. The **Web-ASSISTant** Web site lists a few of these.

Lesson Readiness

Ask students if they have ever heard the expression "A picture is worth a thousand words." While the majority have probably heard of the expression, what it means to each student will vary significantly. Some will say that pictures often show so much that there will be as many interpretations as there are people. The intended end of this activity is to provide a good starting point for storyboards: that it is often easier to describe something visually. Inadvertently, the activity ends up also providing a good starting point for later lessons on visual literacy, and will be referred to at the appropriate place in that chapter.

Another way to orient students toward the differences between writing for television and for other media is to have them follow the instructions in the **Script Quest** activity found on the **Web-ASSISTant** Web site. In this activity, students look for examples of different types of script formats and writing styles.

Closure

Students will be responsible for providing storyboards for future projects as soon as this lesson is completed, which, according to the "Teaching Chronology," occurs just prior to the "Stop Action" video assignment. In addition, there are two or three possible questions on the sample quizzes and exams found on the **Web-ASSISTant** Web site.

Pre-Class Activity

Student Instructions: You may have heard of the following expression:

"A picture is worth a thousand words."

Write down what this expression means to you.

Teacher's Note: The answers you get from this exercise will be very different than what you might expect. Students will come up with several different connotations. Some of your students will be ahead of you and really *get it*. They will think beyond the current problem and recognize that a picture is subject to many interpretations. Although you will want students to focus on the problem of storyboarding, do not discourage that answer. Rather, ask them to *hold that thought*—it falls right into your later discussions on elements of design where you pose the following corollary question:

If a picture is subject to several different connotations, then is it possible to minimize misinterpretations through a structured design approach? Said in another way, is it possible to create an image that guarantees that 100% of your audience interprets it exactly the same way?

Finally, recall the *Understanding Television* video in which the narrator talks about how a video screen is really made up of a thousand pictures, just to portray a single word: CARS. You might want to play this scene again for the students to refresh their memories and to reinforce the point. Challenge students to choose an image (even a square with a circle inside it) and see how many different interpretations they come up with, even for this simple design!

The purpose of this exercise is to orient you to the fact that the major difference between video and other forms of media is the **importance of the visual element**. Visualization can both add to and detract from a viewer's understanding of your premise. To properly plan your visual story, you need to put the major scenes and sequences on to a storyboard so that you may see how your storyline might be subject to (mis)interpretation by your viewers.

Terms

storyboard uses (4)	teleplay
partially scripted storyboard	continuity secretary
fully scripted storyboard	coordinating secretary
	scriptwriter job description

Using a Storyboard to Visualize a Story

Have you ever thought about whether the words you conjure up to describe a picture are the same as the person next to you would use? Have you ever wondered why the expression uses "a thousand words" rather than a hundred or several or a bunch? Have you ever considered how the careful selection of words might play into the idea of a video where there are pictures **and** words?

The primary idea conveyed by the expression "A picture is a worth a thousand words" is that a picture tells a lot. But the idea of a thousand words may also mean that there are so many different ways to look at something that the viewer might just as easily get the wrong idea about the picture as understand all the nuances. Thinking visually, then, means much more than having a picture to go along with your words. If the picture and dialogue are not synchronized they could conflict with each other or give the wrong impression.

A **scriptwriter's job** encompasses two things:

- **writing the dialogue** and

- **deciding how the shots and scenes** are to be visualized.

The storyboard is where these tasks are accomplished. A storyboard is a visual method to plan and outline for a visual medium. The storyboard not only tells what the scenes are going to be but also how they are going to be captured; all the way down to the **mechanics** and **methods** of production. Often there is really nothing that appears on the storyboard to indicate that there are special considerations with the visual portion of the story. The video is simply a reinforcement of the audio. In this case the storyboard would not show the process you went through to make the shot. However, the process needs to be the same, even if you decide that the video has no particular significance: You need to think all your shots through and make those decisions in advance. Because we are learning this process, often a thought will occur to you as you are doing the shoot.

The storyboard is where all your organizational efforts come together. It is where you visually describe the outline of the goals and objectives and the atmosphere that surrounds your production.

If you were a director for a professional production company doing a professional shoot, you would have a **continuity secretary** at your disposal who would note all the scene changes that come about as the shoot progresses. The job of the continuity secretary is to update the storyboard when changes are made.

There are different styles of storyboards, depending on the purpose of the shoot. For example, a newscast requires only the storyline, representation of what inserts you will use, and how they will be inserted.

The storyboard for a news story has fewer pictures and contains more production cues and abbreviations. This is often referred to as a **partially scripted** storyboard.

A storyboard that supports a story or a **teleplay** involves more cuts, and, therefore, more pictures. A teleplay is a script developed for television as episodes or situation comedies. Scripts written for teleplays are referred to as **fully scripted** storyboards. They contain more specific blocking notes for the talent and camera shots and angles for the cameraperson.

Using a Storyboard to Carry Out the Objectives of a Production

As you develop your story line, you should be able to indicate a reason for each cut. The storyboard contains the audio line as well as the **objective** of each scene or segment. As you develop the storyline, not only will you decide the nuance portrayed within the shot, you also have to ensure that there is continuity between and among the shots. Your cuts will have to be appropriately timed to the dialogue. Many different storyboard formats exist. The one used in this course contains room on each frame to indicate the audio cue and the stated objective for each cut to be sure that you focus on their importance.

Teacher's Note: Show the storyboard sample provided in **Appendix I.**

Producing a storyboard in a professional environment can be an involved and elaborate affair. Therefore, quite often the scriptwriter will use a software package to aid in the process. The storyboards used by professionals are much more elaborate because the whole process is more involved. At our level, we are only interested in ensuring that the storyline includes all the scenes necessary to provide continuity between shots and to be sure nothing is left out of the story.

Teacher's Note: You may also wish to discuss how, in a professional environment, the stress and strain of producing a weekly show has forced scriptwriters for television to *package* their work. For example, standard shots and takes are used to show reactions; standard joke styles may be used. That is why the *situations* in situation comedies tend to copy one another. When someone discovers that something works (that is, is well-received by an audience), other shows tend to copy the format. The considerable pressures of producing a weekly show tend to make the show format more and more vanilla. A good example of this process can be found in *Television Today and Tomorrow*, by Jankowski and Fuchs (1996). Chapter 2, "The Creative Product," contains several passages that describe this scenario precisely. Information on to how this book may be ordered can be found in **Appendix J**.

Using a Storyboard to Sequence a Production

When you produce a teleplay, you will not always have the opportunity to shoot scenes or segments in a **linear** fashion (in the same order as the storyline). For example, you might have occasion to shoot location scenes together, even though they take place at different times during the story. This is what happens to television shows like *NYPD Blue,* which intersperse on-location shots with scenes shot at the studio in California. When you view the final product, you see the scenes in their appropriate sequence. However, it is not uncommon for all on-location shots for all episodes for the entire season to be taken care of at the same time over the period of 10–15 days. This saves the producers considerable time and expense. A **fully scripted storyboard allows the producer to shoot out of sequence**. This is something that may make sense, even in our projects. By shooting all of the scenes that require similar clothing, hair styles, time of day, or location, the production crew can save considerable money and effort.

Using a Storyboard to Determine Supply Requirements

One of the most frustrating (and most expensive) moments during a professional shoot is when the entire production crew is assembled and is on location, the talent have learned their lines, the shoot is about to begin, and the director discovers that they have forgotten a necessary prop, a costume, or some other support material (like videotape, batteries, a microphone, or an extension cord). Indeed, this all may be the **ultimate responsibility of the production assistant**. However, in reality, the storyboard is where all this begins. The creative team is responsible for providing enough information on the storyboard so that proper decisions may be made in advance. The **storyboard is a written plan** for the entire production and must be treated as such. **In real life,** mistakes and oversights can be **very expensive. In a school environment, being unprepared could cost a letter grade.**

Using Script Notes

In addition to an accurate storyboard, we need to make **script notes** to log our tapes by which scenes are shot by which camera, and on which tapes. When we put our production together, we refer to these notes about which scenes are found on which tapes. We also add these notes to the index of all the tapes stored for safekeeping. This is particularly important if more than one camera is used. The script notes indicate which camera was used for which shots. The <u>coordinating secretary</u> is responsible for this task on a professional production crew. We will assign one or two people for this task during our *Sweeps* project (#8) at the end of the term. (In reality, we will combine the roles of the coordinating secretary with that of a continuity secretary, a job function we will describe more fully in a later lesson.)

In summary, one can say that a **storyboard affords the scriptwriter the ability** to

- <u>organize</u> the story,

- <u>sequence </u> the production shoot,

- <u>define the objective</u> of each scene or segment, and.

- <u>plan</u> the entire production.

Follow-up Activity

Student Instructions: Throughout this course, you will often hear that television commercials may be the perfect production activity. They may well have to be. Commercials occupy the most expensive block of time in the entire broadcast day. A 15-second spot can run into many millions of dollars to produce and broadcast. Therefore, nothing can be left to chance. No commercial can be successfully produced without extensive planning and a very accurate storyboard. Because television is a visual medium, the visual aspect of the commercial is often more important to the storyline than the audio portion. The production team must be sure every visual second counts in the commercial so that the message gets across to its target audience.

To stress the importance of the storyboard, in this assignment you are to view a television commercial and describe how important the storyboard must have been. You are to describe the commercial and point out the one scene in the commercial that required a crucial video shot without which the commercial would have failed to get its message across. Every commercial has one or more *defining moments* that are crucial to understanding its premise. It may be a close-up, a glance, a single word or phrase, or another visual. Try to find a commercial in which this is very obvious.

Because this is a class about visualization, you should videotape your example and bring it to class.

This assignment is due: _____/_____/_____.

Lesson 4.2

Visual Storytelling in a Teleplay

Lesson Planning Considerations

(**Approx. Time:** 25–35 minutes)

Agenda

Students often groan when you tell them that they cannot go out and just shoot footage. Second only to creating special effects, shooting ad hoc footage around campus is a favorite activity. Apparently, telling them that they have to plan their shoot and write a script makes the exercise seem more like school than fun. To many, scriptwriting is a chore, something a teacher makes them do to take the fun out of things. As a teacher, your challenge is to make this part of the process as much fun as the actual shoot.

Although the trial and error method has its benefits in the early stages of learning how to work the camera, in the long run, a production will be much more successful if it is properly planned. You have to remain firm on this point. The best way to explain that a planned shoot is better than one that is ad-libbed is to point out that even improvisation sessions are the result of hundreds of hours of planning sessions and practice. Indeed, most high school students simply are not very good at ad-libbing. Otherwise, why do drama teachers spend so much time on the subject?

Simply put, a good story is a good story and often carries a program. When people were asked why they returned to see the blockbuster movie *Titanic* several times, most replied that it was because of the love story between the two protagonists. Fewer returned because of the special effects. *Titanic* did not even win the Oscar for best screenplay that year!

The following lessons break down the story-building experience into some very practical steps. They are fundamental and will carry through, regardless of the medium. These series of lessons concentrate on the content of the scripts and storyboards rather than the style or format. The latter will be covered in subsequent lessons.

Objectives and Outcomes

As a result of these lessons, students will be able to

• contrast and compare the writing styles for newscasts and teleplays.

• define five major terms used in newscast scripts,

• describe the three main parts of a script and the corresponding role each plays in the development of a successful storyline, and

• contrast and compare the terms *premise* and *hook*.

Mediated and Textual Support

Twilight Zone videos are used at the beginning of this lesson as an orientation devise and as a supporting resource for this lesson. Rod Serling is a great role model to demonstrate the benefits of good scriptwriting. Many may not be aware of his background, but he was quite a celebrity in his day. Under the guidance and support of Hubel Reynolds, head of entertainment at CBS, Serling made a name for himself on the acclaimed *Playhouse 90* and *Studio One* anthology shows, winning three Emmys for his live broadcasts in the early 1950s. His stories had social connotations. He demonstrated the "charismatic value" of black-and-white television and would have used it "even if color was an option." (CBS, 1995). Reynolds, a patron of anthology television, left CBS in 1959, followed soon afterward by Serling and many other quality writers. Serling was often criticized by his peers and the network censors for his controversial social commentary. After leaving the anthologies behind in New York, he moved to Hollywood and came up with the idea of creating Martians and monsters to say what "Republicans and Democrats could not" (CBS, 1995). *Twilight Zone* was a continuation of his need to make social commentary and a scathing reaction to censorship, housed in a sci-fi setting. His scripts demonstrated a sensibility for the little guy, redemptions, and second chances, often clothed in societal fears and twists of fate. Several episodes may be purchased with performance rights from educational video distributors, any one of which would be suitable for this exercise.

The cyber course at **www.cybercollege.com** provides a module called *Scriptwriting Guidelines* that should help to review. Dr. Ron Whittaker, the Web site designer, provides certain limited copyrights to teachers to use this course, as long as proper references are made.

There are several scriptwriting software packages on the market. They often include automatic formatting and notations specifically designed for television. Some of them are quite expensive, but they may be useful, especially if you wish to place additional emphasis on writing. One such product is Scriptware by Cinovation, Inc. Specific ordering information may be found on the **Web-ASSISTant** Web site on the page that supplements **Chapter 4**.

Lesson Readiness

There are plenty of role models to demonstrate the fundamental concept that television is visual storytelling. Scriptwriters like Rod Serling certainly *got it*. He had very little opportunity to use special effects. As a matter of fact, most of his sets look hokey by current standards. Yet students of all ages still enjoy the opportunity to watch his stories. Why? Because Serling knew how to tell a visual story, even without special effects. An ironic twist at the end became his trademark **hook.** All his shows followed a similar format. They had a specific **beginning** in which the premise was developed, a **middle**, where the story unfolded, and an **end**, which contained the denouement and ironic twist. He stretched one's imagination and made even the most outlandish circumstance appear plausible. That is because he knew how to push the envelope but, at the same time, anchor it in some bit of reality. He played on fears and anxieties common to us all.

This does not mean that Serling would not have used special effects had he had access to them. Who knows what kind of monster team Serling and Spielberg might have made, had they been contemporaries?. What Serling's experience points out is the value of deprivation in the initial stages of teaching students how to make videos. If you let them, kids tend to gravitate toward the technology and focus on gizmos without building a solid foundation based on a solid storyline. Showing any *Twilight Zone* episode is a great way to orient students to the value of great storytelling.

Closure

Lessons 4.3 and 4.4 are a continuation of these discussions on style differences between news and teleplay scripts, in which students will be asked to demonstrate their understanding of the conceptual and stylistic designs of the two forms of writing. They will also be asked to write scripts for all future projects after these lessons are completed.

Pre-Lesson Activity

Twilight Zone Video

Student Instructions: We are going to watch a *Twilight Zone* episode. Many of you are very familiar with this early series but may have never seen one of the original episodes. When you are watching this video, concentrate on how Rod Serling unfolds the storyline, how he economizes on the use of time, and how little a role special effects play in creating the illusions. Serling did not have a lot of technology to work with, yet somehow, this did not detract from the quality of the shows.

What do you think are the most enduring qualities of Serling's writing?

_____

_____.

Terms

three parts to a script:	**premise versus plot**	**hook**
-beginning	**power of suggestion**	
-middle		
-end		

Lesson Notes

Many of the early pioneers thought that television was simply a **radio with pictures**. The early programs were long on dialogue and short on camera movement and special effects. In some respects it is fortunate that this happened, because it gives us an opportunity to see how a storyline is developed.

Television shows today often miss the story development aspects of good storylines. All too often, too much emphasis is placed on special effects to hook an audience. To many of its critics, television has become too much **hook** and too little **premise.**

As we will see in later lessons, the synergy between the video and audio portions of a program is really what makes it effective. But all the recent advances in special effects would not be as effective if the idea of a strong storyline had not been perfected. The storylines of the early TV pioneers like Alfred Hitchcock and Rod Serling came out of episodic radio, for which a strong dialogue was the foundation of the entire program's success. Even Shakespeare understood the concept of a well-organized play. Each performance had distinct **sections or acts**. All played a significant and consistent role in revealing the plot.

The early television series writers understood this. Even continuous series like *The Fugitive* had a distinct beginning, middle, and ending in each episode. The plot was introduced in act one. It was developed and carried to its end in the second act. The final scenes (the epilogue) cleaned up loose ends and carried the plot forward to future episodes. In other words, a good story has three distinct parts: **the beginning, the middle,** and **the ending**. In this type of storyline, each plays an important role. To keep things simple, remember:

- In the beginning, you tell the audience **what you're going to tell them.** In a teleplay, this is where the premise for the story is developed and where the main characters are introduced.

- In the middle, you **tell them.** In a teleplay, this is where all consequential action tasks place.

- In the ending, you tell the audience what **you just told them** (summarize). Often, there will be an epilogue or a resolution to the problems posed in act one and carried out in act two.

Once you learn this developmental style, you will do well in anything you write or present, whether it is a speech, a class you teach, a story you write, or a term paper. The rule of threes is quite important. Even many experts in the field of education agree that people tend to remember things longer after they have seen or heard them three times.

The next thing to understand about building a story is that two underlying principles make it successful. First, there must be a clear **premise**. A premise differs from the **plot.** The premise is the actual, founding idea or concept that you are trying to get across. In our sessions about the production sequence, building a premise was one of the early steps. In fiction, the premise has to be built upon a believable idea, or one that at least starts out as being possible. In a commercial, or a public service announcement (PSA), the premise has to be one the viewer can identify with it as being an important issue or need.

To make the viewer remember or want to stay interested in your premise, you need a **hook**. A hook is what you insert in your segment to catch your viewer's attention. Most movie trailers (those portions of the movie shown as advertising in the theater prior to the feature attraction) are full of hooks. These may be special effects, a superstar, or another attraction like violence or sexual innuendo.

In television, as with any other visual medium, a scriptwriter may add **atmosphere** to the storyline with or without actually having to write it into the dialogue. The atmosphere of the segment is the environment in which the story is set. It may be the mood, the weather, the time of day, the location, and so forth. All these help to complete the the feelings the viewer is supposed to sense, and are certainly considerations while developing a storyboard. In later lessons, we will develop ideas on how to accomplish differing atmospheres using colors, light, camera angles, and so forth.

Because television is a visual medium, the story may either be helped or hurt by its supporting video. A good story is made better when the visual portion supplements the dialogue. In other words, the **video and audio portions should overlap but not duplicate** each other. This is true regardless of the type of show you are presenting: whether it be a talk show, a news show, or a story. A production in which the video and the audio replicate each other becomes quite boring. To understand this you might try this experiment: When a sporting event is being broadcast on the radio and on television at the same time, watch the TV with the volume down and turn the radio volume up. On the radio, the announcer has to describe the action more thoroughly than the television person does. Imagine how boring a regular show or movie would be if the script described not only the dialogue but also the action. With a video portion, the scriptwriter can **economize** on the dialogue.

Even more effective is a show or movie that uses the video portion to **augment** the script. This gives the scriptwriter the opportunity to have characters make implied statements rather than saying them outright. The video shots make or emphasize a point, or reinforce dialogue that is taking place.

For example, a writer might imply that the speaker in the dialogue is telling a lie by inserting **a close-up of the facial expression of someone** who knows the truth. You must have seen numerous examples in shows or movies.

The concept we are trying to get across here is probably best summed up by saying: **what goes without saying . . . probably does!** The <u>power of suggestion</u> is an extremely effective and useful tool. A good visual clue suggests its meaning and is a very powerful tool. It took quite a while for television scriptwriters to figure this out. When they were forced to by the network censors, the early pioneers asked viewers to use their imagination. But the technology at their disposable was limited, something that is no longer an obstacle.

Follow-up Activity

Student Instructions: Following are some examples of how a scriptwriter might supplement a script or storyboard with visual enhancements, which will be covered in more detail in a later lesson. Can you recall specific examples from a recent television show or movie of each one of these techniques?

1. A **close-up** showing an actor's facial reaction to what is being said by another.

    _____.

2. A **focal length transition** between two actors or groups to show their reactions.

    _____.

3. Using **another medium, like a photo or list**. For example, a courtroom scene in which someone is crossing off a list of names of those testifying. A few scenes later, we see that a few names have already been crossed off, indicating that they have already spoken.

    _____.

4. Using **time lapse photography** with a camera to show the passing of time.

    _____.

5. Using **cover/establishing shots** to introduce segments.

    _____.

6. An **audience shot** of laughter or applause.

    _____.

7. Showing scenes leading up to a violent act, but then **fading to black**.

    _____.

Lesson 4.3

Active Versus Passive Voice in News Scripts

Lesson Planning Considerations

(**Approx. Time**: 25–30 minutes)

Agenda

The **Script Writing** exercise (on the **Web-ASSISTant** Web site) points out that there are several differences between scripts written for teleplays and those written for newscasts. Not only do news scripts contain their own notational shorthand, but the writing style varies significantly from other forms of dialogue. When writing dialogue for a narrative story, the key is to write in conversational style. This includes the intentional improper use of grammar and syntax, when appropriate. The tone in a newscast, on the other hand, requires a different style. To enhance the anchor's authoritative demeanor and believability, the news script requires shorter sentences written in the active voice. It is not enough to simply point out the fact that the active voice is a requirement. Younger students generally have not yet crystallized the subtleties of *active* versus *passive* voice. The intent of this lesson is to help students understand that changing a sentence to the active voice is not simply a matter of removing all the forms of the verb *to be*. Rather, it implies a conversion of the entire tone and sentence structure.

After a short introduction on what active and passive tenses are and the importance of the active voice in news writing, the bulk of this lesson is devoted to having students work on two writing exercises. The first is a group of three articles that includes important information about newsworthy events. Students are to try to put together a news story without the use of any form of the verb *to be*. Most will have already experienced an English assignment that was quite similar in nature. However, those who remember such an experience most likely have no idea why they were to write in this manner.

Objectives and Outcomes

At the end of this session, students will be able to

• relate that the preferred writing style for news reporting is the active voice and

• rewrite news stories by removing unnecessary occurrences of the verb *to be*.

Mediated and Textual Support

Several videos focus on teaching how to write the news. Although most concentrate on newspaper journalism, there are enough similarities in style between newspaper and television writing that the content of the videos should prove useful. The Annenberg/CPB Project sponsors a series on news writing. Three videos from this set are particularly useful:

    #1: *What Is News?*

    #6: *Good Writing versus Good Reporting*

    #8: *Broadcast News Writing*

Information on how these may be ordered is included in **Appendix J.** Also, a link has been provided on the **Web-ASSISTant** Web site. Because Internet links are subject to change, check the **Web-ASSIS-Tant** Web site on the "Chapter Four" page for updates to see if this link is still active. Where possible, an alternative will be provided, should this link be removed.

Lesson Readiness

Some students may object to being forbidden to use the verb *to be* in sentences. They might state that they hear it on television all the time. These objections actually make for a great introduction and focal point for this lesson. The idea is that, by striving to cut these out, the sentence structure will automatically become cleaner, even if a sentence or two contains the verb. The goal is not to eradicate the use of the verb but to get a long description of an event down to the required time limit. Sometimes this includes removing some of the other, unnecessary descriptors also.

In essence, you are teaching one of the steps in the news filtering process. Recall the news filtering paradigm from an earlier session. One of the filters news story go through is simple correction of the story. Note that there is a typo in the original news story being used for the students to edit. $10,000 was written incorrectly as 10,00. The editor has to decide whether the original story meant $10,000 or $10. Although $10,000 maybe more obvious in this case, it might not be so clear in other cases.

Closure

Students write up the review exercise, without using the verb *to be*. The review activities in lessons 4.3 and 4.4 were adapted from an exercise handed out during the Florida Institute of Film in Education (FIFE) Annual Convention in 1997.

Lesson Notes

In earlier lessons, we have seen that news scripts contain their own notational shorthand. You may have noticed that the writing style also varies significantly from other forms of dialogue. When writing dialogue for a narrative story, you should mimic conversations that would take place in a given situation. For example, to maintain the **atmosphere**, it is acceptable to use bad grammar if that is how your character usually speaks. Realism plays an important role in maintaining the believability of your dialogue. Much of the distress over the use of four-letter words in movie dialogues is based on concern that expletives are so common in everyday conversation. Some moviegoers do not wish to hear this, so they choose not to go to those movies.

Television, especially a newscast, is meant for general audiences who have less control over what they see and hear. For that reason, the language you use in a newscast is certainly different from that of a movie. But the news format is really much more than simply cleaning up foul language and the proper use of syntax. Over time, a certain **delivery style** evolved that was born out of necessity and business requirements. You may have experienced this during the news reading activities found in **Chapter 6**.

For the longest time, the news bureaus of the major networks were run as entirely separate entities. There would be a president of XYZ network entertainment and a president of the corresponding news divisions. Neither had the power to choose talent, use or deny the use of stories, or even solicit sponsors for the other's division. Although business interests have resulted in this separation becoming less definite in recent years, one thing that has remained separate is the writing style for a news story, which is considerably different from that of a narrative story.

The first thing that you will notice about a news story is that there is very little use of the verb **to be** in any of its forms, whether it is used alone or as a helper for another verb. This does not mean that you will never hear *to be*. But you certainly will hear less of it than you would during a conversation between two people. The rationale behind this is twofold. First, because you are trying to deliver so much information in a short time, it is thought that the fewer words you use, the better.

Second, and most important, an active verb (not modified by the verb *to be*) is more powerful in tone. The industry even went through a period during the 1980s when employees took power writing courses at work. Power writing, as the name implies, means adding directness in style to your words: Do not mince words. Consequently, the direct approach is considered more honest and straightforward. This use of straightforward talk, coupled with the ability to look the audience straight in the eye, supported by the electronic teleprompter positioned right next to the camera lens, gives the appearance of honesty in reporting.

There was a time when the label "honest reporter" was coveted. In fact, during the 1960s a poll was taken asking the television public who they felt was the **most honest man in America. Walter Cronkite**, the news anchor at CBS, won that title from a list that included the president of the country.

With this in mind, we are going to have the opportunity to see for ourselves what it takes to write in the news style and avoid the use of the verb *to be* and all its derivatives. The handout you will be given reviews what the use of this verb is, what it looks like, and how to avoid it. **The exercise is to solidify your understanding of how this change in verbs also changes the tone of the story.**

Teacher's Note: Another good way to teach this lesson might be to put the following two sentences on the board:

>   Tom broke the toy.
>   The toy was broken by Tom.

Ask students to compare them. Tell them that, in this case, really only the number of words differs. Television news writers are continually looking for ways to shorten their sentences. The first choice does that. Then put the next two sentences on the board:

>   I broke the toy.
>   The toy broke on me.

In this case, not only is the second example less efficient, but the meaning changes (the shifting of blame). In this case, there are two reasons why the active voice may be of more use to the news editor.

In-Class Activity

So You Think the Active Voice Is Easy?

Student Instructions: Write a 30-second news story from the facts below. Assume it is for a late evening newscast. Use complete sentences. Use no form of the verb *to be* (**is, am, are, was, were, be, being, been**). Any passive construction contains some form of the verb *to be*. Your story should contain only active voice verbs.

Robbery at First State Bank in Smithville at 10 this morning: man wearing blue jeans, blue jean jacket, tennis shoes, sunglasses, and ski cap is considered the suspect. Didn't show a gun, but teller says she was handed a note claiming he was armed; after being told to do so, the teller (Miss Amy Lou Scaredstiff) put all her money in a sack and handed it over. Official estimate is $10,00 missing; he escaped on foot into a residential area north of the bank. Acting on a tip, Smithville police saw suspect walking along Rogers Street about an hour after the robbery. He was taken into custody; suspect is identified as Ronnie Jones, 38, of Springdale. A sack containing $10,00 was found on him when he was arrested. He is being held under $25,000 bond following arraignment; no injuries were reported.

Possible response:

A robbery took place at the First State Bank in Smithville at 10 A.M. The alleged suspect, a male, wore blue jeans and jacket, tennis shoes, sunglasses, and a ski cap. Although he didn't show a gun, the teller, Miss Amylou Scaredstiff, claims he handed her a note demanding that she put all her money into a sack. Officials estimate that the suspect ran off on foot into a residential area north of the bank with an estimated $10,000.

Police spotted a man who looked like the suspect carrying a sack containing $10,000 walking along Rogers Street about a half hour after the robbery. Police are holding the alleged suspect, identified as Ronnie Jones, 38, of Springdale, under $25,000 bond following arraignment.

Teacher's Note: To make this reader fit into a 30-second time slot, additional changes will have to be made. The suggested answer intentionally does not include those changes. A good follow-up discussion is to have students identify which elements could be deleted to make the writing more tight. These edits include the deletion of what the suspect wore and exactly what he was carrying. Your students will come up with others.

Lesson 4.4

Get the Lead Right

Lesson Planning Considerations

(**Approx. Time:** 25–30 minutes)

Agenda

Expecting first-year students to write short, concise, and energizing *leaders* might be a little too much. However, correcting someone else's work is easier than trying to find fault in one's own. This activity involves taking raw news information similar to that which comes off a newswire and reworking it into a news story fit for a television newscast. Those who have followed the "Teaching Chronology" will have already discussed the news media paradigm in **Chapter 2**. After explaining the process of correcting the copy, one can easily see how there might be communications problems between an ENG and the local news agency, even if either side does not have a personal agenda or the intention to color the news in any way. Care must be taken not to seriously alter the content of the news while correcting its format.

This class is entirely a work session and should be completed within 20 to 30 minutes. If time is a problem, you can divide the topics by groups and have each group work on a different story. To review, each group reads their story aloud for the rest of the class to critique.

Objectives and Outcomes

At the end of this session, students should be able to write a good lead. They are to understand how the lead can act as a **teaser** to gain viewer attention.

Mediated and Textual Support

The Annenberg/CPB Project video series also includes a video titled *Hard News Leads,* which discusses and demonstrates the power of the summary lead. It may be ordered directly from **www.learner.org**, or from the link provided on the **Web-ASSISTant** Web site.

Lesson Readiness

Ask the students to reflect on the previous scriptwriting sessions for newscasts by completing the short questionnaire. They are to list three differences between a script written for a teleplay and one written for a newscast, as discussed to date in class.

Closure

Students are to complete and review the follow-up activity. The in-class review should provide an indication of how well the class absorbed the material and are able to synthesize it.

Pre-class Activity

Student Instructions: So far, we have been discussing the stylistic differences between scripts written for teleplays and those written for newscasts. Besides format differences (e.g., a newscast script is written in all CAPS), we have come up with **three important differences**.

Can you recall what they are? You may use your notes.

- **Active versus passive voice**

- **Avoid the clutter: write clearly and concisely.**

- **Write for the spoken word.**

Teacher's Note: This is a partial list. Students may develop their own list. The important thing is that they are able to differentiate between the two styles.

Terms

leader

teaser

Lesson Notes

Now that we have reviewed the differences in writing styles, we have to investigate one more important distinction: the **lead**. In television, the lead can either make or break the story. There is actually very little difference between a lead and a teaser, except that a teaser might only be one or two sentences. A lead might have as many as three or four sentences. The objective of a **teaser** is to get you to stay tuned to the program through one or more commercial breaks. The objective of a lead is to introduce a story that might go to a remote ENG interview, and so forth. In either case, they need to be concise and to the point. The majority of our time today will be spent rewriting the leads and discussing them in class.

To create a good lead, you have to make certain assumptions about the value of the information you are being provided. This is one of the **filtering** issues we discussed earlier this year. Recall the **newsworthiness** selection criteria for the stories covered in **Chapter 2**:

> - **Timeliness:** How recent is it?
> - **Proximity:** How close is it?
> - **Exceptional quality:** How important is it?
> - **Possible future impact:** How does it affect the future?
> - **Prominence:** How important is the person involved?
> - **The number of people involved or affected:** How many are involved?
> - **Consequence:** What is the impact?
> - **Human interest:** Is there a human interest story there? Question: Are animal stories human interest stories?
> - **Pathos:** Is there human suffering?
> - **Conflict**: Are there people fighting?
> - **Shock value:** Is it shocking?
> - **Titillation component:** Are there sexual overtones?

These criteria relate directly to which information is selected first in the story. Lots of information is provided, much of it extraneous. The less important items follow a strong lead.

In-Class Activity

Student Instructions: Read the four groups of facts below. Then, using the newsworthiness criteria as your content guide, decide on the relevance of the information and relative positioning of that content, and write a suitable broadcast lead for each group.

Objective: Assume these are 30-second reports with no accompanying video. Your lead may be more than one sentence long.

> **GROUP 1:** There has been a fire in the 1400 block of Ross Street. One person was in the house when the fire broke out about 2 A.M. The person is a man. He was burned critically. The house was destroyed.

> **GROUP 2:** An overnight snowfall leaves a coat of ice and about six inches of snow on the roads. All area schools are closed today because of the ice and snow. Temperatures are forecast to be near zero for the next two days.

> **GROUP 3:** The National Telephone Company has asked the state's Public Service Commission for permission to increase its rates charged to private phone customers for local service by 14 percent.

> **GROUP 4:** The deadline for a high school basketball player to sign a letter of intent to attend an NCAA member university on an athletic scholarship was today. The letter is binding and official. Our own Siwash University Simpletons need all the help they can get after last season's 3–27 record. One of their signees today was 7–foot prep all-American Lurch Lumpkins of nearby Centertown.

The Good News Writer's Dazzling Dozen

Lesson Planning Considerations

(**Approx. Time:** 25–35 minutes)

Agenda

When all is said and done, there are really only a few rules to apply to make one a good news scriptwriter. Writing classes often get bogged down in rules of grammar and syntax that sometimes can get in the way. If you are an English teacher who has television as one of your subjects, you may not feel agree with this. However, one writing for a news script usually works from another's storyline that has come in over the newswire. What news writers have to do is rewrite that into good copy. The easiest and most concise way to teach concise writing is simply to have students get down to the task and begin to write short news stories. The following list is very similar to those hints offered to adult learners in workshops on the basics of news writing. They might even help one get through a state-sponsored writing test, as well as helping students understand the basics of good communications.

This lesson reviews the lessons to date, in the form of a checklist to be used with future writing assignments.

Objectives and Outcomes

As a result of participating in this lesson, students will be able to

• list at least four camera/equipment techniques used to visually supplement script action;

• review their own and someone else's writing to improve its style and delivery;

• list at least six good writing techniques; and

• using a checklist, summarize the scriptwriting and storyboarding portion of a video production.

Teacher's Note: Introduce the following list of 12 hints. Students should not be expected to memorize the list. Rather, it is offered to help students with future news scriptwriting exercises.

---

1. **Write factually and accurately.** The best technique and the finest form mean nothing if your facts are wrong.

2. **Write in the active voice.** This technique will make your copy tighter, more complete, easier to listen to, and more interesting. Do whatever you must to avoid the passive voice. We will be discussing the active voice in more detail in our next session.

3. **Write in the present or present perfect tenses.** They make your copy more immediate, and immediacy is more interesting. Avoid the word *today*.

4. **Keep your writing simple. (Use the KISS method).** Choose positive forms over negative forms. Write one thought to a sentence. Avoid searching for synonyms, since repetition is not a sin. Avoid searching for complicated, intellectual language. Give the audience the best possible chance to understand the story.

5. **Be complete and clear.** In your quest for brevity and conciseness, avoid omitting necessary information.

6. **Be creative.** Stick to the rules, but develop your own style. Try to say the "same old thing" in a different or new way. Make use of the Rule of Threes and other writing devices that make copy easier to listen to and more interesting.

7. **Write to be heard.** Maintain a sense of rhythm in your writing. All life has rhythm, and rhythmic writing is easier to hear. Avoid potentially confusing homonyms. Always test your copy by reading it aloud.

8. **Avoid interruptives**. Do not force the listener to make difficult mental connections. Put modifiers next to what they modify. Avoid splitting verb phrases.

9. **Avoid commas.** A comma demands a hitch in reading and the resulting jerkiness frustrates the listener. Avoiding commas also will eliminate subordinate clauses. Such clauses kill the impact of copy, especially if they come at the top of a story or sentence.

10. Avoid **numbers.** The listener has trouble remembering them.

11. Avoid **pronouns**. If you must use a pronoun, make sure the pronoun agrees with its antecedent and appears close to the antecedent.

12. **Write to the pictures but not too closely to the pictures.** Remember that more specific video requires more general writing, and vice versa. Write directly to the video at the beginning of a sequence and then allow the writing to become more general with background information and other facts as the video continues.

Lesson 4.6

How to Write for an Interview

Lesson Planning Considerations

(**Approx. Time**: 15–20 minutes)

Agenda

The interview is also an easy segment to produce. The script requirements are minor in that they do not require as much story-building content. The students can therefore get on camera quite quickly. However, there still is a proven methodology to make the interview tell its story.

In a newscast, the interview does not stand alone as an individual task. It usually is a part of a news segment. The on-air talent introduces the segment. The newscast cuts to the interview, after which the interviewer sends it back to the studio for a wrap-up or conclusion. This three-part segment is a classical example of the notion of the idea of a project having a **beginning, middle, and ending** that was introduced in the scriptwriting sessions, and thus serves to provide students with an additional way to synthesize that concept.

There are two ways to introduce the *Interview* project (#5). The interview could be a stand-alone activity. The students could interview any famous person from television history. This is outlined in the project description. An alternative is to interject an interview into the *Decades* project (#6). That alternative is outlined in **Chapter 6.** The project found in this chapter assumes that it will be done as an individual activity.

Objectives and Outcomes

At the end of this lesson, students will be able to:

• list four differences between writing for news and interviews,

• identify two different interview formats, and

• incorporate an interview into a news segment.

Mediated and Textual Support

The Annenberg/CPB Project sponsors a series of videos covering writing for the news. Video #5, *Dealing with Sources*, covers the interview process. See **Appendix J** for information on how to obtain this video.

Lesson Readiness

The lead-in question should orient students to the need for a well-structured interview plan. The first tape comes from an interview conducted by a former student. Most likely, you will have one that did not go so well, for one reason or another. Then show the video that accompanies the Kyker/Curchy text. It has an example of an interview that should serve as a model of how the interview should look. Students can then write down their impressions.

Closure

Project #5 is an interview. Students will be evaluated on their interview style as well as production techniques.

Pre-Lesson Activity

Student Instructions: In preparation for this lesson, review the video of an interview that was done by a former student. Then review the interview shown on the sample lesson tape. Compare the two and write down your impressions about why the second might be considered more successful than the first.

_____

_____

_____.

Terms

interview preparation steps (7)

Lesson Notes

An interview is an alternative way to tell a story. Unlike writing for history, the plot develops on the fly as the interviewee answers your questions. This does not mean that you do not prepare. In short, you are actually making history with your interview. To make it go as you want, you have to do some planning. If you are prepared, the story should come out well constructed, as you want it to. It will even end up having three parts (a beginning, middle, and ending), just as we discussed.

There are two formats for an interview:

- The first is the traditional method in which the interviewer and interviewee appear together. The former asks questions, which the latter responds to.

- The second type of interview provides viewers only with the answers to the questions. The segment producer assumes that the question is well-understood and is obvious by the response given. Often, this type of interview is interjected into a news magazine format or a storyline, when appropriate.

Both styles require that the producer come prepared. Using the interview worksheet (**Appendix E**) will help you make those preparations. The style of interview will dictate the style of questions.

> ***Teacher's Note:*** Show the "Interview Preparation Sheet" provided in **Appendix E.**

Using the following as a guide, you can see that the major ideas for the interview are essentially a repeat from an earlier session we had about body language.

Preparation Questions

- If you had to decide on **one main theme or goal** for the interview, what would it be?

- Avoid **yes and no** answers, when possible.

- Always have **more questions to ask** than you think you might need.

- Be prepared to **branch away** from a topic if you find the interview going in a particularly interesting direction.

- Ask **interesting** questions; those that the interviewee likes will elicit a better response.

- Ask yourself how you expect the **interviewee will answer** your questions.

- Ask yourself **what you will do** if the answer comes back differently than you expected?

Add these to the list found on the worksheet, and you should have a well-planned interview.

Lesson 4.7

Video Devices to Supplement a Teleplay or Newscast

Lesson Planning Considerations

(**Approx. Time:** 25–35 minutes)

Agenda

Because television is a visual medium, some decisions have to be made by the scriptwriter regarding how the video portion is shot. In a professional environment, final interpretation is often left up to the artistic creativeness of the director. However, a much better connection is made between the director and the scriptwriter if the latter is familiar with industry terminology and understands how to use video equipment as a tool to communicate ideas.

In an educational setting, television teachers want to expose young students to all aspects of creating a product. Often the role of the director is also assumed by the scriptwriter. Beginning students are often totally consumed by simply trying to apply the basics of storywriting. The intensity that often accompanies the creative relationship between a writer and a director may be too much for them to handle in a first-year course. They may have little energy left to think visually on the fly, interact with another interpretation, and still come up with a product that has linear continuity. For that reason, it is a good use of class time to review a few of the standard camera shots and techniques that should be identified by the scriptwriter in the storyboard. In other words, this lesson adds one additional element to the storyboard to the four already outlined: The scriptwriter needs to also indicate (when possible) how visual effects are to be accomplished.

This lesson is also reviewed in the equipment training sessions in **Chapter 3.** This information was put into both chapters to maintain continuity of theme in both.

Objectives and Outcomes

At the end of this session, students will be able to

• relate that the role of the audio track in television is to support the visual images and

• list at least four camera or equipment techniques used to visually supplement script action.

Mediated and Textual Support

Reviewing these techniques is also in keeping with the visual literacy theme. If you have some sample footage, it might be a good idea to demonstrate these. The Zettl *Videolab 2.1* CD offers several examples.

Lesson Readiness

Students are asked during the session to recall certain shots and scenes they have seen that remind them of the type of video device being discussed.

Closure

Students are to fill out the review exercise that summarizes the use of video devices.

Terms

flashback	cover/establishing shot	teaser
bumper music	close-up	long shot
B-roll footage	extreme close-up	dutch-angle shot
over-the-shoulder (OTS) shot	power of suggestion	
closure		

Lesson Notes

Now is probably a good time to review and summarize some of the more typical types of video shots that are used in a production. We may have already used many of these at one time or another, but we have not as yet applied labels to them. As they are (re-)introduced, you can supply your input about when we have used them so far, or if you can think of any significant examples of them in use on network television.

Remember, any of these shots may be accomplished using split frames, fade-in, fade-outs, or a combination to add to the effect. These are decisions you need to be making while planning your production. This is not to say that you cannot experiment during the shoot. You do several takes and then choose the best one back at the studio. This is very common in the real world of television production and moviemaking.

The first shot type we are covering is called a **flashback. Can you think of a show or movie in which this has been used? Forrest Gump**

A flashback is used to recall for the viewer a previous period of time to set up a current situation. If you recall, the whole premise of *Back to the Future* was a series of flashbacks and flash-forwards. One of the unique things about *Star Wars* is that it took place in a later time than episodes released later. To maintain that premise, flashbacks are frequently used. If more than one flashback is supposed to take place during a specific time frame, usually they are all shot at the same time.

A **cover/establishing shot** is a short clip that introduces the viewer to an upcoming segment. In a news story, it is a short clip of the next story. This may be used as a **teaser** to keep the viewer interested enough to stay tuned during a commercial. In a television series, a cover shot is often used to reorient the viewer to the location of the upcoming scene. Often, it is accompanied by **bumper music** (a jingle), which is a musical interlude of very short duration. The combination of the cover shot and the jingle reacquaints the viewer with where the next scene is going to take place.

Can you think of an example of a cover shot that you have seen on television? One example might be Seinfeld or Friends using a shot of their apartment buildings to orient viewers. Each television show has its own example.

Remember, television uses two powerful psychological concepts: **power of suggestion** and **closure**. These two terms will be further described in our lessons on visual acuity. The video portion can create its own reality. Although the cover shot may be shot on location, most often the subsequent scenes actually take place on a set at the studio. This transition of locale is seamless if accompanied by bumper music and other transitional devises.

B-roll-footage has many uses. It is inserted during an interview, an instructional video, even a flashback, and demonstrates visually what is being talked about in the segment. The main portion of the video is referred to as the **A-roll** (or primary). The term comes from the fact that footage is insert edited onto the primary segment as a video box or complete overlay.

Can you name an example of B-roll footage that you have seen on television? Footage of an event inserted over the shoulder of a news anchor while he or she describes it.

A **long shot** is more a style of shot than a type of shot. A long shot is the opposite of a **close-up** and is used for reference. A long shot could be used as a cover shot in a story. This style of shot helps to (re-)orient a viewer.

There are several types of close-ups. An **extreme close-up** is exactly what the name says it is. It is used to get a facial expression or reaction, or to focus on a still object. It is used to elicit emotion.

Can you think of why you would use a medium close-up or tight shot instead of an extreme close-up? Used for a crowd scene—to use for a small number of people to make it look like a whole crowd, or to get a group reaction.

Over the shoulder shots are very useful during interviews. They simply offer a variation in scenery and can help give a depth perspective to an interview.

A **dutch-angle shot** is an upward angle shot in which the subject is also tilted slightly to the left or right. This adds to the sense of superiority or size.

We have learned to use the **strobe setting** on the camera. **Can you think of a use for this technique? To show the character is disoriented, angry, or having an anxiety attack.**

Finally, there is one more device that has come into vogue lately and has been used in cartoons and comic strips for years. **Can you think of an example of a thought bubble (i.e., an insert of a bubble or balloon containing written text of what the on-screen talent might be thinking)?** <u>Pop-Up Videos on VH1</u>

Portfolio Project #2
Stop Action

Project Planning Considerations

<u>Agenda</u>

This activity is intended to give students an opportunity to add knowledge of some of the fundamental editing techniques to newly learned camera operation skills to present a storyline without words. In this project students use the concept of **persistence of vision** that they learned in the "How Television Works" lesson. They will demonstrate their skill in visually and conceptually organizing their thoughts. This time, they use action figures with moving parts, clamation (clay figures used to animate cartoon characters), racing cars, dolls, and so forth. Storyboards become more important because they have to show movement in a continuous series. On the assessment scorecard, continuity becomes more important to the grade. The action is continuous, with no large gaps in the sequence. The final production is rather short (approximately 30 seconds). Some students may feel this is too short. However, after realizing that a half-minute show involves 30 one-second frames, they begin to appreciate the work involved in producing a complete full-length feature animated film.

Again, students should be graded on their ability to frame pictures, assemble edit them into a sequential storyline, audio dub their music, and use the character generator to add the title page. The model assessment scorecard is modified to mirror the change in emphasis to the new skills involved.

Some students may have a problem identifying a main theme or idea for their project. In this case, they try to add too much action. There is a temptation to replicate *War and Peace* all within 30 frames. When you mention that there must be a storyline, most interpret that to mean that there must be some type of elaborate plot involved. All you are trying to get them to do is map a series of movements and conceptualize a storyline. The best way to explain is through example. You will be using this project to reemphasize the importance of a storyboard. Most students overlook an action because they did not follow a set script.

Many may still not understand how assemble editing works. You may or may not wish to tell them about the still button on the camera (if it has one). This project will work either way, because you will have the ability to still the shots on the A-V board during editing. Whether you let them in on this shooting secret depends on how much you want them to learn through discovery and resolving identified problems.

Again, to get students to become more creative, instructions have to be broad. The themes can be on any topic. They can use any music they wish, but this time the teacher can be stricter about how well it relates to the theme.

The remainder of the scoring criteria are the same as for the still shots. You will be making a determination about how well the students display their knowledge of the equipment and your overall impressions of their creativity and understanding of the persistence of vision concept. This is a great project to assess a student's understanding of storytelling. Students tend to overcomplicate things. This is a case where **simpler is better.**

Student Instructions: Stop Action is the second major project. It is an extension of the first one, but with the added complication of restricting each frame to one second. In this case, you will be working with action figures or any other models such as puppets or clamation. Pictures may be used if they are contiguous. In other words, the action shown in each photo must progress in action, from one to the next.

You are to build a 30–45 second video that tells a story. You are still not allowed to use a spoken script, as the story should be visual enough for the viewer to recognize the premise of the story and to understand how it completes. The production may be over or under the time limit by no more than 10 seconds. The allotted time has been restricted to make you aware of the time constraints that often accompany real videography productions. Time limits will become more and more of a factor in your projects as you progress through the course.

You may pick any topic for the production that you want. The music should complement and add to the ambience of the storyline. The story should show that you have a basic grasp of the three-part storytelling concept. The show must have a beginning, middle, and ending, similar to a three-part play. The beginning should orient the viewer. The middle should tell the story. The ending should provide a conclusion to the story. For example, if you were going to show a n encounter between a hero and a victim, the first few frames would introduce the characters. The action takes place in the middle third. A winner might be declared in the final few seconds.

How You Will Be Evaluated

The characteristics of the scorecard (**Appendix H**) are very similar to the *Still Shots* video. However, this time emphasis is placed on the continuity issues. Understanding of balance and symmetry are shown by limiting all the frames to one second each. The scorecard is modified in the following manner:

> **Balance:** Each frame should exhibit some type of symmetry. The pictures should take up the entire frame or be bordered and centered. Each frame is to be one second.

> **Continuity**: Each frame should look the same (i.e., have the same color, lighting, camera effect), unless a difference is needed for emphasis or to make a point. The action should flow from one frame to the next. The action should be relatively continuous, smooth, and not jumpy. No snow should appear between frames.

> **Emphasis**: The storyline should remain constant. There should be no confusion about why any individual shot has been included. The main idea of the storyline must be emphasized throughout.

Portfolio Project #3
Book Trailers

Project Planning Considerations

Agenda

Research has shown that the most common way people choose a book to read is by its jacket. Movie trailers are most often used to persuade potential audiences to purchase tickets to movies. It would make sense, then, to use a visual medium like video to help create a similar persuasive commercial to attract potential readers. There is also considerable research indicating that reading and comprehension could be positively affected by visual readiness activities. Were it not for the fact that most movies are not really true to the original book content, it might make sense on many levels to actually show movies taken from books beforehand instead of afterward. A book trailer appears to be a very good compromise.

The idea is to see whether students can grasp the idea of translating from "page to screen," taking ideas written in text and transforming them into visual representations. This is a continuation of the visual storytelling concepts introduced in the first two projects.

This project can be introduced in one of two different ways. You could either have students do the trailer about their own personal favorite books, or pick one book and have everyone in class do a trailer about it. A drawback of the first option is that they might pick a book that already has a movie created from it, thereby diluting their originality. But at least students will have an incentive because they are working on a story that they are actually attracted to. If you pick the book, it might not be one that is attractive to them. On the other hand, by working on the same book, students will learn that there are multiple points of view about the same topic, when you show in class all the different visual versions of the same book. At a minimum, you should pick (or allow them to pick) a book that appears on your school's recommended reading list.

This project could actually be introduced in the English class. It is a good activity for teachers who wish to have some type of interactive, engaging activity to help solidify the learning experiences of reading. As the television teacher, you could work in conjunction with your English teacher(s) to form a joint project in which your student s act as producers for projects written and developed in English classes.

As publishers become more familiar with the idea of book trailers, you will see more of them. If you want to see examples of existing book trailers and learn more about the concept, go to www. digitalbooktalk.com.

Student Instructions: For this project, you are to create a video trailer for a selected book. This is a trailer that relates the content of the book. It is NOT a trailer for a movie that has been made (or that you think should be made) from the book. Just like any movie trailer, your trailer should contain enough information to tell the story, but not so much as to give the storyline away. The video should be from two to four minutes in length and run true to the storyline. Another way to think about this concept is that if you could write a one- to three-sentence summary about the content, ideas, and concepts of this book, what would you write? Then build those two to three sentences into your trailer.

How You Will Be Evaluated

The characteristics of the scorecard (**Appendix H**) will be used. There is a change in emphasis in that the combination of moving and still (and/or text) images will be used. It is preferred that you choose a book that you know or will be assigned to be read in your English class this year.

Portfolio Project #4
Instructional Video

Project Planning Considerations

Agenda

The need for a detailed storyboard and more elaborate script increases with this project. Students must now show that they understand the concept of the three-part story. The final product should show evidence of a beginning, middle, and ending; each containing the appropriate elements. The video should employ a visual of the function being taught. Insert editing is taught in conjunction with this project. The need for an insert edit may be satisfied with B-roll footage, a second camera angle, or an insert of a photograph. The footage may be produced by the team or be stock footage showing others performing the tasks. For example, the video may be showing how a football lineman blocks his opponent. The footage may be taken from an actual football game.

Mediated and Textual Support

The Kyker/Curchy text (*Television Production: A Classroom Approach*) comes with a supporting videotape containing a model of an instructional video. You may also use projects submitted by prior classes.

Lesson Readiness

Students are to read the appropriate lesson in the *Television Production: A Classroom Approach Text*, and answer the review questions at the end. The questions are to be handed in for a grade and will be covered during the introduction to this activity.

Preliminary Student Activity

Student Instructions: You are to read the lesson in the Kyker/Curchy textbook and answer the review questions. They are to be handed in by the due date found on the assignment board.

An instructional video teaches the viewer how to accomplish a task, a series of tasks, or a function. It has been included as a project because it contains many of the elements of storytelling that we have been teaching, as well as allowing us to take advantage of some new production and editing techniques. This is a how-to video that follows a proscribed format.

You are to produce, write, and complete a three- to five-minute video that describes a task, a series of tasks, or a function. It may be no more than 15 seconds longer or shorter than this limit. The video should contain evidence of your understanding of the three part expository format. It should have a clear beginning, in which you tell the audience what you are going to tell them; a middle, in which you tell them the details; and an ending, in which you summarize one more time. The video should contain a visual in which the function you are teaching is actually shown. The topic may be anything you choose, but it must be physical in nature so that it may be demonstrated.

How You Will Be Evaluated

This video will be assessed in much the same way as the previous projects. **Criterion #1** remains the same: You need to show evidence of the three-part storytelling format, as well as continuity, balance, and emphasis. **Criterion #2** has been modified to include an appraisal of your ability to insert appropriate footage.

RESOURCES

Barnouw, E. 1990. *The tube of plenty.* New York: Oxford University Press.

Jankowski, G., and D. Fuchs. 1995. *Television today and tomorrow: It won't be what you think.* New York: Oxford University Press.

CBS Television Video. 1995. Many of the *Twilight Zone* Videos are available from local retail stores or online at www.amazon.com. Cost: approximately $30 each.

Digital BookTalk. 2004. Available online at www.digitalbooktalk.com.

CHAPTER 5

Developing an Acuity for a Visual Medium

INTRODUCTION AND LESSON GOALS

Following is an old story that you might relate to your students at the appropriate moment. Hopefully, it will help to put the concept of teaching visual literacy in perspective:

Star Struck

Sherlock Holmes and Dr. Watson went on a camping trip. As they lay down for the night,

Holmes: Watson, look up into the sky and tell me what you see?

Watson: I see millions and millions of stars.

Holmes: And what does that tell you?

Watson: Astronomically, it tells me that there are millions of galaxies and potentially billions of planets. Theologically, it tells me that God is great and that we are small and insignificant. Meteorologically, it tells me that we will have a beautiful day tomorrow. What does it tell you?

Holmes: It tells me that somebody stole our tent!

In other words, it is easy to overanalyze things by getting too bogged down in the details. Developing a visual awareness is not rocket science. It is mostly a little bit of self-discipline mixed with a lot of common sense.

TOWARD AUDIENCE ANALYSIS

The role visual awareness plays in a first-year educational program about television is even more fundamental than a purely commonsense approach. Students learn in the ASSURE planning model as described in **Chapter 7** that the first step in the production sequence is to **analyze the audience**. Teachers should not underestimate how daunting a task this can be for a self-absorbed teenager. It is much more difficult (if not impossible) to understand the needs of others if one does not have a tolerance for the fact that everyone does not think the same way, or that it is not a bad thing that others look at things differently. Developing an awareness to satisfy the needs of others is based on the premise that one first understands one's own self-concept. Only after overcoming a natural intolerance of others that comes with immaturity will teenaged students be able to understand what the concept of audience analysis really entails.

It is not the purpose of the lessons in this chapter to implement a self-defense campaign. That is, these are not exercises in negativism. Rather, they are intended to be an integral part of a proactive experience to show students how to use visual imagery to create concrete concepts out of intellectual abstracts, empowering them to become better communicators and expanding their lifelong learning capabilities. In short, they are an attempt to move toward the "acquisition model" advocated by Kathleen Tyner and others. Viewing literacy in this way will provide a framework for questions regarding issues such as

- transferring information to new contexts like home entertainment and viewing (like learning how to read and interpret commercials) or other learning domains and

- integrating visual media production and synthesizing that knowledge to other forms (that is, researching historical information to write a better script for the *Decades* project), which, in turn, may lead to reading skill and practice. (Tyner, 1998, pp. 132–133.)

The acquisition approach is at the heart of the educational goals of this course. Unfortunately, there is a temptation to allow the teaching of media concepts to degenerate into an exercise in media bashing because it is an easier path to follow and often appears to be more fun.

In keeping students on a positive plane, these lessons begin with the basic design concepts of using visual imagery and how it supplements and attempts to communicate. First, students are introduced to an instructional concept commonly known to educators.

Students tend to remember:

10% of what they read,

50% of what they see, and

90% of what they encounter through active participation.

But what does the term *seeing* entail? To understand the full emotional impact of visual imagery, students have to be shown the concept of unnoticed and subliminal stimuli by introducing concepts like **closure** and **persistence of vision**. Because they have been exposed to regular doses of computer usage, students easily understand that a television screen's picture is really made up of pixels and how different a series of dots looks from afar than up close. When they are reminded of times when their eyes saw one thing and their minds caused them to perceive an entirely different thing (like looking up at clouds), students easily understand this concept. Students then learn how to use light, colors, texture, shapes, vectors, and sound. It is during these sessions that students combine all visual factors and put them into practice. They learn to identify the tools others use to create moods and evoke emotions.

TOWARD VISUAL AWARENESS

If **audience analysis** is the key to a successful production, then students must become much more visually aware of how to read people, based on judgments about their demeanor as demonstrated through the continual visual clues they send out during an encounter. The lesson on body language is designed to introduce students to the concept of self-realization. Students are taught that, to someone else, reality of being is almost entirely based on that other person's perceptions, not the first person's impressions. This is easily demonstrated. Students often do not like how they sound on audiotapes or what they look like the first time they see themselves on television. Yet these are the true impressions they leave with others through sight and sound. Once they understand that their own impressions of themselves are different, they are ready to be taught how to read visual clues and the importance of first impressions. The sessions on body language become very real.

STUDENTS USING THEIR KNOWLEDGE

Students use their newly found knowledge of reading body language in their early on-screen activities. First, they read a news script in front of a camera without any previous instruction. They then read for a second time, after they have learned some of the visual concepts like body language and camera movements. Students use their own first attempt in front of the camera as a self-analysis. They are graded on the improvements they make from the first reading to the next. In the second activity, students make their own commercials. The intended objective of project #7 *(PSA/Commercial)* is for students to demonstrate that they can use all these concepts to sell a particular product or gain support for a particular point of view. Making a 30-second commercial is a great way to test a student's ability to integrate what he or she has learned about storytelling with selling a viewpoint to an audience.

In other words, the concept of desconstructing is introduced for positive purposes. Deconstructing refers to breaking something down into its component parts. (In the computer industry, this is often referred to as **parsing**.) Students first learn the tools of the trade for how media are built and then apply that same visual psychology to their own work.

The goal of project #3 *(Book Trailers)* is to teach students something about the concept of **text to screen**. This involves being able to visualize something that is communicated in another medium (text) and translate it to another mode (video). As a by-product, perhaps, students will also learn something about the visualization process involved with reading and acquire some reading skills.

The overall goal of this series of these lessons is to go beyond passive visual acuity to a complete **visual literacy** that shows

- how reading for story differs from reading for information,

- how to translate text-based communications to a visual medium,

- why the visual element is a central part of a complete literacy competency,

- how to select the best form of visual imagery for their own productions,

- how to integrate visual and verbal texts,

- how to select the right visual device to communicate ideas and information, and

- how to use details of graphic design to organize and support meaning.

SUMMARY

In short, the terms **visual literacy** and **media literacy** often mean the same thing. According to Kathleen Tyner, being media aware implies that a student is also visually aware. In other words, the student has the ability to "comprehend and create images in a variety of media in order to communicate effectively" (1998, pp. 94–95). The real educational opportunity that comes with teaching about television is the chance for teachers to help students learn how to become visual thinkers, visionaries in the sense that they understand how to use visual imagery to amplify and supplement the points they are trying to make. Visual awareness supplements the concept of literacy in all its forms, as it is a mechanism that makes students better communicators.

DIGGING DEEPER

Studying visual literacy can lead to studies of many other areas. It is such a new field that educators are just now beginning to understand the role teaching visual literacy can play in creating lifelong learners. Study in visual literacy has led to research in new areas such as **metacognition**, learning how we learn; and **semiotics**, the study of signs and visual communication. Fortunately, there are several excellent Web sites available that make this research fun and convenient.

The **Web-ASSISTant** Web site provides several links to these sites in the "Digging Deeper" section of the page that supports **Chapter 5**. The activity that precedes Lesson 5.1 attempts to introduce younger students to some of these concepts. You may wish to look at some of the supporting Web sites prior to introducing this activity.

A source of information about the elements of film-making is *Understanding Movies*, written by Louis Giannetti. This book, originally published by Prentice Hall in 1972, has had two subsequent revisions (1976 and 1982). The book discusses themes like shots and angles, use of colors, and frames, using modern movies as its models. Although it was written about movies, much of it is transferable to television. There are several images and photos in this book that may be used in class to demonstrate the effects discussed in Lesson 5.4.

Libraries Unlimited has published an excellent text about visual literacy, *Visual Messages: Integrating Imagery into Instruction.* Written by David Considine and Gail Haley, it is a text designed for a variety of classroom applications. The book is loaded with visual illustrations and practical classroom applications.

The International Visual Literacy Association (IVLA) publishes a refereed, scholarly journal twice a year that explores empirical, theoretical, practical, and applied aspects of visual literacy and communication (*Journal of Visual Literacy*). IVLA is an excellent source of information for those interested in visual literacy. Information is available from Dr. Nancy Nelson Knupfer at Kansas State University (e-mail address: **nknupfer@ ksu.edu**).

Herb Zettl's book, *Sight-Sound-Motion: Applied Media Aesthetics,* is an important addition to any television teacher's library. It is published by Wadsworth Publishing and can be ordered from most retail bookstores, or from any of the online vendors.

SEQUENCING THE LESSONS IN THIS CHAPTER

Like those in the other chapters, the lessons in this chapter were written in contextual sequence. That is to say, they have continuity with regard to subject matter and can be taught in the exact order in which they are presented. However, to reach the specific goals of this course, it might be better to consider following the sequence outlined in the "Teaching Chronology" in **Chapter 1**. At a minimum, it makes sense to at least consult the prescribed format to make an informed decision.

Lesson 5.1

The Making of *Citizen Kane*

Lesson Planning Considerations

(**Approx. Time**: 35–45 minutes)

Agenda

The best way to teach students how to accomplish a task is to use models. What better model is there than the movie rated by the industry as the greatest of all time*?* Orson Welles's creative genius in *Citizen Kane* shows in its script, acting, and cinematography. The latter is what we focus on. It is said that you can actually watch this movie without sound and still understand the plot; at least with regard to the relationships among characters (that is, the dominant character in a relationship versus the submissive person). This black-and-white film introduces all sorts of discussion opportunities about the use (or lack of) color, shading, light, and so forth. It makes the later discussions on design elements that much easier. An interesting aspect of this class is that, after seeing how the film was made, students actually want to watch this movie, something that might not be true otherwise. In today's world of high tech special effects, a simple story like *Citizen Kane* would have difficulty competing.

Objectives and Outcomes

After viewing this video, students should be able to

• identify three contributions Orson Welles made to movie making,

• use contrasting light and shadows to set a mood, and

• identify the aspects of camera angles and vectors to identify relationships between characters in a production.

Mediated and Textual Support

Support for this lesson comes from the video *Citizen Kane,* specifically, the version produced by Turner Classic Movies (1996), which includes a 20-minute segment called *The Making of Citizen Kane.* That piece is the basis for this class. It should be shown first. The segment lends itself very well to the introduction of the visual awareness concepts that form the basis for these lessons. Specifically, it explains the techniques Welles used and points out overall how significant a contribution this movie made to movie making.

Lesson Readiness

The video is an advanced organizer and an outcome. Most teachers use the *Making of Citizen Kane* as an orientation and show the story in its entirety as the lesson activity. If this session is done correctly, students can actually view the story in fast forward and still understand the value of the camera work. The introductory activity is intended to get students thinking about how often the word *see* is used in our everyday vocabulary and, how important the role of being able to visualize is in our lives.

Closure

Students are asked to complete the review questions after viewing this video. They are discussed in class.

Pre-class Activity

Student Instructions: Have you ever heard the following phrases? Write down what you think they mean.

I *see* what you mean. _____.

Seeing is believing. _____.

Let's *see* . . . _____.

What you *see* is what you get._____.

Can you come up with any more expressions involving the word *see* on your own?

_____.

Why do you suppose we have so many expressions in our culture that include the use of the verb *to see*?

_____.

Lesson Notes

Being able to visualize something is an incredibly important part of our lives. To demonstrate how powerful visual imagery is, we are going to watch a movie without sound and get an understanding of the interrelationships of the main characters.

In this activity, you are going to watch a video on the making of the movie, *Citizen Kane*. To be sure you have understood it and that you have paid attention, you are being asked to write out and turn in your answers to the questions that follow this paragraph. *Citizen Kane* represents several very important aspects of how one can use nonverbal criteria such as camera angles, lighting, coloration (or the lack thereof), and rudimentary special effects to accomplish the objectives the producer has set for certain scenes. Even though the medium is motion pictures, rather than video, the technical aspects of how to use visualization to accomplish goals remain the same.

Questions

Respond to the following ideas based on information gathered from watching the video:

1. In the video, those being interviewed refer to *Citizen Kane* as the greatest movie ever made. Recently, the Screen Actors Guild also voted it the greatest movie of all time. Please list two reasons why others feel this is such a classic.
   a) **Combination of camera effects**
   b) **Great script and use of talent**

2. List three camera angles or tricks used in the filming of this movie as explained on the video.
    a) <u>**Fading**</u>
    b) <u>**Overlapping audio**</u>
    c) <u>**Cutting hole in floor for camera angles**</u>

3. According to the video, why did Orson Welles sweat so much during the screen test he had with his leading lady?
    a) It was hot on the set.
    b) He was a big man.
    c) <u>**It was his first acting job, and he was very nervous.**</u>
    d) He had a fever.

4. Why do you think Welles chose to make this movie in black and white even though color cameras did exist at the time? <u>**He used contrasting light and darkness for emotional effect.**</u>

5. What technique(s) did Welles use to create moods? <u>**Camera angles, use of light**</u>

6. This movie was a *fictional* account of the life of William Randolph Hearst, the newspaper mogul. Why was Hearst so upset by this version? <u>**It painted a bad picture of him.**</u>

7. In the movie, there was an important scene transition where the camera came down through the skylight. Name two effects techniques Welles used to create this transition.
    a) <u>**Fading from real image to a model**</u>
    b) <u>**Use of a moving camera (trucking + 300m)**</u>

8. Who wrote the screenplay (script) for this movie? <u>**Herman Mankiewicz and Welles**</u>

9. Who played Citizen Kane, the main character? <u>**Orson Welles**</u>

10. Who directed the movie? <u>**Orson Welles**</u>

11. Whose production company produced this movie? <u>**Orson Welles's**</u>

Short Answer (5 points):

This movie has been hailed as one of the greatest movies of all time. Even though you have not seen it yet, you have been presented with some convincing arguments. Based on what you have seen of this movie during the preview, do you agree or disagree? Write one or two sentences defending your position. <u>**Could include anything, as long as they include valid reasons.**</u>

Lesson 5.2

Lesson Planning Considerations

(**Approx. Time**: 25–35 minutes each)

Agenda

In this session, students **will learn how to deconstruct the visual clues** they receive during an encounter with someone else. Body language is an integral part of everyday communication. Learning about how to read body language is a practical exercise that reinforces and develops one's visual awareness skills.

During this session students will learn what the term *body language* means and how to identify basic body language signals.

As a follow-up to general comments about body language, the class will be in a position to appreciate information given to them about what can be done to improve on-screen performance. Most students believe that those who do well in front of the camera are naturals at it and that there is little or nothing one can do to actually become better. The first thing you need to get across to students is that it is perfectly natural to feel self-conscious and nervous in front of the camera and that most people feel that way initially. Very few people are able to perform well without practice. Those who appear to perform well have spent time perfecting their skills. It is common to not like the way you look the first time you see yourself on camera. In fact, even some very famous movie stars **never** like their own performances and seldom watch themselves on camera.

This does not mean that students need to fear being on camera. There is no magical solution but, once a few basic techniques are learned, students will find that it is not that hard. Armed with the confidence-building information found in this session, students should do very well.

Nonverbal communication is a key element in today's visual world. It can make the difference between an effective newscast or one that loses its meaning through sending the wrong visual signals. Everyone communicates with his or her body. Here is what you can do to become a more effective communicator, especially when on camera during a newscast or interview.

This lesson is divided into three sessions and is intended to relate the discussions on body language directly to on-camera performance. The lesson finishes with a checklist that should help the on-screen **talent** perform better. It is the last session before introducing project #5, *Interview for a News Magazine.*

Objectives and Outcomes

At the end of this lesson, students will

- know that body language is a form of communication and

- be able to use body language to improve the visual appearance of their on-screen personality.

Mediated and Textual Support

The Internet provides several sites on body language that can help form the basis for this subject. Check the **Web-ASSISTant** Web site ("Chapter Five" page) for links.

In addition, there are several videos available that go over many of these same body movements. *Speak Up on Television,* produced by the National Education Association, provides insight into how to prepare to communicate and how to prepare statements that will survive news editing. The tape also covers other topics such as how to handle a crisis and conduct a press conference.

Lesson Readiness

Students generally already have some idea what the term *body language* means. But many of these preconceived ideas are incorrect. Some may have already had lessons on body language in other classes. Orient students by asking them to name some of the body language indicators they know about. Ask them why some people seem to get away with lying and others always seem to get caught. A good strategy might be to use the **K-W-L** method: Ask them what they **k**now about body language, then what they **w**ant to **l**earn about body language. Follow up the session by asking students to repeat what they learned about body language during the current session (Kizlik, 1998).

Closure

Students will be evaluated on the use of body language in projects #5 and #6. Quiz #5 questions on body language may also be included.

Lesson 5.2A

Body Language

Pre-lesson Activity

Student Instructions: Answer the following questions in preparation for this lesson:

1. Have you ever noticed that some people always seem to get away with telling a fib but others always seem to get caught? Why do you think this happens?

_____

_____

2. Why do you think actors warm up in front of a mirror?

_____

_____.

Teacher's Note: You may want to relate at this time the following story about Martha Graham, a famous choreographer from the 1930s and 1940s:

At one of her grand openings, as she was being praised for her wonderful work, a reported asked her:

> **"Ms Graham, that dance was wonderful! But, just what does it mean?"**

and she was reported to have replied:

> **"Honey, if I knew how to say it, I wouldn't have danced it!"**

There are several ways to communicate without words. The converse is also true. Sometimes words cannot express what you want to communicate. Can you remember any case when you had something to say but did not know the correct words? Have you ever had an idea about something that you were sure you could not put into words, even if vocabulary were not an issue?

Communication and human expression sometimes are nonverbal. That is the purpose of the lessons that follow. We are going to focus on visual communication. Body language is just one form of that type of expression.

Terms

handshake   body perceptions

common gestures   body language

powers of observation

Lesson Notes

Whether you know it or not, you are continually telling others what you are thinking, even though you are not speaking to anyone. No, we are not all psychics, nor do we have ESP. Just by existing in a world full of others, people communicate with one another through their **body language**. A person's body language speaks volumes. By observing somebody's **posture, eye movements, breathing,** and/or **skin coloration**, you can gain a lot of information about what he or she is thinking. You can get similar information just by listening to someone else's tone of voice.

Over the years, the subject of body language has created a lot of interest. Several books have made best-sellers' lists. It is a huge topic, and to master it requires a good deal of training and experience. It is not our intent to make you experts at it but to present the basics that can be readily noticed.

Without knowing what all the different body movements mean, you can simply notice when there is a change in someone's attitude through simple **powers of observation.** You may or may not immediately know what that change means, but by noticing it, it will help you figure out how to deal with it. For example, if a person has been sitting perfectly still and then suddenly starts twitching or moving his or her eyes, that person's attitude probably has changed. Or if someone's breathing rate changes, that is an indication of change in the person's attitude.

People often demonstrates interest in what you are saying based on the direction in which they are leaning. If you are speaking to them and they are interested in your topic, they will **lean forward** in your direction. If they become uninterested, they may lean **backward** or slouch.

You cannot be sure, just from a specific body motion, what is going on. But you can get a good idea. For example, you notice your discussion partner daydreaming and you ask, "What are you thinking about?" The person suddenly leans back, indicating that whatever he or she is thinking about is an external matter. The partner is thinking about something far away in time or distance.

Body perceptions can be broken down into **pictures, sounds,** and **feelings.** When we access an item in our minds, body language tends to reflect the kind of information we are recalling. Emotions and feelings have a **low frequency**; they are slow and deep. A person will **breathe deeply** and slowly when a mood takes over or his or her state of mind is in the process of changing, or he or she is thinking about an emotional moment from the past. On the other hand, a person will breathe **shallowly** and **high in the chest when accessing intellectual or visual information**. A person will tend to speak faster and at a higher pitch when accessing this type of information than when accessing other kinds of information.

These body language qualities show up in various ways:

• When **thinking** about something visual, a person tends to **look up, straighten up,** and **make gestures** into space.

- When **listening** to music or playing a song in their heads, people will tend to **look to the side**, maybe **slant** their **heads** and **cross** their **arms**.

- When thinking about an **emotional moment**, or when someone's mood is changing, he or she will tend to **look down** and **slump over** and **speak** in a **lower, slower tone** of voice.

With practice, you can become well-versed in interpreting another's body reactions. You do not really need to become an expert, just learn to notice the changes in people's bodies and how they react to what you are saying. Learning to read body language is nothing more than interpreting feedback about what another person is doing in your presence.

Here are a few gestures that are easy to spot and read:

Gesture	What It Means
1. The hand to the mouth.	**The person is not at ease.**
2. Arms folded across the chest.	**A major defensive posture; the person does not like what you are saying or is angry.**
3. Hands on hips	**Combative stance; watch out!**
4. Eyes moving back and forth.	**The person is thinking up stuff (not necessarily lying).**
5. Eyes looking up to the right	**The person is trying to recall something real.**
6. Eyes looking down to the left	**The person is making something up or winging it (possibly lying).**

To summarize, there are many nonverbal clues that allow you to figure out what is happening during a conversation with another person. Nervousness is the easiest to spot because it provides the most telltale signs. Reading body language is one tool used by lie detector experts.

There is one last gesture to be mentioned, and although it does not relate directly to body language, it is an important gesture. Creating a good first impression is crucial. You want to make people feel comfortable and you certainly want to provide an impression that you mean business. The **handshake** is an important body language signal you use almost every day. Make sure it is not too hard and not too soft. Pay close attention to how you are shaking someone's hand.

It is also important to provide body language clues during a broadcast, whether you are reading the news or conducting an interview.

The following is a basic set of principles:

Someone who is **engaged** in listening will display one or more of the following body language clues:

- lean forward

- open body

- open arms, open hands

- smile

Someone who is **listening** will often

- tilt his or her head

- maintain eye contact

- nod

- blink his or her eyes regularly

Someone who is **bored** will often be

- staring into space

- slumped or in a relaxed posture

- doodling

- tapping his or her foot

- sitting head in hand

- droopy eyed or stare blankly

Someone who is **lying** might

- touch his or her face

- put his or her hand over his or her mouth

- pull his or her ear

- keep his or her eyes down

- glance at you

- shift in his or her seat

- look down and to the left

Someone who is **nervous** may

- clear his or her throat

- cover his or her mouth when speaking

- tug at his or her ear

- stare with darting eyes

- twitch his or her lips or face

- have his or her mouth slightly open

- play with objects or fidget

- shift his or her weight while standing

- tap his or her fingers

- wave his or her foot

- pace

- whistle

Lesson 5.2B

Using Body Language on Camera

Teacher's Note: This and the subsequent lesson consist of the essential body movements used to positively affect appearance on camera. Although it is not a script, it might be easier to cover these lessons as they are written. Student comments and conversations might cause a deviation to the schedule. As long as the discussions do not go too far off track, any side conversations may be an alternative way to cover this material.

What to Do in Front of a Camera

How does one learn to **project** the correct image during a broadcast? One must first learn what visual clues are and then learn to picture them in one's own mind. It takes some practice to perfect one's on-screen personality, but a few basic characteristics will make a huge initial difference for those who are just beginning.

Remember: Body language by itself only tells part of the story. Everyone communicates with his or her body. You must blend a reading of the individual signals or signs a person gives off with your knowledge of the situation. Using your knowledge of how to read someone else will help you react better to that person. Knowing how to project these clues will also help you provide the proper visual clues when in front of the camera. Here is what you can do to become a more effective communicator, especially when performing before a camera during a newscast or an interview:

> **Open posture:** Keep your back straight, arms, legs, and feet relaxed and uncrossed. Slouching creates an image that you are uninterested or simply winging it.

> **Lean forward:** Leaning slightly forward shows you are interested. Leaning backward demonstrates aloofness or rejection.

> **Mirroring:** Pay attention to people's breathing and the pace that they are talking. Is it fast or slow? Mirror what they do. For example, if during an interview the interviewee crosses his or her legs, do so, too.

> **Direct eye contact:** Direct eye contact is a compliment to most people and builds their trust in you. You must learn how to do this while reading a script on camera.

> **Look at the camera frequently:** This is made possible through learning how to read ahead on the script.

One of the most frequent mistakes made by inexperienced talent is that they stop when they make a mistake. This happens more when a show is being taped than during a live performance. If you make a mistake, you must **keep going**. The director or producer will decide whether it has to be redone.

<u>Read as if you are telling a story:</u> Your inflection will be your own, but don't talk in a dry monotone. A good way to learn this is to take a short news article and summarize it aloud in your own words. Try to recall the inflection and then read the story with details.

<u>Practice, practice, practice:</u> Once you feel comfortable, the cameras will roll. Everyone gets two tries before recording for real.

<u>Develop your own on-screen personality:</u> Very few professionals act the same way in front of a camera as in real life.

Lesson 5.2C

How to Conduct an Interview

Lesson Notes

Much of the preparation for an interview involves writing good questions and planning. If this sounds like scriptwriting, it certainly shares many of the characteristics of good scripts we covered in those lessons. Solid preparation translates into a higher sense of confidence, which then also translates into proper body language.

Some important points to remember when preparing for the interview questions include the following.

Primary Preparation Question

First, if you had to decide on **one** main theme **or** goal for the interview, what would it be?

Preparation Hints

After the primary question has been answered, you should look at the following to determine how the interview will proceed, should it take some unexpected turns:

• Avoid questions that elicit simple **<u>yes and no</u>** answers, when possible.

• Always have **more questions to ask** than you think you might need (this is the old "plan B" concept).

• Be prepared **to branch** away from the topic if you find the interview going in a particularly interesting direction.

• Ask **interesting** questions.

• When preparing the questions, ask yourself, "How do I expect the interviewee to **answer** my questions?"

• Ask yourself **what you will do** if the answer comes back differently than you expected.

On-Camera Hints

- Always **look interested** in what the interviewee is saying; look directly at the interviewee and nod slightly to show your interest.

- **Use index cards** to remind yourself of the questions.

- Try to look at the **next question** before it comes up to keep the flow going.

- Maintain a good **pace**.

- Try the interview **twice**, once with you next to the person, and once with over the shoulder shots (you will pick the best ones in post-production edit).

- Do not forget to point the microphone **directly** at the interviewee when he or she is talking and bring it back to yourself when you ask the questions.

Lesson 5.3

Principles of Visual Design

Lesson Planning Considerations

(**Approx. Time**: 25–35 minutes)

Agenda

In this session, students will learn how to **deconstruct the visual clues that are always present** in any presentation, painting, photograph, movie, or video product. There are some general guidelines that artists tend to use as standards to evoke certain responses, but there are no hard and fast rules. For example, most believe that yellow is the color one would use to evoke the feeling of jealousy. However, many have heard the expression "green with envy." This is where artistic license comes into play.

In this lesson, students will **synthesize design standards** and apply them to a fictional product that they may create. Class discussions are intended to **solidify their understanding** and to provide the creative corral in which they may operate. Students will learn to take their knowledge of the standards **to actually produce a commercial** that is based on evoking an emotion through the use of colors, lines, shapes, or lighting to sell their product or concept.

Objectives and Outcomes

In this session, students will learn how to

- use colors, shapes, lines, and texture to manipulate visual materials;

- think, discuss, and read about the content of visual materials in terms of the emotion or mood they are trying to elicit;

- become more aware of visual images in their world; and

- develop a vocabulary to use in discussing images.

Mediated and Textual Support

Much of the material covered in this session can be found on the Internet. The visual design site sponsored by the University of Toronto should be of significant help (**www.oise.utoronto.ca/~bposer/ vl/elements.htm**). It is an interactive site that provides the opportunity for participants to learn more about the way they think.

Because Internet links are subject to change, check the **Web-ASSISTant** Web site "Chapter Five" page for updates to see whether this link is still active. Where possible, an alternative will be provided, should this link be removed or.

Lesson Readiness

1. Use a picture that contains some abstract quality. It would help in preparing for the discussion if the picture includes some written information about the intent of the photographer or artist.

2. Recall the opening question in the lesson on storyboards. Some students probably came up with the idea that, if a picture is worth a thousand words, then it might be subject to interpretation. In this activity, we orient students to the problem this causes and pose it in the form of a question. The picture you use should be one that is abstract enough to elicit discussion. This should get students thinking about how they might design a product that is received by its viewers as intended.

3. The *Auchtung! Alles Lookenspeepers* passage in the student instructions is not really German but a made-up group of phrases. Actually, it is a joke. This sign appeared in many computer rooms around the country during the early 1970s. Computer operators were becoming increasingly upset by all the visitors who invaded the computer rooms in awe of those gigantic mainframe computers with their blinking lights. They would come in, touching and feeling everything, sometimes breaking things. Most students will fall for the trap. It looks like German but will not sound like it, once they read it out loud. Using the passage makes the point that visual images often change meaning when accompanied by sound, a very important point that is often missed in classes about visual literacy.

Closure

Students are to participate in a follow-up activity to learn about themselves. They also should be able to answer one or two questions on a quiz regarding visual perception.

Pre-Lesson Activity

Powers of Observation

Student Instructions:

1. You are to look at a picture introduced by your teacher. Write down on a sheet of paper what you think it means. Also, identify any element in particular that caused you to come up with your answer, such as color, shape, or texture.

_____

_____

_____.

2.   Recall our discussions about storyboards and the comment concerning a picture being worth a thousand words. Some of your classmates came up with the idea that any picture is subject to several different interpretations. Do you think it is possible to create a picture that is *not* subject to individual interpretation? If so, how? (What elements must the picture have to have the best chance for a single interpretation?)

_____

_____

_____.

3.   Look at the following statement and read it to yourself. What do you think it means? Then read it aloud to see if your impressions about the meaning of the passage changes. If it did, why do you think it changed? .

AUCHTUNG! ALLES LOOKENSPEEPERS

DAS COMPUTENMACHINE IS NICHT FÜR GEFINGERPOKEN UND MITTENGRABBEN. IS EASY SCHNAPPEN DER SPRINGERWERK, BLOWENFUSEN, UND POPPENCORKEN MIT SPRITTZENSPARKEN. IST NICHT FÜR GERWERKEN BY DAS DUMMKOPFEN. DAS RUBBERNECKEN SIGHTSEEREN, KEEPEN DAS HANDS IN DAS POCKETS—RELAXEN UND WATCH DAS BLINKENLIGHTS.

_____

_____.

Terms

tone	line characteristics	using shapes
intensity	-location	-circles
cool colors	-direction	-square
warm colors	using vectors-still images	-triangle
hue	using textures	
tone		

Lesson Notes

Certainly, visual interpretations vary. In the exercises that introduced this lesson, we saw that accurate interpretation depends on some type of preconceived notion we have about the colors, shapes, and so forth. We also saw that sight alone can fool us. A visual image will change dramatically when accompanied by appropriate sound (like the sound of our own voice that interpreted the pseudo-German passage). In this lesson, we are going to see which design elements can shape and color (pun intended) our interpretations.

Colors

Technically speaking, color is simply your brain's response to a wavelength of light reflected from a surface. In practicality, color is much more than that. Color has several properties including **hue** (the actual color), **tone** (the quantity of light a color reflects), and **intensity** (the quality or purity of light a color reflects). Color has a strong emotional and psychological impact on the viewer. Color is often referred to in terms of the **mood** it invokes.

The color wheel is based on three primary colors from which all other colors can be made. This should not be confused with the primary colors (red, blue, and green) used in scanning a video. They were chosen for an entirely different purpose. The three primary colors on the color wheel are **red, blue**, and **yellow**. All other colors are made from these basic colors Other colors may be considered complementary or contrasting. Have someone ever told you that the clothes you picked out are complementary or contrasting? There is a reason for this. Complementary colors are those colors that are across from each other on the color wheel. Red and green, blue and orange, yellow and violet are complementary colors. You see these combinations quite often in school colors used for athletic uniforms.

Value or tone is the quantity of light a color reflects. A wide range of color tones may be produced by using one hue and modifying it with the addition of black or white. When a hue is lightened with white, it is referred to as a **tint**. When darkened with black, it is called a **shade**. In black-and-white videos or pictures, shading and lighting create specific moods all by themselves. Often an artist (remember our class discussions concerning *Citizen Kane*) uses only black-and-white images to accomplish a task.

Red, yellow, and **orange** are considered warm colors. These colors are usually associated with sun, fire, and blood and often are used to denote **aggression, excitement**, and **danger**.

Blue, green, and **violet** are considered cool colors. These colors are usually associated with **air, sky,** or **water** and are considered passive colors.

Lines

Lines are very important to a picture or video frame. In addition to the obvious shape of a line, we often interpret a line based on its **edge**, a meeting of its areas, or a change in the **plane** of its surface. A **repetition** of lines creates patterns that add an emotional impact to the visual image. The location of the line, the direction of the line, and the character of the line are considered its three main physical properties. Lines create a vector in a frame that pinpoints for the viewer the most important element.

The **location** of lines can unify, divide, create symmetry, or imbalance in an image or frame. This is done through placement and thickness. There are an infinite number of combinations of long or short and thick or thin lines.

Lines can take only three basic directions: horizontal, vertical, and diagonal. Horizontal lines are generally thought to be **serene, stable,** and **static**. They appear familiar and demand little attention. Vertical lines are thought to be full of poise and movement. They demand and hold our attention because they are an interruption of the norm. **Diagonal** lines create the strongest vectors. They make the strongest impression on our senses and demand the greatest concentration from the viewer.

Character of line is related to how it is created. Each line has its own qualities. A pencil line may be hard or soft; a brush line wet or dry; a felt tip pen thin, thick, or chiseled. These different characters of line can be described as **bold, thin, feathered, soft, rigid, strong, rough, fluid, or scratchy**. Lines do not figure heavily in video, except in backdrops or in combination with other video techniques.

Shapes

Shape is a design element that is directly related to specific areas of space, rather than the lines that create it. Shapes come in an infinite variety, although most often shapes are defined by the use of lines. They range from symmetrical to asymmetrical, posed to awkward, static to dynamic, and outgoing to retiring. The three basic shapes are the **circle**, the **square,** and the **triangle**. Each shape is thought to imply a specific meaning:

The **circle** gives a feeling of **protection, infinity,** or **motion**.

The **square** reflects an attitude of **honesty, equality,** and **organization**.

The **triangle** is representative of **action, aggression,** and **conflict**.

Size, Mass, and Volume

The measure of an object or image is directly related to its size or mass. In two-dimensional viewing (like on current standard television sets), shapes are often not **accurately measurable**. Creating a three-dimensional perception in standard television is very difficult. This should be corrected when high definition television becomes perfected. The implications of mass and distance provide the viewer with a sense of the size and measurement of the image and the space between images. Mass adds a sense of volume to the visual image. The mass and the shape together provide a relationship with other elements. Space between images provides an implication of mass and distance.

Texture

Texture is another element dealt with by television. It is very difficult to create an image on video that accurately reflects the feel of the surface of that material. Texture is used to create a pattern and hence evoke a tactile response from the viewer. Simulated texture is created through the rendering of **light** and **dark** patterns created by a surface character such as clouds, rocks, glass, earth, velvet, wood, satin, or water (this, adding another dimension for the use of color).

Vectors

There are additional considerations to take into account because we are dealing with moving images. The movement of the image can either add meaning or detract from the message that the image is trying to convey. Too much movement can interrupt the flow and interfere with communications. A vector is a psychological force the creator of an image is trying to impose on the viewer. We have talked about vectors previously when discussing headroom, nose room, and so forth. We stated that the frames of pictures have a natural vector of their own. Vectoring can even be in the form of words: having a billboard make the statement "Made ya look!" implies that billboards by nature are automatic vectoring devices. The message implies that they have a draw of their own and your advertisement needs to be on this particular billboard. If the movement of an object in a picture draws the viewer's attention in a certain direction, it is doing its job.

All the previous design principles (shapes, color, size, texture, and lines) have the power to cause vectors. A triangle, for example, can cause the viewer to look in a certain direction or at certain portions of a picture. Colors can also have the effect of drawing a viewer's attention. A sudden change in texture or size can have the same effect.

Teacher's Note: Ask the following: You already know what vectors are. Can you think of a color or series of colors, lines, shapes, or textures that can cause a vector?

All the previous design principles (shapes, color, size, texture, and lines) have the power to cause vectors. A triangle, for example, can cause the viewer to look in a certain direction or at certain portions of a picture. Colors can also have the effect of drawing viewer's attention. A sudden change in texture or size can have the same effect.

Questions

1. List five possible ways the design principles discussed above can enhance an image:

    Color: based on commonly understood principles

    Shape: use correct symbols

    Direction of lines: use horizontal line for stability

    Shading: dark characters

    Size: distance, separation of characters depicts loneliness

2. List five possible ways the design principles discussed above can detract from or interfere with an image:

    Color: use color that doesn't match the mood (e.g., blue for anger)

    Shape: use triangle for stability

    Direction of lines: use vertical for stability

    Shading: use black and white for a happy occasion

    Size: relative size of characters out of synch

3. How do the design principles discussed above help provide a link with the audience? **Answers will vary.**

    _____

    _____.

4. In what way can the design principles discussed above help establish a style for your video (or get in the way)?

    _____

    _____.

Teacher's Note: Now might be a good time to review Zettl's *Videolab 2.1* CD, specifically under "Screen Forces" (tape #5), under "Cameras" on the "Control Panel." The tapes on **vectors, frame edge, horizon**, and **balance** all apply to this lesson.

Follow-up Activity

Finding out About Ourselves

<u>Agenda</u>

The main reason visual awareness has been introduced in this television production course is to help students understand how they perceive images. By developing an awareness about their own thinking and a consciousness of the process of learning, students will be better able to apply themselves to new situations. Audience analysis is the first task a production team takes on after a new project is assigned. Audience analysis is really very much like any other learning taxonomy. New facts are learned, analyzed, and eventually synthesized into an end-product.

In this exercise, you may use any picture or photograph. The idea is to have students look at it and immediately write down their first impressions. Then they should be shown the picture a second time. This time allow them more time to look at the picture and think about their answers. Any picture can be used, as long as it is contains many of the conceptual design elements previously discussed.

Student Instructions: In this exercise you will look at a picture (a video frame or an image), then be asked to answer a few questions. There are no right or wrong answers. Your answers will be compared to answers given by others in your class. This will help you understand two things:

- It will tell you something about yourself and **how you perceive** things.

- It will tell you **how others perceive things** and that they might not see things the same way you do.

This is an important aspect of learning about audience awareness and how others perceive things. In our lessons on production planning and sequencing, we will learn that first thing you do when preparing for a segment is **analyze your audience** and their needs.

Look at the images and answer the following questions:

1. When looking at each of the images the first time, what did you pay attention to at first? Describe what you see:

    _____

    _____

2. When you were looking at the image for the second time, what different perceptions did you have? Do you see anything now that you missed the first time?

    _____

    _____

3. Are there any inherent vectors in the image that draw your attention naturally?

    _____

Now, answer some general questions about yourself:

4. What is your favorite color? Do you look for this color first? What about shapes and lines?

    _____

    _____

Teacher's Note: For interesting discussions on favorite colors and how they relate to one's personality, read *What Color Is Your Personality?: Red, Orange, Yellow, Green . . . ,* by Carol Ritberger, published by Hay House, 1999.

---

5. How would you combine all the elements (line, shape, mass, color, texture) into one interpretation of an image?

    a) to create a sense of sadness _____

    b) to create a sense of anger? _____

    c) to create a sense of happiness? _____

    d) to create a sense of jealousy? _____

Lesson 5.4

Using the Camera to Manipulate Moods

Lesson Planning Considerations

(**Approx. Time**: 25–30 minutes)

Agenda

This segment of the class is more or less a rap session in which students can relate some examples of their own about how the editing process has helped or hurt their projects so far. Although much of what is covered here may be obvious, it needs to be gone over because it sets the scene for later discussions regarding visual and media literacy. As more technology is introduced to the editing process, these fundamental discussions are necessary so that students realize what is happening to them and why there is so much alarm and concern on the part of parents and educators for their welfare.

This session makes a good follow-up to all our sessions on visual literacy. It incorporates an understanding of the principles behind visual awareness and synthesizes their use into the television medium. Having spent some time on the design elements and deconstructing commercials, the students should find the activity in this session fun and interesting. In fact, this activity may even be used as a graded, written exercise.

Lesson Notes

Many call post-production the *make-it or break-it* phase of production. However, in terms of what a videographer can do to manipulate audiences, it might be more accurate to assume that all the steps along the way have their role to play. No project is any good if the audience has not been analyzed first, or the premise and hook are not well thought out in advance. Even a great actor cannot hide a very bad script. Post-production editing can make up for a lot of sins. Many video projects have been saved because the sound editor was able to cover over audio problems. We have already seen that assembly editing can resolve problems.

You now know that a variation in the type of transition you use between shots can set up the mood of either the before or after segment. You have seen firsthand how adding music can help to amplify or detract from the mood of your sill shots and stop action videos.

Let's review how the following techniques help or hurt a video in relationship to some of the effects we have already learned for the camera. Notice that the list is a lot longer for the post-production phase:

What kind(s) of emotional responses can you elicit from each of the following camera actions?

- camera angles **superiority or inferiority, heroism, strength**

- camera shots (close-ups versus medium shots) **emotional ties with actor**

- lighting **sadness or happiness, passion, spirituality**

- slow motion **tiredness, use of drugs, etc.**

- strobe **stop action, drug use, etc.**

- filtering of image (like using a stocking over the lens) **romance, aging, etc.**

- focus transition between two people or one person and a group (rack focus) **person overhearing conversation**

- quick zoom **surprise, astonishment**

- others?_____

What kind(s) of emotional responses can you elicit from each of the following post-production activities?

- fade to black **depression/death**

- cut to black **violence**

- insert of a picture of a doll or clown without music **child's play**

- insert of a picture of the same doll with Marilyn Manson music in the background **fright, danger, monsters**

- the use of different background colors on a CG (blue versus red versus purple versus green versus yellow) **cold, heat, rage, envy, cowardice**

- off-centered or dutch angle **kooky, crazy, uneducated, off-balance, impending disaster**

- quick cuts **passion, excitement**

- using the chroma key **surreal, artificial**

- insert edit of a close-up of a someone's reaction to what is being said **reinforces the statement**

- filtering the image (like using a cheesecloth or sand to age the image as in *Citizen Kane*) **romance, aging, etc.**

- others? _____

On-Camera Activities
News Readings

Activity Planning Considerations

Agenda

A large part pf developing visual awareness with students involves their becoming aware of their own images and improving their opinions of themselves. Younger students are very self-aware, to the point of being self-conscious. These three activities provide an opportunity to turn that energy into something positive and useful. The first activity is to have students read a news script in from of the camera. Without any pre-planning or instruction, announce to your students that you are running auditions to see who can read well and that they are to read a news script in from of a camera. The script may be written on paper or presented on a teleprompter.

If you need a teleprompter, the **Web-ASSISTant** Web site links to a Web page that offers a shareware program paid for on the honor system. It is not a sophisticated program, but it is sufficient for the purpose of providing students with a chance to fell what it is like to read from a teleprompter, just like the professionals do on television. There are also several sites on the Internet that contain actual news scripts from local newscasts. The **Web-ASSISTant** Web site lists links to those sites. Rigging a teleprompter is easy. If you place the computer screen close to the camera (or, even better, attach it to a television monitor through a scan converter), students can practice reading the script from the teleprompter software. One thing to remember: The farther from the camera lens the reader is, the less likely it is that the viewer will notice that the reader is using a prompter. This has a lot to do with the viewing angle of the camera in relationship to the reader.

News Reading #1

The best learning opportunity comes from students reading the news script without any print instructions regarding how one is to read on camera. You then have the opportunity to sit down one-on-one with the student and watch the video. Together, you can review the video. You can offer a critique to supplement the student's own observations. about the performance. Experience has shown that you will have the student's undivided attention throughout this session. Students are very interested in doing better, and you are providing assistance in a nonthreatening way. This session is not about earning a grade. Rather, like many other competencies in this course, student simply receive points for attempting the reading. A majority of your students will probably never wish to appear on screen again. This exercise is your one opportunity to provide constructive feedback to your students. They receive follow-up points for the second reading, in which they offer their own critiques of how or whether they improved from the first reading.

If you are following the "Teaching Chronology," this part of the activity will be introduced approximately one to two weeks prior to students receiving their first instruction on body language and other on-camera techniques. This will make the comparisons much more striking and therefore, meaningful to them.

News Reading #2

After you have had a chance to review the reading individually with each student, you can tell the students that everyone received points for attempting the reading and that no actual assessment grade was given. Next, set a goal for each student to redo the reading using the suggestions in your written assessment. This time, the reading will be graded and added to their portfolios. This project is a very positive experience that returns more than a self-critique. While watching, the students notice the camera work done by their peers. They notice the symmetry and vectoring considerations discussed in class. Students thus elevate their visual awareness and begin to synthesize their knowledge of camera techniques to an analytical level. This is much more rewarding and a better learning environment than simply memorizing facts presented in class during direct instruction. Most of the time set aside for this activity is to provide an opportunity for each student to get in front of the camera and read a script. Therefore, the allotted time will depend on the number of students in your class.

Student Instructions: Part of developing a visual awareness is to develop a sense of how you look when you appear on television. Like anything else, being effective in front of the camera requires that you develop the ability to see yourself in your mind's eye and learn to recognize that you are displaying certain traits. That is why you often see a monitor placed in a professional studio where the talent can see themselves.

It is well known that not everyone likes to appear in front of the camera. It is not a requirement of this course that every student develop an affection for this function, only that they gain an appreciation for what it entails. That is why you are asked to complete this activity whether you plan on making a career out of being an on-air talent or not. One of the premises of the script readings is to provide an early opportunity for you to get involved in this function of television. Developing self-awareness is a major anticipated outcome for this course. You will certainly improve in this area as the course progresses. Who knows, you might even learn to enjoy it! This may be a mortifying experience for some. But you need to promise that you will at least try it. Everyone needs to do this once, even those more comfortable behind the camera.

You are going to participate in two readings. The first will take place early in the course. Like many of the other early activities, this first reading is intended to establish a benchmark from which you will be able to evaluate your own progress in this area. Your first reading will take place prior to receiving any instruction on the subject. You will not be allowed to use a studio monitor to see yourself on-camera for the first reading. The monitor actually makes most people feel more self-conscious, anyway. A normal result might be that you will feel very self-conscious and be more focused on your own image than on the script, the camera, the crew, or your director's directions. You will need, to practice prior to recording onto your portfolio tape. You will receive a passage to read. It will be either on paper or on a teleprompter. You are to practice the script until you feel comfortable with it. Then your partner is to record you reading the script on your portfolio tape.

The second reading works the same way. The major difference is that you will complete it after you have received some instruction on body language, the dos and don'ts of on-air behaviors, and on-air etiquette. You will probably feel much more comfortable with the second reading. This time, you may use a studio monitor.

Both readings will be quite short (30 seconds to one minute). They may include some names that are difficult to pronounce. These types of names and places are often included in the scripts you receive while recording audition tapes. The idea is to provide you with as real an experience as possible.

How You Will Be Evaluated

You will receive points for the first reading simply by getting the recording onto your portfolio tape on time. It will be used in a one-on-one meeting with your teacher in which you both critique your performance, according to the on-air checklist developed for class. These points will be made to facilitate skill development so that the second reading will show growth.

The second reading will be graded according to a growth scorecard. The majority of the grade will be awarded for showing an improvement from the first reading. In other words, you will receive points for how well you address the shortcomings noted from the first reading, as well as a grade for your overall performance. This way, everyone has the opportunity to receive a good grade for this activity regardless of desire to complete it or overall ability. You are only competing against yourself, not others in the class who may have a natural flair for the task or have had a lot of practice.

Portfolio Project #5
Interview for a News Magazine

Project Planning Considerations

Agenda

In essence, this project demonstrates the basic building blocks of creating a newscast or a news magazine format in cookbook fashion. The goal is to provide a logical method for students to follow to build an interview that will be inserted into a segment for the main show. An interview is easy to begin with and adds content depth and sophistication in a student's first full segment. Students have already covered the three main aspects of writing for a news show. Now they have the opportunity to use the list of newsworthiness criteria to develop valid questions to build a premise. They also get to plan their video shots, using those presented in Lesson 4.6 in **Chapter 4.** A special checklist is provided that summarizes the concepts. Students are asked to review the checklist and consider which video devices and newsworthiness criteria they plan to use as a premise. This provides a great review and allows them to sue their creativity to figure out a way to make a good interview.

The topic for the news segment and accompanying interview is a historical event, a prominent person, or an invention related to the development of radio and television, per the history lessons. Generally, those who have followed the "Teaching Chronology" will have covered at least through Lesson 6.9. Students may choose any idea they wish but must consider how the interview is to fit into the *Decades* project in **Chapter 6.**

Using one of these events, person, or inventions provides a means for students to actually use some of the facts they have been taking notes on during class. This activity provides the opportunity to synthesize cognitive information to accomplish a task.

The checklist ensures that students use the concepts that were presented in the class sessions that covered scriptwriting and how to do an interview. Using the history lessons as the subject matter adds another planning dimension. Because we are essentially redefining the term *news,* students will have to make decisions about how to make the subject timely, as some of these events took place almost 100 years ago. Other decisions will involve selecting appropriate video and writing styles.

Students are assessed using the same project scorecard used for earlier projects. Section 1 of the scorecard provides a space to check off whether the news segment checklist found in **Chapter 4** was included with the project submission. Section 2 contains a space to check off whether the student understands the building block concepts brought out in the news segment checklist.

Mediated and Textual Support

Because the subject of the interview comes from the history lessons, students may use information gathered during those sessions to write their scripts. They may also use any materials found in the school's media center, such as books, CDs, and videos, for research. The **Web-ASSISTant** Web site contains a "Hall of Fame" page that has links to several sites for many of the individuals discussed in class.

Student Instructions: Interviews look easy to build. Not much shows in the way of creativity. However, a lot goes into making an interview work, from pre-production, to the shoot, and even in post-edit. The scriptwriting portion of the interview is not too difficult and is a significant part of the pre-planning. Ask the wrong questions and the whole interview may fail. How the talent acts on camera is crucial also. An interview tests the resourcefulness of the talent in reacting to questions that are not answered according to script or when some other unexpected event happens. In post-production, the interview must correctly tie in to the main part of the show, be of correct length, and be edited for technical flaws. That is why this project is introduced as a part of the lessons on production.

Your team is to conduct a taped interview. The interview is to be slated into a news magazine show format called the Decades project. The format and premise for *Decades* are explained more fully in project #6. The talent in *Decades* will introduce the interview, cut to it, and then wrap it up afterwards with an appropriate summary or segue. The whole segment (including interview) should last no more than four or five minutes. The person you interview should be (or a relative of) someone from broadcast history that we discussed in class. Therefore, the questions and corresponding responses should be placed in the proper context. To prepare for the interview, use the interview checklist found in **Chapter 4.**

How You Will Be Evaluated

The project will use the same scorecard as earlier projects. Additional consideration will be taken into account under **Criterion #1** for segment continuity. Points will be awarded for the introductory and concluding segment properly tying into the interview. Points are also awarded for a script and storyboard, as well as how well the interview ties to the decade chosen for project #6.

RESOURCES

Kizlik, R. *Strategic teaching, strategic learning, and thinking skills.* Available: www.adprima.com/strategi.htm. (Accessed September 14, 2004).

Tyner, K. 1998. *Literacy in a digital world: Teaching and learning in the age of information.* Mahwah, NJ. Laurence Erlbaum Associates.

CHAPTER 6

The Birth of Radio and Television: A Condensed History of Broadcasting

INTRODUCTION AND LESSON GOALS

Getting young students interested in history can sometimes be a daunting task, especially when they discover that the teacher is attempting to teach academics in a course that was supposed to be fun. Yet becoming literate in media and broadcasting requires background knowledge in at least **some** of the situations and major events that led up to current circumstances. The ultimate goal of these history lessons is to lend cognitive support for an "arts-based approach to media education" as proposed by Kathleen Tyner in *Literacy in a Digital World*. Tyner warns that "one danger of a media arts approach is that in the process of learning by doing, students often fall into a technicist trap by marginalizing the analysis component in the quest for production" (1998, pp. 32–34). History is one such analysis component. Because it is essentially an ebb and flow or pendulum that swings back and forth between actions and public reactions to those events, knowing something about the history of broadcasting is both a comfort and a warning signal.

It is a comfort to know that dramatic changes do not always portend the end of the world as we know it. But we also learn that not all change is good, nor is its content always original. Students should learn that history has a tendency to work in repeating parallels, as can be clearly demonstrated by looking at the "Hall of Fame" page on the **Web-ASSIST-ant** Web site. There, a very coincidental comparison is made between David Sarnoff and Bill Gates, both historical icons of their time. Sarnoff's motives for television were intended to ensure that history did **not** repeat itself. He did not want what happened to radio to happen to television: There would be no ham (i.e., amateur) television operators while he was alive and in control. Yet it is interesting to note that, now that television is finally coming into full bloom with hundreds of options, local access channels run by nonprofessionals will be a major part of television's future.

The warning comes from realizing that certain events can lead to harmful results, if left unchecked. In these sessions, students learn about RCA's attempts to monopolize the radio industry. Were it not for several coincidences and twists of fate, radio may never have evolved into the entertainment device they now know. Students also learn that, although it is very difficult to monopolize an entire industry, it can happen. (It is interesting to note that most high school students do not even know what a monopoly is, let alone understand why they should be concerned about the problem.) The publicity surrounding Microsoft's attempts to control the communications industry is both a bane and a blessing.

No matter what the subject is, teachers often have trouble justifying why history should be taught. At first glance, television and broadcasting is no exception. Students often sign up for television production as an elective course in an attempt to augment their GPA. Their notion of how class time should be spent more than likely would not include anything that smacks of academic endeavors. In some regard, this view may not be an incorrect one. Adding history lessons runs the risk of turning students off and losing focus on the real purpose of the course.

A television teacher has an opportunity that can often be lost in the academic environment: to make the subject matter relevant to the students' real-world environment. Because television is so much a part of their everyday world, students are often naturally curious about how the media became so ingrained in our culture. Once they see that all the media hoopla and the current state of our media-rich society actually are the result of some extraordinary coincidences, circumstances, or luck, they become infatuated with its story. Television history is rich with all those things, characterized as it is by attempted monopolization, uneven governmental regulation and interference, and the sometimes down and dirty tug of war between the technical dreamers and doers from big business. The sad story of the competition between Philo Farnsworth and David Sarnoff, as told by the video *Big Dream, Small Screen,* is particularly interesting to students.

The circumstances surrounding the growth of radio also play a significant role in how the television genre evolved. At no time during the twentieth century was public interest in current events not directly influenced by audience infatuation with an electronic communication medium. Even today, the influence of televised news events in our daily lives is sometimes incalculable. A student of television does not stand a chance of understanding the traditions in this industry without getting at least some cursory overview of its history.

If, indeed, the futures of the telephone, television, and computer are all somehow intertwined, then knowledge of their independent histories is crucial to foreseeing their potential combined prospects. Although television was dreamed about during the late 1800s, it did not become a technical reality until the late 1920s, it did not become a consumer product until the end of the 1930s, and it certainly did not reach its **golden age** until the 1950s. It is only now that technological advances are allowing the medium to reach its real potential. It is important to understand the reasons for the many delays in its development and to know why some of the regulatory controls that were once considered very necessary are now being shredded as fast as the megamergers of large corporations are taking place. History will provide the basis for understanding what Alan November referred to as a new **"digital combine"** (1998). Technology is certainly fomenting cultural changes in this country that will far surpass those that came about during and after the Industrial Revolution.

Historians often refer to history as being a giant pendulum. Things come and go out, and many "changes" are simply a return to previous ideas that went out of favor. This is particularly true in the television industry. The monopolies of the 1920s pale in comparison to the size and scope of the industrial giants created today by megamergers. What makes big companies okay today? Why were they completely wrong for the 1920s? Our history lessons might offer a clue. One thing remains constant, whether we are considering the newspapers, radios, television, or the Internet: It is all about managing and potentially manipulating information. The phrase "knowledge is power" is morphing into something like *"managing the information flow* is the real power." To understand this concept, students need to understand the evolution of media.

The historical topics covered in this module are aimed at the media and visual literacy goals set forth in the very first training session. The timeframe is limited to the bulk of the twentieth century, beginning with Guglielmo Marconi coming to America to cover the yacht races. The breaking points are arbitrarily set at decades, realizing that no issue ceases to exist just because the decade changes. These time limits offer a fairly logical breaking point. Each lesson carries a theme representing the one or two major events that took place during that time that shaped or influenced the outcome or historical perspective. Each lesson has a catchy title to help students remember the significant influencing event or thought process of the important individual during that time.

To ease possible tensions in the very first session, tell your students that they are getting the summarized version (which may be referred to as the *Reader's Digest* version). The miscellaneous facts, dates, and names have been condensed down into only those who made a significant contribution or were involved in a *critical path* development without which television would not have been a success. You can also tell them that they will not be required to memorize a numerous dates, names, or inventors. The goal of these lessons is to present and discuss the *chronology* of events; the curious coincidences and twists of fate; and the major backroom deals that made people, the broadcasting industry, and the government react in certain ways. Many of those reactions have become the foundation for the traditions, laws, regulations, and media literacy issues that are current media events today.

The chapter is broken down into 12 short lessons (approximately 25 minutes each), and two general follow-up discussions about the future of television. The breakdown is as follows:

Lesson 6.1	The Pre-Marconi Era	1870–1900
Lesson 6.2	Everyone Gets into the Act	1900–1919
Lesson 6.3	The Birth of Broadcasting	1920–1940
Lesson 6.4	Babes in Broadcastland	1920–1930
Lesson 6.5	Making Order out of Chaos	1927–1934
Lesson 6.6	Go for Broke	1935–1945
Lesson 6.7A	The Birth of Television	1945–1975
Lesson 6.7B	Go West, Young Man	
Lesson 6.7C	*Quiz Show*	
Lesson 6.7D	Beyond Prime Time	
Lesson 6.8	The Last Great Ride	1975–1985
Lesson 6.9	The Birth of Tabloid and "Reality" Television	1986–?
Discussion #1	Has the Chaos Returned? (The Telecommunications Act of 1996)	1996– ?
Discussion #2	What's the Big Deal about 2006?	2000–2006

The sessions are short enough to allow for some other activities within a single class period, even for those on a standard 50-minute schedule. For those on the 4 x 4 block, students will have about one hour during each class session to work on projects.

Unless otherwise noted, the supporting resources for these lessons are the same. Several references are made in this first lesson to photographs of paintings. These pictures are found in the book *The Tube of Plenty,* written by Eric Barnouw. It is one of several books that are used as references. There are couple of ways to allow students to view these pictures: Insert them into a PowerPoint® presentation or show them on an overhead projector. Although understanding the concepts does not require that these specific pictures be used, they certainly clarify the points.

An introduction to the most influential individuals in these lessons can be found at the "Hall of Fame" page on the **Web-ASSISTant** Web site. Each has a summary introduction and links to sites at which additional information about them can be found.

Many lessons are preceded by introductory passages with review questions. The goal of having the students read these passages is to encourage them to become actively involved in classroom discussions.

Projects #5 and #6 are introduced at the end of this chapter for students to synthesize material and demonstrate their understanding of audience analysis. In project #6, through the use of footage, pictures, and other information provided throughout the lessons, student teams produce a five- to eight-minute video that presents visually their concept of what it was like to live during their chosen decade. Because there is not much in the way of available video footage, recordings, and so forth for earlier eras, students naturally gravitate toward the 1950s through the 1990s. This decision process is actually a lesson about the value of television. Students learn the value of having video footage with which to present information.

DIGGING DEEPER

To obtain further details about the events that are described in this chapter, the following books may be of great use:

Auletta, Ken. 1986. *Three Blind Mice: How the TV Networks Lost Their Way.* New York: Random House.

Barnouw, Erik. 1990. *The Tube of Plenty.* New York: Oxford University Press.

Tartikoff, Brandon. 1992. *The Last Great Ride.* New York: Turtle Bay Books.

Internet links and other information about how to obtain copies of these texts is included in **Appendix J**.

SEQUENCING THE LESSONS IN THIS CHAPTER

The lessons in this chapter were written in contextual sequence. That is to say, they have continuity with regard to subject matter and can be taught in the exact order they are presented. However, to reach the specific goals attempted by this course, it might be better to follow the suggested sequence outlined in the "Teaching Chronology" in **Chapter 1**. At a minimum, it makes sense to at least consult the prescribed format to make an informed decision.

Lesson 6.1

The Pre-Marconi Era
1870–1900

Lesson Planning Considerations

(**Approx. time:** 25–30 minutes)

Agenda

This session is entirely about Guglielmo Marconi, although some of the early information on how he got to America is included. What the title refers to is the events that led up to his coming to this country and setting up one of the most significant corporations in broadcasting history, RCA. Almost all the events leading up to the founding of RCA and subsequent to its role in the development of television were the results of the people, events, and interesting twists of fate during this time. This session covers about 30 years in about 25 minutes. The most important and relevant events are included.

Objectives and Outcomes

The objectives for all the direct instruction lessons are the same. As a result of these discussions, students will learn the following:

- People dreamed of someday having a video projection device in their living rooms as early as the 1870s.

- The term *radio* did not always refer to an entertainment device, as it does today. It was first conceived of as a military device to communicate at sea during wartime and later used commercially.

- Marconi arrived in America through some very ironic twists of fate.

- Paul Nipkow's spinning disk was the invention that gave people the idea that transmitting a visual image was possible. It became the basis of John Logie Baird's work on mechanical television in the United Kingdom.

Mediated and Textual Support

Additional information on Marconi may be found at the "Hall of Fame" page on the **Web-ASSIS-Tant** Web site. *The Tube of Plenty* has several pictures showing the various paintings discussed in this lesson. Showing them to students should help to stimulate their interest and curiosity.

Lesson Readiness

By reading the opening passage and participating in the discussions, students should begin to focus on the following:

- In many cases, a g*olden age* follows very closely to the time when new technologies are first introduced to the public. This was true of radio and the Internet. However, this did not happen with television. The question is: *Why not?*

- A *golden age*, by definition, does not necessarily refer to the best works. Rather, it represents a time defined by the most growth and creative energy. Often, the best works follow this era. This is especially true of those things supported by technology.

- Early radio was more like a telephone than the entertainment device common in today's world.

Closure

Much of the learning about history is a cognitive activity and is demonstrated through successful completion of written tests and quizzes. Questions regarding this lesson appear in quizzes and exams throughout this course.

Introductory Reading

If we wanted to make this class a full review of the historical events that led up to modern communications, we would have to go back to the Gutenberg printing press. Certainly the histories of newspaper, radio, and television are intertwined. However, we have chosen to start with the invention of the telephone and telegraph as our jumping off point. We mention this only in passing to use it as a backdrop to describe **Marconi's real invention: the discovery of how radio waves could be made to travel through the air without the use of wires**. In short, it was the world's first wireless telephone. **To be more exact, it was a wireless telegraph**. Wireless voice transmissions had not been figured out yet, so a special coding of a series of *dots* and *dashes* had to be used to carry data. This is why **American Telegraph and Telephone (AT&T), the country's largest provider of wired transmission services, viewed this new invention as a competitive threat.**

First let's introduce the text that we will use as the basis of our history sessions: *The Tube of Plenty*, by Erik Barnouw. This is a college-level text with lots of pages. Our task is to give you a *Reader's Digest* (condensed) version. The most salient points from this book have been summarized to lead to our discussions about how television got to its current state and its design for the future. The good news is that we are not going to cover history in great depth or memorize a lot of people's names or a huge list of dates. That is not what history is really all about. **Historical references best serve to provide perspectives and to answer certain questions**. When we are done, you will understand the intimate relationships the radio and television industry had with the military and certain shipbuilding industries, and why those came about. You will understand that people dreamed of someday having a video projection device in their living rooms as early as the 1870s. You will find that *radio* did not always refer to the entertainment device it is today. Numerous people helped pave the way to television. We will only look at a few individuals who made the most significant contributions. You will learn that the new enhancements and a surge in the use of radio and television were often the result of ironic twists of fate rather than of thoroughly designed plans or business propositions.

The first thing you have to understand is that the golden age of television did not occur until the late 1950s. Yet, the idea of television was almost 100 years old at that point. Our sessions will show you why it took so long to develop. The term *golden age* does not necessarily equate with being the **best** age. Rather, it refers to the era of the greatest increase in use, a time when creative energy was at its highest level. Many say that television is much better today than during the 1950s. However, based on a percentage of new users and new shows that came on to the scene, the 1950s have been historically referred to as the *golden age of television*.

Today, inventions and technological advances are cropping up so fast and furious that it may be difficult to imagine a time when developments took decades to unfold. People were indeed afraid of change and progress.

Questions

1. What communications device is used as the jumping-off point for our discussions into television? **<u>Early radio experiments</u>**

2. What is the name of the book used as the basis for these sessions? **<u>The Tube of Plenty</u>**

3. What is meant by the phrase "Historical references best serve to provide perspectives and to answer certain questions?" **<u>history often repeats itself; history is a giant pendulum, etc</u>.**

4. What does the term *golden age* refer to? **<u>A time when the most new development takes place</u>**

5. When was the Golden Age of Television? **<u>1950s</u>**

6. When was the concept of transmitting visual images into the home first conceived? **<u>1870s</u>**

Terms

Nipkow's Disk	**John Logie Baird**	**black box**
British Marconi	**wireless telephone**	**Morse code**
America's Cup	**Guglielmo Marconi**	

Teacher's Note: The pictures described below come from *The Tube of Plenty*. If you decide to purchase the book for use in class, you may wish to show the pictures to your students.

Lesson Notes

Regarding change, people can generally be broken down into two groups: those who look forward to and are excited by it, and those who fear or loathe it. Perhaps you know someone who is always complaining about change and who wishes things cold go back to "the good old days." You probably know others who cannot wait for new things to happen. This is very typical. Evidence of those who feared technology intruding into their lives can be seen as early as the 1870s, when a picture entitled *Terrors of the Telephone* appeared. This picture does not exactly paint a picture of calmness. People were terrified of technological changes and perceived the telephone as an invasion of privacy into their homes. Hopefully, this might help you to see that everything is relative. Today, we talk of computers doing exactly the same thing.

On the other hand, there are those who long for the future and cannot wait for new technology to be invented. In 1876, **George du Maurier** painted a picture that depicts a family sitting in front of the fireplace watching moving images projected on the wall. By 1882, another picture appeared in print, painted by **Albert Robida** depicting essentially the same thing. Imagine a flat screen video device 50 years prior to the first television! Talk about *Star Trek*!

About the same time (1879), Paul Nipkow came up with the first of the many inventions that we will be discussing in class. Remember, breakthrough inventions usually occur at the end of a long line of previous innovations giving the inventor an inkling that their device would actually work. **Nipkow's Disk** was one such early invention. For the first time, people got the idea that transmitting an image from one location to another was actually possible. As you saw in *Understanding Television,* Nipkow's Disk is like a spinning peephole in which light is transmitted and converted into energy. All the initial experiments in television were based on Nipkow's Disk. In fact, **John Logie Baird**'s work in England was totally based on the spinning disk idea. Just like the video showed us, not until decades later, when it was discovered that the disk would have to measure 14 feet across to work on a full size set, did the idea fall out of favor. The invention showed that transmission was possible, even if it would have to be done differently.

The main question we are going to answer in this session is

Why did television take so long to develop?

There are many reasons. Before we can get to some of them, we need to look at how **Guglielmo Marconi** came to America. His idea of how to transmit a message without using a cable or wire was an important concept that eventually made possible the development of television. The fact that he came to America is important to the development of the broadcasting industry in this country. Yet his coming here was due more to coincidence than planning. Marconi was an average kid who spent a lot of time thinking about what were then called *hertzian waves* (named after Heinrich Hertz, the German scientist who first demonstrated their existence). His ideas were further intensified through analysis of static electricity. He spent hours developing his **black box**, a device that transmitted **radio waves** to another receiving device across the room. Once he convinced his parents that it was for real, they took him to people they knew in Italy to see what the future might hold for this new invention. Unfortunately, Marconi's parents could not find anyone interested in Italy because no one could figure out what to do with this thing.

Marconi's parents sent Guglielmo to England. During his visit, an important member of the French government was murdered with a bomb. Thinking that it was an explosive devise, the customs officials in England confiscated Marconi's box, the only working model, and destroyed it. Marconi had to start from scratch. Fortunately, he found financial support from members of the British Post Office. They set up a new company, **British Marconi,** with a small amount of seed money.

Marconi's work did not go unnoticed in America. About that same time (1898–1899) the Spanish American War broke out. This was the first war in which ships were used extensively in a strategic deployment. The U.S. military was having a difficult time communicating with its vessels. Hearing about Marconi's device, they realized that it might be an excellent strategic military tool. This concept of the black box being a military secret weapon increased its popularity with the government as well as making it a closely guarded secret. That view remained unchanged for decades.

Understand that the box was more like a **wireless telephone** than anything else. First, it was a **one-to-one communication**. The concept of a broadcast did not come along until a quarter-century later. Second, there was no voice. The communication was done with **Morse code**, a combination of long and short tones that, when used in series, made up words that were translated. Voice did not come into play until the early 1920s.

After the war, the first commercial use for the box was conceived. The *New York Herald* newspaper was at that time sponsoring the **America's Cup Yacht Race** outside of New York Harbor. Someone there came up with the idea that, if they could somehow station Marconi with his box at the finish line, they could actually get the results of the race published even before the ships returned to harbor. Yes, it was sort of a publicity stunt, but it worked! Marconi was invited and did what the newspaper had hoped. The *Herald* gained tremendous publicity and word spread like wildfire about Marconi's box. He had found an important new market for his product.

Next session, we will talk about what happened during the first 10 years after Marconi's arrival in the United States, the new American company he set up, and the struggle by the U.S. military to maintain control over this new strategic, (not-so) secret weapon.

Lesson 6.2

Everyone Gets into the Act
1900–1919

Lesson Planning Considerations

(**Approx. time:** 25–30 minutes)

Agenda

After the success of the America's Cup experiment, Marconi's Wireless of America was formed. This single act opened up an era of unparalleled activity and development not unlike what we are experiencing today with the Internet. The major theme of this session is to point out **how the new invention gradually turned from being viewed as merely a not-so-secret military weapon into the massive entertainment machine broadcasting is today**. To understand how remarkable an accomplishment that was, students must understand that the early radio did not employ voice transmissions, let alone broadcasting methodology.

The second point that is important to understanding any history is that **successful breakthrough inventions are not the result of any one, single act of genius.** Usually, they are the result of a long line of previous innovations leading up to the final idea. Also, the one who usually gets the credit for the invention is not the one who actually thought of the idea. Often, the one who made the new idea a commercial success is credited with the invention. This was certainly true of Robert Fulton and the steamboat, for example. Television is no exception. Not only did we have a whole cast of characters who contributed to the eventual development of television, but the man who really came up with the idea for how television in America would be based (Philo Farnsworth) was almost overlooked by history. If David Sarnoff had the vision to keep RCA focused on the eventual goal of driving the television industry, then Mr. Farnsworth was the vision.

Objectives and Outcomes

At the end of this lesson, students will learn

• how it came to pass that AT&T, GE, the military, and Westinghouse got involved in the radio business;

• who ham radio operators were, and what role they played in the development of the radio; and

• who David Sarnoff was, and how he got started in the broadcast business.

Mediated and Textual Support

Additional information on the early radio may be found on the "Digging Deeper" section of "Chapter Six" on the **Web-ASSISTant** Web site.

Lesson Readiness

The reading passage found at the beginning of this lesson is intended to reorient students to what has transpired to date and to point out how the early radio was looked upon by the military and American business. It is also intended to point out how this new invention was used during its early days. In its early form, the radio was more like a wireless telephone or telegraph than anything else.

Closure

Much of learning about history is a cognitive activity and is demonstrated through successful completion of written tests and quizzes. Questions regarding this lesson appear in quizzes and exams throughout this course.

Introductory Reading

The success of the America's Cup experiment unleashed an era of unparalleled development in the communications industry in this country similar to what were are now experiencing with the Internet. By 1901, Marconi Wireless of America had been formed, with British Marconi maintaining a 30 percent ownership. This is an important point. Because the military thought of early radio as being mostly a strategic weapon, the fact that it was owned by a company based in a foreign country was very bothersome. You should also note that **AT&T considered this new wireless telegraph** a **competitive threat** because they made money by selling parts, and they feared a world without wire would put them out of business.

Radio broadcasting as we know it today did not yet exist. Technology had yet to deal with range limitations and the ability to transmit actual voice. Recall that the original transmissions were nothing more than wireless telegraphs that communicated via Morse code.

Questions

1. What was Marconi Wireless of America? **Company formed by Marconi in America**

2. Who owned 30 percent of this new company? **British Marconi**

3. How did the military look upon of the new invention of the radio-telephone? **As a strategic weapon**

4. How did AT&T think of it? **As competition**

5. True or False: The original radio/telephone was capable of voice transmission.   T   (F)

Terms

Reginald Fessenden	**Westinghouse**	**Radio Relay League**
audion tube	**AT&T**	**David Sarnoff**
WWI	**Lee DeForest**	**United Fruit Company**
hams	**GE**	

Lesson Notes

By 1906, an engineer for Westinghouse Electric (the major parts supplier to AT&T), Canadian born **Reginald Fessenden**, was experimenting with **voice transmissions**. He established the National Electric Signaling Company (NESCO). Fessenden might have been a genius, but he did rather poorly in two areas: he failed to convince the buying public that his idea would actually work (they originally ridiculed it), and he was a poor businessman. His company eventually failed and he sold his patents to **Westinghouse**. In the meantime, he was the one who eventually came up with the name *radio*. He referred to it as a **radio-telephone**, which was shortened to **radio-phone**, and eventually simply to **radio**. Although Westinghouse finally added voice around 1922, the idea of broadcasting still had not occurred to anyone.

Voice transmissions required the radio to be more powerful. Some type of power boost was required. Along came another inventor who happened to work for General Electric, the company that Edison founded to carry on his business plans with the light bulb. In 1907, **Lee DeForest** had the idea that the light bulb essentially performed the function of boosting power to produce light. He came up with the idea that this same type of functionality could also boost radio waves. His **audion tube** came about in 1909. In essence, the audion tube was an amplifier that permitted voice transmissions to travel great distances. Unfortunately, DeForest could not finance the idea commercially on his own. He sold his invention to AT&T. Thus, **GE** joined **AT&T** and **Westinghouse** and as a player in this fledgling industry.

Because shipping companies were the main customers for this new form of communications, several began to form their own invention factories to develop ways to enter the market using their own technologies. The **United Fruit Company** was one of the most successful. Several of their engineers contributed interim inventions that helped further develop and better the ways that radio worked. Because of their early successes, they, too, joined the GE, AT&T, and Westinghouse triad as a major player in this market.

In the meantime, the **military** was feeling that the field was getting too crowded. It still jealously held onto the idea that radio was a strategic weapon. It wished to control any public use of the radio for commercial purposes. The military needed AT&T, GE, and Westinghouse to provide technology and parts. This was the beginning of a long and enduring tight relationship between the U.S. government and these companies that has lasted nearly 100 years.

By 1912, chaos was reigning. The airwaves were filled with crackling codes and voices. It was a period of uncontrolled growth. There is an uncanny parallel in the growth and development during the early days of the radio industry and the current growth of the Internet. No one *owned* the airwaves, therefore, no one could control them. Those involved in the industry in the really days were a fairly well organized group of amateurs called **hams,** a term that in not unlike the current *nerd* or *geek*. All this was going on while the military grew even more frustrated and impatient because of its contention that the radio was nothing more than a strategic device that needed to be controlled.

The radio came into its own as a news-carrying device for the American public when, in 1912, the *Titanic* sank. A then unknown 21-year-old clerk of Marconi Wireless made a name for himself by staying on top of the news about the *Titanic* and feeding this information to the newspapers. His name: **David Sarnoff**. Remember this name. We will be hearing a lot more about him in later sessions.

Teacher's Note: For years there have been rumors about David Sarnoff and whether this story is true. Other apocryphal stories arose from time to time, also giving credit to Sarnoff for inventing the concept of broadcasting. Whether they were true or not, Sarnoff did nothing to quell these rumors and actually encouraged them. These rumors add to the myth of the man who did more than anyone to develop broadcasting as a commercially viable business.

By 1918, the military's concerns were realized due to a significant event: **World War I.** Many have credited U.S. communications abilities, brought on by the wireless radio, for helping us win the war. The war also brought home the idea to AT&T, GE, and Westinghouse that wars actually make some folks a lot of money. Due to the thousands of radios and millions of parts needed for the war effort, these three companies became very rich.

The concept of a **military-industrial complex**, as it was referred to during the late 1960s and early 1970s, was forming. Much of the distrust younger Americans had for the government during the Vietnam War was because many thought that we kept that war alive simply for big business to make big money. The kind of money made by AT&T, GE, and Westinghouse in World War I helped sow the seeds of that economic reality.

The military kept up its pursuit of monopolizing the radio industry for its own purposes. It would have won its case were it not for a group of **hams** called the **Radio Relay League**. This group made a name for itself helping the military win the war. Later they would save the radio for the American public, as we shall discuss in our next session. The idea was that the hams would organize a formal call chain (the first person agrees to call 10 others; those 10 call 10 others, and so on). This organized method of mass communication allowed these amateurs to be in control of the flow of information about the industry, more so than the professionals involved in the industry. In short, the military lost its battle for the monopoly, but it eventually appeared to win the war. It got Congress to set up a publicly held company: RCA (the Radio Company of America). On its boards of directors were (not so surprisingly) **AT&T, GE, United Fruit Company,** and a **military general.**

What happened to Marconi and Westinghouse? What were they going to do? Stay tuned to our next session to find out.

Lesson 6.3

The Birth of Broadcasting
1920–1940

Lesson Planning Considerations

(**Approx. time:** 25–30 minutes)

Agenda

If the period right after WWI could be referred to as radio's infancy, it was really nothing more than what Eric Barnoux called it: the "toddler period." The amazing thing about it is that the golden age began almost simultaneously with its early development as a full-fledged broadcast medium. Several significant milestone events led to the explosion in the number of radio broadcast stations that appeared on the air almost overnight. This phenomenon will compare significantly to the golden age of television, which happened almost 50 years after television's first appearance as a technical reality. This significant teaching point needs to be stressed during the next few lessons.

Depending on the age group of your students, you will have to teach two important vocabulary terms as part of these lessons: **monopoly** and **golden age**. Experience has shown that first-year high school students have heard of these two words but cannot explain them in their own words. The lesson script assumes that these terms have already been discussed.

Objectives and Outcomes

At the end of this lesson, students will learn

• that GE bought up all the assets of American Marconi, paving the way for Sarnoff;

- how Westinghouse finally got invited to join the monopoly;

- how, in the initial years, the monopoly was failing; and

- how the monopoly finally overcame the head start of the amateurs and took control.

Introductory Reading

State of the art in radio by 1920:

- Radios were still one-to-one communication devices until 1920.

- People were already talking about a visual radio right after WWI.

- The government tried to monopolize the radio.

- The Radio Relay League established its method of networking information during WWI.

- RCA's board of directors was composed of members from AT&T, United Fruit, GE, and the military.

- There were no preconstructed radios for consumer use. All radios had to be constructed part-by-part each time one was needed.

Questions

1. Explain in your own words what a monopoly is: **One company controls an entire industry**

2. Before 1920, radios were capable of broadcasting.   T   (F)

3. The idea of television is a new one.   T   (F)

4. How did the Radio Relay League provide the initial ideas for broadcasting and networking? **Relayed messages using a call chain**

5. Why did the government try to monopolize the radio? **They thought of it as a strategic weapon.**

Terms

> **Frank Conrad**   **broadcasting**   **preassembled radios**
> **killer app**

Lesson Notes

When RCA was set up, it appeared to be just like any other publicly held company. Stock was sold and it looked as though it would compete in the marketplace. What was not generally known at the time was that AT&T, GE, United Fruit, and the military figured that there would be no competition. Any time the military needed products, it would only purchase them from this company. **AT&T** took control of all transmissions. **GE**, which owned the rights to Marconi's black box at this time, took control of the parts business and any antennae that might be required. Marconi Wireless, as you may recall, was partly owned by British Marconi. As a part of its articles of incorporation, the government got the board to agree that only U.S. citizens could become officers. **GE** eventually bought all interests of **Marconi Wireless of**

America with all its patents and assets (including employees like Sarnoff). Over time, United Fruit Company eventually dropped out of the business, leaving everything to the remaining three. **Westinghouse** was left out of the loop.

What saved Westinghouse was one of its engineers, **Frank Conrad.** Taking his lead from the idea born of the networking concept demonstrated by the Radio Relay League, Frank Conrad came up with the idea that the radio, too, could actually communicate **one-to-many**. This concept, later known as **broadcasting,** came into being in Conrad's garage. He would experiment with sending signals for many to hear and would eventually entertain hundreds each Saturday evening playing the piano, playing classical music from his record player, inviting neighbors over to sing, and so forth. These originally informal concerts grew into regularly scheduled *Saturday Night* programs.

To make a long story short, Conrad convinced Westinghouse that the broadcasting idea would work. Westinghouse secretly came up with an idea for a consumer type of **preassembled radio** that would sell for $10. In 1920, Horn's Department store, in Pittsburgh, Pennsylvania, ran an advertisement in the local newspaper for these preassembled wireless radios. They were an overnight success. Many of their customers purchased this new Westinghouse Radio Receiver. Within two years, there were more than 500 radio stations on the air.

This was the **killer app** that Westinghouse (and RCA) needed to make the industry take off. (Killer app is a term in use in the computer industry. It relates to a software application that helps solidify or validate a computer's niche in the marketplace). To keep control of the monopoly, **RCA had no choice but to ask Westinghouse to join its empire**. Westinghouse finally got in the club! Westinghouse would control the receiver end of the business, AT&T was to *own* the transmitter end, and GE was to sell all the parts and antennae.

The monopoly was apparently safe. The golden age of radio was beginning. The monopoly had *total control* (or so it thought) of the entire industry. But an interesting thing happened on the way to the empire. By 1922, over **$60 million** of annual equipment sales had taken place, but only **$11 million** went to RCA. This does not sound like a monopoly.

What Went Wrong?

An uncanny series of events, greed, and unfortunate circumstances led to the initial failure of the monopoly:

1. First, Lee DeForest retained rights to sell his parts to his **hams/amateur friends**. DeForest considered himself one of them and wanted to continue doing business with them. For whatever reason, GE went along with the idea.

2. After the war, there was a tremendous **surplus of parts**. Amateurs could purchase an unlimited supply of parts sold wholesale to army/navy stores.

3. The amateurs had an advantage. Besides being able to get parts cheaply, their entire not-for-profit motivation and operation led to **cheaper broadcasts**. **They didn't pay royalties** and all the employees worked for free. This amateurism eventually evolved into professionalism with all its increased costs. (We will see how this happened in our next sessions.)

4. Until this point, **the only way to make money in radio broadcasting was to sell parts**. At this time, commercials and advertising did not exist and were not necessary. This also changed later, as we shall see. If the parts company (RCA) could not make money because the amateurs were **purchasing their parts elsewhere**, their major source of income would disappear.

What was to happen next? Stay tuned for our next session.

Lesson 6.4

Babes in Broadcastland
1920–1930

Lesson Planning Considerations

(**Approx. time:** 20–25 minutes)

Agenda

The purpose of this review is mostly to lock in with your students the reasoning and rationale behind the formation of RCA and to help them understand why the Radio Act of 1927 was so momentous. Because it is mostly a review session, you can use the time to make sure students understand that the early radios were really not thought of as entertainment gadgets but rather commercial communications devices and military strategic weapons. The relationship between the RCA monopoly and the government was really tight and is one example of the military-industrial complex that would become the subject of protests during the late 1960s and early 1970s.

At the end of this session, students should be able to define in their own words what is meant by the term *golden age*, why the Radio Act of 1927 became necessary, and what the events were that led up to the establishment of the National Broadcasting Company (NBC).

Objectives and Outcomes

At the end of this lesson, students will have learned

• how NBC was born,

• how Westinghouse got into broadcasting and opened KDKA, and

• how the rivalry between RCA and AT&T finally ended with the formation of networks and the concept of selling advertising space.

Introductory Reading

The state of the union in radio in the early 1920s:

• **Westinghouse's** outlook appeared bleak.

• Frank Conrad began *Radio-Phone* (*Saturday Night*) Concerts.

• These concerts actually carried out what **DeForest** had envisioned.

• Many others followed suit.

• Amateurs were broadcasting **cheaper**.

• The **monopoly** was not working.

- In 1920, Horn Department Store ran a newspaper advertisement for a **$10 radio receiver**.

- Westinghouse saw the light, beginning production of premade, ready to use radios. Because of its success, Westinghouse was **asked to join RCA**

Questions

1. The monopoly between RCA and the government was working well: T   (F)

2. Why were Westinghouse's prospect for joining the monopoly looking bleak? **Westinghouse had nothing to offer.**

3. What invention eventually got Westinghouse invited to join? **Preassembled radios**

4. How were the amateurs able to make their broadcasts cheaper than the monopoly? **Did not pay royalties; used spare parts; donated labor**

Terms

army surplus	royalties	ASCAP
KDKA	toll broadcasting	golden age of radio
network stations	NBC	compromise
advertising space		

Lesson Notes

Earlier we discussed the fact that amateur radio stations were producing shows frequently and cheaply, and that the monopoly interests were quite worried. Not only were the amateurs purchasing parts cheaper from **army surplus**, but their talent pool worked gratis. No **royalties** were being paid, and no one was enforcing copyright laws. The free ride did not last, however. What started out as a hobby ended up being just as complicated and just as expensive in the long run as a commercial enterprise. In 1923, an **A**ssociation for **S**ongwriters, **C**omposers, **A**uthors, and **P**ublishers was formed: **ASCAP**. Within a few years, this organization grew to become one of the most powerful and influential unions in the country. Even today, ASCAP wields tremendous influence and power over the protection of creative works. Concurrent with its rise in power was a natural inflation. The free ride was over for the amateurs.

At the same time, the U.S. government began to get aggressive by issuing licenses. Unfortunately, these early attempts at regulation had very little policing power. The licenses **had no teeth.** Also, once a license was issued, it never expired. There was little or no language regarding how a station would actually lose its license.

The first fully licensed station was established in **Pittsburgh,** as a result of Conrad's efforts. To this day, Westinghouse owns station **KDKA.** Within two years, there were over 500 stations on the air. We call this time period the **golden age of radio** because there was so much growth. Going from zero to 500 stations represents a 500 percent growth in a very short time. Corporate creative juices were flowing as to how to take advantage of the golden age. But how were all these broadcasts going to be paid for? Recall, RCA was not exactly making the lion's share of profits. Until this time, the only way the monopoly could make money was **to sell parts**. Would there be a government tax? That was considered but quickly rejected. Some tried a donations theme. Just like public broadcasting today, people tend not to donate in sufficient amounts for an entity to be self-sufficient.

About the same time, AT&T was beginning to experiment with **toll broadcasting** (remember, they owned rights to airwaves). Their idea was to replicate in broadcasting what had made them a lot of money in the telephone business. People would pay for usage. To add value, they devised a plan to **network stations** using long distance lines between cities. (See Figure 6.1.)

Figure 6.1. AT&T's Early Radio Network Concept.

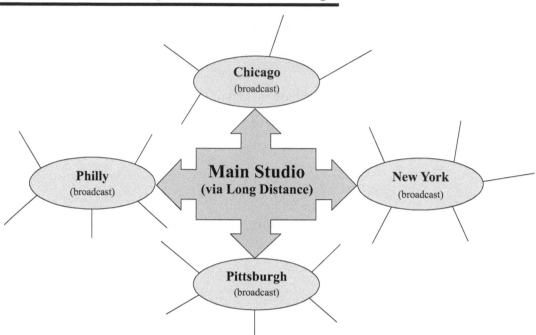

The networking idea failed initially. Partially by accident, they stumbled on the idea of selling **advertising space**. Although this did not work immediately, the idea picked up steam. By 1923, the networking concept added value to an advertiser's sponsorship. AT&T seemed to be in power with its **networked stations** idea.

As an aside, we have to mention that television experiments were also being tried. These experiments were spurred on by the early successes in radio.

Meanwhile back at RCA corporate headquarters, GE and Westinghouse were becoming extremely worried that **AT&T** was gaining too much power. AT&T began to stop buying **receivers** from Westinghouse or **parts** from GE and began building their own. Making matters worse, Westinghouse and GE feared that this might also extend to television and did not want to be left out. GE & Westinghouse went to court to stop AT&T . . . **and won!** But, that did not stop AT&T. The fighting was extremely bitter, public, and lengthy, lasting for over two years.

To make a long story short, the government worked out a **compromise**. For each party to protect its own interests and businesses, a broadcasting company would be formed for the exclusive purpose of keeping the monopoly alive and well in the broadcasting world. In 1926, **NBC** was born! **GE** and **Westinghouse** were the majority shareholders. **AT&T** did not get any stock, but it would receive an annual royalty. As this was mostly a broadcasting entertainment venture, the military had no seat on the board. However, the interests of RCA were certainly there, and that company carried on its businesses as usual. The government still had a **very close relationship** with this emerging business that would last until the 1970s.

Thus, we see that AT&T got out of the broadcasting business and how Westinghouse and GE remained. If we spin quickly ahead in time to 1998, we see that things have come full circle. GE still owns RCA and NBC. Westinghouse got out of broadcasting briefly and then got back in with its purchase of CBS in the early 1990s. Now, Westinghouse has spun off all its military and commercial businesses and renamed itself CBS. Westinghouse, as a company, no longer exists. AT&T got back into broadcasting in 1998 with its purchase of TCI, one of the largest cable operators in the nation.

As the old saying goes:

The more things change, the more they stay the same.

Lesson 6.5

Making Order Out of Chaos
1927–1934

Lesson Planning Considerations

(**Approx. time:** 25–30 minutes)

Agenda

This lesson is followed by a short deliberation about the need for the Radio Act of 1927 and a discussion about the need, in general, for regulation. This is intended to set the scene for a later lesson in which students are introduced to the Telecommunications Act of 1996, which, in effect, removed all these regulations. The lesson and review questions should take about 20 minutes to complete. This leaves about 10 minutes for the discussions. At the end, students should be able to form a preliminary opinion about whether the industry should be overseen by the FCC or be left to self-regulate.

Objectives and Outcomes

At the end of this lesson, students will have learned how the government finally put some teeth into its regulations.

Closure

Students answer the review questions at the end of the lesson to ensure they have understood the information.

Terms

Red and Blue networks	commercials	**CBS**
talkies	**RKO**	**Radio Act of 1927**
Paramount Studios	licenses	**antimonopoly**
	simulcasting	**federal radio commission**

Lesson Notes

This is a reading lesson. Instead of the passage serving as an introduction, it serves as the lesson itself. Read the following and see if you can fill in the blanks with the appropriate words from the list. Then answer the review questions at the end.

By 1927, NBC had two radio networks: **Red** and **Blue,** because communications traffic was so heavy. NBC still appeared to have total control of all broadcasting outlets; there was no competition.

This became an era of increased interest in **commercials** by the country's largest corporations. We shall see in later lessons that the industry became so commercialized that a public outcry erupted to limit commercial time during broadcasts, and Congress was compelled to offer a compromise plan. Eventually a peace came over the broadcasting industry, since there was no apparent competition and the radio industry appeared to be under control. The fights that characterized the earlier years within RCA finally calmed down.

However, in a capitalistic society, money begets money; and money also begets competition. A new competitor entered the arena in 1927 and shook things up again: **CBS**. Although not as big as NBC, it did cause a lot of concern for the other broadcasting companies.

The peace at RCA/NBC did not last. The corporate mentality of the titans in this industry was that they wanted to have sole control of anything that had to do with communications. With television just on the horizon and the movie industry heating up, the partners started going out on their own again in order not to be left behind. GE began to experiment with television on its own.

Teacher's Note: NBC/Universal is now a wholly owned subsidiary of GE.

AT&T was up to its old tricks again. Because of the invention of the **talkies**, AT&T got into sound business with the major movie studios without advising its partners. GE & Westinghouse (i.e., **RCA**) felt left behind, so they teamed up with **Kaufmann** and **Orpheus** (a company that opened up movie theaters all over the country) and formed the **RKO** movie theater chain, one of the largest and most successful in the country. **Music** was becoming important to movies, so, RCA bought two small music companies in 1927 and 1928 and formed the RCA record label.

Experiments with **television** appeared in the late 1920s, using stop action pictures and a **radio for sound.** Is this the origination of **simulcasting**? (The practice of displaying the video portion of a show on television and simultaneously airing the audio portion on radio.) What had happened with radio (amateurs, etc.) was beginning to recur with television. Was the chaos going to resume? Many people, especially those in Congress, thought so.

The earlier acts passed by Congress had no enforcement power. However, in 1927 Congress passed one of the most significant and comprehensive communications laws to date: **the Radio Act of 1927**. Unlike previous laws, it had enforcement powers. It included such things as

- establishing the **Federal Radio Commission** (oversight agency to enforce the rulings);

- requiring **licensing** for each channel (they were no longer perpetually owned);

- including **antimonopoly** regulations (limiting the amount of financial holdings companies were allowed so that no one company could obtain total control of any aspect of the business);

- limiting the **number of outlets** per market;

- limiting **the power** of each station; and

- including a clause for **television.**

In response to increasing financial troubles, CBS sold 40 percent of its interests to **Paramount Studios**. The seeds were sown for the tie-in of radio and television with the movie industry. From that day forward their paths would travel together, so much so that, by the 1950s, the movie industry would re-enter the television marketplace and change the landscape of television forever. (Again, history repeats itself. After later having to divest itself of all interests in CBS, Viacom, the parent company of Paramount, bought controlling interests in CBS in 1999.)

Teacher's Note: CBS is now a wholly owned subsidiary of Viacom.

David Sarnoff made a prediction in 1929 that within **five years**, there would be a television set in every household. He was in a position to know. He was secretly saving money to pay for research and development efforts in television. His prediction was off by about 50 years; a couple of events got in the way that even he could not have forecast:

The Great Depression & WWII

Questions

1. What invention caused the movie companies to form relationships with RCA? **Talkies**

2. Name two instances in which a joint business effort between members of the radio industry and a major movie studio was formed: **CBS & Paramount; RCA and RKO**

3. How did the early movies and television experiments get their sound? **Simulcasting from radios**

4. Why did NBC form a second network? **There was too much traffic for one.**

5. What was the major motivation for Congress passing the Radio Act of 1927? **The industry was getting out of hand.**

6. Name four pieces of regulation that were part of the Radio Act of 1927 that added "teeth" to it: **It limited licenses, limited broadcasting power of each station, limited number of stations per market, and had antimonopoly regulations**.

7. Do you think there was a need for the government to intercede in the radio industry? Yes /No Why/why not? **Possible response: Otherwise the industry would become chaotic, too few companies would control it and become monopolies).**

Going for Broke
1935–1945

The Philo Farnsworth Story

Lesson Planning Considerations

(**Approx. time:** 50–60 minutes. This may be covered in five separate sessions.)

Agenda

Both the successes and failures of radio during the 1920s shaped what was about to happen in television. In the end, radio produced consistently huge profits for the RCA cartel, which was finally beginning to show signs of a real monopoly. David Sarnoff grew to become head of RCA and all of its businesses, including NBC. RCA's control over broadcasting was so strong that any business that wanted to participate in the industry had to pay RCA a royalty. The royalty concept became the founding principle on which the commercial industry was built. Advertisers would, in fact, pay a royalty for the privilege of having their names mentioned on the air. As much as RCA finally controlled broadcasting, Sarnoff was paranoid about making the same mistakes in television as were made in the early days of radio. There would be no **ham television operators** if he could help it. No amateurs need apply.

If any inventors came along with any concept that hinted at becoming competitive with RCA, Sarnoff either bought them out or devised a plan to otherwise take control of the new idea. This is the basis of the rivalry between Sarnoff and Philo Farnsworth, the real inventor of electronic television. It may also been one of the reasons for Farnsworth's downfall. Farnsworth did not want to compromise with Sarnoff and naively thought he could challenge the power of RCA. He was offered money to sell his invention to RCA, but he held out for a royalty, a concept Sarnoff rejected.

Project #5, *the Interview*, coincides with the completion of this lesson. The interview format used in the supplementary video to save time introduces students to an alternative way of accomplishing this project. It also provides the first visual images of the major players in the industry: David Sarnoff, Vladimir Zworkyn, Philo Farnsworth, and so forth. These visual images serve as models for students to use in the interviews of famous people in the industry.

This lesson uses the PBS video *Big Dream, Small Screen: The Philo Farnsworth Story,* following it up with group discussions. It may be played in one sitting in its entirety (it is 60 minutes in length) or be broken up into four or five smaller sessions. From earlier sessions, students know who Sarnoff is. They understand the problems the monopoly had in the early days, and how Lee DeForest outsmarted them. They also know a little about the audion tube, so, when they are shown on the video how Farnsworth perceived the early picture tube would work, they can relate to it quite easily. The video reinforces visually what they have already discussed in class. Spacing its viewing over several days treats it like a serial; students anxiously wait for the next installment to see what happens. This video will make a significant impression on your students.

Objectives and Outcomes

At the end of this lesson, students will be able to

- describe the relationship between Philo Farnsworth and David Sarnoff and how Farnsworth, until very recently, never received recognition for his ideas;

- describe the differences between Farnsworth's and Logie Baird's inventions; and

- describe why the commercial development of television took from 1939 to the 1950s to reach its golden age.

Lesson Readiness

The entire lesson is really a learning set for the video and adds closure to the lesson.

Closure

After viewing the video, students answer the review questions. You may also wish to spend some time discussing the hardships inventors often face getting their products to market. Another excellent discussion opportunity is to ask students how it was that Farnsworth never received credit for his invention.

Terms

John Logie Baird	**Paul Nipkow**	**effects of the Great Depression**
ABC	**serials**	**mass communications**
Edwin Armstrong	**PBS**	**setbacks to introduction of television**

Lesson Notes

We are going to watch a video over the next few days. It is *Big Dreams, Small Screen: The Philo Farnsworth Story*. We are going to see how Farnsworth came up with the idea for his version of television. As you may know, there were several other inventors who were working on different concepts. For example, **John Logie Baird** in the United Kingdom. was working on a mechanical model that took its idea from the spinning disk invented by **Paul Nipkow**. The remarkable things about Farnsworth's idea are that

1. he discovered and researched it on a farm that did not even have its own source of **electricity,** and

2. he was only **14 years old** when he came up with the idea of electronic television.

Before watching this video, we need to be brought up to date with what was happening during the early 1930s and into the 1940s. This is the backdrop, or canvas, on which we will paint the Farnsworth picture:

> In 1929, the **Great Depression** began.
>
> The monopoly was getting out of hand:
>> too much greed
>> too many scandals

Because of the **effects of the Depression**, public sentiment against **big business** was probably as high as it would be during any other time in U.S. history. In 1933, the Justice Department finally began to break up the broadcasting monopoly. RCA was now a separate company from NBC, and the FCC required RCA to divest one of its networks. **ABC** came from the Blue Network.

During the Depression, the only links people had to the outside world were their **radios**. People would give up their furniture first before parting with their radios. This was the age of the radio **serials** (continuous storylines throughout many episodes). The airwaves were full of commercials. The question was, did advertisers sponsor the programs, or were the programs simply a vehicle to keep listeners' attention until the next commercial break? There were no truth-in-advertising laws. The regulations introduced in the Communications Act of 1934 added **PBS** to balance things. The FCC was challenged with the task of managing the electromagnetic spectrum based on phrases like "public trust" and "localism," which exist to this day.

Teacher's Note: Thus, the Communications Act of 1934 was a very important piece of legislation. Not only did it establish public radio, but it also brought into the vernacular the famous phrase "in the public trust," which carries forward to this day. This phrase indicates that the rights to a certain slice of the electromagnetic spectrum will always remain free and be managed by the government, similar to how certain portions of land and the environment are preserved through the National Park Service.

Edwin Armstrong came up with **FM radio,** which had much better sound. RCA fought it because Sarnoff thought it would interfere with the development of television. Even though the Great Depression stalled the introduction of television, the U.S. audience's dependence on **mass communications** grew. Radio gradually replaced newspapers as the primary way they received news and information.

How did we break the Great Depression? Yes, that's right, with another war. World War II did divert efforts for commercial use of television, but **technological advances** developed in the war helped in the end. RCA got into the **radar** business.

Meanwhile, CBS was doing some interesting things just to survive. **Paramount Studios** owned 40 percent of CBS. To fill dead air time, they were willing to take chances, and they

- developed better newscasts and

- purchased old *Amos & Andy* and *Jack Benny* shows from the radio.

As a result, RCA was making all the money, but CBS was winning all the awards.

As a review of our previous lessons, the following are offered as a summary of the **setbacks to the introduction of television as an entertainment medium to the masses:**

- **WWI** (during the 1910s)

- **Great Depression** (during early 1930s)

- **Antimonopoly sentiments** (during the 1930s)

- **WWII** (during the 1940s)

- **McCarthy hearings** (during the early 1950s)

- **Cold War** (during the late 1950s)

Why the marketplace was finally ready for television right after WWII:

- **Technical developments** during the war.

- **Spare parts** at army surplus.

- The **economy** in the United States was finally ready.

- The **baby boomers.**

- People became interested in **the news;** they wanted information.

- Television shows easily transferred from **radio.**

Now, on to the Farnsworth video. As you watch this video, pay particular attention to the surroundings in which Farnsworth was raised. Decide whether if it were you, you would have had the fortitude and money to bring your ideas forward against the odds that appeared to be stacking up against Farnsworth.

In this video, you are going to find out how Farnsworth came up with the idea; how it is that, until recently, few really knew who he was; and the trials and tribulations he went through to bring his idea to life. It is a remarkable story.

Questions

1. What triggered the idea of electronic television in Farnsworth's mind? **Plowing his fields reminded him building a screen one line at a time. He was very well versed in electronics through the magazines he read. Electronics were covered in every magazine.**

2. Looking back on mechanical television, do you think it ever had a chance to succeed? If so, why? If not, why not? **No. It was too bulky and slow.**

3. Which of the following do you believe were some of the reasons behind Farnsworth's failures? **Circle those that apply.**

    He was undercapitalized.

    His idea did not work.

    He had no formal education.

    Mechanical television was a better idea.

    Sarnoff had a better idea.

    No one wanted television.

    Television was too expensive.

    Sarnoff was a better inventor.

    Farnsworth was naïve.

4. Why do you think Sarnoff was so bent on making sure that RCA controlled all aspects of broadcasting? **Possibly, he learned his lessons from radio (remember DeForest?).**

5. What, if anything, could Farnsworth have done differently to become a success? Do you think he should have sold his invention to Sarnoff? **Possibly, to get more capital and form an alliance with Sarnoff, Vladimir Zworykin, or both**

6. Do you think Sarnoff was a positive or negative impact on broadcasting? **Both. Although he tried to squash Farnsworth, he did lead the way at RCA for several decades.**

7. Who do you think is really the father of American television, Sarnoff or Farnsworth? Why? **Both played a role.**

Lesson 6.7

Lesson Planning Considerations

(**Approx. time:** 25–30 minutes each)

Agenda

In some regards, this series of four sessions is the pay off for all the time the class has spent on history to get to this point. Because there is considerable video available, it is quite easy to actually visually demonstrate many of the events that helped shape history during this period. Certainly, most students are already familiar with several of the prominent television shows from this era through watching reruns and nostalgia networks such as TVLand. There are also many videos that can be purchased with performance rights that you can use in class to show students what television was like in those days.

Prior to taking this course, few students, if any, seem to understand why the 1950s are considered the "Golden Age." Most students come into class with a preconceived opinion about what constitutes good television (high reliance on special effects, extraterrestrial beings, and so forth). They do not quite "get it" with regard to classic television and why there is so much hype about the "good old days" in television land. They certainly do not understand that the baby boomers are driving a lot of the romantic sentiment about the 1950s. They also will not understand that television did not depict life as it was like during the 1950s. The movie *Pleasantville*, through its satire, also provides many discussion points about the good old days. The humor will be lost, however, unless you spend some time going over what really happened during that era.

If you have covered broadcast history, as prescribed in the previous sessions, you will be able to relate to the reasons why there was so much pent-up demand for television and why the market was primed at that particular moment in time. The first session begins with a review of those concepts. As mentioned during the discussions about the radio golden age, younger students are not quite sure what constitutes a golden age. Therefore, the second goal of these sessions is to remind students of the factors that make an era "golden."

It has already been seen, during the showing of the PBS video on Farnsworth, that providing a prior understanding of the historical events surrounding the invention of the television made the showing quite enjoyable to most students. Similar experiences will occur when you discuss the 1950s if students have a basic understanding of the times that the shows depict.

A note about the format: This and the succeeding lessons have the note-taking blanks already filled in. This is to accommodate the *Decades* project, which follows at the end of this chapter. Having the notes already filled in provides flexibility on how these lessons are to be covered. One method may be to introduce the project after showing the film *Quiz Show*. The note pages for Lessons 6.7 through 6.9 can be used as aids to help students find materials. Covering the lessons may take the shape of a review of completed projects. Students then have an objective of making their videos cover the topics well enough to use them in class in place of the lectures. This also helps to move the class away from direct instruction and involves students more in their learning.

Mediated and Textual Support

Because there is so much material available on video, there are several opportunities in these last few history sessions to play the programs in class. This is certainly a worthwhile practice. In fact, specific programs or movies are referenced as examples in this chapter. One word of caution: Be sure to obtain performance rights for anything you want to show in class. One way to do this is to attach a form with all orders that describes your intentions to purchase the videos for in-class use.

Lesson 6.7C is based on the movie *Quiz Show*. If you obtain performance rights to this movie, it is an excellent opportunity to show a high-quality production that represents a clear picture of what things were like during the 1950s. Most videos that students see relating to that era are in black and white and present a rather drab visualization. As a result, students' are turned off by the lack of color. Generally speaking, students like this film; can relate to Robert Redford, the producer; and recognize many of the actors. In short, they easily identify with the film, enjoy watching it, and learn something in the process.

A cautionary note: There are one or two spots in the film where the language needs to be reviewed for student consumption. You should watch the film first to identify the areas in question.

This movie can be purchased with in-class performance rights, if it is ordered properly using the correct distribution channel. Teachers should check with their compliance officials to determine how this might be done

The Annenberg/CPB Project sponsors a video series on filmmaking that includes one of particular interest. *Film & the Television Age* traces the way film and television have influenced each other beginning with the Golden Age of television. This session discusses that relationship in some depth.

The Teacher's Video Company distributes a set of seven videos about series television from the 1950s, *Classic Television*, showing clips from the *Lone Ranger, Roy Rogers, Howdie Doody,* and other popular programs.

Objectives and Outcomes

After watching this movie, students will be able to

- discuss the Charles van Doren scandal and relate its impact on television and the American public,

- describe the close relationship that existed between RCA and the U.S. government,

- explain why providing answers ahead of time to contestants is not in the best interests of the viewing public,

- discuss NBC's rationale for providing these answers, and

- explain the impact television had on the viewing public.

Lesson 6.7A

The Birth of Television
1945–1975

Terms

Joseph McCarthy	blacklists	anthologies
quiz show scandal	early television pioneers	Edward R. Murrow
Charles van Doren		majestic mission

Student Instructions: In this lesson, the class will be watching two videos. *Quiz Show* and *45/85: America Since WWII*. There are review sheets for both of these videos. You are asked to show your understanding of the concepts in these lessons through your participation in the *Decades* project, which will be introduced in the next few days.

The McCarthy Era

Throughout the early 1950s, television stations made their debuts and were joined together by coaxial cable and radio relay. The three national television networks took shape (NBC, ABC, and CBS) using a technology similar to that radios first used during the 1920s. Schedules expanded, and sponsors made their moves. The mass acceptance that David Sarnoff had predicted was finally taking place.

Throughout the course of history, inventions come along that people just sense will be a successful, even though no knows, at first, what use it can be to people. Radio was one of these technologies, and so are the cell phone and personal computer. Television appears to have joined this group right from the beginning. Although no one was sure what to do with it (another solution looking for a problem to solve), everyone was sure that they needed it. The first groups within the broadcasting companies to use the new a medium were the newsrooms. For the first time, people could watch the news in their living rooms. These close and early ties to the news brought resulted in a special significance to the role many perceived that television should play in our lives. Television, it seemed, was bigger than life, and carried with it a special august purpose, or **majestic mission** for the American public. This perception persisted into the late 1980s and early 1990s, when television evolved into what we shall see in later lessons is a gigantic money machine. Television was an instant hit, possibly because there was so much pent-up anticipation. Recall, it was first introduced to the public in 1939.

With all the good that was happening in television, several very negative events took place that clouded the era. First was the series of Senate hearings on communism held by a committee headed by **Joseph McCarthy**. Several performers, producers, and writers from the entertainment industry were called to testify. Many were accused of being Communists and were **blacklisted**. Some never recovered. McCarthy's efforts expanded into the FCC. He purged the FCC of its existing membership, replacing them with those loyal to him. Most of his accusations were based on rumors. (Lucille Ball was even accused but later cleared in a much ballyhooed pronouncement.) History has shown that McCarthy was probably correct in many of his assumptions. His downfall was how he implemented his solutions.

Episodic Series Came to Television from the Radio World

Better known as **anthologies,** episodic series finally came to an end due to pressure from their sponsors. Advertisers were selling **magic** (their own view of reality. Recall our discussions on deconstructing commercials?) and were in constant conflict with the serious nature of the anthology series. As these sponsors became more powerful, they interfered more and more with scripts. In 1953–1954, five anthologies ranked in the top 10 shows. By 1955, none showed up. From these episodic anthologies evolved the **television series, but it was** seriously altered. All America's problems, it seemed, had to be solved in 30 minutes to suit the sponsors.

Early Television Pioneers: *Studio One, TV Playhouse,* Paddy Chayefsky

The evening news format (15 minutes) became *very* popular. News cameras and **visual images** became more important than what was said (unlike radio, where **audio** was king). Sponsors still displayed impressive control. For example, Camel cigarettes was a major news show sponsor. They did not allow cigars to be photographed in any news story, nor were there any **no smoking** signs. Some of the news anchors who became famous during the 1950s were

John Cameron Swayze	Edward R. Murrow
Dave Garroway	Douglas Edwards

Edward R. Murrow, in particular, is an interesting story. In his *See it Now* show, he exposed McCarthy for what he was. Murrow was able to do on television what no one else seemed able or willing to do. **This one show established television as a viable and indispensable medium**. The television excitement of 1953–1955 and rising viewership were bringing in many new sponsors.

The Real $64,000 Question

As many awards as he won, Edward R. Murrow had to concede to the rising popularity of the quiz show. The size of the award was **big money,** and the concept of **holding the contestant over** extended the show's excitement. By 1957, five of the top ten shows were **quiz shows**. They drew a phenomenal 84.8 percent share of the market. The quiz-show era ended in 1958 with the **Charles van Doren** scandal on the program *Twenty One.* The movie *Quiz Show* depicts that scandal.

The movie *Quiz Show* depicts that affair.

Lesson 6.7B

Go West, Young Man

Terms

Nikita Khrushchev	importance of Westerns	telefilms
The Untouchables	television moves to Hollywood	
	show themes of the 1950s	

Lesson Notes

The Press Was Almost an Arm of the Government

Throughout the 1950s, networks only broadcast what was *released* to them by the government. This type of behavior did have its foundations in earlier times. For example, very few people knew that FDR had polio, because he was never filmed in his wheelchair.

Eisenhower used the power of the media **to introduce his diplomacy initiatives**. All news about the government that was to appear on television was rehearsed beforehand. It was not until the late 1950s that news conferences were actually shown live. **Broadcasting topics and coverage were literally controlled by the government's wishes**. Whatever was stated by government sources was considered the truth. CIA operations were disguised and not made public, including our early involvement in Vietnam during the late 1950s.

There was a vacuum of truth. It was so deep that whatever the government said, had to be the truth because there was no other party who would dispute the information made available. (Recall our earlier discussions about misinformation and disinformation.)

All this was done in the name of defeating communism. Television, it would appear, was perceived by the government as a military weapon (sound familiar? Remember our discussion about radio during the early 1900s?).

Telefilms

By the end of 1957, however, television had entered an new era. The entertainment aspects of the medium started to take hold. What brought us there were the **telefilms**. By the end of that year, more than 100 series of these television films were on the air or were in production.

By the end of the decade a surge in **crime mystery shows** modeled after the gigantic success of *Dragnet* took over. These shows included *Highway Patrol, Perry Mason, Official Detective, The Vise,* and *Richard Diamond.*

As international intrigue surged, so did **superhero** shows, including *Captain Gallant, Captain Midnight, I Led Three Lives, A Man Called X, Superman,* and *Passport to Danger.*

But Westerns dominated. They included *Hopalong Cassidy, Lash Larue, Gene Autry, Roy Rogers, Jim Bowie, Annie Oakley, Cisco Kid, Gunsmoke, Wild Bill Hitchcock, Fury, Lassie, My Friend Flicka, Tales of Wells Fargo, Rin Tin Tin, Have Gun Will Travel, Tombstone Territory, Restless Gun, Zane Grey,* and *The Lone Ranger.*

By 1958, **30 Westerns** were on in prime time. There was violence (people got shot), but the shows always included a redeeming social value: **The bad guy always lost**. Not only was he arrested (it was always a "he" in those days), but he often made a break for it and had to be killed. There was an unspoken premise that evil must always be conquered and subdued by the hero and that the normal processes of justice were inadequate. This spawned the first concerns about violence on television.

In 1958 Nikita Khrushchev became Premier of the Soviet Union. His presence in world politics only helped to further the goals of those in government who wished to control the media. It should be no wonder that

- television played a crucial role in shaping public opinion about world events,

- it would be possible for the government to use the media to hide its activities, and

- we could become so fixated on stopping communism regardless of the cost.

In 1959, Vice President Richard Nixon agreed to go to Moscow. During his visit, he and Khrushchev entered into a **live debate in a kitchen** exhibit that was part of a cultural exchange between the two countries. They both agreed to do it without cuts and editing, something unheard of previously in world politics. What followed was a 16–minute encounter that is remembered to this day: one of the initial rounds of the decades-long **Cold War**. Khrushchev was quoted as saying during one of his meetings with the U.S. ambassadors, "We will bury you!"(*The Ukrainian Weekly*, 1960).

Meanwhile, Back at the Ranch . . .

Westerns continued their assault in the entertainment arena. In 1959, of the top 10 shows, Westerns accounted for five. It was also in 1959 that the famous quiz show scandals came to light. This meant more to the shaping of what the purpose of the television industry was to be than anything that came before it. As a result of the scandals, **television executives decided to eliminate quiz shows from their lineups and replaced them with telefilms produced in Hollywood**. Thus, one of the principal remnants of New York television disappeared. It was the use of stock movie footage in the Westerns that caused the television industry to move west also. The entire television industry reached a crossroads:

Thus, in the wake of the quiz scandals, a split-personality pattern was becoming the network norm. One part, the *news division*, was always prepared for, and welcoming, the grandstand interruptions that had become its specialty. The other part, the real money-making part, went ahead with normal business. An inter-network battle that was suddenly turning savage (violent). (Barnouw, 1990, pp. 246–248)

ABC was still in third place. Many cities still did not even have an ABC outlet, but in 1960 the big news was ABC's release of a new show, ***The Untouchables.*** After that, every evening carried with it an action-adventure telefilm, all extremely violent by the then-current standards.

Lesson 6.7C

Quiz Show

Student Instructions: Today, you are going to watch the movie *Quiz Show*. It takes place in the mid-1950s when television was just coming into its own. People were beginning to establish viewing habits, and television producers were just beginning to understand its power. The scandal depicted in this movie would change the face of television forever.

The game show *Twenty-One* was the most-watched show of its time. Producers realized that they could get more viewers hooked if their champion remained on over the course of several weeks. They became so greedy that they actually helped the contestants with the answers. As a result of the ensuing scandal surrounding Charles van Doren, new rules were put in place that limited the time a champion could reign on a quiz show. Only recently have these rules been relaxed (as on *Jeopardy!*).

Teacher's Note: The quiz show *Jeopardy* recently instituted a change to this procedure, allowing champions extended appearances on its shows. Note that it took almost 50 years for the van Doren scandal to go away.

You are watching the show for two reasons:

- To get an idea of how television was perceived in its early days. (This movie is a period piece. It does a good job showing what the United States was like during the mid-1950s. As one of the few films you have seen about this era that is in color, it should be more realistic to you. Note the sets and props; even the old-style cameras used on the studio set.)

- To understand how television producers perceived their role in society, especially with regard to how they thought they had the power to manipulate the viewing public. Television was perceived to be entertainment, rather than a news outlet for the government. That line of thinking would later permeate even how some networks would perceive the news. The movie demonstrates the alleged low opinion television executives had of the American viewing public.

The movie will provide you with the answers to the following questions. As you watch this movie, please write down your impressions.

Questions

1. Who was Charles van Doren? **A college instructor at Columbia University**

2. Since he was from a prominent family, why is it so significant that he would actually agree to learn the answers ahead of time? What convinced him to do so (what was his rationale)? **He was trying to make a name for himself and escape living in his father's shadow. Then the lure of being under the lights got to him, and vanity set in.**

3. What was the rationale behind the network passing the answers along? **Television is not real anyway; it's only entertainment. Their rationale was that it would be good for the cause of education.**

4. Compare Charles van Doren to Herb Stempel, his competitor on the show. Do you think the differences in their appearance might have had something to do with Van Doren's popularity? **Van Doren: very photogenic; Stempel: smart but geeky. Definitely: television is an image-conscious industry.**

5. At what point does the movie reveal the close relationship between RCA and the federal government that we have been discussing in our earlier history classes? **When the special investigator Richard Goodman from the attorney general's office confronted the president of NBC (Kittner) in front of the elevator.**

6. There are several camera moves and effects in this movie that are interesting. There is one special effect in particular that is quite unique. When Charles van Doren was in the isolation booth, he had an anxiety. How did Robert Redford (the movie's director) produce this effect? **They zoomed the background out on a blue screen while keeping van Doren's image fixed.**

7. In your opinion, why was it so wrong for the network to provide answers to the contestants? After all, to paraphrase NBC, *it's only entertainm*ent. **There are several possible answers. One might be that the audience placed so much faith in what they saw on television. It represented one further example of how the morals in our country were possibly falling apart.**

Lesson 6.7D

Beyond Prime Time

Terms

Newton Minnow   two-headed monster   mid-1960s shows

early 1960s shows   official government lie   late 1960s shows

Lesson Notes

Television in the 1960s was a **two-headed monster**. On one hand, ABC ran counterprogramming to **gain** ratings. They used a lot of violent shows like *The Untouchables* and everyone else followed suit.

In 1961, in a speech in front of the National Association of Broadcasters (NAB), **Newton Minnow**, the newly appointed chairman of the Federal Communications Commission, referred to television as a **vast wasteland** and a **cultural desert.** This seems to demonstrate that people have badmouthed television for its perceived failure to accomplish its "majestic mission" since its beginnings. Minnow said there was no **redeeming social value** in daily programming, and that the broadcasters were making fortunes on it. It seems as though the majestic mission was turning into one gigantic money machine (Jankowski and Fuchs, 1995).

On the other hand over half of the U.S. population now received its news via television. Television was helping shape American opinion about world events. This created a situation in which television actually played a significant role in helping decide the outcome of the 1960 presidential election.

Other developments:

- 1961–1962 gave rise to **animated telefilms** like *The Flintstones* and many copycats.

- The United States launched its first **telecommunications satellites**, which set the scene for cable television in the 1970s.

TV Prime Time's Evolving Line-up:

Shows that appeared on early 1960s television included:

- *The Andy Griffith Show*

- *The Beverly Hillbillies*

- *Bonanza*

- *The Dick Van Dyke Show*

- Of the top ten shows, five were Westerns

Shows that appeared on mid-1960s television mirrored the Cold War with spy shows such as:

- *I Spy*

- *Get Smart*

- *Mission Impossible*

In the late 1960s shows began mirroring the Vietnam War and turned to spoofs about war such as:

- *McHale's Navy*

- *F-Troop*

- *Gomer Pyle*

- *MASH*

- *Wild Wild West:* a unique show that combined spy gadgetry with a Western motif.

Other television developments in the late 1960s include:

- First Super Bowl in 1969.

- CBS buying the New York Yankees in 1967, signaling a change in the way media did business.

- The rise in popularity of soap operas.

- A perceived overcommercialization (40–50 spots per two-hour block).

Meanwhile, Vietnam War was beginning to be broadcast at the dinner table every night. With the introduction of shows like *Mission Impossible,* the premise for the **official government lie** was born: "Jim, we will disavow any knowledge. . . "(quote from opening of *Mission Impossible* television show).

To paraphrase a famous line from the quiz show *To Tell the Truth*, which ran for more than 15 years on television:

Will the real television please stand up?

The Last Great Ride
1975–1985

Lesson Planning Considerations

(**Approx. time:** 20–25 minutes)

Agenda

The title for this lesson comes from the book of the same name, written by Brandon Tartikoff, president of NBC entertainment division during the late 1970s and 1980s. He describes a time when television was a much simpler place. The title depicts a time in television history just prior to the advent of cable television during which the three major networks dominated home viewing; a time when Sweeps winners actually captured the total market, not just a portion of the market. In the early 1970s, newcomers like HBO and other premium channels began to compete for attention and viewership (Tartikoff, 1992).

The goal of this lesson is to point out a time when the world of television was much simpler. The media invasion really did not happen until the 1990s. Some say it has not even arrived yet. Most students only know this era through reruns that appear on the Nostalgia and TVLand channels.

Mediated and Textual Support

As mentioned, *The Last Great Ride* serves as the major resource for this lesson. The **Web-ASSIS-Tant** Web site provides an online link to a Web site set up specifically to review this book. Clicking on the menu frame for the "Hall of Fame" page takes you to a picture of Brandon Tartikoff. By clicking on his image, a direct link to the Web page is provided.

Further information for this portion of media and broadcast history can be found in *Three Blind Mice*, written by Ken Auletta. This book depicts what the author refers to in his preface as the "decline of American network television" (1986).

Specific references for these two books are included at the end of this chapter. Information on how these two books may be obtained may be found on the **Web-ASSISTant** Web site, on the **Chapter 6** "Digging Deeper" page.

Terms

rabbit ears/antennae	national anthem	premium channels
Brandon Tartikoff	television shows of the 1970s	the Apple IIe

Lesson Notes

In this series of lessons, you will be watching video clips from some of the shows from this decade. You are to participate in discussions regarding television's influence on society. The big change from the 1950s is that television was beginning to reflect the true values of society, rather than escapism. It is your task to decide if that evolution has progressed too far, to the current situation in which television may be too real.

Television 20 years ago was not the vast universe it is today. Following are some of the features that have come and gone:

- Television **antennae/rabbit ears** (representing that there was no cable TV). Television viewers had these on top of their sets and moved them around for each channel they selected. People only received their local channels, and reception was not consistently good.

- Playing of the **national anthem** (television shut down at midnight and always played the anthem to end its broadcast day). Now, with 24/7 television, one hardly ever hears this song except at sporting events. When television first came on in the early 1950s, programming often didn't begin until 5:00 PM (making the introduction to the *Howdy Doodie* show particularly exciting).

In short, it was the last time period during which the three networks dominated television viewing (thus the title of the book, *The Last Great Ride*). By the end of the decade, **premium** channels like HBO had arrived on the scene. With cable television the face of television would change forever.

Because of the creative programming that first appeared in the mid-1960s, ABC took over first place in the ratings, followed by CBS. By the mid-1970s, CBS had captured the ratings. Meanwhile, NBC finished so far behind that the joke was that NBC came in **fourth** in a three-network race. In 1975, NBC hired away ABC's head of entertainment division, Fred Silverman. Silverman brought along with him a young, creative talent who revolutionized NBC's schedule: **Brandon Tartikoff**. By the end of the decade, NBC was back in first place with quality shows like

- *St. Elsewhere,*

- *Hill Street Blues,*

- *Cheers,* and

- *Saturday Night Live.*

The Thursday night schedule became known as *owned* by NBC.
Emmy winners in 1977 included:

- *The Mary Tyler Moore Show*: A show about a single woman out on her own. It was an early show that referenced the 1970s as a time that witnessed the changing role of women. It was one of the first prime time network shows in which a woman appeared in the starring role.

- *All in the Family*: A comedy show that mirrored changing attitudes toward intolerance

- *Saturday Night Live*: This show, featuring a satirical look at current events and mores, began in 1975, and is one of Tartikoff's longest-running hits. The idea was to re-create the live atmosphere prevalent in the 1950s when shows originated from New York and were live, just like the original Saturday radio concerts originated by Frank Conrad in the 1920s.

- *Roots*: A miniseries that depicted the struggles of blacks in this country from slavery through the twentieth century. It premiered in January (on NBC). This was the most-watched miniseries in television history.

First timers that started in 1977 included:

- *Love Boat*: A show that took a lighthearted look at the sexual revolution.

- *Love American Style*: Ditto.

- *Soap*: A parody that introduced Billy Crystal, who portrayed a homosexual, the first such character on prime time television.

- *Welcome Back Kotter*: A show whose view of the outcasts in the student body of a school was probably one of the first series to redefine the meaning of the term "bad."

Many considered the 1970s the best years for the movies since 1939. Releases included:

- *Star Wars*

- *Close Encounters of the Third Kind*

- *Oh God!*

- *Smokey and the Bandit*

The 1970s were also good years for songs and albums. Their resurgence in popularity is credited to things like disco and groups like

- The Eagles

- Abba

- The BeeGees

1977 also brought to market one other small, insignificant invention: **the Apple IIe.**

Lesson 6.9

The Birth of Tabloid and "Reality" Television 1986–?

Lesson Planning Considerations

(**Approx. time:** 20–25 minutes)

Agenda

From a purely historical perspective, television finally became an entity in its own right during the 1990s. No longer can it be simply referred to as a radio with pictures. Now, instead of being historically linked with radio, television's future has become the foundation of a new technology-filled communications medium. Computers are becoming interactive televisions. It may or may not be a coincidence that the term *tabloid TV* came about approximately at the same time that Rupert Murdoch, a publisher of tabloid newspapers, entered the broadcasting arena with the FOX television network. It also may or may not be coincidental that television technology took a great leap forward about the same time the FOX network introduced many new, creative, and inventive visual aids to its sports broadcasts. Different approaches, like the florescent hockey puck, several new camera shots at baseball games, new statistical graphics, and sound effects all came into existence when FOX entered television broadcasting. New and inventive shows aimed directly at the teenaged audience were also introduced. FOX led the way with its "capture-a-single-night-then-move-forward" approach to programming. Several other start-up networks copied this concept.

Although technology certainly has had a positive impact on increasing television's ability to communicate visually, television content has not all been positive. Talk shows have evolved into sideshows. Shows carrying labels like "reality television" have, in some cases, become an excuse to titillate. This is not to say that all recent changes in television are negative ones. There have been tremendous improvements, especially in delivery capabilities and increased program choices brought about by communications satellites. The addition of special interest channels automatically stratifies markets for advertisers who seek to segment television audiences so they can target the marketing of their goods and services.

Change, in itself, is not the problem, and should not be presented as such. Most people understand that change is inevitable. Students should be introduced to the fact that it is the rate of change that matters, and it is disconcerting to many. Technology is bringing about rapid changes. Society is usually slow to react to change and needs time to absorb new things. Rapidity makes learning and analysis extremely difficult. It appears that, for the first time, many of the historical perspectives will no longer serve. Fads come and go quickly, making them difficult to analyze.

The rate of technological change has increased the need for literacy education. New, nonlinear editing capabilities provide a means for advertisers to manipulate moods and emotion. The line between reality and "virtuality" is becoming less defined. Talking animals, dancing babies, and surreal environments make believable what was once fantasy. Television has become a totally constructed medium. What made television so endearing during the 1950s was that it was live. People would watch just to see what would go wrong. Today, airtime is so expensive that producers and advertisers leave nothing to chance. Instead of being solely an entertainment medium, television is becoming, again, a means to manipulate.

Because they are living through them, teenagers probably do not notice the speed of changes brought about by technology and have accommodated for it. Certainly they do not understand the need to be able to step back and view historical events in perspective. Therefore, this particular lesson provides an opportunity for you to ask students to attempt to critically examine current events to see how they would analyze them in an historical perspective, based on information you have supplied in previous lessons. An alternative would be to simply present the above information as a background, make a list of events, and ask students to do one of the following (either by themselves or in groups):

- Sort them in order of importance.

- Identify the top five or six, in their opinion, that have had the most impact on our lives.

- Relate certain events to television programming.

- Make value judgments about the positive or negative effects selected events have had on our lives.

By doing this, you provide students with their first lesson in audience analysis, the first rule in the ASSURE production planning model that is introduced in **Chapter 7**. Kathleen Tyner points out in *Literacy in a Digital World* that "synthesis of analysis and practice is the key to media education" (1998, pp. 32–34). Video producers must be able to synthesize current events and trends and capitalize on them to properly target their products. At a minimum, students will learn the difficulty of this job.

Mediated and Textual Support

Support for the point of view presented in this lesson comes from materials that have been used throughout the course. The Discovery Channel School video, *Headlines & Sound Bites*, may have new and increased meaning if replayed, even if only in part. A very effective introductory technique is to play sound bites from the video to reintroduce the current state of affairs in the communications industry and ask students whether they can equate what is happening today to any other period(s) in their previous lessons.

The CD produced by the New Mexico Media Literacy Project might offer some opportunities to discuss how the media have affected our lives recently. If you have a video of classic commercials, you might want to compare these to current commercials from the CD and ask students whether the differences in approach to marketing products are simply based on new technology, or whether mores and ethics have changed since the original commercials aired. You might find that the original commercials used hyperbole freely and that current truth in advertising requirements actually make commercials better and less intimidating.

Because media and technology have combined into one entity, they have become more than a method of presentation of information. Paul Zane Pilzer calls technology "the actual definition of knowledge"(1991, p. 121). The New Mexico Media Literacy Project CD also covers the role of technology in the media in detail.

Objectives

As a result of participating in this lesson, students will be able to

- list five of the most important events that have happened in the past decade to shape television;

- sort these five into a priority list, based on their importance; and

- explain their reasoning for the selection and sort sequence.

Closure

By participating in the discussions, students should be able to demonstrate sound reasoning for their responses and deliver an informed opinion about whether television is better or worse today than it was in its golden age.

Terms

Wrestlemania   tabloid television   talk shows
sound bites   spin doctors   57 Channels and Nothin' On
media circus   paparazzi
                                                            infotainment

Lesson Notes

Although television has been the focus of our discussions, it is only one form of media. In our earlier discussions, we have talked about how television, the telephone, and the computer are all combining into one. That evolutional aspect is the basis for our discussions in this lesson. We have to talk about the changes in television over the past decade. While doing so, we also have to direct our attention to what is happening to the process of delivering information rather than spending time on specific types of television shows that have come along, as we did when we covered previous decades.

Recall that the first order of business when designing a video production is to **analyze the audience**. This has to be done before the objectives and goals for the video can be completed.

In this lesson, we are going to look at the events surrounding television differently. Instead of taking notes, you are to prioritize the list of events and programs below, according to the instructions provided by your teacher. For this session, you need to discuss each selection with your team, then be prepared to discuss each topic in class. Yours are opinions and will be treated as such. However, you should base your decisions on some logical foundation that is representative of a group consensus.

Teacher's Note: Select one of the initiatives from the list below as the basis for class discussions. This is a group assignment. Allow class time for the groups to get together and come up with their decisions. Decisions must be based on some logical or historical foundation from class notes or readings. Ask your students to

_____ sort them in order of importance.
_____ identify the top five or six that have made the most impact on our lives.
_____ relate certain events to television programming.
_____ make value judgments about the positive or negative effect they may have had on our lives.

The two basic questions that you are asked to answer are:

Has television finally lost its "majestic mission" tag?
If so, what do you think has replaced it?

Recent Trends in Television

Yes, there have been some great shows, like *Seinfeld, ER*, and so forth. However, these appear to be in the minority. There is **increased nudity, graphic gore, and violence** (versus shows in the early 1980s such as *The A-Team* in which bullets were fired, but nobody got shot), even on quality shows like *NYPD Blue* and *Law and Order.*

By 1983, as a result of an antitrust lawsuit by the U.S. Treasury Department, the National Association of Broadcasters (NAB) had all but abandoned the code of ethics they had fostered in the 1950s. **Tabloid television,** in which news and entertainment cross the line, is one result. Examples include *COPS* and *Real TV.*

However, the real story is the **change in style of shows.** Talk shows such as *Oprah* and *Rosie O'Donnell* have proliferated.

By the end of 1999, quiz shows had returned to the scene. Based on the success of *Who Wants to Be a Millionaire* (at one point the show aired almost every night of the week), others followed, including *The Weakest Link.* NBC even tried to resurrect *Twenty-One*, the show that ended it all in the late 1950s. Fortunately, this phase didn't last long.

By the end of the century, a new format had evolved. Enter "reality (?)" television. While the inference is that viewers could view real people involved in real, unscripted situations, the fact is that nothing on television is by accident. Yes, the shows run videotape continuously, but it is the show's producers who select the scenes to be shown and, in some cases, contrive the "plot line." Some, like *Survivor*, have been extremely successful, and according to many, quite entertaining. Others were mere copycats and fell by the wayside.. Luckily, there was a mutual attraction between the network executives and their audiences. The latter loved the shows and felt that anyone had the ability to participate, whether by being in the shows or voting at home. Television executives love the concept because the audiences respond to them and they are relatively cheap to produce (as compared to a half-hour sitcom). Recall that one of the significant characteristics of a digital society is participation.

Teacher's Note: The term "reality" is deceiving. Probably the best definition this author has ever heard (source unknown) is reality that is manipulated for the sake of good storytelling; after all, it's still an **entertainment** medium. Doesn't this remind us of the *Quiz Show* scandal of the 1950s?

Whether reality TV is merely a fad or has staying power remains to be seen. But like the quiz show mania of the 1950s, there isn't a night that goes by when new a reality show or two shows up. Besides *The Bachelor, The Osbournes, Average Joe, Survivor, The Simple Life*, and *American Idol*, new entries for the winter 2004 line-up included *House of Dreams, Average Joe: Hawaii, Airline, Made in America, The Real World, Celebrity Moll, The Surreal Life, American Chopper, America's Next Top Model, The Bachelorette, Star Search, My Big Fat Obnoxious Fiancé, Todd TV, Till Death Us Part, the Apprentice*, and *Extreme Make-Over*—all premiering within two months of each other.

Changes in Personality Types

Johnny Carson retires—enter David Letterman, Jay Leno, and Conan O'Brien. With this change, the shape and format of late night television changes. No longer does television shut down at midnight. Today, television is a 24-hour-a day operation. The talk shows have also evolved into choreographed peeks at a seamier side of life, such as *Ricki Lake* and *The Jerry Springer Show*.

Animated features **aimed at younger audiences** have included:

Beavis and Butthead

South Park

Celebrity Death Matches

The Simpsons

Wrestling has moved to **prime time** in shows such as *Wrestlemania*.

The Last Great Ride Revisited

At the 1998 Emmy Awards, HBO collected the second-most Emmys after NBC (87). During the summer of 1998, news shows outpaced reruns; reruns advertised heavily (They're new to you!).

One thing has always been a certainty in television, if a show is popular, copycats are sure to follow. Just like bell-bottoms, trends come and go. "New" shows are often remakes of previous genres in "new clothing." One example is *American Idol,* which is essentially a mix of *Ted Mack's Amateur Hour* of the 1950s and the *Gong Show* of the late 1970s. Amateurs perform and are critiqued, with Simon being the "gonger." *Idol* is amazingly popular. The twist on this show is that viewers across the nation can call or e-mail in their votes, often jamming the phone lines. One show, for example garnered over five million votes.

Other Changes

Television not only reports the news but creates it. For example, shows like the *Today Show* report cuts from earlier interviews in previous segments of the show as news events in subsequent segments.

Politicians have learned to use television to manage news and to create new persona just for the medium. A new lingo has evolved. Recall our discussions in **Lesson 2. 3** about the terms that entered into broadcasting vocabulary during this decade:

• **Sound bites**

• **Spin doctors**

• **Media circus**

• **Paparazzi**

Teacher's Note: You might wish to have students recall the definitions of these words as a review.

Movies such as *Wag the Dog* and *Primary Colors* also presented this new view of politics.

Recall Bruce Springsteen's song from the 1980s, **"57 Channels and Nothin' On."** We have moved from three networks to 57 channels, and on to over **500 channels** (some say that there is *still* nothing on), and satellite television with a channel for every interest (the *Anything You Want* Channel?). This automatically provides target audiences for advertisers to market their products. What does this do for the ratings business? Television has finally evolved from being simply radio with pictures into a genre of its own right.

Teacher's Note: The second significance of this phrase relates directly to Newton Minnow referring to television as a "vast wasteland" in 1961 (see **Lesson 6.7D** for citation). When students are told how terrible television is today, remind them that some people have **always** thought of television as a waste.

Music certainly has changed, including such themes and groups as devil worship, counterculture, rap, hip-hop, punk rock, Marilyn Manson, and Rob Zombie. Yes, music is coming full circle: Swing is back!

In radio, FM evolved from being only for PBS and long-hairs (those who like classical music) into being the preferred place for teens. AM radio reverted to talk shows. Enter digital satellite radio (XM, Sirius, etc.). Did you ever think you would be paying $10 per month to listen to radio in your car?

The third question we need to ask and try to answer:

Is television better or worse today than it was during its golden age?

Teacher's Note: Probably the best answer is **both**. This short discussion will give you the opportunity to discuss the fact that television was called a "vast wasteland" even back in the 1960s. Maybe story content has worn thin, but technology is getting better. With all the new channels, people have many more choices. However, all the options have thinned out the talent pool. There is no correct answer to this question, but some class time should be spent in discussion as an important step toward accomplishing one of the stated media goals: for each student to establish his or her own individual relationship with the media. **Remember, this is a discussion class, based on previous notes and opinion.**

Follow-Up Discussions

Discussion Planning Considerations

Agenda

Discussion #1.—The Telecommunications Act of 1996 was as far-reaching as any other communications legislation in the twentieth century. In essence, it reversed all the regulations imposed by the Radio Act of 1927. No longer are there requirements for limiting the number of outlets permitted in each market. Nor are there restrictions on the cross-over between media ownership formats. A newspaper can now own a radio or television station, and vice versa.

As with all deregulation, there are bound to be many problems initially. The basis for discussion in this lesson is to try to get students to express opinions regarding the value of regulation. There are two schools of thought. Many believe that regulation is an important aspect of the government's role in our society. Others believe in free trade.

Another important aspect of the 1996 Act is support for reinstituting a voluntary code of ethics, something that has yet to come about.

For first-year students, the conversation will not run very long or be very deep. For the most part, they have limited knowledge upon which to base their opinions. On the other hand, if you have discussed the radio Act of 1927 and how it was necessary then, your students might surprise you and have some understanding of the impact of this new act.

The second aspect of the review is the naming of conventions for the various acts and how they have evolved as the industry changed. Before the 1920s, the acts were referred to as "telephone acts". In 1927, the term *radio* became synonymous with *communications*. In 1934, the new laws included the word "communications" because they were to encompass television. In 1996 the "Telecommunications" Act was passed, because it covers cable, satellite, and digital convergence of television, telephony, and computers.

Discussion #2.—Discussions on digital television (DTV) will prove very interesting. Students are quite up to date on anything digital and are interested in the future. Now that you have spent some time on the past, they should be in a better position to do some predicting.

Mediated and Textual Support

There is a lot of information available on the Internet on the Telecommunications Act of 1996. The FCC hosts a Web site (**www.fcc.gov/telecom.html**) that explains it in great detail. Because Internet links are subject to change, check the "Chapter Six" page of the **Web-ASSISTant** Web site for updates to see if this link is still active. Where possible, an alternative will be provided, should this link be removed or changed.

Digital Television, a Crash Course, a half-hour video produced by PBS Home Video in conjunction with Samsung and Best Buy, features Robert Cringley, a self-professed geek. Cringley takes audiences behind the scenes of a visual revolution, illustrating the advantages of digital television. It is available at the PBS Web site, which can be linked to via the **Web-ASSISTant** Web site.

Several electronics retailers have added information on their Web sites regarding DTV. In fact, much of the information presented here came from one of those sites. In addition, links to other sites have been added to the **Web-ASSISTant** Web site on the page that supports **Chapter 6.**

Much of the content for Discussion #2 comes from a PowerPoint presentation found on the **Web-ASSISTant** Web site: *From Garage Cinema to Desktop Television: Literacy in the Digital Age.* Feel free to use the slides from that presentation in your classes.

Discussion 1—Has the Chaos Returned?
The Telecommunications Act of 1996

Student Instructions: In 1996, the FCC passed a new set of regulations that, among other things, essentially removed all prior restrictions on ownership of broadcast media. This is why we are seeing so many new mergers being announced. AT&T, for example, has recently purchased TCI, the second largest cable television operator in the country. You will see more and more cross-ownership of media outlets.

Do you think this is all good? Do you think there is a danger that one or two companies will buy up all the media outlets in an area and essentially control the news?

As you can see from your lessons, the government has vacillated in regulating the communications industry (Radio Act of 1927, Communications Act of 1934, and so forth). With all the challenges provided by the Internet, do you think the FCC will finally step in and regulate it? Be prepared to explain your answer.

A third, and more important, aspect of the 1996 Act was an attempt to put back in place a television code of ethics, which was all but abandoned by the NAB in 1989. Unfortunately, this section of the act has been overlooked by the industry and remains a sore point with many (Grossman, 1999, p. 53).

In class, you need to be prepared to discuss these changes from the perspective of whether they are good or bad.

The Telecommunications Act of 1996 created much more change than is currently evident. Included in the provisions were tactics to be used to help broadcasters recapture much of their significant investment in new equipment and to reestablish public interest obligations. This included a pledge by the government to remove many of the barriers to cross-ownership, a commitment by broadcasters to draft a voluntary code of conduct, a set of minimum public interest requirements, and full funding for public television.

Teacher's Note: For complete details visit the "Digital Beat" on the Benton Foundation Web site (**www.benton.org/ DigitalBeat/db121800.html**). See also "Charting the Digital Broadcasting Future: The Second Anniversary of the PIAC Report," by Kevin Taglang.

Discussion 2—What's the Big Deal About 2006?

Student Instructions: Read the following passages and be prepared to participate in a class discussion. Use the questions at the end of the readings to guide you.

The FCC has ordered that all television stations and networks convert to digital format. Scheduled to arrive by 2006, digital television (DTV) represents the largest change in television formats since color television was introduced in 1957. DTV is a new broadcast standard based on digital signal transmission that will eventually replace existing analog signals. The edict to convert was issued, essentially, for financial reasons. Because DTV uses less wavelengths and at higher frequencies, the existing frequencies will then be freed up for resale to new users like the ever-expanding cellular phone network suppliers.

DTV provides up to five times the picture quality and ten times the color information of current analog signals. Viewers will be able to watch on a cinema-like picture format (16:9 aspect ratio) and listen with CD-quality sound with Dolby Digital. The improved signal will provide multiple channels of surround sound, with picture and sound quality similar to a movie studio.

You might also be hearing a lot about another format called high definition television (HDTV). Like DTV, HDTV also carries five times the visual information detail and ten times the color information as analog and more than double the horizontal and vertical resolution, as well as CD quality audio. However, the full range of capabilities will not be available to HDTV sets via over-the-air broadcasts until digital transmission signals are in place.

Essentially, DTV refers to the signal transmission, whereas HDTV refers to the resolution and sound reception qualities of the sets.

What will make HDTV and DTV most interesting is that the improved signal will provide PC compatibility. In other words, the formats for your computer and television sets will be identical, further evidence of the pending digital combine discussed earlier.

The conversion will not require that everyone purchase new sets (at least not right away). Standard television sets (SDTV) will continue to function, but users will have to purchase a converter box to change the digital signal back to SDTV. SDTV users will not be able to take full advantage of sound quality, aspect ratios, and improved picture quality. They will also see their programs with the black lines at the top and bottom of their screens, just like a movie that has not been converted for television use (i.e., "letterboxed") .

Many of the television markets are already beginning to make the conversion. Ten markets converted in 1998. The plan is to have at least 85 percent of the households in the country capable of receiving a digital signal in one fashion or another (through over-the-air broadcast, cable, or satellite). The first sets will be very expensive (in the $2,500 range). As more people convert, the cost is expected to rapidly decrease to about $800.

Teacher's Note: The plan is to have at least 85 percent of U.S. households capable of receiving the digital signal in one fashion or another by the year 2006. It might appear that cable and satellite subscription television will obviate the need for this plan. However, some have placed the number of households that will still rely solely on over-the-air broadcasts as high as 30 percent by 2006.

Questions

1. With this new information you have just read, what do you think television will be like by, say, 2010? _____ .

2. Do you expect television and computer usage to merge? _____
_____ .

3. Do you think all these changes will be good? _____
_____ .

4. What is your impression of the concept called the *digital combine*? _____
_____ .

Portfolio Projects #5 and #6
Interview and Decades

Project Planning Considerations

Agenda

The objective of this project is to support students' conclusions regarding the influence television has on everyday life. There is a lot of debate about whether television has been influenced by what was going on in the world, or events of the time are accurately reflected in the shows of that time. Students are asked to answer the basic question: Does TV accurately **portray** the world we live in, or does television **influence** events, styles, and activities?

This can be investigated by comparing the types of shows that appear(ed) during any particular time period and to the lifestyles of that time. Students are also afforded the opportunity to show how much they have learned about evoking emotional stimuli using television or video as a medium.

This project is a news magazine in which students **incorporate an interview**. The goal or end of this project is to become the wrapper for the interview. In other words, the person being interviewed should come from the decade chosen for this project. The decades portion serves as an introduction and wrap-up for the interview. In short, the *Decades* project is the news magazine show in which the interview appears. This project should contain the footage and music, with or without a host who introduces the interview. Use the information provided in the **scripts** lessons on writing interviews and the checklist on how to prepare for the interview in **Chapter 5**.

Mediated and Textual Support and Other Resources

Information may come from a number of sources: videos from the class archives, books and magazines, the Internet, or any other electronic medium made available to you. You may use any of the several links to Internet sites already provided on the **Web-ASSISTant** Web site, or you may find others on your own.

Videos may come from any sources used so far this year in class, or students may find their own in the public or school library.

Student Instructions: In this project, you are to support the conclusions that you came to during our discussions on the influence television has on everyday life. You need to answer the basic question:

Does television accurately **portray** the world we live in, or does it **influence** events, styles, and activities? (Note: This portrayal and influence can be investigated by comparing the types of shows that appear during any particular time-period with lifestyles of that time.

This is a team project. Your team is to produce a four- to five-minute video in the form of a news magazine that covers one 10-year period, as agreed upon with your teacher. The video should present what it was like to live during that era, using pictures, video clips, and sounds. Your video can depict any 10-year period you choose, but should generally pertain to a single decade. As you know, one period did not necessarily end just because a decade changed. Therefore, you may run over from one decade to the other by a year or so, if it is necessary to properly depict the information you are trying to present. (Most books and reference materials artificially structure themselves on specific decades.)

The 10-year time frames have been arbitrarily divided to begin and end at the end of each decade. However, you will not be required to pay strict adherence to specific cut-offs. You may borrow some concepts from an earlier or later decade if it is beneficial to complete the continuum.

The video should include such things as fashion, fads, music, movies, and of course, television. Your video should be supported by footage, still photos, and multimedia from products at your disposal (Hyperstudio, the CG, Director, or PowerPoint).

This project will include an interview, using the checklists provided. Therefore, one goal will be to provide a way to properly introduce that interview by setting the mood and premise for that interview. This project will also become the summary or conclusion of that interview.

How You Will Be Evaluated

Your project will be reviewed and assessed according to the standard criteria found on the **Project Scorecard (Appendix H).**

Under **Criterion #1: Content and Format,** you will be graded on whether your

- music supplements and correlates to topic or main idea;

- content relates to the topic and shows understanding of main themes of the era;

- project contains sounds, images, and some degree of animation; and

- interview contains at least two different camera angles.

RESOURCES

Auletta, K. 1986. *Three blind mice: How the TV networks lost their way.* New York: Random House.

Barnouw, E. 1990. *The tube of plenty.* New York: Oxford University Press.

Grossman, R. 1999, March. Making a mess of digital TV. *Columbia Journalism Review.* Available: www.cjr.org/. (Accessed March 15, 1999).

Hickey, N. 2004, March. So long analog broadcasting and hello to digital, which may spell good news for viewer—and plenty of it. *Columbia Journalism Review* Available: www.cjr.org/2004/2/hickey-tv.asp. (Accessed September 22, 2004).

Jankowski, G., and D. Fuchs. 1995. *Television today and tomorrow: It won't be what you think.* New York: Oxford University Press, p. 125.

November, Alan. 1998, March 7. The end of the job: Major bummer or fantastic opportunity? Presentation delivered at Florida Educational Technology Conference. Orlando, FL.

Pilzer, Paul Zane. 1991. *Unlimited wealth: The theory and practice of economic alchemy.* New York: Random House.

Tartikoff, B. 1992. *The last great ride.* New York: Turtle Bay Books.

Tyner, K. 1998. *Literacy in a digital world: Teaching and learning in the age of information.* Mahwah, NJ. Laurence Erlbaum Associates.

The Ukrainian Weekly. 1999. Archives. Available: www.ukrweekly.com/Archive/1960/1796005.shtml. (Accessed September 22, 2004).

CHAPTER 7

The Production Process: Production Planning as a Variation on a Common Theme

INTRODUCTION AND LESSON GOALS

The following quote is attributed to Henry Ford, who is said to have made one response when asked about model options for his newly mass produced vehicles:

> *"The customer can have any color he wants. . . . So long as it's black."*—Model T Ford Club, 1999

Ford meant that he was going to only make one color of car, regardless of the requests he received. This quote can be related to production theory: Production and planning might be presented in many different formats or models, but they all come down nothing more than many variations of the same idea. Almost all production plans consist of five or six similar phases, regardless of the industry they pertain to. Planning, development, implementation, review or evaluation, and correction or re-vamping are commonly used production phases whether the topic is airplane manu-facturing, television production, or educational development. The steps may be labeled differently for each industry, but they are essentially the same. Inasmuch as production planning is relevant to any industry, the lessons in this chapter are perti-nent not only for television production but also for *any* school-to-work training. The goals and outcomes transcend television production, and that is how the les-sons in this chapter are presented.

SWEEPS: A DIFFERENT APPROACH

Production may be taught in many different ways. Most experienced teachers are likely to already have a preferred approach. As are most of the lessons in this book, those in this chapter are presented so as to accommodate those who wish to pick and choose, taking them out of the prescribed context and incorporating them into their own established curricula. However, for those who choose to follow the "Teaching Chronology" more closely, production training in this chapter is also presented in "cookbook" fashion. Students get to use their newly found knowledge to carry out a Sweeps competition, in which they put together a five- to ten-minute competitive teleplay that is broadcast campuswide and voted on by their peers. Because Sweeps is competitive, students also learn about product marketing, which connects directly to the acquisition model for media literacy they have learned about in **Chapter 2.** Class discussions are designed to encourage students to assign the job responsibilities taught in the lessons and to resolve problems as they arise. Students are responsible for deciding on show format and content, creating each segment, and creating an organizational chain of command. Class time is allotted for student teams to work on prospective segments. Each segment team reports to the class through a daily briefing on its progress. Decisions on show content and timelines are made as a class group at these daily briefings. As they are elected, student leaders run the meetings under the guidance of the teacher, who acts as the executive producer.

According to the "Teaching Chronology," students first learn how to produce a single segment, as demonstrated in projects #1 and #2. Projects #3 through #8 interject the planning problems associated with having many simultaneous projects to complete. By the time they are assigned the *Sweeps* project, students will have gone through all the lessons on basic equipment operation, scriptwriting, and the literacy issues. Therefore, Sweeps is largely about requiring students to pull several unrelated segments together into a coordinated production. In addition, it acts as a catalyst to teach students how to meet deadlines because the broadcast date is firmly established and advertised ahead of time. The show airs, regardless of condition, on the prescribed date. One thing is for sure: Students do not care to be embarrassed by a poor showing. Deadlines rarely ever are an issue for television students during *Sweeps*.

In short, students are introduced to project planning in a simulated real-life setting. Students come up with a show format, respond to questions in class about important aspects of the show, and then translate those into tasks. They identify critical path items and establish lead times. Once all these are noted, students then learn that the final step is to simply plug that information into a calendar. Thus, a planning calendar is developed. Students learn that a seemingly complicated and large project has a much better chance of success once it is broken down into smaller, more manageable steps. Often the most difficult task is to come up with a show format that includes opportunities for the whole class to become involved with the production. This challenge translates into the opportunity to show that most television shows are essentially several smaller segments that are glued together by a single premise. During class discussions on show format, there are often as many opinions about what a good show format should be as there are students in the class. Lively discussions are likely to follow. Students are challenged to produce a show made up of several potentially disjointed topics strung together with a common format.

HOW PRODUCTION IS TAUGHT IN LIGHT OF THE "TEACHING CHRONOLOGY"

The production lessons in this chapter are divided into three categories:

- **pre-production** (planning and analysis),

- **production** (shooting footage), and

- **post-production** (editing).

Information on the actual operation of the equipment for the video shoot and post-production is included in **Chapter 3**. The lessons in this chapter generally follow the higher learning categories espoused by Bloom: **synthesis** and **evaluation**. Specifically, they require students to use equipment to accomplish some of the aspects of production discussed in the chapters on scriptwriting and visual literacy.

As in other chapters, many of the lessons are broken down into multiple sessions covering several class periods. Those lessons are divided up into separate sessions to minimize the amount of time taken up by discussions in any single class period. This leaves more time for students to work on other assigned projects. If the "Teaching Chronology" is being strictly followed, several projects will open simultaneously. For students to be able to work on multiple projects at once, they should be shown some basic planning techniques. Thus, the lesson on production scheduling should be introduced fairly early in the course, not only for the sake of being able to juggle simultaneous projects but also to encourage cooperation among student teams. At the heart of being able to carry out the goals and objectives of this course is to successfully implement a cooperative learning environment in which students are able to work both independently and in groups. Students, especially in the earlier high school grades, are in constant need of feedback and encouragement to progress in projects that stretch over several days. Large class sizes and the resulting amount of hands-on effort required will also consume considerable time. Because many high school students have not developed good independent work skills, they need to be taught how to break down large projects into manageable units, assign priorities, and commit to time schedules.

The lesson on production scheduling (**Lesson 7.3**) is particularly helpful to the goal of making students accountable for the completion of their projects and is aimed at presenting students with the task of providing weekly, basic task-level commitments to their teacher. In fact, according to the "Teaching Chronology," it is introduced out of sequence and very early in the term. In this session, students learn how to develop and commit to accomplishing a rudimentary plan for the upcoming week. At the end of the same week, they document what they have actually accomplished. The teacher can then assess each student's participation in any of the projects based on the student's own documentation. This method allows students to participate in their own assessments.

On the other hand, cooperative groups solve many of the class equipment problems. Chances are pretty good that there will be more students in each class than there is equipment to go around. Sharing equipment by assigning teams can also alleviate problems with lack of progress due to equipment shortages, which, by the way, are not simply limited to the education arena. Equipment shortage is very often a problem (and common stumbling block to successful, timely project completion and preventing budget overruns4) that can plague real-world television production. Ultimately, this helps student understand the importance of scheduling and accomplishing tasks within given time frames. These newly learned production-scheduling concepts also act as an anchor upon which the teacher can then build when covering material in the subsequent planning sessions.

DIGGING DEEPER

There are several excellent sources for books on production. It is difficult to choose only one or two, because most texts on the subject do an excellent job. There are several references on the **Web-ASSISTant** Web site.

The online course at **www.cybercollege.com** covers most of the production issues presented in this chapter, but in much greater depth. The cyber course was designed for higher education but is a great resource, and it is mentioned throughout this chapter. In addition, Dr. Whittaker has published a handbook, *Television Production* (Mayfield Publishing), after which the online course was designed. It be obtained at the Web site or any major bookstore.

Another online source is Video University, found at **www.videouniversity.com**. It contains articles on production, history, and all sorts of other topics. Check this site regularly.

As Internet links are subject to change, check the "Chapter Seven" page of the **Web-ASSISTant** Web site for updates to see if this link is still active. Where possible, an alternative will be provided, should this link be removed or changed.

Another good way to learn about the interdependencies of production scheduling is to work with any one of the excellent software products on the market. Some software publishers offer free trial download copies. The "Chapter Seven" page of the **Web-ASSISTant** Web site has links for obtaining copies of. Information on how to obtain other mediated and textual resources is also provided.

SEQUENCING THE LESSONS IN THIS CHAPTER

Like the lessons in the other chapters, these are presented in contextual sequence. That is to say, they have continuity with regard to subject matter and can be taught in the exact order in which they are presented. However, to reach the specific goals of the course, it might be better to follow the suggested sequence as outlined in the "Teaching Chronology" found in **Chapter 1**. At a minimum, it makes sense to at least consult the prescribed format to make an informed decision.

Lesson 7.1

The ASSURE Planning Model

Lesson Planning Considerations

(**Approx. Time**: 15–20 minutes)

Agenda

Much has been written about how to begin a video project and put it into production. Dirk Shouten and Ron Watling, in *Media Action Projects,* discuss whether the best way to begin a project is to "simply begin"(1997, p. 14). Professor Ron Whittaker, on his Web site, suggests that the sequence begin with an identification of the purpose of the project. (1999, p.6). The common thread in all discussions about production planning (and what most seem to agree on) is that some type of analysis should take place.

The planning model presented in this lesson is an adaptation of the **ASSURE instructional development model** developed at Purdue University (Heinrich, Molenda, and Russell, 1994). Being able to use an instructional model for television production points out that production planning is, essentially, a common theme in any industry, whether it be television, teaching and learning, or software development. The core principles remain the same. In the instructional model, as first developed and later as modified, ASSURE is an acronym containing the following interpretation:

- **A**nalyze the needs and characteristics of students.

- **S**tate instructional objectives.

- **S**elect appropriate media.

- **R**equire participation.

- **E**valuate and revise, based upon feedback. (Russell, Sorge, and Brickner, 1994, p. 6)

An instructional model was chosen and adapted for two reasons. First, it is assumed that many teachers are already familiar with the planning concepts associated with instructional development, especially the ASSURE model. In fact, the lesson format used throughout this book is based largely on that model. Second, instructional development shares many common traits with other design sciences. Even though the ASSURE model is conceptually oriented toward classroom instruction rather than a planning system or product, its value is in its simplicity. Planning models tend to go into great detail to cover every possible complication, something that is not necessary in an introductory high school production class. It was relatively simple to adapt the ASSURE model to the needs of this course, requiring only changing the words that make up the original acronym to fit television production terminology.

Even though ASSURE is oriented toward delivering classroom instruction, it is based on concepts that closely relate to sequencing tasks common to all production planning. It should be noted, however, that the order in which the specific planning tasks occur does vary from model to model. For example, Professor Whittaker, in his online course at **www.cybercollege.com**, promotes the idea that deciding on an objective should be the first point to consider (this is point 2 on the ASSURE model). Teachers are cautioned to avoid getting bogged down in details, so long as a formal planning model is followed.

Students should be able to easily grasp the six steps that the ASSURE model follows. ASSURE is easy to teach and is adaptable to any planning situation. Because this is probably the first time most students will have encountered a formal planning tool, it is not that important that they remember the specific details of every planning step. Rather, it is more important that they discover that planning models do exist, and that they include several smaller planning steps to make larger projects easier to accomplish. Students' first encounter with planning should provide them with a key for breaking down large projects into smaller, more manageable steps.

One thing to stress while presenting the ASSURE model for the first time is that it is only a *model*. Revisions in projects are common, and they can happen at any point in the process. Project plans are by nature iterative. The best productions are generally the result of changes that continue in some cases even after the project deadlines. In fact, it is not uncommon for the final program to bear very little resemblance to how it was first conceived, especially on this level. That is why requiring that students always come up with a working title is so important. It helps keep the program focused on its overall direction.

The concept of planning cam be introduced at any time during the semester. Some feel that it should not be done until all the foundation learning principles have been covered. Something can be said for the idea that students seem to learn better after they have made mistakes. Their interest is keener when you are showing them ways to save time and energy. The "Teaching Chronology" has a lot of this thinking in it. Some material is presented during the first couple of weeks. Initial projects are delayed mostly to provide the opportunity for teachers to get to know their students' work habits to assist in forming groups. However, after 10 days or so, students are generally very anxious to get started on their projects. For this reason, the *Still Shots* project is introduced very early. Although the results might be better when providing some instruction on the benefits and aspects of planning time beforehand, the project is simple enough that it would not be harmful to allow students to get started with minimal instructions. The goal of this first video activity is then extended to also cause students to demonstrate what they know about sequencing and planning, at least in minimal terms. If introducing the ASSURE model is delayed until after completing the *Still Shots* project, students are then also given a problem-solving opportunity. Asking them to apply the model retrospectively to the outcome of their project and to decide what they might have done acts as an advanced organizer for **Lesson 7.1**.

Objectives and Outcomes

As a result of this lesson, students will be able to

• list the planning steps found in the ASSURE model modified for television production,

• describe how knowing the objectives and target audience for a product is an important aspect of determining its success,

• write a cohesive storyboard that clearly reflects the show's objectives and audience needs, and

• write a production plan.

Mediated and Textual Support

There is not much need for computer support, videos, or other mediation when covering planning and production. Because the projects are on a relatively simple scale, there is little need for using sophisticated computer-based planning software products other than to show how they operate. The Zettl *Videolab 2.1* CD covers some of the production tasks but does not cover the planning aspects in much detail. Dr. Ron Whittaker's Web page at **www.cybercollege.com** also provides some information. Because

Internet links are subject to change, check the "Chapter Seven" page of the **Web-ASSISTant** Web site to see if this link is still active. Where possible, an alternative will be provided, should this link be removed or changed.

The **Web-ASSISTant** Web site lists several additional Internet locations to help shape the lesson content and add information for those who wish to dig deeper into this subject.

Lesson Readiness

When confronted with large tasks, people often become overwhelmed. The orienting question addresses being able to take relatively large tasks and break them down into smaller, more manageable tasks. Students will learn very early in the term that they will have to adopt some type of planning model, because the "Teaching Chronology" introduces several simultaneous projects and activities very early in the cycle. Once they begin to stumble and miss a couple of deadlines, they will easily grasp the need for planning. You will get their attention very early if you stress the importance of deadlines from the beginning.

Closure

Students will write up a product plan for the *Sweeps* project at the end of the term, based on the ASSURE components, to show that they fully understand production planning.

Terms

working title	**premise**
hook	**ASSURE planning model**

Lesson Notes

Planning is one the most important skills you will take with you from this course. The term *production* implies that some systematic plan has been executed that the team has used to produce a product or service. Planning your work is just a part of the production process that should come naturally to you.

In real life, every successful project has benefited from a well-executed plan. Any success that comes otherwise was purely coincidental and the result of luck. In this class, we are going to take a general planning tool and adapt it to the television production situation.

We call our planning model **ASSURE.** For purposes of our discussions on production planning, the word **ASSURE** stands for

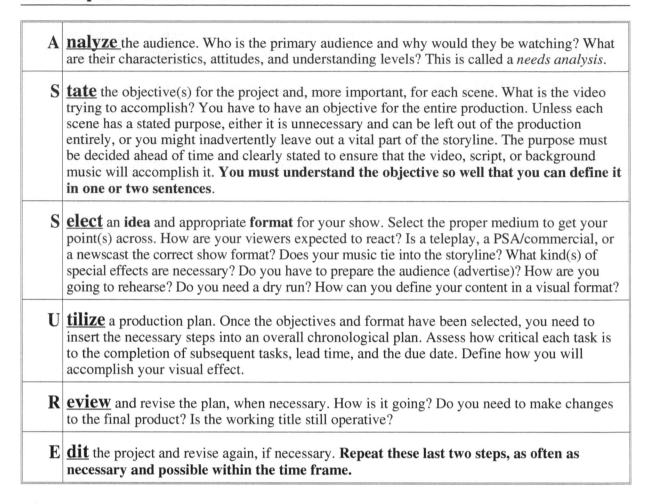

A **nalyze** the audience. Who is the primary audience and why would they be watching? What are their characteristics, attitudes, and understanding levels? This is called a *needs analysis*.

S **tate** the objective(s) for the project and, more important, for each scene. What is the video trying to accomplish? You have to have an objective for the entire production. Unless each scene has a stated purpose, either it is unnecessary and can be left out of the production entirely, or you might inadvertently leave out a vital part of the storyline. The purpose must be decided ahead of time and clearly stated to ensure that the video, script, or background music will accomplish it. **You must understand the objective so well that you can define it in one or two sentences.**

S **elect** an **idea** and appropriate **format** for your show. Select the proper medium to get your point(s) across. How are your viewers expected to react? Is a teleplay, a PSA/commercial, or a newscast the correct show format? Does your music tie into the storyline? What kind(s) of special effects are necessary? Do you have to prepare the audience (advertise)? How are you going to rehearse? Do you need a dry run? How can you define your content in a visual format?

U **tilize** a production plan. Once the objectives and format have been selected, you need to insert the necessary steps into an overall chronological plan. Assess how critical each task is to the completion of subsequent tasks, lead time, and the due date. Define how you will accomplish your visual effect.

R **eview** and revise the plan, when necessary. How is it going? Do you need to make changes to the final product? Is the working title still operative?

E **dit** the project and revise again, if necessary. **Repeat these last two steps, as often as necessary and possible within the time frame.**

What you need to do for each project from this point is think about what you want to do, fill out the Segment Checklist/Scorecard sheet found in **Appendix G,** and turn it in as a part of the package. You will receive all your points for doing the worksheet initially. We will discuss the plan and adjust it, and you will then resubmit it with your final projects. Filling out the form is actually pretty easy; simply answer the questions. These should lead you to the answers you need to properly lay out the production. Time has been allowed in our production schedules to let you make changes and revise, if necessary. The ASSURE plan and your production scheduling are as important to your overall success as your creativity.

Even with good planning, there are no guarantees of success. However, following a logical blueprint such as the one that the ASSURE model offers will certainly increase your chances for success. Remember, any good plan should be **flexible, adaptable, diverse,** and **time efficient**.

Teacher's Note: Students can add any words here they want. As a matter of fact, they might come up with some better ones! Having them supply the missing adjectives adds to their ownership of the planning model.

The plan should not be locked into one set pattern or time frame. You will often run into difficulties and delays. You need to be adaptable. The plan should take into account as many possible situations and roadblocks as you can think of. Finally, remember that your project will probably take longer to complete than you expect.

Getting Started

1. To get started, and to maintain focus, you need to come up with a **working title**. This can change as often as needed, but it is important to keep it in front of you to be sure you are on track. Post it on a board or wall somewhere in the room where you are doing most of your scriptwriting and editing.

2. You need a **premise**, main concept, or idea that carries throughout the storyline.

3. It is also a good idea to come up with a **hook**, a device that will get the viewer's attention. It should be something that will make potential viewers want to watch your program.

Teacher's Note: The following item is a suggestion from Tom Schroeppel's book, *Video Goals: Getting Results with Pictures and Sound*. It is a legitimate series of questions that pertain directly to the "Set Objectives" item on the ASSURE model. Also note how closely these principles mimic the three teaching domains: cognitive, affective, and psychomotor. Corporate trainers often refer to these as KSAs (knowledge, skills, attitudes).

---

4 Ask yourself, how are you going to make your **viewers react**? Are you planning on simply having them understand or know something? Do you plan to change their minds? Do you want them to take action? Or is the video for simple entertainment? Each involves invoking a change in action, attitudes, or knowledge.

Lesson 7.2

Implementing the Project Plan

Lesson Planning Considerations

(**Approx. Time:** 35 minutes)

Agenda

The first order of business is to learn what the individual planning steps are. So far, students have been introduced to the equipment. They have learned how to tell a story with the use of that equipment. The next step is learning how to put together and follow a production plan. Project and production planning boils down to learning how to be a team player, the naming conventions for the types of shots being used, on-screen and behind-the-scenes etiquette, and time management. There is very little technical training going on per se; it is more procedural in nature. Often, television production courses focus on this aspect. In an entry-level course, production is only one of many aspects to be explored.

Several elements go into the actual sequencing of events leading up to a production. For expediency, this particular set of lessons assumes that the first several phases of the production sequence have taken place, as pointed out in previous lessons. The justification for the show has already been made and a script has already been planned out and written. The sole remaining planning step is to decide on a format.

This session, then, continues the discussion about the **production sequence**, focusing on the **implementation cycle**: script-reading rehearsals, production crew job responsibilities, and post-production editing. These include ancillary discussions about studio etiquette, and so forth—all items that make up the visual awareness and literacy portion of the course.

Because this is a first-year introductory course, most of the items are not covered in any great depth. In addition, some of the lesson topics relate more to rudimentary background procedures that might be assumed and otherwise overlooked in a second- or third-year course.

For example, one of the lessons reviews the elements of good script reading, whereas another covers how to conduct and validate an opinion questionnaire. Assessment activities include written exercises (quizzes), a script-reading contest, and having students conduct a couple of surveys. The culminating activity is to produce book trailers that will be added to each student's video portfolio. This is the first bit of production that requires a small script to be written. The real scriptwriting activities in **Chapter 4** (the interview and instructional video) do not actually take place until later in the term.

Objectives and Outcomes

At the end of this session, students will be able to

- describe the importance of production scheduling, especially in a work environment that includes multiple simultaneous projects; and

- create weekly production schedules than plan time and use of equipment.

Mediated and Textual Support

All these lessons are supplemented with online resources. Some alternative references may be found on the **Web-ASSISTant** Web site, on the "Digging Deeper" page under "Chapter Seven." The cyber course found at **www.cybercollege.com** provides a module on production planning. Dr. Whittaker provides limited copyrights to teachers, as long as proper attribution is made.

Closure

The teaching plan calls for assigning completed production schedules by the fourth week. Students are to estimate their schedules on Mondays and turn in completed schedules on Fridays. They will most likely fall short in writing the necessary amount of detail on the production schedules to indicate that they have actually planned their time. Once the first few have been graded, the feedback from you will quickly orient students to the importance you place on planning.

Terms

project plans	Murphy's Law	chronological sequence
interdependencies	critical path items	productions steps (4)

Lesson Notes

Project plans, whether they be for producing a television program, developing and releasing a new software, or completing a science project for school, all have very much in common. They are all based on three simple principles:

1. Identify the **key steps** that make up the overall project.

2. Arrange the steps into a chronological sequence that takes into account **critical path** items, those tasks that have to be completed before the next ones in the sequence can be attempted.

3. Establish **lead times** and **due dates**.

Once these principles have been determined, the only thing left is to put the key steps onto a calendar, based on their chronology and sequence, and voilB: You have the framework for an operating plan to complete any project. Is this process really that simple? If it is, why do we constantly read about projects that do not complete on time? The making of the movie *Titanic*, for example, finished months late, and the film cost millions more to produce than originally estimated. The answer to the question is really *yes* and *no* at the same time.

Delays and overruns normally occur because of unexpected circumstances that affect any one or all three of the basic principles. Therefore, any good plan has to take one more thing into consideration:

Murphy's Law:
"**Whatever can go wrong . . . will . . . and at the worst possible moment**."

Actually, the law mentioned above is Murphy's Law number 3. The first two are:

1. Nothing is as easy as it looks.

2. Everything takes longer than you think.

This relates to the original point: Planning only **looks** easy (actually, some say it is and blame all problems on bad execution). The message here is simple: A **bad** plan is still better than **no** plan at all. Contingency planning is important.

Identify the Key Steps That Make up the Overall Project

The biggest oversight is to fail to list important steps. You may wonder how you can list all the steps of a project when you have never done this before. The idea is to start somewhere and list as many steps as you can. As you discover more, add them and readjust your overall schedule. For our purposes there are four main steps in television production:

1. **Analyzing (using ASSURE) and planning**.

2. **Laying out the storyboard and scriptwriting**.

3. **Shooting**

4. **Post-production**

In a professional environment, there are a few more. For our purposes, you only need to know about these four. At the end of this session you will receive a checklist that helps you organize them.

Arrange the Steps into a Chronological Sequence That Takes into Account Critical Path Items

The most frequent mistakes made here are to arrange the steps **out of sequence** and to miss the **interdependencies**. Again, you may ask how you can know these if you have not done this before. The answer is the same: You need to start somewhere. Even if you miss some, chances are your thinking about it will cover the majority. Add the steps as you discover them and reevaluate your schedule.

Establish Lead Times and Due Dates

You may notice a common thread in these discussions: the idea that you can readjust a schedule. Sometimes this is not possible, because you have been given an impossible deadline to begin with. When possible your schedule should include some padding that leaves room for readjustments. This means that, if you are lucky and do not encounter problems, then you will finish early. No one was ever criticized for finishing a good project early. If your project is normal, you will probably be running a tight schedule, no matter how good your plan was. Murphy's Law will, more than likely, ensure that an early plan will complete on time. An on-time schedule will most assuredly be late!

Plan for Changes

Changes to the plan are inevitable. Things will come up, teammates or other students who have agreed to be your talent will be absent, equipment will not work properly, and so forth. Alternate plans are needed to handle unexpected occurrences. This is where the expression *going to plan B* comes into play. Whenever delays occur, you will need to make adjustments on the written schedule.

Lesson 7.3

Production Scheduling

Lesson Planning Considerations

(**Approx. Time:** 25–30 minutes)

Agenda

Production schedules are a large part of the life of all employees involved in jobs in which projects or building an end product is involved. If you are following the "Teaching Chronology," the concept of production schedules will have been discussed several weeks before this lesson is scheduled. Students should be shown how to fill out the schedule (see **Appendix F**) to use as a part of their weekly paperwork submission requirements. By the time they take this class, students will be familiar with the concept and will have had the opportunity to see how this portion of the process works. If your students are like most, you will notice how sketchy the schedules are and how little thought they generally put into them. However, they will be able to discuss problems that poor scheduling causes. More than likely there is not enough equipment to go around. Students will have encountered scheduling conflicts when they wished to use equipment. This is an opportunity to show how important advanced planning is and relate it to practical matters like equipment scheduling conflicts. Later schedules will most likely be filled out more completely as a result of this session.

The purpose of this lesson, then, is to introduce the planning concept to the class and to establish a formal production schedule format for the class projects. Although there should be no question that the schedules are required, there might be some discussion about when they should be completed. It really does not matter whether they are completed at the end of the week during a reflection and goals writing session or at the beginning of a new week. This is a matter of personal preference. Some teachers like the wrap-up session to help wind things down while things are fresh in the students' minds. Others seem to think that goal-setting is best done at the beginning of the week, to help the students focus on their work.

Either method will work, as long as the production schedule becomes a regular practice. Some students may have a hard time with it at first, mostly because they do not want to spend the time getting the right amount of detail into their plans. There is a grading rubric for the scheduling portion, but it might be wise not to impose it in the beginning. However, as time goes on, the rubric becomes a regular portion of the class schedule and provides students with completion points. The rubric also provides you with the opportunity to provide formative feedback to each team about how they are progressing with their projects. Your feedback gives students an opportunity to find out fairly early in the cycle whether they are on schedule, rather than finding that out when it is too late.

Finally, it appears as though production schedules, just like class notes and journals, are self-fulfilling prophesies. Those students who are well organized seem to do better in the course and get better grades. Those who are not organized may get good grades, but they are in the minority. (The fact that students can receive a grade for the condition of their *Student Workbook,* and that all the tests and quizzes are open-note or open-book assessments, also contributes to this coming true. At the same time, the rationale for these assessments speaks to the need to become organized.)

Objectives and Outcomes

As a result of this session, students will be able to

• describe the importance of production planning and

• produce a weekly production schedule.

Mediated and Textual Support

Module 4: Production Sequence at **www.cybercollege.com** may be of some help in finding additional background materials. Because Internet links are subject to change, check ("Chapter Seven" page of the **Web-ASSISTant** Web site for updates to see if this link is still active. Where possible, an alternative will be provided, should this link be removed or changed.

The Kyker-Curchy text we have been using (*Television Production: A Classroom Approach*) also provides some materials on planning tips and techniques throughout the book. The Zettl *Videolab 2.1* CD also offers a complete chapter on this topic. None of the resources follows exactly the same planning path. The lesson in this book is an adaptation from many different sources.

Closure

The "Teaching Chronology" calls for students to begin filling out production schedules very early in the term. The schedules that students fill out throughout will be evidence of their increased knowledge of production planning. The first ones are not likely to be very complete and will lack details. However, as the term progresses, so too will students' ability to consider how to juggle priorities associated with having more than one project due.

Terms

production schedules   relationship to ASSURE

Lesson Notes

Developing production schedules is an important part of being able to complete projects on time. It is so important that points will be awarded each week for their successful completion. As the term progresses, you will be involved with projects that will take several days to complete. Also, because of problems with availability of equipment, you will be faced with working on more than one project at the same time, with differing commitments and due dates.

This is not unlike the real world, in which you, as an employee, will be managing several jobs, whether you work for a software company, a publisher, a manufacturer, or an e-television production studio. This problem is so acute that several successful software packages have been developed that specialize in production planning and scheduling. Many of the job descriptions written in the various want ads in the newspapers indicate that employers are looking for people who can balance multiple priorities.

Teacher's Note: This class is based on the "Project and Activity Planning Sheet" in **Appendix F**, which should be handed out prior to class.

The schedule we use in class in a simplified and modified one common to schedules used in a production environment in industry. If you plan on working in any of these environments, knowing how to use and manage these types of schedules will certainly make you a better employee. It will also give you an appreciation for what is behind large production projects. The purpose of all this paperwork is to get you into a mindset for record keeping, which plays a significant role in the daily life of a television and radio studio. As you will see in our discussions about FCC regulations, stations have a considerable record-keeping burden to maintain their broadcast license. For example, they must prove to their customers that an advertisement ran as scheduled, or they must prove that they performed the minimum required public service by logging what happened every minute of every day. This log becomes a legal document for future reference. A focus on detailed record keeping, then, is a required trait for any broadcaster

This lesson is to introduce you to the "Project and Activity Planning Sheet" (**Appendix F**) that we will be using in class and to set up a program in which you will be responsible for turning in a completed schedule each week

On this schedule, you will note what you plan to complete during this week and also comment on how you did on last week's plan. There is a place for you to list the **name of the projects** your team is working on, a place by day of week for specific **interim steps** to completion, and **the equipment** you believe you will need to complete each step. Besides helping you to plan out your work, the schedules will also help your teacher make available specific equipment. Any conflicts can be resolved ahead of time.

Once your schedule is approved, you may then sign up for the use of the **equipment** according to the schedule. On the bottom of the form is a place for you to enter all the projects you are working on and the number of **class days available** until their due dates. This will help you focus and prioritize projects based on when they need to be completed.

The steps you enter on your sheets consist of two parts. First, you should put the **sequence category** of the phase you are in. These are the ones we discussed during the lesson covering the production sequence. Those categories relate to the ASSURE model. The abbreviations are:

- Audience analysis   **A**
- Formal plans and objectives   **S**
- Storyboard/script/media selection   **S**
- Use plan to shoot footage   **U**
- Review progress   **R**
- Edit (post-production)   **E**

You must make an entry for each day of the week. You also must make an entry for any class discussions or activities that are planned for each day. All planned class activities will be put on the schedule board in the front of the class for the entire week on Monday (or Friday, if that is the day you do your planning). For each of the categories, write a sentence or phrase that describes what you plan to accomplish. Finally, to indicate which pieces of equipment (if any) you will need each day. This will help us plan equipment use. Once I meet with you on the project plan, you will then be able to sign up for the equipment for that day. If there are any conflicts, your schedules will help us resolve them ahead of time.

At the bottom of the form, be sure to enter the number of class days you have remaining until the due date(s) of any outstanding projects. This will help you focus and prioritize your work. If you find that you do not have enough days left, it is better to discover that when there is still some time to make adjustments so that you have the opportunity to complete your projects on time.

These schedules are to be placed in each week. They will receive points according to the grading scorecard found on the bottom of the back of the schedule.

Lesson 7.4

Production Crew Responsibilities

Lesson Planning Considerations

(**Approx. Time**: 45–50 minutes)

Agenda

The next step in the planning process is to introduce the various jobs and job titles of the tasks that must be accomplished during a normal show production. This lesson does not present all tasks but rather only those that are typical for a small high school production. The list can be modified as needed. In the model presented, some jobs have been combined (such as the cameraperson and director) to give as many students as possible opportunities to participate in the production.

Try to avoid having the same person take the same responsibilities for every broadcast. Younger students tend to gravitate to those tasks they like best and avoid others. You need to ensure that everyone gets the opportunity to experience all the jobs.

The normal list of jobs most likely will be modified for student productions, depending on how many students there are in each class and the amount of detail you wish to include. Many of the positions are quite subjective. You also may want to draw a different line between roles you want to play with a beginning group and those you are willing to delegate. Chances are you will be covering a lot of these, especially in the beginning.

Objectives and Outcomes

As a result of this class, students will be able to

• list and identify job responsibilities for the television production crew and

• identify the jobs that will be required to complete the *Sweeps* project

Mediated and Textual Support

The list of jobs is not exhaustive, but it does represent a good starting point. There are sites accessible from the **Web-ASSISTant Web** site that show slight variations. These are in the "Digging Deeper" section of the "Chapter Seven" page.

Closure

Some of the job titles should appear on a quiz. However, the best way to finalize the responsibilities is to assign them during the *Sweeps* project and review their performance during its execution.

Terms

producer	writer	talent
director	camera operator	technical director
CG operator	sound engineer	grip
lighting director	videotape operator	audio technician
		continuity secretary

Lesson Notes

In a class production situation, we will use the following job functions:

• The **Producer** is the person who is generally in charge of the entire production. He or she implements the program concept, lays out the timetable for the production, and keeps the project on task. This person needs to know how to work with all the personalities—the writers, the key talent, and the director—while at the same time guiding the general direction of the production.

Teacher's Note: In a classroom setting, program concept is generally provided by the teacher, school traditions, or class discussions. Because this person is the team leader, it is not generally a good idea to allow just anyone from the class to play the role of producer.

• A **writer** writes the script. A script tells you what people **say and do**.

> *Teacher's Note:* This is usually best done in teams of two or three per segment. This is the job everyone seems to hate. If you get someone in class who likes to write, consider yourself lucky. In some situations, you may try to subcontract this out to an English class (depending on content), but generally you have to enforce getting a script written.

- **Talent** refers to anyone whose voice is heard or who appears on camera: actors, reporters, hosts, guests, and off-camera narrators.

> *Teacher's Note:* You will find those who love to be on camera, and those who hate it. You will be tempted to use the same people all the time. Although this may be efficient, it defeats the goal of teaching everyone visual awareness.

- **Camera operators** do more than just operate cameras; they typically set up the cameras and ensure their technical quality; work with the director, lighting director, and audio technician in blocking (setting up) and shooting each shot; and (on a field production) arrange for camera equipment pickup and delivery.

- In a professional studio the **director** is the person in charge of working out pre-production (before the production) details, coordinating the activities of the production staff and on-camera talent, working out camera and talent positions, selecting the camera shots during the production, and supervising post-production work.

- The **technical director** assists in the control room and typically operates the video switcher. The technical director, or TD, is also responsible for coordinating the technical aspects of the production.

> *Teacher's Note:* You will probably modify this to have the roles shared between the producer and director. It generally works better when you select someone to be a floor manager, who supervises what happens on the floor of the studio during production. The producer would take care of the rest of the list.

- The **CG operator** (electronic character generator operator) programs (designs/types in) opening titles, subtitles, and closing credits into the CG. Occasionally we may decide to use PowerPoint® or Hyperstudio® in place of the CG.

> *Teacher's Note:* You will probably have a team of two or three running the board, including the recorders, and the character generator. While one of them might be the most proficient on the equipment, normally the team works in a cooperative manner with no one really being the boss.

- The **lighting director** (LD) arranges for the lighting equipment needed and sets up and checks the lighting. This person may also play the **sound engineer,** responsible for making sure the set has working mics and that they are balanced, and so forth, and then strikes (disassembles/ removes) the audio recording equipment and accessories after the production. This same person also may play the role of a **grip**, the one who holds the boom mic in place during production.

- The **videotape operator** (VTO) arranges videorecording equipment and accessories, sets up video recordings, performs recording checks, and monitors video quality. Sometimes all that is involved is queuing up the tapes and then pressing the (un)pause button when necessary.

Teacher's Note: You may wish to discuss the following jobs, but they are not necessary in most high school productions: a **set designer,** along with the producer and director, designs the set and supervises its construction, painting and installation; a **makeup person;** and **a wardrobe person.**

These jobs only account for the major functions of the studio team. If we are sending people out of class to gather interviews and/or footage, then we have, in effect, an **ENG** (electronic newsgathering) team consisting of at least a **cameraperson** and **talent**. If you are lucky enough to have good field-level audio equipment with a mixer, then you probably will include an **audio technician** with the team.

Teacher's Note: Students need to know that there is another field-level production team in the industry that will probably never experience in a school setting. This is called an EFP (electronic field production) team; it includes just about every production studio job description listed above. These are most often used for major events like a Super Bowl, the Winter Olympics, and so forth. The organization generally has its own satellite dishes, production trucks, and so forth to be able to accomplish in the field whatever one might be able to do within a studio operation.

Major production crews also employ a **continuity secretary** (CS), who makes notes on continuity details as each scene is shot to ensure that details remain consistent between scenes. Once production concerns are taken care of, the continuity secretary is responsible for releasing the actors after each scene or segment.

Lesson 7.5

Capturing Footage
Simple ENG Assignments

Lesson Planning Considerations

(**Approx. Time**: 20–25 minutes)

Agenda

We have already covered the differences between ENG and EFP assignments. The intent here is not to go into any great detail about the makeup of the teams but rather to discuss procedures for getting organized, documenting scenes and takes in the footage log, and shooting. For teenagers, shooting footage is basically a social experience. Many perceive it to be an excuse to get out of class, walk around campus, and capture whatever shots they like as they run into their friends. It is important to stress early on that this assignment is meant to be fun but also has a purpose.

The first issue to cover is whether a written storyboard is needed prior to allowing students out on campus to shoot footage. There are advantages and disadvantages to having a formal, written plan. Making students write storyboards before going out for a shoot does take a lot of the fun and spontaneity out of it, but it keeps them on track. They should at least have an objective or purpose for the shoot. It is also a good idea to be sure that good records are kept. Students do not innately know how tapes should be labeled and dated. Chances are that the school owns a large number of scratch tapes that are reused frequently. One of the most frustrating aspects of editing a show is either losing the footage tapes or having to review a dozen scratch tapes to find a small scene. Therefore, the field footage log becomes an important part of classroom procedures.

Objectives and Outcomes

As a result of attending this session students will be able to understand and operate within the confines of the class organizational system. The system is based on the following:

- A separate location has been set aside to store unused scratch tapes. Students should know that they may go to this location and use any tape without asking permission beforehand.

- Another secure place should be set aside for each class to store footage tapes (scratch tapes that are currently in use). Students are to learn that under no circumstances are they to use these tapes without permission. The teacher, or a designated student, should take responsibility for controlling the use of these tapes and for regularly recycling them from the secure location after they are no longer needed.

- A standardized labeling system should be developed. There are rewritable labels on the market that accommodate reuse.

- A logging system should be introduced. The sample field footage log found in **Appendix D** is sufficient for this purpose.

Mediated and Textual Support

Unfortunately there is not a lot written about this portion of production. In the past, most teachers have had to fend for themselves in developing a system for shooting footage, as well as storing and labeling scratch tapes. The system presented in this lesson is somewhat rudimentary but should suffice for most circumstances.

The Kyker-Curchy text used throughout this course (*Television Production: A Classroom Approach*) is accompanied by a video with student models for the teacher's to use in class. There are examples of interviews and remote segments that were a part of a news broadcast. You might wish to bring in examples of local newscasts or national news programs.

Closure

As they say, "The proof of the pudding is in its eating." If students follow the system then the objectives will be met. It is up to you to provide time in class for reflection and group discussion.

Terms

footage tape	scratch tape
SMPTE	field footage log

Lesson Notes

For a minute, visualize yourself as a producer of a large television studio or video production house. If your company is successful, you continually have several projects going on at the same time. Imagine the problems you must contend with: assigning and scheduling people to be at the right place at the right time, capturing footage accurately, assembling the production schedules, and so forth. Such businesses do not need to be concerned with the frustrations of having to remember which tapes have been used for each shoot, where to store them, and how to label them each time they have to go out on another shoot. That is why most successful businesses put in place some simple but effective procedures for taking care of scratch tapes, recycling them after use, and storing them in a secure place when they are being used.

Today we are going to cover some of the more logical and simple procedures that we need to implement if we are going to be successful in our projects. We don't need to be as organized as a busy production house, but we need to have some basic procedures just the same. Keep in mind that we are only dealing with simple ENG assignments. The field production teams have problems and needs on a much larger scale. You may think that some procedures we are going to discuss may only be associated with larger productions. This might be true to some degree, but it is important that we all agree on a few things before we get into the busy schedules associated with completing our projects.

First, we have already agreed where to find all scratch tapes. The rule is that this is the only place from which you may select scratch tapes to use. Unless you have permission, no one should be using tapes that are stored anywhere else. It also follows that any tapes left in this location are considered fair game. That means that they may be used without penalty. So, if any production tapes are left there, it is at the owner's risk.

A tape that is being used for preliminary recording is, for the purposes of this class, called a **footage** tape. These are tapes that are in use and are deemed off-limits, unless permission is granted to use them for something else.

To reiterate:
Scratch tapes are fair game. **Footage** tapes are off limits.

Sometimes tapes will inadvertently be left around or in a camera. To be sure we are able to distinguish scratch tapes from footage tapes, we need to establish a **labeling** format. Labels should contain a small title, the name of the cameraperson, and a date. This will facilitate their being placed in the proper storage location. All tapes found lying around will be placed on the teacher's desk for 24 hours. After that, they will be recycled into the scratch bin. Everyone should understand that this is a procedure and that accidents do happen. If footage tapes do get reused, that is a risk that the owner takes. The only secured footage tapes are those properly stored in the footage bin.

Final, edited tapes should be transferred to **portfolio** tapes. Because we want to use tapes that are closest to original generation as possible, this transfer may not take place until after they are completely assembled for the project or production deadline.

Teacher's Note: The pace of the transition from analog to digital environments in the schools makes this section particularly difficult to write. Although many schools have completely converted to digital editing and production, there are several schools still using all analog or some combination of analog and digital production techniques. Even with a digital editor, cameras still rely on tapes of varying styles and formats. DV tapes still have to be recorded and cataloged the same ways that VHS tapes are. Most digital editors provide many EDL and cataloging capabilities. In these cases, if there is enough storage capacity on your editing computers you may wish to teach students how to use the editing software to catalog the footage clips you intend to use.

Last, we have to deal with being able to easily find the proper footage tape. There are several procedural problems associated with gathering footage that need to be addressed. Recall, from our discussions about the advantages of storyboards, that footage might not be shot in sequence. Also, we might have to shoot all the parts of the footage over several different days, we may be reusing the same footage tape for several different projects, or we may be assembling the final tape from pieces and parts of other footage. We need a means to log our tapes. It is very frustrating and time-consuming to relocate footage. If it is not properly logged, it is possible to lose the footage all together. Finally, we need a means to ensure that all the scenes dictated by the storyboard are actually recorded. Recall that the storyboard is used to plan the entire shoot. **Planning** is the responsibility of the scriptwriter. Making sure that the footage has actually been recorded is the responsibility of the **ENG team**.

Therefore, we have several uses for the **field footage log**:

Teacher's Note: Show the field footage log provided in **Appendix D.**

On this log, we record the date, time, content, a short description, and the <u>**SMPTE**</u> (Society of Motion Picture and Television Engineers) setting for each scene. The log is then stored with the footage tape. A good way is to physically wrap the log around the tape and secure it with a rubber band.

Most cameras have a meter setting that can be reset. Care should be taken to ensure that the proper reading is used. This may have to be done at the time that the footage is reviewed back at the studio. This is a second reason to review footage after the shoot. The first, of course, is to be sure that the correct footage was actually recorded, framed properly, and contains the correct sound levels.

Before going out for a shoot, there are a few pre-planning items to be checked:

___ Do I have tape?

___ Do I have back-up batteries?

___ Do I have sound (is the microphone working)?

___ Do I understand the objective of each scene to be shot, according to the storyboard?

Normally, the ENG team has been assigned a very specific purpose for each shoot and should have a very clear understanding of what that is. However, this is not to imply that there is no room for spontaneity. This is the responsibility of the ENG team. Although they have to accomplish the shoot according to directions on the storyboard, they do have the freedom to be creative. Sometimes the storyboard itself is altered because problems need to be dealt with or a new concept is discovered during the shoot.

Lesson 7.6

<u>In-Studio Etiquette</u>

Lesson Planning Considerations

(**Approx. Time**: 25–30 minutes)

<u>Agenda</u>

This lesson is dedicated to reviewing the exercises from the supplementary text. It is important that students have a general understanding of studio terminology because most of it will come up again during the ensuing lessons.

Right after teaching the production job descriptions might be a good time to introduce requirements regarding dress code and studio etiquette. You need to decide what special clothing, if necessary, will be appropriate for on-screen talent, what types of music you will be allowing (see **Chapter 2**—Rights and Responsibilities), and student behavior during studio shooting. You need to review terms like "quiet on the set!" and what they mean. This short session can make or break your studio productions. A strict adherence to protocol is a must.

<u>Objectives</u>

After this lesson, students will be able to

• demonstrate understanding of studio etiquette, as outlined by the teacher and through its use during production.

Mediated and Textual Support

Footage showing how directors work in a real-life environment would be helpful. The video *Understanding Television* includes some of this.

Closure

Students will demonstrate their knowledge by correctly following class rules.

Lesson Notes

To maintain control, the teacher, the director, or the producer takes care of the countdown. This is a simple sequence of counting backward from five in one-second intervals, calling out each second loudly with accompanying hand signals visible to the talent and back room personnel.

"QUIET ON THE SET!"

"STAND-BY!"

"FIVE! . . . FOUR! . . . THREE!. . . ."

At *two,* the count goes silent, at which time only the hand signals indicate the continuation of the countdown. After a one-second pause after the silent *one* count the floor manager or director points at the talent to begin talking.

At the end of the segment, the floor manager or director begins a silent three count with his or her fist clenched high in the air. At the end, he or she announces "And we're clear." It is not until this point that the segment is considered over. The talent sits completely still, staring into the camera until the *we're clear* signal is given.

Meanwhile in the back room the videotape operator has begun the tape recording (and the sound engineer has brought the mics up) at the silent *two* count. The videotape operator (VTO) continues taping until the *we're clear* signal, but the technical director has faded to black and the audio engineer has closed down the mics by the time the all clear is given. This gives enough time to capture the entire segment on tape with room for post-editing.

After shooting is completed the editors take the videorecordings and blend the segments together, adding music and video and audio effects to create the final product.

Teacher's Note: The first activity in preparing for any of the following lessons is to have students, either individually or in groups, review the Kyker-Curchy text and Modules 10–15 at **www.cybercollege.com**, or whatever text is selected to accompany these lessons.

Lesson 7.7

Lesson Planning Considerations

(**Approx. Time:** 35–40 minutes each)

Agenda

The importance of editing to the success of a production is far greater than most people realize. As we will see in this next lesson, an editor can make or break a production. Some assert that technology is making the concept of post-production obsolete. Those that make that assertion feel that nonlinear editing (using software packages like Adobe Premier and After Effects) allows producers to manage the process as an assembly line that actually evolves as a simultaneous process of constructing a final video. Because of advances in camera equipment, footage may be digitized and manipulated in the process of being gathered. No post-shoot mechanical editing using videotape recorders is needed. We discuss this in some detail in **Chapter 6**. We take the position that most schools do not have the computer technology required to fully implement a nonlinear editing process even if post-production were passé (which it is not).

Even if your school has some nonlinear editing capabilities, for educational purposes it's better to break down the production process into segments. For this reason alone, a post-production unit has merit. In addition, because you are dealing with a significant number of students at once (probably more students than there is available equipment), you need to break the job functions down into segmented parts to allow the working teams to contribute to the process.

Post-production entails finalizing your footage into a finished product. For the purposes of this lesson, footage is defined as unedited videotape as it comes out of the camera. It may be too long, without any manipulation of the order or quality of the video or audio output. Editing, then, is the process of manipulating and processing footage.

If you are following the "Teaching Chronology," you know that this class, in many cases, comes after you have actually been working with the process on earlier projects (i.e., the *Still Shots* and *Stop Action* videos). You also probably know that this is deliberate. The teaching basis for this idea is that students do not necessarily need to know titles for things while they perform a process. They are also more likely to remember the names of a process once they have a frame of reference for that process.

Audio dubbing has traditionally been simply the process of adding or changing audio. In later lessons, we will introduce some more sophisticated processes that have come along, thanks to technology. Although it is possible that the types of audio dubbing discussed here will not be used in the industry by the time your students get jobs, it is important that they have a foundation in order to understand the impact that these new technologies have had on the industry.

It also should be noted that we are not really dealing with the concept of manipulating the sound in these lessons. That process is left for **Chapter 6,** in which we discuss multimedia and animation. There are several excellent sound manipulation software products on the market that will be covered in later lessons. We are dealing here solely with the process of adding quality sound to the video, regardless of how that sound was constructed prior to our getting it.

Objectives and Outcomes

As a result of this class, students will be able to

• recite the various steps involved in post-production;

• recite the differences and uses for wipes, swipes, cuts, and fades;

• explain the differences between insert and assemble editing;

• demonstrate how to add audio to a tape through audio dubbing;

• identify the qualities of a good audio track; and

• demonstrate how to use an edit description list (EDL) in the post-production process.

Mediated and Textual Support

This lesson is based on the Kyker-Curchy text (*Television Production: A Classroom Approach*) and the cyber college Web site (**www.cybercollege.com**). The Web site has modules, *Composition, Graphics, Virtual Sets, Audio,* and *Editing,* which relate to the various functions normally associated with post-production. Because Internet links are subject to change, check the "Chapter Seven" page on the **Web-ASSISTant** Web site for updates to see if this link is still active. Where possible, an alternative will be provided, should this link be removed or changed.

There are several Internet sources that describe the editing functions and how they fit into the production plan, especially as they relate to EDLs. On the "Digging Deeper" page for this chapter at the **Web-ASSISTant** Web site are links to sites that describe in detail what an EDL is. Again, because Internet links are subject to change, check the "Chapter Seven" page on the **Web-ASSISTant** Web site to see if this link is still active. Where possible, an alternative will be provided, should this link be removed or changed.

Lesson Readiness

Students are to complete the appropriate Kyker-Curchy lesson prior to the class session. The review questions are to be handed in for a grade. They will be reviewed as a part of the discussions on post-production.

Closure

Students will be graded on their completion of the Kyker-Curchy review questions. Many of the concepts in this lesson are also assessed on Quiz #6. The student "Competency Checklist" will be updated for audio dubbing and insert editing tasks.

Lesson 7.7A

Post-Production

Pre-Class Activity

Student Instructions: Read the appropriate lesson in the Kyker-Curchy text (*Television Production: A Classroom Approach*). Answer the questions at the end. These questions are to be completed and handed in on the due date on the assignment board.

Teacher's Note: For background and demonstration purposes, we rely on a supplementary program like Zettl *Videolab 2.1.* The **Web-ASSISTant** Web site suggests other resources that may be substituted. Whichever mediation is chosen, classes will be more effective if they are provided with some type of visual aid that introduces the editing process.

Terms

audio dubbing	editing types:	edit decision list (EDL)
white space	- insert	character generator
symmetry	- assemble	transition
balance	- linear	cut
fade	- nonlinear	wipes or swipes
footage	matte	

Lesson Notes

For purposes of our class discussions, <u>**footage**</u> is defined as unedited videotape as it comes out of the camera. As you probably have noticed in your early use of the camera, this tape is not to be considered a finished product. Most likely it requires some type of polish. We have already seen during our *Still Shots* and *Stop Action* projects that we need to fix up the tape because several things have gone wrong:

- It is too long.

- It has sounds on it we need to get rid of.

- We want to add music.

- We want to add footage captured at a different time, etc.

This process of fixing up our videotapes to make a completed product for our viewers is called **post-production** in the industry.

There are two major processes associated with post-production: **editing** for video and **audio dubbing** for sound. For now, we will assume that all our post-production work must take place on the audio board and videotape recorders we have in our studio. When we discuss using software products on the computer to accomplish some of these tasks, we will modify our terminology. At this point, however, think of only these two concepts.

> <u>**Editing**</u> refers to the process of **manipulating** the video portion of **footage**.

> <u>**Audio dubbing**</u> is the process of replacing old audio with new audio **while leaving the video portion intact**.

Let's take editing first. <u>**Linear editing**</u> refers to using the standard practices that have been around in the industry for 20 years, namely taking your video and fixing it as the tape physically passes along through the machine in a linear fashion. **Nonlinear editing** most often refers to a process of digitizing the video images and reconstructing them in any fashion or in any order that suits you. Because they are digitized, the images do not have to be done in any specific order. This is very much like the difference between typing a term paper on typewriter and on a word processor.

Teacher's Note: Although it's true that this book is about television in the digital world, the following section was left in this second edition for several reasons. First, we are in a state of transition. Not all school programs are at the same place, and there are several schools that still do analog editing. Second, there are many teachers who feel that learning about analog editing is the proper foundation to teaching nonlinear editing. Third, many of the nonlinear editing programs use prompts and menus that assume users know the terminology associated with former forms of editing. Therefore, it was a conscious decision to leave this section in this edition.

In a noncomputerized world, there is only one video image on videotape. Likewise, there are two types of editing: **assemble** and **insert**.

Assemble editing is the kind of editing you have already done with your *Still Shots* and *Stop Action* projects. For example, you had to make your footage exactly one second each on your *Stop Action* videos. Try as you might, you were not able to capture exactly one second each. In fact, for the most part you were instructed to shoot three to ten seconds, just to be sure you had enough. When you came into the back room and retaped your footage onto your portfolio tape, you learned how to reassemble it into the exact number of seconds and in the exact order to tell your stories. This is assembling editing.

Insert editing is a process some of you may have already learned how to do, depending on what happened during the course of putting our earlier projects together. Insert editing is the process of taking a video that is already in the right order but needs some other video overlaid. This could be a correction or simply another image. Insert editing will allow you to insert onto a tape, for example, a second or third shot of you during the interviews while the conversation carries on. It is insert editing that will allow you to put in a segment that demonstrates a process you are explaining during your instructional videos.

Teacher's Note: Students often better understand the concept of assemble versus insert editing after being shown screen displays from nonlinear software, such as Adobe Premier. If students are having a tough time conceptualizing the difference, spending a few moments showing these screen displays may help.

As we do our projects associated with this lesson series, we will learn the exact steps to perform both these types of edits. Your interview and instructional videos will require at least one insert edit each. Because most of you have already learned how to assemble edit, you will only have to do one more project to prove that you know how that is done. This will be done in groups. You will be asked to take a videotape with numbers on it and place them in a specific order on your portfolio tapes.

Teacher's Note: Review the project and activities instructions before teaching this session.

Edit Decision Lists (EDLs)

<u>Edit decision list</u> (**EDL**) refers to a list that is made by a videotape editor while putting together a television program. Most programs that are made for commercial television are naturally divided into a number of separate acts or segments. An EDL cuts down drastically on wordiness used to describe the scene take that is to be used as a final cut by the editor. For example, we can describe a scene using a lot of words:

> *Scene I we will use is the one by the soda machine at school, where Bill, this cool due wearing light pants and Hawaiian shirt, looks closely into his friend's eyes and says his line better this time, so it can be used as a final cut.*

Or, we can use an EDL that logs a scene number, the SMPTE code for starting and ending time (recall the *mark-in, mark-out* instructions from the editing lessons in **Chapter 3**) from the footage log (see Appendix D), and a brief description of the action.

The EDL is much more precise and requires fewer words to describe the actual scene that needs to be included in the final edit. In a professional environment, **an EDL is a shot-by-shot document** (either on paper or in a specific computer format) **that is generated during the rough cut edit and used as a plan for editing in more expensive online post-production editing facilities, where equipment time is rented and the creative decision-making process can be quite costly**. The EDL expedites online editing and reduces costs.

We will use the EDL as a teaching vehicle to graphically describe and to learn more about the thinking process that goes into editing. An EDL is normally used during the editing stage of a video to sequence footage clips. During the shoot, it is typical for much more footage to be created than will actually be used in the final product. This results in **different takes**, **bloopers**, **angle shots**, and so forth. Creating the EDL requires those making editing decisions to sift through all of the footage and decide which takes should be used, and in which order they should appear on the final edited version. The programs we are about to look at use an EDL to create a final cut scenario of an actual television program.

Teacher's Note: At this point, go to the EDL Internet sites linked to the "Chapter Seven" page on the **Web-ASSISTant** Web site and display them to the class. Where possible, an alternative will be provided, should this link be removed or changed.

All this may sound complicated. However, the most difficult part is the choices the editor has to make about which takes are to be used. Writing the actual list is straightforward. There are many software programs available on the market that take the EDL and create the finished, fully edited production tape. In short, the most highly critical phase of the task, and one that takes a person who is armed with a critical point of view for the final product, is the editing decisions themselves.

Manipulating Images

Other than editing, there are only a few other manipulations of the video image that we will be learning about this year and using in our projects. For example, we may want title screens or a rolling or scrolling text. We use the **character generator (CG)** to accomplish this. Characters are defined as a letter, a number, a special character (like a dollar sign), or a space. Again, most of us already know how to do this, but what we may not have known until now was what the machine was called. Some of you have used PowerPoint to accomplish this. Most of you also need to learn another term associated with this machine: **white space.** White space is not always white. It refers to the background of your screen, regardless of its color. It comes from a term used in the print media that refers to the background of your screen. In practical terms, it refers to not putting too much content on a single page. We have already reviewed the concepts of symmetry and balance. Adding **symmetry** and **balance** to a CG screen means that you do not have too many words or too much information on the screen at once.

Another set of processes we use to manipulate the video image includes terms. A **transition** is moving or changing from one segment to another. If the change is quick (appears to have no transition), it is called a **cut**.

There are several other types of transitions in two general classifications: **wipes or swipes** and **fades.** A wipe or swipe is a transition in which the image from one scene or segment is gradually replaced with the next one. There are many shapes and special effects that can be obtained while doing these, which will be shown to you.

A fade is a transition in which the scene gradually changes to a blank screen. Typically, this fade is to black. However, current AV boards provide many colors. The blank colors are referred to as a **matte.** This ability to fade to colors provides directors with another tool to project an image on their videos. A fade to black, for example, may project a feeling of depression or death. We will discuss this in detail in a later session.

Review Activity

Creating an EDL

Student Instructions: The goal of this exercise is to create on paper an EDL for a fictitious scene, using the following scenario.

Scenario

In this scenario, we have four different imaginary videotapes that have been used in different cameras, on different locations, from different perspectives, and so forth. Tape 1 contains shots on the bus before arriving, which are all frontal shots. Tape 2 contains the same on the bus scenes but as over-the-shoulder and through the window of the bus taken from a camera hung on the outside of the bus. Tape 3 contains shots of the bus arriving, and over-the shoulder shots of two students getting off the bus. Tape four is taken from the bus landing zone at school.

Working in teams of two, assume you have logged the footage as you shot it so you know approximately where on each reel the different sections of our video are. You need to decide which takes to use, and in what order. Make up imaginary meter readings for each scene.

Scene Description

John and Mary arrive at school just before class. John is asking Mary how he should approach Jane, a common friend, whom he wants to ask to the dance on Friday. He is nervous and shy about bringing up the subject. John finally gets up the nerve to ask Mary about Jane. The scene ends when Mary, after making John sweat it out a little, confides that Jane really likes John and wants him to ask her out.

Scene Order	Reel Time	Action

Your job is to create an EDL for the first scene of this imaginary television program, using the following format. The time code is the actual time, as logged from the tape recorder meter (STMPE format). You start the conversation on the bus, approximately two minutes before the bus arrives at school. The scene should flow naturally and be complete with dialogue shots and close-up shots of John fretting and Mary smiling to herself as she senses what he wants to ask and toys with him for a while. Scene order refers to when you want the scenes to appear in the final piece, not where they are on the reels: reel location is referred to by time, in the format 00:00:00, for hours:minutes:seconds.

When these tasks have been completed, you are to write the same information out in longhand showing, in the same detail, how the segments should be edited. Then be prepared to discuss a comparison of the two in class.

Teacher's Note: Do not be too critical of the SMPTE format. The idea is to have students create a fictitious EDL that indicates how the scenes should be edited in as precise detail as possible. Some students have trouble with the SMPTE coding structure. The goal is for students to see how more precise an EDL is and how anything else might be subject to interpretation. (Recall class discussions about a picture being worth a thousand words in **Chapter 5.**)

This exercise is provided so we can find specific portions of the tape using the time counter. It is therefore very important to make sure the tape has been rewound and the time counter reset to 00:00:00 before composing the EDL.

Lesson 7.7B

Adding Sound in Post-Production

Terms

calibrating	set to zero	Vu Meter
volume	mixer	feedback
gain	potentiometer	

Lesson Notes

The process of replacing old audio with new audio while leaving the video intact is called **audio dubbing**. Many of you already know firsthand what happens when you press the wrong buttons on the editing equipment. If you press the (un)pause button or the record button on the recorder instead of the audio dub button, **you will erase the video as well as the audio**.

Unlike the video portion, all videotapes have **two** audio tracks (mostly for left and right channels for stereo). There is only **one** video track. Therefore, there is a specific procedure you must follow to ensure that both the left and right audio tracks are overwritten.

Processing video on our AV board is not as complicated or sophisticated as using computers.

The first thing we have to understand about the audio is that we have to ensure that the input side is tuned in with the output side. In other words, we can have the mic turned up all the way and still not get the right amount of sound on the tapes. Getting the sound right involves two things: using the correct mic (if we are recording a live subject) and pointing it in the right direction (if necessary), balancing the input side with the output side. The process of balancing the sound is called **calibrating**, which we will demonstrate on our CD.

Audio tracks are considered **fully calibrated** or in balance when all measurements for inputs and outputs for all equipment are **all the same when they are all set to zero**. This is very similar to the fade button on your car radio. Note that the balanced position is sometimes referred to as zero on the adjustment settings.

Calibrating is quite difficult without the use of an electronic device that measures the sound waves. This device is called a **VU Meter.** The older meters have a needle that moves left or right and stops at points along a scale, based on the voltage put out by the mic or recorded sound. The newer ones represent the volume in a linear scale (either horizontal or vertical).

There are a couple of additional terms you need to know when dealing with adding audio. First, you need to know that there is a difference between **volume** and **gain**. Simply put, **volume** refers to **loudness** or softness. **Gain** refers to the **amount of coverage** area that a microphone picks up. In other words, setting the volume louder may not allow the mic to pick up a wider coverage area. More gain will not make your subject easier to hear. Too much gain, and it could be picked up by the loudspeakers. Because the mics and the speaker's polarity are the opposite, their sound waves actually can be heard repelling each other (like placing the same end of two magnets together). This repelling, where the mic and the speaker "hear" each other, is called **feedback**. Turning the volume down will not necessarily solve a feedback problem; it will only make the feedback softer or louder. **To correct a feedback problem, you need to adjust the gain.**

Usually you make these adjustments on what is called a **mixer.** The mixer has adjustment knobs called **potentiometers**.

Lesson 7.8

Visual Techniques Used to Advance a Story

Lesson Planning Considerations

(**Approx Time:** 40–45 minutes)

Agenda

This session is a precursor to the "UB the Director" activity that follows. It is an important introduction to one of the areas that is missing in most books on video production: the role of a producer or director and how he or she can influence the outcome of a broadcast. Note that the roles of producers and directors are combined here, even though in reality they are two distinct functions. In a high school environment, most often the teacher plays the role of the (executive) producer, especially with younger age groups. It is recognized that every so often, a "star" student comes along who can handle the producer role. The distinctions are blurred for efficiency, but it is certainly acceptable to keep them separate. It depends solely on the level of sophistication and abilities of the students you are working with. This particular lesson focuses on the narrative, because there is so much to tell and it relates well to the kinds of movies students are likely to be watching. After this lesson, there is an optional lesson (The Segment Checklist) that can help tie things together.. This lesson is a thinking piece that brings out subtleties of shooting, editing, and the whole thought process behind the actual production routines demonstrated in the "Segment Checklist."

Objectives and Outcomes

As a result of this session, students will understand and be able to express

• the concepts of sequence analysis,

• the storytelling value of certain camera moves and techniques,

• the value of sound in a production, and

• the job functions of a producer or director.

Lesson Readiness

Ask students to develop a list of potential job functions for the director in terms of camera shooting, editing, and acting. Sometimes a famous actor or director is interviewed on Bravo's *Inside the Actor's Studio*. Any one of these episodes might help to stimulate the discussions.

Closure

Students will participate in the "UB the Director" activity that follows.

Terms

cinematography   mise-en-scène

dramatic arc   sequence analysis

dramatic beats

Lesson Notes

Storytelling is not the sole purview of the scriptwriter. In fact, the whole production team is involved. The only way a story can be correctly told is for the entire team to focus on the concept. It is the director's job to make sure that happens. Each member of the creative team has a role and normally makes suggestions, but the director is usually responsible for the final decisions. In our discussions today, we will take one small liberty. We will combine the role of the director and the producer, even though in the real world this is rarely done. We can spend some time on the differences in the roles at a later time. For now, whenever you hear the term *director*, I am referring to the combined position.

Teacher's Note: *Small* is a relative term. It is in fact a major departure to combine the roles of producer and director, but it may be necessary in a class of students with limited experience. The teacher could also play the role of executive producer in add support of a student producer or director.

Following are ways that others on the production team can help advance a storyline.

What Camera Work/Staging Can Do to Advance the Story

- In major television series and movies, a production designer is usually assigned to arrange, select, and construct the set or locale. The costume designer takes care of the costumes. The dialogue coach helps with any foreign accents or language or slang expressions. The director makes sure all these functions are coordinated. The lighting director sets the lights. The scriptwriter and director combine on the "blocking" (movements of all objects in the frame including animals and people) and decide on the appearance and movement of people: acting, dialogue, gestures, and positioning of the characters. The term **mise-en-scène** refers to anything that shows up in front of the camera to be shot.

- The cinematographer plays a subtle but crucial role in telling a story. The term **cinematography** refers to things like shooting techniques; color, black-and-white, or tinting; lenses and changes in focus (deep focus, shallow); camera angles (high, low, or straight-on); camera movement (panning, tracking, zooms), framing; shot duration; and distance of camera to objects (close-ups, medium and long shots).

Post-Production Techniques Used to Advance a Story

- **Editing** (as a storytelling technique) refers to the frequency, smoothness, jumpiness, rhythm, and logic of shot-to-shot relationships; classical continuity editing (the dramatic linking of the various elements of the plot to provide a maximum amount of continuity); and montage (the thematic linking of various seemingly unrelated scenes or shots within a sequence to create a particular association).

Teacher's Note: The term *montage* has been used in two different ways in this text. A rapid montage video is like a kinestasis film (rapidly presented images appearing on the screen). The definition used here is more of cinematic.

• <u>Sound</u> refers to the music, speech, any noise (music, dialogue, sound effects); voice-overs; commentary; or use of silence.

Difference(s) Between Video and Movies

Although cinematic elements are important, it is also useful to know that there are subtle technical output differences between film and video footage. For example, video holds up well in close-ups but begins to break apart in very wide shots. The primary distinction is projection. Video projection is limited, and frame sizes in video (especially for the Web) are better suited for close-. (These differences will only become more stark in the short run with the advent of the 16/9 aspect ratio).

Therefore, when shooting video it is advisable to avoid stark color contrast, such as white backdrops and red costumes, white blows out and red bleeds. With video it is almost impossible to shoot into the sun. Rapid screen movements and varying lights will become much more of a distraction with digital video, and pixilation will be the norm.

Scene Analysis

In a post-production mode, the director has to make certain decisions about each scene (this is why there are often more scenes shot than will actually appear in the finished product.). If a scene doesn't do at least one of these, it will end up on the cutting room floor (time or run-length is money in the real world). The director asks:

Does the scene or shot

• advance the story and expand the viewers' awareness of the characters and conflicts?

• properly follow the previous scene or shot?

• properly lead to the next scene or shot?

• advance the dramatic arc of the character? (What do we know that we didn't before?)

• give information about characters?

• give important information to the audience?

• resolve the dramatic need of the main character?

The Shooting Plan

In short, the director plays an extremely important role in the production. To develop a shooting plan that fulfills his or her storytelling functions, the director needs to:

- **Know the script:** How does each scene fit into the overall plan? Why is this scene here; how is it crucial to the telling of the story? What would happen if the scene were removed? How does it advance the arc of the characters? What do we know now that we didn't know before?

- **Know the theme:** How does it follow from the previous scene? How does it connect to the next scene?

- **Know the character(s):** Know what each character wants in the story (that is the character's objective (either conscious or unconscious). The story needs to develop a history of the main characters In this regard, the director knows the **back story** (what characters might say or have said in other scenes that may or may not have taken place). The director knows the **dramatic arc** (a goal, obstacle, or resolution). Last but not least, the director has a flair for **dramatic beats:** a dramatic moment, a significant moment of change.

Summary

The director's storytelling role boils down to what is commonly called **sequence analysis,** a term generally used in the creation and critiquing of videos. Sequence analysis can also be a proactive function. It is important to logically order the shots in to a series, which creates your story. When analyzing the sequence, whether it be during the shoot or in post, the director needs to determine

- what logic was used in the editing of the shot sequences in a particular scene and how it works,

- how well the scene or shot works in developing a character and relating that to the rest of the story,

- how effective the editing of a particular montage is, and

- whether all visuals match the sound accompaniment.

Follow-up Activity

UB the Director

Background

The director is the storyteller, who tells the story through the placement of the camera and the actors. Every creative decision flows from the director's vision of the script. The director defines this vision by developing a profound understanding of the script and a clear sense of its theme or central idea. The director's preparation for principal photography centers on breaking down the script into shots. This shooting plan, or shot list, is an important factor in finalizing the shooting schedule. The process of converting the script into a visual plan is called previsualization and can be done with an extremely detailed, shot-by-shot storyboard or with a more general summary coupled with floor plans. The director translates the script into shots by previsualizing it on paper.

Student Instructions: Your assignment is to create a general summary with a description of a floor plan for the following scene. You are to incorporate information from the lessons regarding how visual design, contextual development, sound, and camera activities should help to tell a story. Read the scene and decide how the visual and audio elements should be organized to supplement a script. In some cases, you are given the opportunity to make choices.

It was the worst day of her life. Not only was it her first day at a new school, but it was also the first Monday of daylight savings time. Boy, was she tired! Riding on this bus, in the dark, with all these strange people was a real drag. Lidia could hardly keep her eyes open. What a scene: the bouncing bus, a low murmur of strange people saying strange things in a strange language that she could not understand.

The boy next to her was obviously tired, too. His head kept drooping down and leaning toward her shoulder. Lidia made an uncomfortable attempt to move his head in the other direction, toward the aisle, but like a bouncing ball, it kept coming back to her. . . yuck!

Coming from Puerto Rico, she did know some English, but she was no-where close to being fluent. "These Gringos all speak too fast," she thought. Their inflection is so intense! Except for this new "friend" who was using her shoulder as a pillow, she felt so alone!

Boy, was she tired. She began to think about the beaches in San Juan, the beautiful sand, the blue waters, the warm sun bathing her body. These Flo-ridians think their beaches are so great. They have no idea how murky their water is. She could hardly believe her parents had made her move right in the middle of her senior year! Everything seemed to slow down. She imag-ined being on the beach with her friends, dancing and having a lot of fun.

Suddenly, she awoke with a start! The bus, apparently, had hit a pot hole.

Based on the scene, decide which video device(s) or effect(s) should be used to tell the story, vary the shots, and add emotional value to the video. Decide on what background music and bumper music, if any, would be appropriate. Remember, not everything written into the story has to be literally translated onto the video. Use your imagination for how to use the camera and editing to tell the story. In some cases, dia-logue can be added; in others, spoken words will not be necessary or appropriate because you have cap-tured the idea visually.

Questions

Answer the following questions to help serve as a guide:

Cover shot: How would you orient your viewers to what is happening?

Central camera effect: Which of the following shot(s) would you use for this scene? (Circle all that apply.)

| flashback | OTS shot | B-roll footage | long shot |
| two shot | medium shot | extreme close-up | cross shot |

Explain your decisions: _____
_____
_____

Cut to next scene: Describe what method(s) you might use to end the scene (e.g., fade, dissolve, cut to black or other color, gradual fade to another scene, zoom in or out, pedestal, pan or tilt, etc.).
_____
_____
_____

What camera move would you use to present the relationship between the two characters? Select two of the following shots and describe how you would use them.

| Tilt | Pedestal | Pan | Dolly | Truck | Zoom |

_____
_____
_____

How would you effect the dream sequence?
_____
_____
_____

How would you bring the viewers back to reality?
_____
_____
_____

What other effects (colors versus black-and-white, chroma, etc.) might you use to complete the mental picture?
_____
_____
_____

What narrative methods would you use to help the storyline?
_____
_____
_____

Audio

What might you do to increase the effect on the following music segments? (If not applicable, then place "NA" in the space provided.)

Bumper Music:

_____

_____

Background Music (with or without voiceover):

_____

_____

Credits/Title Page

What colors and fonts would you use on the credits/title pages? (If not applicable, then place "N./A" in the space provided.)

_____

_____

<u>Optional Lesson</u>

The Segment Checklist

Lesson Planning Considerations

(**Approx. Time:** 25–30 minutes)

<u>Agenda</u>

This session recapitulates in many ways what has already been covered in earlier sessions. Review never hurt anyone, especially young students. The purpose is to introduce a basic worksheet that works equally well for a segment as for a multisegmented program such as *Sweeps*. The checklist contains many of the assessment criteria used to evaluate the earlier projects. Often students feel that, just because they are working on a larger project, the fundamentals somehow change. The checklist serves to reassure them that the basics are the same, regardless of project size. The entire checklist boils down into one or two questions to be answered:

- What is/are the objective(s) of the scene or segment?

- Is/are that/those objective(s) accomplished by the camera work, editing, and audio?

Although this lesson is housed within the series covering production, it is actually a review of several different subject areas found in earlier chapters. In fact, the term *production* really refers to a culminating activity that embodies several others, including scriptwriting, camera techniques and operation, and visual acuity. The checklist in Lesson 7.8 provides a good place to review the most important aspects of bringing together a production and serves as an opportunity for the student to integrate and use many of the concepts taught earlier. It does not cover new material in any great detail. Rather, it concentrates the most meaningful ideas that one would expect a first-year student to master.

The checklist includes references to the chapters and lessons in which the concept was originally taught, in case you want to go back over them in greater detail. It also provides a frame of reference for your students so they may refer back to the appropriate lesson.

The project or segment checklist covers most of what one might expect to find on a checklist developed for a full in-studio production. In fact, it actually could serve as one. This is done because the projects in this course could be accomplished in-studio or with ENG teams, depending on individual circumstances. The only difference between this list and one designed for a studio production is that it does not split up the responsibilities for a floor director or producer.

This checklist is an excellent short list that can be used as an additional assessment tool to review students' individual performance. All previous projects were assessed as individual assignments, even though many were done on a team basis. The one shortcoming of the scorecards for six of the seven projects (all but the *Still Shots*) is that the focus was generally on the team rather than the individual. *Sweeps* (project #8) is a class project, making it even more difficult to determine individual contributions. The following checklist rates outcomes by function. During your planning sessions, you probably assigned job functions to individual students. The rating sheet, then, will by default allow you to assess individuals while you simultaneously apply a grade to the project as a whole. Students will then come to learn how an individual output contributes either positively or negatively to an overall project outcome.

Objectives and Outcomes

As a result of this session, students will

• express the need for a "Segment Checklist" and

• use a checklist for future projects.

Lesson Readiness

Because this is a review session, students will already understand the concepts behind it. They will have had to juggle many projects by this time, so they will also understand the need for some type of checklist.

Closure

Students are expected to use the checklist during the *Sweeps* project.

Terms

cover	**continuity**	**context**

When we originally discussed how to shoot segments, we spent a great deal of time looking at three concepts that are important in any scene:

- symmetry

- balance

- continuity

These three were so important, in fact, we added them as a check-off on all assessment scorecards.

Also, recall our four-step project completion process:

1. Analyzing (using ASSURE) and planning

2. Laying out the storyboard and scriptwriting

3. Shooting

4. Post-production

Now that we are assembling scenes and segments and putting them into a production, we need to establish a new set of contextual guidelines. The original scene-development principles remain. We are only adding another layer that takes into consideration a new set of circumstances. Remember, building a program is best done in layers. A scene is made up of individual camera shots, a segment is built by assembling several scenes, and a program contains several segments. The guidelines for each layer remain:

- A camera shot should have proper head room, lead room, angles, color, vectors, and so forth.

- A segment requires symmetry, balance, and continuity

Now, we must consider the guidelines for building a program made up of several segments. The segment-building guidelines are best remembered as the three Cs:

Cover	Each new scene must include a provision to orient or reorient your viewers. Otherwise, they will not be able to follow the action. We could use a cover shot, dialogue, or special effect.
Continuity	There should be some consistency between and among the scenes or segments. There needs to be some similarity of visual style so that viewers do not feel that they missed the point somewhere along the way.
Content/context	The storyline must have some contextual glue that keeps the program together. This is the umbrella concept that ties all the scenes together. Each scene must have a purpose or objective, which ties back to the overall context.

If you keep these three principles in mind each time you build your program, follow the planning guidelines we discussed in the last class, and maintain the integrity of each shot and scene or segment, your overall program will also obtain its goals. This is basically a cookbook approach to building your program. It's simple, yet effective.

To help keep these concepts in mind during the shoot, we have developed a checklist.

Teacher's Note: The formatted version of the checklist in **Lesson 7.8** is laid out differently from the final formatted version. This unformatted version is designed to accommodate additional teacher's notes, when appropriate. A sample of the formatted version used to evaluate the *Sweeps* project is in **Appendix G.**

Step 1: Analyze and Plan

Analyze the Project

What are my objectives? _____

What are my time frames? _____

What are the critical path items? _____

Analyze the Audience

Who is the target audience? _____

What is the purpose or premise? _____

What is the hook or teaser? _____

Step 2: Lay Out the Storyboard and Write the Script

Link the Content

_____ Did I link the content to a context, event, or concept that the audience understands or has heard of before?

Analyze the Content

_____ Did I use any words my audience may not understand?

Organize the Content

_____ Do I have a beginning, middle, and end?

_____ Did I sequence the content so the most important information is first?

_____ Did I avoid the passive voice?

_____ Do I have short, concise sentences?

Storyboard the Content

_____ Have I accounted for each scene or sequence? (Have I coordinated with the content to be sure there is a scene for each critical point in the storyline?)

_____ Have I established an objective for each scene?

___ Have I established how am I going to accomplish each objective (visually, verbally, or a combination)?

___ What visuals need to be provided?

Step 3: The Shoot

Which Camera Shot or Angle(s) Should Be Used?

___ Head room (medium shot)?

___ Nose room (profile shot)?

___ Extreme close-up?

___ Other shot/angle?

General Criteria

___ What are my cut-off points? (closure).

___ How is the lighting? (Check it on a monitor; the viewfinder lies).

___ Is the camera at the right height?

___ How are the symmetry and balance?

___ Are there any visuals to insert? (Where? The alignment changes).

___ How is the focus? (Be sure to zoom in all the way to check it out.)

___ Do I have sound?

Things the On-camera Talent Needs to Consider

___ How is my speech? (Slow down! Your perception of how fast you are going is grossly underestimated. If it sounds too slow to you, it is probably just right!)

___ Do I integrate reading with looking at the audience?

___ Do I look right in the eye of the camera? (You will be more believable. Your audience will perceive you are talking to each of them individually.)

___ Do I *say it* rather than *read it*?

___ How is my body language?

___ Posture? (Sit up straight; slouching makes your viewers believe you are bored.)

___ Do I smile, when appropriate? (It relaxes your viewers.)

___ Do I align my head with my chin and look straight at the camera? (This conveys that you know what you are talking about.)

___ When interviewing someone, do I look right at the interviewee and acknowledge his or her responses?

___ Other ideas (from our review) _____

Step 4: Post-Production

Things the Technical Team and Post-Production Editors Need to Consider

_____ Does the show have title and credits page(s)?

_____ Is there any snow between cuts?

_____ Arc all visuals accounted for?

_____ Do scenes or segments match storyboards?

_____ Does the music complement or detract from the scene(s)?

_____ Does the show meet minimum and maximum time frames?

Portfolio Project #8
Sweeps

Project Planning Considerations

Agenda

In the real world of television, Sweeps plays a very large role in determining the content of television schedules, how much everyone earns, and what viewers discuss around the water cooler at work. The _Sweeps_ concept also provides a significant culminating learning activity for students.

Although the _Sweeps_ shows are a culminating activity, they actually represent a full year (or session) of activities and learning experiences. Each television class produces a competing show that is broadcast to the entire campus and voted on by students' peers. Students learn about the real world, where _Sweeps_ winners are determined by how well their shows are received by their audience, not by the award-winning camera or editing techniques or scriptwriting. The technical aspects help determine their grades, however. In this way, students are evaluated and rewarded in the appropriate manner. Good audience analysis and corresponding content wins the T-shirt. Proper planning, writing, and technique determine the trophy or, in this case, grade. Awards are announced to the student body during a subsequent broadcast, with T-shirts going to the winners.

Planning

As this is most likely the first full show the class has put on, the teacher will probably provide significant guidance, especially for the first few days of shooting. All planning should be done as a class group. Each student should be asked to bring in a show idea for the initial brainstorming meeting. These can be placed on the board and discussed. An important objective of these initial meetings is to arrive at a show format. More than likely, the class will not be able to agree on a single content. The alternative is to come up with a variety show or other format in which several different kinds of segments can be pieced together to formulate a show. If the show is made up from several different segments, an umbrella format will be needed to tie all segments together with continuity. Then, a **working title** must be agreed upon. The concept of the working title cannot be underestimated. It should be discussed every day to help students maintain focus. As the show context changes (and it certainly may . . . several times), the title should be revisited.

Assigning Roles

Once the planning is done, jobs should be decided. A student producer should be selected. A team should be assigned for each segment, with a team leader (producer) for each one. Scripts and storyboards should be written and approved. This might take a few sessions. Once all segments are arranged, another class meeting should take place to review integrity and continuity issues. It is a good bet that the individual segments will not tie together very well in the beginning. This is where revisiting the working title comes in handy. The plan should be updated to be sure there is enough time to get the shoot done with time left over for post-production.

Shooting

The storyboard makes it possible to shoot out of sequence. However, it might be a good idea to complete the opening sequence or a single segment with the whole class watching before attempting to do others. This provides a model for the class so that they understand how everything will fit together. Shooting the opening sequence is when show continuity issues will appear. Students begin to understand the need for cover shots or scripting that allows viewers to understand what is happening. Unless the premise is established early in the program, viewers will become disoriented. After students view the opening sequence, they have a better idea how their segment fits into and contributes to the show. It is not uncommon for many new issues to crop up during the opening shoot. Often the working title is changed to reflect a new premise or focus of the program. Production is an iterative process. The show format evolves slowly. Being flexible is important. Keep things on schedule. Be sure to allow a couple of extra days for the shoot, because people will be absent, if Murphy's Law has a say in it, probably right in the middle of an important sequence when you cannot shoot around that person. Have a back-up plan.

Post-Production

This is the area in which most people underestimate the required time commitment. It is also the area in which the teacher can be of most help. To make *Sweeps* an entirely student-run production requires an extraordinary group of students who have some previous experience. A teacher's major accomplishment with *Sweeps* will be to use the process of putting on a program to demonstrate how all the production pieces fit together. The teacher will most likely play the role of director, editor, and producer at one time or another so that deadlines will be met. This is okay, as long as someone is always working alongside to learn as the process progresses. Experience has shown that the most editing help and guidance will be needed on the opening sequence. Once it has been fully edited, this should serve as an excellent model. Students often have trouble picturing a finished product simply by viewing raw footage. The most mileage will be gained by showing the day's shoot at the end of each period and then showing what can be done through editing to finalize the product. Editing can fix many mistakes and add another dimension to a visualized storyline.

Objectives and Assessment

Sweeps is the culminating project for the entire course. It is also a class project in which students play as large a role as they wish. The level to which the objectives will be met is based entirely on how much an individual contributes. Most of the determination about whether objectives have been met relates directly to a student's participation level in the *Sweeps* production. For this reason, a three-tiered assessment has been developed in which an overall project grade is given, a second grade is provided to those who demonstrate competencies in specific equipment operation, and a third grade is assessed based on the student's level of participation. The latter is accomplished via a daily worksheet that the student fills out and is assigned an average grade, based on the teacher's assessment of the student's participation and the student's honest self-assessment. The class project grade is provided on the assessment scorecard that is similar to the scorecards for each of the previous projects. The competency assessment is in the form of a checklist that indicates that each student knows how to operate the specific equipment outlined in the competency objectives found in **Chapter 1**. The "Equipment Competency Checklist" is in **Appendix C**. The teacher should use personal discretion when deciding whether the competency was shown by the student during a particular production or as a separate, graded exercise.

Student Instructions: In the television industry, Sweeps is a significant determinant of just about everything that happens: how long the shows stay on, how much money they earn, when they are shown, and so forth. We are using Sweeps as a core element of our television curriculum. Each class will enter a show in competition with the other classes. You will ask your peers to vote for their favorite show. As is the case with ratings in real life, your final grade will be partly determined by your overall vote count. This means that, besides producing a quality show, you have the task of getting your peers to vote for your show. You will need to figure out how to hook your audience, arrange for publicity, and work in teams to accomplish your goal.

Each class will produce a five- to seven-minute show in any one of several formats: a news broadcast, a news magazine format, a storyline, a talk show, a skit, and so forth. To help you, we have provided a few links on the **Web-ASSISTant** Web site.

The subject may be anything you choose but must demonstrate knowledge of the three parts of any storyline (a beginning, a middle, and an end). You are encouraged to advertise your show in any manner you see fit (a video commercial, posters, an audio PA announcement, etc.).

You will first make up a storyboard and write a short paragraph that describes the main focus of your segment. The objective is to for you to tell your story. Remember, the video should be in focus and properly framed, according to the techniques we have learned in class.

How You Will Be Evaluated

You will receive three different grades for this project: class assessment, individual participation, and equipment competency.

Class Assessment

Each of your previous projects has been evaluated using an appropriate scorecard. *Sweeps* is no different. However, because this project involves so many additional aspects of planning a whole production, additional criteria have been added. In addition, the point value associated with *Sweeps* is doubled to take into account the importance of teamwork, planning, and day-to-day cooperation. The class, as a whole, will receive the same grade for this portion.

Section one of the minimum requirements has additional criteria. Also included are points for general teamwork, advertising methods, storyboards, and scripts, as appropriate. Individual evaluations will closely follow the checklist covered in Lesson 7.2. Grades will be given for each individual role a student plays, according to the checklist.

Individual Participation

You will be filling in a daily participation sheet that includes your contributions to the project. You are to fill in your accomplishments and assign a grade for each day. If you were absent, indicate that. Overall, your participation grade will be the average of the grade you assign yourself and a grade your teacher gives you. The teacher's grade will take into account your honesty and sincerity in the self-grade, as well as points for your actual participation. If there are any serious discrepancies, an individual conference with the teacher will be arranged.

Equipment Competency

Each student will be evaluated for his or her ability to operate the equipment. This will be in the form of a *yes* or *no* marked next to the basic competencies on a checklist that will be filled out at the end of the term. Demonstration of these competencies may come from participation in *Sweeps*, another project, or as a separate demonstration in which the student shows to the teacher that he or she knows how to perform the specific task.

RESOURCES

Heinrich, R., M. Molenda, and J. Russell. 1994. *Instructional media and the new technologies of instruction.* (4th ed.). New York: Macmillan.

The Model T Ford Club. 1999. *Great quotes by and about Henry Ford.* Available: www.modelt.org/tquotes.html. (Accessed September 21, 2004).

Russell, J. D., D. Sorge, and D. Brickner. 1994, April. Improving technology implementation in grades 5–12 with the ASSURE model. *T.H.E. Journal.*

Shouten, D., and R. Watling. 1997. *Media action projects: A model for integrating video in project-based education, training, and community development.* University of Nottingham, UK: Urban Programme Research Group, School of Education.

Whittaker, R. 1998. *Television production: A comprehensive on-line cybertext in studio and field production. 15 production steps: The production sequence (Module 4).* Available: www.cybercollege.com. (Accessed September 21, 2004).

APPENDIX A

List of Terms and Corresponding Lessons

Note: The chapter titles listed here reflect the main concept of each chapter and are not exact titles for the chapter in the "Table of Contents."

Term	Chapter	Lesson
ABC	Chapter 6 - Television History	Lesson 6.6
ADVERTISING SPACE	Chapter 6 - Television History	Lesson 6.4
ALLEGEDLY	Chapter 2 - Media Literacy	Lesson 2.3
AMERICA'S CUP	Chapter 6 - Television History	Lesson 6.1
ANALYZE THE AUDIENCE	Chapter 2 - Media Literacy Chapter 7 - Production Process	Lesson 2.5A Lesson 7.1
ANTHOLOGIES	Chapter 6 - Television History	Lesson 6.7A
ANTIMONOPOLY	Chapter 6 - Television History	Lesson 6.5
APPLE IIe	Chapter 6 - Television History	Lesson 6.8
ARMSTRONG, Edwin	Chapter 6 - Television History	Lesson 6.6
ARMY SURPLUS	Chapter 6 - Television History	Lesson 6.4
ASCAP	Chapter 6 - Television History	Lesson 6.4
ASPECT RATIO	Chapter 3 - Equipment Basics	Lesson 3.2A
ASSEMBLE EDITING	Chapter 3 - Equipment Basics Chapter 7 - Production Process	Lesson 3.5 Lesson 7.7A
ASSOCIATED PRESS	Chapter 2 - Media Literacy	Lesson 2.1A
ASSURE	Chapter 7 - Production Process	Lesson 3
ASSURE PLANNING MODEL	Chapter 7 - Production Process	Lesson 7.1 Lesson 7.3
AT & T	Chapter 6 - Television History	Lesson 6.2
AUDIO DUBBING	Chapter 3 - Equipment Basics Chapter 7 - Production Process	Lesson 3.5 Lesson 7.7A
AUDIO TECHNICIAN	Chapter 7 - Production Process	Lesson 7.4
AUDION TUBE	Chapter 6 - Television History	Lesson 6.2
A-V BOARD	Chapter 3 - Equipment Basics	Lesson 3.3A
BAIRD, John Logie	Chapter 6 - Television History	Lesson 6.1 Lesson 6.6
BALANCE	Chapter 7 - Production Process	Lesson 7.7A

BANDWAGON	Chapter 2 - Media Literacy	Lesson 2.5B
BIG LIE (THE)	Chapter 2 - Media Literacy	Lesson 2.5B
BLACK BOX	Chapter 6 - Television History	Lesson 6.1
BLACKLISTED	Chapter 6 - Television History	Lesson 6.7A
BNC CABLE	Chapter 3 - Equipment Basics	Lesson 3.3B
BODY LANGUAGE	Chapter 5 - Visual Literacy	Lesson 5.2A
BODY PERCEPTIONS	Chapter 5 - Visual Literacy	Lesson 5.2A
BRIBERY	Chapter 2 - Media Literacy	Lesson 2.5B
BRITISH MARCONI	Chapter 6 - Television History	Lesson 6.1
BROADCAST	Chapter 3 -Equipment Basics	Lesson 3.6
BROADCASTING	Chapter 6 - Television History	Lesson 6.1
B-ROLL FOOTAGE	Chapter 4 - Script Writing	Lesson 4.6
BUMPER MUSIC	Chapter 4 - Script Writing	Lesson 4.6
BUST SHOT	Chapter 3 -Equipment Basics	Lesson 3.4A
CALIBRATING	Chapter 3 - Equipment Basics Chapter 7 - Production Process	Lesson 3.1B Lesson 7.7B
CAPTURE/ACQUISITION	Chapter 3 -Equipment Basics	Lesson 3.6
CAMCORDER	Chapter 3 -Equipment Basics	Lesson 3.2D
CAMERA OPERATOR	Chapter 7 - Production Process	Lesson 7.4
CARTIOID	Chapter 3 - Equipment Basics	Lesson 3.3A
CBS	Chapter 2 - Media Literacy Chapter 6 - Television History	Lesson 2.1A Lesson 6.5
(CCD) CHARGED COUPLE DEVICE	Chapter 3 - Equipment Basics	Lesson 3.1B
CG OPERATOR	Chapter 7 - Production Process	Lesson 4
CD-ROM	Chapter 3 - Equipment Basics	Lesson 3.2
CD-RW	Chapter 3 - Equipment Basics	Lesson 3.2
CHARACTER GENERATOR (CG)	Chapter 3 - Equipment Basics Chapter 7 - Production Process	Lesson 3.5 Lesson 7.7A
CHRONOLOGICAL SEQUENCING	Chapter 7 - Production Process	Lesson 7.2

CINEMATOGRAPHY	Chapter 7 - Production Process	Lesson 7.8
CIRCLES - WHAT THEY MEAN	Chapter 5 - Visual Literacy	Lesson 5.3
CLOSE-UP	Chapter 3 - Equipment Basics	Lesson 3.4A
	Chapter 4 - Script Writing	Lesson 4.6
CLOSURE	Chapter 3 - Equipment Basics	Lesson 3.4A
	Chapter 4 - Script Writing	Lesson 4.6
COLOR BARS	Chapter 3 - Equipment Basics	Lesson 3.2a
COMMERCIALS	Chapter 2 - Media Literacy	Lesson 2.1a
	Chapter 6 - Television History	Lesson 6.5
COMMON GESTURES	Chapter 5 - Visual Literacy	Lesson 5.2A
COMPROMISE	Chapter 6 - Television History	Lesson 6.4
CONDENSER MICROPHONE	Chapter 3 - Equipment Basics	Lesson 3.3A
CONFLICT	Chapter 2 - Media Literacy	Lesson 2.1B
CONNECTORS	Chapter 3 - Equipment Basics	Lesson 3.3B
CONRAD, FRANK	Chapter 6 - Television History	Lesson 6.3
CONSEQUENCE	Chapter 2 - Media Literacy	Lesson 2.1B
CONSTRUCT	Chapter 2 - Media Literacy	Lesson 5
CONTEXT	Chapter 7 - Production Process	Lesson 7.8
CONTINUITY	Chapter 7 - Production Process	Lesson 7.8
CONTINUITY SECRETARY	Chapter 4 - Script Writing	Lesson 4.1
	Chapter 7 - Production Process	Lesson 7.4
COORDINATING SECRETARY	Chapter 4 - Script Writing	Lesson 1
COPYRIGHT LAWS	Chapter 2 - Media Literacy	Lesson 2.2
COVER	Chapter 7 - Production Process	Lesson 7.8
COVER/ESTABLISHING SHOT	Chapter 4 - Script Writing	Lesson 4.6
CRITICAL PATH ITEMS	Chapter 7 - Production Process	Lesson 7.2
CROSS SHOT	Chapter 3 - Equipment Basics	Lesson 3.4A
CUE	Chapter 4 - Script Writing	Lesson 4.1

CUT	Chapter 3 - Equipment Basics	Lesson 3.5
	Chapter 7 - Production Process	Lesson 7.7A
DEFINITION OF MOVIES	Chapter 3 - Equipment Basics	Lesson 3.2A
DEFINITION OF TELEVISION	Chapter 3 - Equipment Basics	Lesson 3.2A
DE FORREST, LEE	Chapter 6 - Television History	Lesson 6.2
DÉTENTE	Chapter 6 - Television History	Lesson 9
DEVISING COMMERCIAL RATES	Chapter 2 - Media Literacy	Lesson 2.1A
DIFFERING MEANINGS	Chapter 2 - Media Literacy	Lesson 2.5A
DIRECTOR	Chapter 7 - Production Process	Lesson 7.4
DISINFORMATION vs. MISINFORMATION	Chapter 2 - Media Literacy	Lesson 2.1A
DISNEY	Chapter 2 - Media Literacy	Lesson 2.1A
DOLLY	Chapter 3 - Equipment Basics	Lesson 3.4C
DOTS	Chapter 3 - Equipment Basics	Lesson 3.2A
DRAMATIC ARC	Chapter 7 - Production Process	Lesson 7.8
DRAMATIC BEATS	Chapter 7 - Production Process	Lesson 7.8
DIGITAL CONVERGENCE	Chapter 3 - Equipment Basics	Lesson 3.6
DIGITAL VIDEO DEVICE (DVD)	Chapter 3 - Equipment Basics	Lesson 3.2
DUTCH-ANGLE SHOT	Chapter 4 - Script Writing	Lesson 4.6
DYNAMIC MICROPHONE	Chapter 3 - Equipment Basics	Lesson 3.3A
EARLY-1960s SHOWS	Chapter 6 - Television History	Lesson 6.7D
EARLY TELEVISION PIONEERS	Chapter 6 - Television History	Lesson 6.7A
EDIT DECISION LIST (EDL)	Chapter 7 - Production Process	Lesson 7.7A
EDITING	Chapter 7 - Production Process	Lesson 7.7A
EFFECTS OF THE GREAT DEPRESSION	Chapter 6 - Television History	Lesson 6.6
EFP	Chapter 2 - Media Literacy	Lesson 2.1A
ELECTROMAGNETS	Chapter 3 - Equipment Basics	Lesson 3.2A
EMOTIONAL TRANSFER	Chapter 2 - Media Literacy	Lesson 2.5A

EMPHASIS	Chapter 7 - Production Process	Lesson 7.5A
ENG	Chapter 2 - Media Literacy	Lesson 2.1A
EXCEPTIONAL QUALITY	Chapter 2 - Media Literacy	Lesson 2.1B
EXTREME CLOSE-UP	Chapter 3 - Equipment Basics Chapter 4 - Script Writing	Lesson 3.4A Lesson 4.6
FADE	Chapter 3 - Equipment Basics Chapter 7 - Production Process	Lesson 3.5 Lesson 7.7A
FEDERAL RADIO COMMISSION	Chapter 6 - Television History	Lesson 6.5
FEEDBACK	Chapter 7 - Production Process	Lesson 7.7B
FESSENDEN, REGINALD	Chapter 6 - Television History	Lesson 6.2
FIELD FOOTAGE LOG	Chapter 7 - Production Process	Lesson 7.5
FIELD OF VIEW	Chapter 3 - Equipment Basics	Lesson 3.4A
57 CHANNELS & NOTHING ON	Chapter 6 - Television History	Lesson 6.9
FIXED-LENGTH LENS	Chapter 3 - Equipment Basics	Lesson 3.1
FLASHBACK	Chapter 4 - Script Writing	Lesson 7.7B
FOCAL LENGTH	Chapter 3 - Equipment Basics	Lesson 3.4A
FOOTAGE	Chapter 3 - Equipment Basics Chapter 7 - Production Process	Lesson 3.2B Lesson 7.7A
FOOTAGE TAPE	Chapter 7 - Production Process	Lesson 7.5
FRAME RATE FOR MOVIES	Chapter 3 - Equipment Basics	Lesson 3.2A
FRAME RATE FOR TELEVISION w/ SOUND	Chapter 3 - Equipment Basics	Lesson 3.2A
FRAME RATE FOR TELEVISION w/o SOUND	Chapter 3 - Equipment Basics	Lesson 3.2A
FRAMING	Chapter 3 - Equipment Basics	Lesson 3.4A Lesson 3.4B
FREQUENCY	Chapter 3 - Equipment Basics	Lesson 3.2A
FÜHERPRINZIP	Chapter 2 - Media Literacy	Lesson 2.5B
FULLY-SCRIPTED STORYBOARD	Chapter 4 - Script Writing	Lesson 4.1
GAUSING	Chapter 3 - Equipment Basics	Lesson 3.2A

GE	Chapter 2 - Media Literacy	Lesson 2.1A
	Chapter 6 - Television History	Lesson 6.2
GOLDEN AGE OF RADIO	Chapter 6 - Television History	Lesson 6.4
GRIP	Chapter 7 - Production Process	Lesson 7.4
GROUP DYNAMICS	Chapter 2 - Media Literacy	Lesson 2.5B
HAMS	Chapter 6 - Television History	Lesson 6.2
HANDSHAKE	Chapter 5 - Visual Literacy	Lesson 5.2A
HEADROOM	Chapter 3 - Equipment Basics	Lesson 3.4A
HIGH DEFINITION TELEVISION (HDTV)	Chapter 3 - Equipment Basics	Lesson 3.2A
HOOK	Chapter 4 - Script Writing	Lesson 4.1
	Chapter 7 - Production Process	Lesson 7.1
HOW STATIONS/AFFILIATES MAKE MONEY	Chapter 2 - Media Literacy	Lesson 2.1
HUE	Chapter 5 - Visual Literacy	Lesson 5.3
HUMAN INTEREST	Chapter 2 - Media Literacy	Lesson 2.1B
HUMOR	Chapter 2 - Media Literacy	Lesson 2.5B
IMPEDANCE OR RESISTANCE	Chapter 3 - Equipment Basics	Lesson 3.3B
INFO-TAINMENT	Chapter 6 - Television History	Lesson 6.9
INSERT EDITING	Chapter 3 - Equipment Basics	Lesson 3.5
	Chapter 7 - Production Process	Lesson 7.7A
INTENSITY	Chapter 5 - Visual Literacy	Lesson 5.3
INTERDEPENDENCIES	Chapter 7 - Production Process	Lesson 7.2
INTERACTIVE VIEWING	Chapter 3 - Equipment Basics	Lesson 3.6
INTERVIEW PREPARATION STEPS (7)	Chapter 4 - Script Writing	Lesson 4.5
INVENTION OF THE PC	Chapter 6 - Television History	Lesson 6.8
JACK vs. PLUG	Chapter 3 - Equipment Basics	Lesson 3.3B
JFK	Chapter 6 - Television History	Lesson 9
KDKA	Chapter 6 - Television History	Lesson 6.4

KRUSHCHEV, Nikita	Chapter 6 - Television History	Lesson 6.7B
KILLER APP	Chapter 3 - Equipment Basics	Lesson 3.6
	Chapter 6 - Television History	Lesson 6.3
LAND	Chapter 3 - Equipment Basics	Lesson 3.2
LATE 1960s SHOWS	Chapter 6 - Television History	Lesson 6.7D
LAVELIER	Chapter 3 - Equipment Basics	Lesson 3.3
LEAD	Chapter 4 - Script Writing	Lesson 4.3
LEAD ROOM	Chapter 3 - Equipment Basics	Lesson 3.4A
LENS vs. F-STOP	Chapter 3 - Equipment Basics	Lesson 3.1B
LICENSES	Chapter 6 - Television History	Lesson 5
LIGHTING DIRECTOR	Chapter 7 - Production Process	Lesson 7.4
LINE CHARACTERISTICS	Chapter 5 - Visual Literacy	Lesson 5.3
LINEAR EDITING	Chapter 3 - Equipment Basics	Lesson 3.5
LOCAL MARKET	Chapter 2 - Media Literacy	Lesson 2.1A
LONG SHOT	Chapter 3 - Equipment Basics	Lesson 3.4A
	Chapter 4 - Script Writing	Lesson 4.6A
MACRO LENS	Chapter 3 - Equipment Basics	Lesson 3.1B
MAGNETIC TAPE	Chapter 3 - Equipment Basics	Lesson 3.2B
MAJESTIC MISSION	Chapter 6 - Television History	Lesson 6.7A
MANIPULATION/PROCESSING	Chapter 3 - Equipment Basics	Lesson 3.6
MARCONI, GUGLIELMO	Chapter 6 – Television History	Lesson 6.1
MASS COMMUNICATIONS	Chapter 6 – Television History	Lesson 6.6
MATTE	Chapter 7 - Production Process	Lesson 7.7A
MAYBE	Chapter 2 - Media Literacy	Lesson 5
MCCARTHY, JOSEPH	Chapter 6 - Television History	Lesson 6.7A
MEDIA CIRCUS	Chapter 2 - Media Literacy	Lesson 2.3
	Chapter 6 - Television History	Lesson 6.9
MEDIA MARKET	Chapter 2 - Media Literacy	Lesson 2.1A
MEDIA PARADIGM	Chapter 2 - Media Literacy	Lesson 2.1A

MEDIUM SHOT	Chapter 3 - Equipment Basics	Lesson 3.4A
MICROPHONE vs. "MIC"	Chapter 3 - Equipment Basics	Lesson 3.3
MICROSOFT	Chapter 2 - Media Literacy	Lesson 2.1A
MICROWAVE-BASED FREQUENCIES	Chapter 3 - Equipment Basics	Lesson 3.2A
MID-1960s SHOWS	Chapter 6 - Television History	Lesson 6.7D
MINNOW, NEWTON	Chapter 6 - Television History	Lesson 6.7D
MIS-EN-SCENE	Chapter 7 - Production Process	Lesson 7.8
MIXER	Chapter 7 - Production Process	Lesson 7.7B
MIXING	Chapter 3 - Equipment Basics	Lesson 3.3A
MORSE CODE	Chapter 6 - Television History	Lesson 6.1
MURDOCH, RUPERT	Chapter 2 - Media Literacy	Lesson 2.1A
MURPHY'S LAW	Chapter 7 - Production Process	Lesson 7.2
MURROW, EDWARD R.	Chapter 6 - Television History	Lesson 6.7A
NAME CALLING	Chapter 2 - Media Literacy	Lesson 2.5B
NARROWCAST	Chapter 3 – Equipment Basics	Lesson 3.6
NATIONAL ANTHEM	Chapter 6 - Television History	Lesson 6.8
NATIONALISM	Chapter 2 - Media Literacy	Lesson 2.5B
NBC	Chapter 6 - Television History	Lesson 6.4
NETWORK STATIONS	Chapter 6 - Television History	Lesson 2.1A
NIELSENS	Chapter 2 - Media Literacy	Lesson 2.4B
NIPKOW'S DISK	Chapter 6 - Television History	Lesson 6.1
NONLINEAR EDITING	Chapter 3 - Equipment Basics	Lesson 3.5
NORMAL SETTING	Chapter 3 - Equipment Basics	Lesson 3.4A
NOSE ROOM	Chapter 3 - Equipment Basics	Lesson 3.4A
NOSTALGIA	Chapter 2 - Media Literacy	Lesson 2.5B
NUMBER OF PEOPLE INVOLVED	Chapter 2 - Media Literacy	Lesson 2.1B
OFFICIAL GOVERNMENT LIE	Chapter 6 – History of Television	Lesson 6.7D
OMNIDIRECTIONAL MIC	Chapter 3 - Equipment Basics	Lesson 3.3A

OTS (OVER-THE-SHOULDER SHOT)	Chapter 3 -Equipment Basics	Lesson 3.4A
	Chapter 4 - Script Writing	Lesson 4.6
PACING	Chapter 2 - Media Literacy	Lesson 2.5A
		Lesson 2.5B
PAN	Chapter 3 - Equipment Basics	Lesson 3.4C
PAPARAZZI	Chapter 2 - Media Literacy	Lesson 2.3
	Chapter 6 - Television History	Lesson 6.8
		Lesson 6.9
PARAMOUNT STUDIOS	Chapter 6 - Television History	Lesson 6.5
PARTIALLY SCRIPTED STORYBOARD	Chapter 4 - Script Writing	Lesson 4.1
PASSIVE VIEWING	Chapter 3 – Equipment Basics	Lesson 3.6
PATENTS	Chapter 2 - Media Literacy	Lesson 2.2
PATHOS	Chapter 2 - Media Literacy	Lesson 2.1B
PEDESTAL	Chapter 3 - Equipment Basics	Lesson 3.4C
PERIPHERAL VISION	Chapter 3 - Equipment Basics	Lesson 3.4B
PERSONALITY TYPES	Chapter 5 - Visual Literacy	Lesson 5.4
PHANTOM POWER	Chapter 3 - Equipment Basics	Lesson 3.3A
PHASING	Chapter 3 - Equipment Basics	Lesson 3.3B
PHOSPHOROUS COATING	Chapter 3 - Equipment Basics	Lesson 3.2A
PIT	Chapter 3 - Equipment Basics	Lesson 3.2
PLUG	Chapter 3 - Equipment Basics	Lesson 3.3B
PORTFOLIO TAPES	Chapter 7 - Production Process	Lesson 7.5
POSSIBLE FUTURE IMPACT	Chapter 2 - Media Literacy	Lesson 2.1B
POST-PRODUCTION	Chapter 3 - Equipment Basics	Lesson 3.5
POTENTIOMETER	Chapter 7 - Production Process	Lesson 7.7B
POWER OF SUGGESTION	Chapter 4 - Script Writing	Lesson 4.1
		Lesson 4.6
POWERS OF OBSERVATION	Chapter 5 - Visual Literacy	Lesson 5.2A
PRE-ASSEMBLED RADIO	Chapter 6 - Television History	Lesson 7.1

PREMISE	Chapter 7 - Production Process	Lesson 6.8
PREMIUM CHANNELS	Chapter 6 - Television History	Lesson 6.8
PRODUCER	Chapter 7 - Production Process	Lesson 7.4
PRODUCTION SCHEDULE	Chapter 7 - Production Process	Lesson 7.3
PROJECT PLAN	Chapter 7 - Production Process	Lesson 7.2
PROMINENCE	Chapter 2 - Media Literacy	Lesson 2.1B
PROXIMITY	Chapter 2 - Media Literacy	Lesson 2.1B
PUBLIC BROADCASTING (PBS)	Chapter 2 - Media Literacy	Lesson 2.1A
PUBLIC DOMAIN	Chapter 2 - Media Literacy	Lesson 2.2
QUIZ SHOW SCANDAL	Chapter 6 - Television History	Lesson 6.7A Lesson 6.7C
RABBIT EARS/ANTENNAE	Chapter 6 - Television History	Lesson 6.8
RACK FOCUS SHOT	Chapter 3 - Equipment Basics	Lesson 3.4C
RADIO ACT OF 1927	Chapter 6 - Television History	Lesson 6.5
RADIO RELAY LEAGUE	Chapter 6 - Television History	Lesson 6.2
RADIO WAVES	Chapter 3 - Equipment Basics	Lesson 3.2A
RASTERS	Chapter 3 - Equipment Basics	Lesson 3.2A
RATINGS	Chapter 2 - Media Literacy	Lesson 2.4B
RCA (PHONO) CABLE	Chapter 3 - Equipment Basics	Lesson 3.3B
RECORDING/STORAGE	Chapter 3 - Equipment Basics	Lesson 3.6
RED & BLUE NETWORKS	Chapter 6 - Television History	Lesson 6.5
REDEEMING SOCIAL VALUE	Chapter 2 - Media Literacy	Lesson 2.3
REPETITION	Chapter 2 - Media Literacy	Lesson 2.5B
RESISTANCE	Chapter 3 - Equipment Basics	Lesson 3.3B
RESOLUTION	Chapter 3 - Equipment Basics	Lesson 3.2A
RF-CABLE	Chapter 3 - Equipment Basics	Lesson 3.3B
RGB CHROMA	Chapter 3 - Equipment Basics	Lesson 3.2A
RKO	Chapter 6 - Television History	Lesson 6.5

ROYALTIES	Chapter 6 - Television History	Lesson 6.4
S-VIDEO CABLE	Chapter 3 - Equipment Basics	Lesson 3.3B
SARNOFF, DAVID	Chapter 6 - Television History	Lesson 6.2
SATIRE	Chapter 2 - Media Literacy	Lesson 2.5A
SCANNING	Chapter 3 - Equipment Basics	Lesson 3.2A
SCRATCH TAPES	Chapter 7 - Production Process	Lesson 7.5
SCRIPTWRITER'S JOB DESCRIPTION	Chapter 4 - Script Writing	Lesson 4.1
SEQUENCE ANALYSIS	Chapter 7 - Production Process	Lesson 7.8
SERIALS	Chapter 6 - Television History	Lesson 6.6
SET TO ZERO	Chapter 7 - Production Process	Lesson 7.7B
SET-BACKS TO INTRODUCTION OF TELEVISION	Chapter 6 - Television History	Lesson 6.6
SHAPES	Lesson 5 – Visual Literacy	Lesson 5.3
SHIELDING	Chapter 3 - Equipment Basics	Lesson 3.3B
SHOCK VALUE	Chapter 2 - Media Literacy	Lesson 2.1B
SHOW THEMES OF THE 1950s	Chapter 6 – Television History	Lesson 6.7B
SIMULCASTING	Chapter 6 - Television History	Lesson 6.5
SMPTE	Chapter 7 - Production Process	Lesson 7.5
SNOW	Chapter 3 - Equipment Basics	Lesson 3.5
SOUND BITES	Chapter 2 - Media Literacy Chapter 6 - Television History	Lesson 2.3 Lesson 6.9
SOUND ENGINEER	Chapter 7 - Production Process	Lesson 7.4
SPIN DOCTORS	Chapter 2 - Media Literacy Chapter 6 - Television History	Lesson 2.3 Lesson 6.9
SPONSORS	Chapter 2 - Media Literacy	Lesson 2.1A
SQUARES- WHAT THEY MEAN	Chapter 5 - Visual Literacy	Lesson 5.3
STACKING THE DECK	Chapter 2 - Media Literacy	Lesson 2.5B
STORYBOARD USES (4)	Chapter 4 - Script Writing	Lesson 4.1
SWEEPS	Chapter 2 - Media Literacy	Lesson 2.4

SYMMETRY	Chapter 3 - Equipment Basics	Lesson 3.4A
	Chapter 7 - Production Process	Lesson 7.7A
TABLOID TELEVISION	Chapter 2 - Media Literacy	Lesson 2.3
TALENT	Chapter 7 - Production Process	Lesson 7.4
TALENT RELEASE FORM	Chapter 2 - Media Literacy	Lesson 2.2
TALK SHOWS	Chapter 6 - Television History	Lesson 6.9
TALKIES	Chapter 6 - Television History	Lesson 6.5
TAPE GENERATIONS	Chapter 3 - Equipment Basics	Lesson 3.2D
TARTIKOFF, BRANDON	Chapter 6 - Television History	Lesson 6.8
TEASER	Chapter 4 - Script Writing	Lesson 4.6
TECHNICAL DIRECTOR	Chapter 7 - Production Process	Lesson 7.4
TECHNIQUES	Chapter 2 - Media Literacy	Lesson 2.5A
TECHNO EFFECTS	Chapter 2 - Media Literacy	Lesson 2.5A
TELE FILMS	Chapter 6 - Television History	Lesson 6.7B
TELEPLAY	Chapter 4 - Script Writing	Lesson 4.1
TELEVISION CODE OF ETHICS (THE)	Chapter 2 - Media Literacy	Lesson 2.3
TELEVISION MOVES TO HOLLYWOOD	Chapter 6 - Television History	Lesson 6.7B
TELEVISION SHOWS OF THE 1970s	Chapter 6 - Television History	Lesson 6.8
TESTIMONIALS	Chapter 2 - Media Literacy	Lesson 2.5B
TEXTURES	Chapter 5 - Visual Literacy	Lesson 5.3
THREE PARTS TO A SCRIPT	Chapter 4 - Script Writing	Lesson 4.2
TIGHT SHOT	Chapter 3 - Equipment Basics	Lesson 3.4B
TILT	Chapter 3 - Equipment Basics	Lesson 3.4C
TIMELINESS	Chapter 2 - Media Literacy	Lesson 2.1B
TITILLATION COMPONENT	Chapter 2 - Media Literacy	Lesson 2.1B
TOLL BROADCASTING	Chapter 6 - Television History	Lesson 6.4
TONE	Chapter 5 - Visual Literacy	Lesson5. 3

TRADEMARKS	Chapter 2 - Media Literacy	Lesson 2.2
TRANSITION	Chapter 7 - Production Process	Lesson 7.7A
TRANSMISSION/DISTRIBUTION	Chapter 3 - Equipment Basics	Lesson 3.6
TRIANGLES - WHAT THEY MEAN	Chapter 5 - Visual Literacy	Lesson 5.3
TRIPOD OR STICKS	Chapter 3 - Equipment Basics	Lesson 3.1
TRUCK	Chapter 3 - Equipment Basics	Lesson 3.4A
TWO-HEADED MONSTER	Chapter 6 - Television History	Lesson 6.7D
TWO-SHOT	Chapter 3 -Equipment Basics	Lesson 3.4A
UNIDIRECTIONAL MIC	Chapter 3 - Equipment Basics	Lesson 3.3A
UNITED FRUIT COMPANY	Chapter 6 - Television History	Lesson 6.2
UNTOUCHABLES, THE	Chapter 6 - Television History	Lesson 6.7B
VALUE MESSAGES	Chapter 2 - Media Literacy	Lesson 2.5A
VAN DOREN, CHARLES	Chapter 6 - Television History	Lesson 6.7A
VARIABLE LENGTH LENS	Chapter 3 - Equipment Basics	Lesson 3.1B
VECTORING	Chapter 3 - Equipment Basics	Lesson 3.4B
VECTORS	Chapter 5 - Visual Literacy	Lesson 5.3
VHS	Chapter 3 - Equipment Basics	Lesson 3.2B
VIDEOTAPE OPERATOR	Chapter 3 - Equipment Basics	Lesson 7.4
VIEWFINDER-WHAT IT DOES	Chapter 6 - Television History	Lesson 3.1B
VOLUME vs. GAIN	Chapter 7 - Production Process	Lesson 7.7B
VU METER	Chapter 7 - Production Process	Lesson 7.7B
WESTERNS	Chapter 6 - Television History	Lesson 6.7B
WESTINGHOUSE	Chapter 6 - Television History	Lesson 6.2
WHITE BALANCE	Chapter 3 - Equipment Basics	Lesson 3.1B
WHITE SPACE	Chapter 3 - Equipment Basics Chapter 7 - Production Process	Lesson 4 Lesson 7.7A
WHO OWNS WHAT?	Chapter 2 - Media Literacy	Lesson 2.1A
WIDE-ANGLE LENS	Chapter 3 - Equipment Basics	Lesson 3.1B

WIPE OR SWIPE	Chapter 3 - Equipment Basics	Lesson 3.5
	Chapter 7 - Production Process	Lesson 7.7A
WIRELESS TELEPHONE	Chapter 6 - Television History	Lesson 6.1
WORKING TITLE	Chapter 7 - Production Process	Lesson 7.1
WRESTLEMANIA	Chapter 6 - Television History	Lesson 6.9
WRITER	Chapter 7 - Production Process	Lesson 7.4
WWI	Chapter 6 - Television History	Lesson 6.2
XLR CABLE	Chapter 3 - Equipment Basics	Lesson 3.3B
YPbPr	Chapter 3 – Equipment Basics	Lesson 3.3B
Z-AXIS	Chapter 3 - Equipment Basics	Lesson 4
ZOOM	Chapter 3 - Equipment Basics	Lesson 3.5
		Lesson 3.1B
ZOOM LENS	Chapter 3 - Equipment Basics	Lesson 3.1B
ZWORYKIN, VLADIMIR	Chapter 6 - Television History	Lesson 6.6

Daily Activity Sheet

Daily Activity Sheet

For the period: ____ /____/____   through: ____/____/_____

Day/Date	Accomplishments (Max. 5 pts per day)	Total Points
1. __/__/__		
2. __/__/__		
3. __/__/__		
4. __/__/__		
5. __/__/__		
6. __/__/__		
7. __/__/__		
8. __/__/__		
9. __/__/__		
10. __/__/__		

(Circle one)

Name: Period: 1   2   3   4   5   6   7   8   Total pts:

Checklist

NAME: _____   PERIOD: _____

COMPETENCY   **DATE CHECKED** _____

Character Generator	___/___/___
Assemble Edit	___/___/___
Insert Edit	___/___/___
A-V Board:	
Audio	___/___/___
Audio Dub	___/___/___
Wipes/Swipe	___/___/___
Fade	___/___/___
Effects:	
Mosaic	___/___/___
Nega	___/___/___
Paint	___/___/___
Multi	___/___/___
Trail	___/___/___

APPENDIX D

ENG/Segment
Footage Log

ENG/Segment Footage Log

Title: _____   Page _____ of _____

Tape No: _____   ENG Team: _____

Scene	Take #	Time code	G	NG	Description/Comments
		: :			
		: :			
		: :			
		: :			
		: :			
		: :			
		: :			
		: :			
		: :			
		: :			
		: :			
		: :			
		: :			
		: :			
		: :			

APPENDIX E

Interview Worksheet

Worksheet

PROJECT TITLE: NAME:

DATE OF INTERVIEW: LOCATION:

QUESTIONS TO BE ASKED

1. _____
2. _____
3. _____
4. _____
5. _____
6. _____
7. _____
8. _____
9. _____
10. _____
11. _____
12. _____
13. _____
14. _____
15. _____
16. _____
17. _____
18. _____
19. _____
20. _____

INTERVIEW TIPS

1. Prepare yourself.
2. Ask focused questions.
3. Ask simple one-answer questions.
4. Ask questions that require an answer.
5. Ask intimate questions in broader terms.
6. Think of the order and intensity of questions (first earn the interviewee's trust).
7. Set the interviewee at ease and ready to talk.
8. Warn the interviewee of possible interruptions.
9. Rehearse questions with the interviewee.
10. Tell the interviewee how you would like the questions answered.
11. Pay attention to what's being said.
12. Always have your next question ready
13. Ask follow-up questions.
14. Never rush the interviewee; let the person answer the question at his or her discretion.
15. Always dress appropriately.

Project and Activity Planning Sheet

Planning Sheet

Team members: _____   Period: _____

For the week of: _____/_____/_____

	Planned Activities	**Equipment**	**Accomplishments**
MONDAY Project Title(s):			
TUESDAY Project Title(s):			
WEDNESDAY Project Title(s):			
THURSDAY Project Title(s):			
FRIDAY Project Title(s):			

Open Projects

Proj. #/Title	**DUE DATE**	**# DAYS TO COMPLETE**
1.		
2		
3.		

APPENDIX G

Segment Checklist/Scorecard

Checklist/Scorecard

135 points Total

Things the scriptwriter needs to consider:

Analyze the audience   **(5 pts each: 15 pts total)**

Who is the target audience? _____

What is the purpose/premise? _____

What is the "hook/teaser"? _____

Link the content   **(10 pts)**

____ Did I link the content to a context, event, or concept that the audience understands or has heard of previously?

Analyze the content   **(2 pts)**

____ Did I use any words my audience may not understand?

Organize the content   **(2 pts each: 8 pts total)**

____ Do I have a Beginning/Middle/End?

____ Did I sequence the content so the most important info is first?

____ Did I avoid passive voice?

____ Do I have short, concise sentences?

Storyboard the content   **(5 pts each: 20 pts total)**

____ Have I accounted for each scene/sequence? (Have I coordinated with the content to be sure there is a scene for each critical point in the story line)

____ Have I established an objective for each scene?

____ Have I established how am I going to accomplish each objective? (visually, verbally, or a combination)

____ What visuals need to be provided?

Things the *camera operator* needs to consider:

Which **camera shot/angle** should I use?

How well do I vary from standard-full front shots?   **(5 pts)**

___ Head room (medium shot)

___ Nose room (profile shot)

___ Extreme close-up?

How well are the shots **constructed?**   **(3 pts each: 21 pts total)**

___ What are my cut-off points? (Closure).

___ How's the lighting? (Check it on a monitor—the viewfinder lies).

___ Is the camera at the right height?

___ How is the symmetry/balance?

___ Are there any visuals to insert? (Where? The alignment changes).

___ How is the focus? (be sure to zoom in all the way to check it out).

___ Do I have sound?

Things the *on-camera talent* needs to consider: **(3 pts each: 24 pts total)**

____ How is my **speech rate**? (Slow down! Your perception of how fast you are going is grossly underestimated. If it sounds too slow to you, it is probably just right!)

____ Do I integrate **reading** with **looking** at the audience?

____ Do I look right in the **eye of the camera**? (You will be more believable. Your audience will perceive you are talking to each one of them individually.)

____ Do I "**say it**" rather than "read it"?

How is my **body language?**

_____ Posture? (Sit up straight—slouching makes your viewers believe you are bored.

_____ Do I smile, when appropriate? It relaxes your viewers.

_____ Do I align my head with chin and look straight at the camera? (It provides an image that you know what you arc talking about.)

_____ When interviewing or talking to someone else, do I look right at the interviewee and acknowledge their responses?

Things the *technical team* and *post-production* editors need to consider: **(5 pts each: 30 pts total)**

_____ Does the show **have title and credits page**(s)?

_____ Is there any **"snow"** between cuts?

_____ Are **all visuals** accounted for?

_____ Do scenes/segments match storyboards?

_____ Does the **music complement,** or detract from, the scene(s)?

_____ Does show meet minimum/maximum time frames?

Portfolio Assessment Scorecards

Assessment Scorecard 1

Portfolio Projects # 1 & 2: Still Shots/Stop Action

Name: _____   Date: ____/____/____

Criterion #1

Checklist   Total Points (5)

____ Meets time requirements: (length = _____).
____ Contains title page/credits screen.
____ Content demonstrates understanding of visual story-telling.
____ Content demonstrates understanding of
    ____ Balance/symmetry/equilibrium
    ____ Unity/continuity (proper relationship between frames).
    ____ Emphasis (the premise is clearly understandable).
Total: _____

Criterion #2

Quality Rating   Total Points (6)

Use of Equipment & Formats

3	2	1
Demonstrates clear understanding of use of equipment. No apparent technical glitches. Clearly demonstrates knowledge of production techniques.	Project somewhat hard to follow. Reveals occasional technical errors and/or proper use of equipment and/or inconsistencies.	Unintelligible use of techniques. Process shows major flaws in technique and/ or use of equipment.

Content/Creativity

3	2	1
Content demonstrates understanding of use of storytelling techniques.	Shows general understanding of use of story-building techniques; partially analyzes material.	Unintelligible concepts. Missing one of required parts (begin/middle/end). Storyline " doesn't fly."

Total: _____

Criterion #3

Overall Impressions   Total Points (9)

9	7	6	3
Clearly Outstanding	Above Average	Average	Below Average

Total: _____
Overall: ____/out of 20

Assessment Scorecard 2

Portfolio Project # 3: Book Trailer

Name: _____   Date: ____/____/____

Criterion #1

Checklist   Total Points (5)

____ Meets time requirements (length = 1 ½ -2 min).
____ Project clearly marked with title screen.
____ Content demonstrates understanding of script writing & storyboards.
       Content demonstrates understanding of
       ____ Balance/symmetry/equilibrium
       ____ Unity/continuity (proper relationship between frames).
       ____ Emphasis (the premise is clearly understandable).
Total: _____

Criterion #2

Quality Rating   Total Points (6)

Use of Equipment & Formats

3	2	1
Demonstrates clear understanding of use of equipment. No apparent technical glitches. Clearly demonstrates knowledge of production techniques.	Project somewhat hard to follow. Reveals occasional technical errors and/or proper use of equipment and/or inconsistencies.	Unintelligible use of techniques. Process shows major flaws in technique and/ or use of equipment.

Content/Creativity

3	2	1
Content demonstrates understanding of use of storytelling techniques.	Shows general understanding of use of story-building techniques; partially analyzes material.	Unintelligible concepts. Missing one of required parts (begin/middle/end). Storyline " doesn't fly."

Total: _____

Criterion #3

Overall Impressions   Total Points (9)

9	7	6	3
Clearly Outstanding	Above Average	Average	Below Average

Total: _____
Overall: ____/out of 20

Assessment Scorecard 3

Portfolio Project # 4: Instructional Video

Name: _____   Date: ____/____/____

Criterion #1
Checklist   Total Points (5)

____ Meets minimum time requirements (length = ____).
____ Project clearly marked with title screen.
____ Content demonstrates understanding of three-part storytelling.
Content demonstrates understanding of
    ____ Balance/symmetry/equilibrium
    ____ Unity/continuity (proper relationship between frames).
    ____ Emphasis (the premise is clearly understandable).
Total: _____

Criterion #2
Quality Rating   Total Points (6)

Use of Equipment & Formats

3	2	1
Demonstrates clear understanding of use of equipment. No apparent technical glitches. Clearly demonstrates knowledge of how to insert B-roll footage.	Project somewhat hard to follow. Reveals occasional technical errors and/or proper use of equipment and/or inconsistencies in insert edits.	Unintelligible use of techniques. Process shows major flaws in technique and/or use of insert edit techniques.

Content/Creativity

3	2	1
Content demonstrates understanding of use of storytelling techniques.	Shows general understanding of use of story-building techniques; partially analyzes material.	Unintelligible concepts. Missing one of required parts (begin/middle/end). Storyline " doesn't fly."

Total: _____

Criterion #3
Overall Impressions   Total Points (9)

9	7	6	3
Clearly Outstanding	Above Average	Average	Below Average

Total: _____
Overall: ____/*out of 20*

Assessment Scorecard 4

Portfolio Project # 5: Interview

Name: _____ Date: ____/____/____

Criterion #1

Checklist   Total Points (5)

_____ Shows segment continuity.
_____ Properly ties to *Decades* project.
_____ Content demonstrates understanding of visual storytelling.
Content demonstrates understanding of
_____ Balance/symmetry/equilibrium
_____ Unity/continuity (proper relationship between frames).
_____ Emphasis (the premise is clearly understandable).
Total: _____

Criterion #2

Quality Rating   Total Points (6)

Use of Equipment & Formats

3	2	1
Demonstrates clear understanding of use of equipment. No apparent technical glitches. Clearly demonstrates knowledge of production techniques.	Project somewhat hard to follow. Reveals occasional technical errors and/or proper use of equipment and/or inconsistencies.	Unintelligible use of techniques. Process shows major flaws in technique and/or use of equipment.

Content/Creativity

3	2	1
Content demonstrates understanding of use of storytelling techniques.	Shows general understanding of use of story-building techniques; partially analyzes material.	Unintelligible concepts. Missing one of required parts (begin/middle/end). Storyline " doesn't fly."

Total: _____

Criterion #3

Overall Impressions   Total Points (9)

9	7	6	3
Clearly Outstanding	Above Average	Average	Below Average

Total: _____
Overall: _____/out of 20

Assessment Scorecard 5

Portfolio Project # 6: Decades

Name: _____   Date: ____/____/____

Criterion #1

Checklist   Total Points (5)

_____ Music, sounds, images all supplement and correlate to topic.
_____ Content relates to theme.
_____ Content demonstrates two-camera interview technique.
Content demonstrates understanding of
    _____ Balance/symmetry/equilibrium
    _____ Unity/continuity (proper relationship between frames).
    _____ Emphasis (the premise is clearly understandable).
Total: _____

Criterion #2

Quality Rating   Total Points (6)

Use of Equipment & Formats

3	2	1
Demonstrates clear understanding of use of equipment. No apparent technical glitches. Clearly demonstrates knowledge of production techniques.	Project somewhat hard to follow. Reveals occasional technical errors and/or proper use of equipment and/or inconsistencies.	Unintelligible use of techniques. Process shows major flaws in technique and/ or use of equipment.

Content/Creativity

3	2	1
Content demonstrates understanding of use of story-telling techniques.	Shows general understanding of use of story-building techniques . . . partially analyzes material.	Unintelligible concepts. Missing one of required parts (begin/middle/end). Story line "doesn't fly."

Total: _____

Criterion #3

Overall Impressions   Total Points (9)

9	7	6	3
Clearly Outstanding	Above Average	Average	Below Average

Total: _____
Overall: _____/out of 20

Assessment Scorecard 6

Portfolio Project # 7: PSA/Commercial

Name: _____   Date: ____/____/____

Criterion #1 _____

Checklist   Total Points (5)

____ Meets maximum time requirements (length = 15 or 30 seconds).
____ Project clearly marked with title screen.
____ Content demonstrates understanding of use of (tool: _____).
Content demonstrates understanding of
____ Balance/symmetry/equilibrium
____ Unity/continuity (proper relationship between frames).
____ Emphasis (the premise is clearly understandable).
Total: _____

Criterion #2 _____

Quality Rating   Total Points (6)

Use of Equipment & Formats

3	2	1
Demonstrates clear understanding of use of equipment. No apparent technical glitches. Clearly demonstrates knowledge of production techniques.	Project somewhat hard to follow. Reveals occasional technical errors and/or proper use of equipment and/or inconsistencies.	Unintelligible use of techniques. Process shows major flaws in technique and/ or use of equipment.

Content/Creativity

3	2	1
Content demonstrates understanding of use of story-telling techniques.	Shows general understanding of use of story-building techniques . . . partially analyzes material.	Unintelligible concepts. Missing one of required parts (begin/middle/end). Story line "doesn't fly."

Total: _____

Criterion #3 _____

Overall Impressions   Total Points (9)

9	7	6	3
Clearly Outstanding	Above Average	Average	Below Average

Total: _____
Overall: ____/out of 20

Assessment Scorecard 7

Portfolio Projects # 8: Sweeps

Name: _____   Date: ____/____/____

Criterion #1

Checklist   Total Points (5)

____ Meets time requirements (7 to 10 minutes).
____ Content shows use of script and storyboards (_____).
____ Story line demonstrates continuity between scenes.
____ Content demonstrates understanding of
    ____ Balance/symmetry/equilibrium
    ____ Unity/continuity (proper relationship between frames).
    ____ Emphasis (the premise is clearly understandable).
Total: _____

Criterion #2

Quality Rating   Total Points (6)

Use of Equipment & Formats

3	2	1
Demonstrates clear understanding of use of equipment. No apparent technical glitches. Clearly demonstrates knowledge of production techniques.	Project somewhat hard to follow. Reveals occasional technical errors and/or proper use of equipment and/or inconsistencies.	Unintelligible use of techniques. Process shows major flaws in technique and/ or use of equipment.

Content/Creativity

3	2	1
Content demonstrates understanding of use of story-telling techniques.	Shows general understanding of use of story-building techniques . . . partially analyzes material.	Unintelligible concepts. Missing one of required parts (begin/middle/end). Story line "doesn't fly."

Total: _____

Criterion #3

Overall Impressions   Total Points (9)

9	7	6	3
Clearly Outstanding	Above Average	Average	Below Average

Total: _____
Overall: ____/out of 20

Storyboard Worksheet

Team: _____

Project (Working Title): _____   **Due Date:** ____/____/____

Objective: _____

_____

Cue: _____

_____

_____

Objective: _____

_____

Cue: _____

_____

_____

Objective: _____

_____

Cue: _____

_____

_____

Objective: _____

_____

Cue: _____

_____

_____

Objective: _____

_____

Cue: _____

_____

_____

Objective: _____

_____

Cue: _____

_____

_____

Objective: _____

_____

Cue: _____

_____

_____

Objective: _____

_____

Cue: _____

_____

_____

Objective: _____

_____

Cue: _____

_____

_____

Mediated Resources Used in This Course

The goal of making recommendations for using outside resources has been to find those that are relevant, inexpensive, and available. This book was written as a turnkey course guide that could stand on its own merit. As such, the course content can be taught without making additional expenditures. However, for those who want to obtain some or all of the recommended materials, the following list has been provided. Keep in mind, that the materials may have to be found in other places. To keep this book current, the **Web-ASSISTant** Web site will provide updates as they become available.

PRINT RESOURCES

Auletta, Ken. 1986. *Three blind mice: How the TV networks lost their way*. New York: Random House. **Cost: approximately $15**. This book may be ordered from any retailer or online at **www.amazon.com**.

Barnouw, Erik. 1990. *The tube of plenty*. New York: Oxford University Press. **Cost: approximately $25**. This book may be ordered from any retailer or online at **www. amazon.com**.

Brinkley, Joel. 1997. *Defining vision: How broadcasters lured the government into inciting a revolution in television*. New York: Harcourt Brace. Available on Amazon.com. **Cost: approximately $35**.

Considine, David M., and Gail E. Haley. 1999. *Visual messages: Integrating imagery into instruction*. Englewood, CO: Libraries Unlimited. **Cost: approximately $20**. May be ordered from most bookstores, online at **www.amazon.com**, or from the publisher directly at **www.lu.com**.

Davies, John. 1997. *Educating students in a media-saturated culture*. Lancaster, PA: Scarecrow Education. **Cost: approximately $25**. It can be ordered from any retailer, online from **www.amazon.com,** or directly from the publisher. Davis promotes the use of popular music, movies, videos, and both commercial and educational television to help students and teachers study how all media affect children on both the cognitive and emotional levels.

Giannetti, Louis. 1982. *Understanding movies*. This book about setting up scenes for movies has considerable applicability to video. It was originally published by Prentice Hall in 1972 and has had two subsequent revisions (1976 and 1982). **Cost: approximately $25**. It may be ordered from any bookstore, online from **www.amazon.com**, or directly from the publisher.

Jankowski, Gene, and David Fuchs. 1995. *Television today and tomorrow: It won't be what you think*. New York: Oxford University Press. **Cost: approximately $20.** It may be ordered from any bookstore, online at **www.amazon.com**, or directly from the publisher.

Katz, Steven. 1991. *Film directing shot by shot: Visualizing from concept to screen*. Ann Arbor, MI: Braun-Brumfield. A text-to-screen masterpiece. **Cost: approximately $30**. Can be purchased at **www.amazon.com**.

Katz, Steven. 1992. *Film directing cinematic motion: A workshop for staging scenes*. Ann Arbor, MI: Braun-Brumfield. A great book that teaches how movies come alive. **Cost: approximately $25**. May be purchased at **www. amazon.com.**

Kyker, Keith, and Christopher Curchy. 1995. *Television production: A classroom approach*. Englewood, CO: Libraries Unlimited. **Cost: approximately $30**. It may be ordered from most bookstores or from the publisher directly at **www.lu.com**. The book is accompanied by a videotape to supplement the text and serves as a model for some of the projects included in the text.

Masterman, Len. 1980. *Teaching about television*. London: Macmillan Press Ltd. *Teaching the media*. London: Comedia/MK Media Press. These two books detail the early ideas about how media should be dealt with. They are compendia of thought on the issues surrounding media education and the problems students and teachers face when trying to participate in media education programs. **Cost: each approximately $25.**

Murray, Janet. 1998. *Hamlet on the holodeck: The future of narrative in cyberspace.* Cambridge, MA: MIT Press. A dynamic look at how the digital domain will change how we look at media. **Cost: approximately $40.**

Schroeppel, Tom. 1998. *Video goals: Getting results with pictures and sound.* **Cost: approximately $10.** It may be ordered directly from the author at: 3205 Price Avenue, Tampa, FL 33611.

Schroeppel, Tom. 1998. *The bare bones camera course for film and video.* **Cost: approximately $10.** It may be ordered directly from the author at: 3205 Price Avenue, Tampa, FL 33611.

Smith, F. L., J. W. Wright, and D. H. Ostroff. 1998. *Perspectives on radio and television.* (4th ed). Mahwah, NJ: Lawrence Erlbaum Associates. A thorough text on the regulatory history of broadcasting. **Cost: approximately $50.**

Tartikoff, Brandon. 1992. *The last great ride.* New York: Turtle Bay. This book is out of print but may be found as a special request at **www.amazon.com**.

Theodosakis, Nikos. 2001. *The director in the classroom: How filmmaking inspires learning.* San Diego: Tech4Learning. **Cost: approximately $40.**

Tyner, Kathleen. 1998. *Literacy in a digital world: Teaching and learning in the age of information.* Mahwah, NJ. Laurence Erlbaum Associates. This is a wonderful book that belongs in any educator's library for background on how the digital age will change how media literacy should be taught. **Cost: approximately $30.** It may be ordered from any retail bookstore, online at **www.amazon.com**, or directly from the publisher.

Whittaker, Ron. 1990. *Television production.* New York: Mayfield Publishing Company. This book may be ordered from Dr. Whittaker's online Web course at **www.cybercollege.com**.

Zettl, Herb. 1998. *Sight-sound-motion: Applied media aesthetics.* New York: Wadsworth Publishing. This book is an important addition to any television teacher's library. **Cost: approximately $98.** (Amazon.com has used copies for $5.) It may be ordered directly from the publisher at **www. wadsworth.com**.

ONLINE RESOURCES

Because Internet links are subject to change, check the **Web-ASSISTant** Web site ("Chapter Seven" page) for updates to see if these links are still active. Where possible, an alternative will be provided, should these links be removed or changed.

Cybercollege. (**www.cybercollege.com**). This is an online version of Professor Whittaker's book and may be used by any educational concern. Check the Web site for special copyright considerations.

Center for Media Literacy. *Is seeing believing? How can you tell what's real.* Posted at **www. medialit.org/.** It is a wonderful product that examines issues surrounding the digital manipulation of photographs. The product comes with videotape, a poster, and a teacher's guide.

Digital beat. In *Charting the digital broadcasting future: The second anniversary of the PIAC.* Report by Kevin Taglang. Posted on the Benton Foundation Web site: **www.benton.org/DigitalBeat/ db121800.html**.

Federal Communication Commission. This agency hosts a Web site (**www.fcc.gov/ telecom.html**) that explains the Telecommunications Act of 1996 in detail.

Media College, www.mediacollege.com, contains a wealth of information on the production and technical aspects of all media, including analog and digital.

Media History Project, www.mediahistory.com, provides timelines, information, and history on media issues. It was used for the timeline surveys in **Chapter 2.**

New Mexico Media Literacy Project (NMMLP). *Understanding media* is an interactive CD that outlines general and specific deconstructing tools and also provides class discussion topics with possible answers. It comes with a newsletter and **can be purchased for $30** directly online at **www.nmmlp.org.**

Radio & Television News Director Association, http://www.rtnda.org/ethics/coe.shtml, publishes an electronic journalist's code of ethics that is worth reading and referring to.

Video University, **www.videouniversity.com,** contains articles on production, history, and other topics.

VIDEO RESOURCES

Annenberg/CPB Project is an educational organization dedicated to producing videos and other mediated aids for classrooms. Many of the videos come with curriculum guides and/or lesson plans. Many are a part of a series and can be ordered separately; some cannot be ordered alone. These are identified below.

Against all odds (Tape #13). Part of a series, but the tape on blocking and surveying may be ordered separately. (Item #ANAASCK). **Cost: $199 (individual tapes costs around $30 each).**

Broadcast news writing. Part of a series on news writing; sold as a set or individually. (Item #ANNWSVEH). A series of 15 half-hour lessons. **Cost: $299. (individual tapes cost around $30 each).**

American cinema. Part of a series on various aspects of cinema to include screenwriting, but can be ordered separately. (Item #ANACSVE) **Cost: $320 (individual tapes cost around $30 each).**

Information on how to obtain the Annenberg/CPB catalog may be found at the Web site, **www.learner.org**. Also, a link to the appropriate page has been put on the **Web-ASSISTant** Web site.

CBS Television Video. 1995. Many of the *Twilight Zone* videos are available from local retail stores or online at **www. amazon.com**. **Cost: approximately $30 each.**

Discovery School Channel. The following two videos distributed by this company were used in this course:

Understanding Television. (Item #717686). Television is the primary source of both news and entertainment for a majority of people, but not many of us understand how this wondrous invention works. This video takes the viewer on a journey through the medium that changed the course of communications industry. **Cost: approximately $35.**

Headlines & Soundbites. (Item #717314). Walter Cronkite takes an unsentimental look at the media. Viewers hear from some of the biggest names in the business how news is selected, packaged, and presented. **Cost: approximately $30.**

These videos may be obtained directly from the Discovery School Channel Web site, **www.school.discovery.com.**

GPM, at the University of Nebraska at Lincoln. *Signal to Noise* is a three-part series that premiered on public television during the summer of 1996. It takes a critical look at the power, business, and allure of television. The videos are broken down into manageable segments that hold the students' attention. The segment approach empowers the teacher to control the time commitment for the specific literacy aspect and still leaves class time to work on projects and activities. **Cost for the set: approximately $90.** It may be ordered directly from the center at **www.gpm.org.**

National Educational Association. n.d. *Speak up on television.* **Cost: approximately $40.** It is available from **www.nea.org**.

Paramount Pictures. 1995. *Quiz show.* **Cost: approximately $25.** It may be ordered from any online video reseller or local retailer. Check local school usage policies for performance rights.

PBS Video. The following videos may be ordered from PBS: The item numbers used designate those with public broadcast rights. A PBS home video version is available and may be an option. Check local appropriate use policies to decide which version to purchase.

Big dreams, small screen. (Item # AMEX-996–F9A). This is the Philo Farnsworth story; it describes the rivalry between Farnsworth and David Sarnoff. The video discusses Philo's life and how he finally came to be known as the father of electronic television. **Cost: approximately $60.**

Digital television: A crash course. (Item # DITV-101–F9A). Robert Cringley takes an irreverent look at the importance of this newest breakthrough in media technology. **Cost: approximately $30.**

Both videos may be ordered directly from the PBS site, **www.pbs.org**.

Teacher's Video Company, Scottsdale, AZ. The following videos may be used as a substitute for the *45/85* video used in **Chapter 6**. These tapes are only sold in sets and can be rather expensive (anywhere from $90 to $200 per set). However, they are representative of the types of videos that are available. The best of the lot appears to be the *Classic television* video, which show clips of some of the great programs from the 1950s.

Unforgettable 50s (item #UFIF)

Memories of the 60s (item #MOSI)

Fabulous 60s (item #FSSS)

Sensational 70s (item #SSSE)

History of the 80s (item #HOTE)

Classic Television (item #CTYF)

The tapes may be ordered directly from Teacher's Video Company, P.O. Box ENF-4455, Scottsdale, AZ 85261. Phone: 800-262-8837. Fax: 602-860-8650.

Turner Classic Movies (TMC) Video. *Citizen kane.* 1996. This video contains a segment at the end called *The Making of Citizen Kane*, which introduces concepts important to the visual literacy lessons in **Chapter 5. Cost: approximately $39.** It may be purchased from most educational video distributors or local video retailers.

Vestron Video. *45/85: America since WWII.* 1986. Houston, TX. This video may be out of print but is often available from the local library. Check local school usage policy for performance rights. If this video is unavailable, the Teacher's Video Company tapes may be used as a substitute.

SOFTWARE RESOURCES

Cinovation, Inc. *Scriptware* is a software package used by professional scriptwriters. It automatically formats the text into specific formats and adds script notes, where required. It is expensive (around $300), but could be quite useful to those who are interested in scriptwriting.

Tom Snyder Productions. *Decisions/decisions: Violence in the media* is a computer simulation game. It explores the complexities of grappling with television violence and provides a firsthand opportunity to make decisions that will affect an outcome, causing students to have to live with the results. **Cost: approximately $80.** It may be ordered directly from the publisher.

Zettl, Herb. *Videolab 2.1.* This CD is an interactive version of Zettl's handbook. **Cost: approximately $80.** It may be ordered directly from the publisher at **www. wadsworth.com**.

REFERENCES

Auletta, K. 1986. *Three blind mice: How the TV networks lost their way.* New York: Random House.

Barnouw, E. 1990. *The tube of plenty.* New York: Oxford University Press.

Davis, M. 1997, February. Garage cinema and the future of media technology. *Communications of the ACM.* 40 (2).

Desmond, R. 1998. Media literacy in the home: Acquisition vs deficit models. In K. Tyner, *Literacy in a digital world: Teaching and learning in the age of information.* Mahwah, NJ: Laurence Erlbaum Associates.

Driscoll, R. 1994. The act of discovery. *Harvard Educational Review* 31 (1): 21–32.

Feller, M. 1994. *Studies in educational evaluation: Open-book testing and education for the future,* vol. 20.Oxford: Elsevier Science Ltd Available: www.ehhs.emich.edu/ ins/open.perf. (Accessed September 21, 2004).

Freed, K. n.d. *Deep media literacy: A proposal to produce understanding of interactive media.* Available: www.media-visions.com/ed-deepliteracy.html/. (Accessed September 21, 2004).

Glasgow, J. N. 1994, March. Teaching visual literacy for the 21st century. *Journal of Reading* 37 (6): 494–500.

Grossman, R. 1999, March. Making a mess of digital TV. *Columbia Journalism Review.* Available: www.cjr.org/. (Accessed March 15, 1999).

Heinich, R., M. Molenda, and J. Russell. 1994. *Instructional media and the new technologies of instruction.* (4th ed.). New York: Macmillan.

Kizlik, R. 1998. *Strategic teaching, strategic learning, and thinking skills.* Available: www.adprima.com/strategi.htm. (Accessed September 21, 2004).

Model T Ford Club. Great quotes by and about Henry Ford. Available: www.modelt.org/ tquotes.html (Accessed September 21, 2004).

National Communications Association. 1996. Adopted at an Aspen Institute Workshop. Available: www.natcom.org/publications/K-12/K12Stds.htm. (Accessed March 1999).

Ontario Ministry of Education. 1996. *The common curriculum, Grades 1-9.* Toronto: Government of Ontario Bookstore Publications.

PBS Broadcasting. 1995. *Rod Serling, Submitted for your approval: Interviews with colleagues (television show).* American Masters Series. Aired December 29, 2003.

Pilzer, Paul Zane. 1991. *Unlimited wealth: The theory and practice of economic alchemy.* New York: Random House.

Schroeppel, T. 1998. *Video goals: Getting results with pictures and sound.* (Available from the author at 3205 Price Avenue, Tampa, FL 33611.)Shouten, D., and R. Watling. 1997. *Media action projects: A model for integrating video in project-based education, training, and community development.* University of Nottingham, UK: Urban Programme Research Group, School of Education.

Tartikoff, B. 1992. *The Last great ride.* New York: Turtle Bay Books.

Tyner, K. 1998. *Literacy in a digital world: Teaching and learning in the age of information.* Mahwah, NJ. Laurence Erlbaum Associates.

Tyner, K., and D. Leveranz. 1998. *The media literacy institute guide.* Houston, TX and San Francisco: Southwest Alternate Media Project and Strategies for Media Literacy.

Vestron Video, Inc. 1986. *45/85: America since WWII* [Video]. Stamford, CT.

INDEX

CPSIA information can be obtained
at www.ICGtesting.com
Printed in the USA
LVHW062227191121
703869LV00017B/124